Firsthand Louisiana

Firsthand LOUISIANA

PRIMARY SOURCES IN THE HISTORY OF THE STATE

SELECTED AND EDITED BY

JANET ALLURED, MCNEESE STATE UNIVERSITY
JOHN KEELING, MCNEESE STATE UNIVERSITY
MICHAEL S. MARTIN, UNIVERSITY OF LOUISIANA AT LAFAYETTE

WITH THE ASSISTANCE OF
LINDSEY DELAUGHTER, UNIVERSITY OF LOUISIANA AT LAFAYETTE
AUGUST MCQUEEN, MCNEESE STATE UNIVERSITY
MARY KATE CORE, MCNEESE STATE UNIVERSITY

2020
UNIVERSITY OF LOUISIANA AT LAFAYETTE PRESS

ISBN 13 (paper): 978-1-946160-67-6
(ebook): 978-1-946160-83-6

http://ulpress.org
University of Louisiana at Lafayette Press
P.O. Box 43558
Lafayette, LA 70504-3558

Printed on acid-free paper in the United States
Library of Congress Cataloging-in-Publication Data

Names: Allured, Janet, editor. | Keeling, John R. (John Robert), 1967- editor. | Martin, Michael S., 1972- editor.
Title: Firsthand Louisiana : Primary Sources in the History of the State / selected and edited by Janet Allured, McNeese State University, John R. Keeling, McNeese State University, Michael S. Martin, University of Louisiana at Lafayette ; with the assistance of Lindsey Delaughter, University of Louisiana at Lafayette, August Mcqueen, McNeese State University, Mary Kate Core, McNeese State University.
Description: Lafayette, LA : University of Louisiana at Lafayette Press, 2020. | Includes bibliographical references.
Identifiers: LCCN 2020021303 | ISBN 9781946160676 (paperback)
Subjects: LCSH: Louisiana--History--Sources.
Classification: LCC F369 .F47 2020 | DDC 976.3--dc23
LC record available at https://lccn.loc.gov/2020021303

Cover images courtesy of:
Armand Duplantier Letters, Mss. 4914, Louisiana and Lower Mississippi Valley Collections, LSU Libraries, Baton Rouge, LA.

Library of Congress, Prints & Photographs Division, photograph by Carol M. Highsmith [LC-DIG-highsm-24848].

Table of Contents

Introduction ix

Part One: Colonized Louisiana, 1682–1803

1682: La Salle Reaches the Mouth of the Mississippi River 3
1699: Excerpts from Iberville's Diary 7
1721: Administrative Ordinances of the Company of the Indies 17
1721: Le Gac on "the Situation in Louisiana" 21
1722: Charlevoix's Louisiana 25
1724: Excerpts from the *Code Noir* 27
1728: Marie-Madeleine Hachard's View of New Orleans 37
1729/1751: Bossu on the Natchez Revolt 43
1758: Le Page Du Pratz on "the Negroes of Louisiana" 53
1764: Jean-Jacques-Blaise d'Abbadie on the Indian Response to the Peace of Paris 63
1764–1766: Correspondence Regarding the Acadians 67
1768: Governor Ulloa and the Creole Revolt 81
1769: O'Reilly Brings Order to Louisiana 87
1770: An Outsider's Perspective on Louisiana 91
1779: José de Gálvez on Military Plans 93
1792: Governor Carondelet on Slaves in Louisiana 97
1792: Seeking Refuge from Saint-Domingue 99
1793: Governor Carondelet on the French Revolution 103
1795: Treaty of San Lorenzo 111
1796–1802: James Pitot on Louisiana Commerce and Sugar 121
For Further Reading 127

Part Two: The Nineteenth Century, 1803–1900

1802/1803: Letters from President Jefferson about the Louisiana Purchase 133
1804: The War of the Quadrilles 139
1812–1862: The Slave Trade in New Orleans 147
1814: Prelude to the Battle of New Orleans 153
1835–1841: Antebellum Politics and the Second Party System 159

1841–1845: Expansion of Suffrage and the Constitution of 1845 165
1840–1860: Antebellum Women in Politics and Reform 171
1841–1842: The Brig *Creole* Revolt 177
1839–1856: Nativism in Antebellum Louisiana 183
1860: Rev. Benjamin Palmer's Thanksgiving Sermon 189
1861: Louisiana Secedes 197
1862: Butler's "Woman Order" 203
1862–1863: Sarah Morgan and Baton Rouge during the Civil War 209
1865: A Sugar Planter and the End of the Civil War 215
1866: The New Orleans Massacre 219
1868: A Reconstruction Constitution 227
1868: Elections and Violence 231
1868–1893: The Louisiana State Lottery Company 237
1874: Opposition to Radical Reconstruction 243
1891–1896: Populism in Louisiana 249
1896: *Plessy v. Ferguson* 257
1898: A New Constitution and Disfranchisement 263
1900: Robert Charles and the New Orleans Race Riot 271
For Further Reading 279

Part Three: Twentieth- and Twenty-First-Century Louisiana, 1897–2017

1897–1917: The Story of Storyville 285
1898/1903: The Convict Lease System 289
1910: Jean Gordon and Social Justice for Children 293
1912: Brotherhood of Timber Workers and the Grabow Riot 301
1912: Eleanor McMain and Kingsley House 311
1913–1920: Kate Gordon and Woman Suffrage 319
1930: A Union Organizer's Memories 323
1929: Articles of Impeachment against Huey Long 329
1933: Excerpts from Huey Long's *Every Man a King* 335
1942: Racial Violence during World War II 347
1942: Robert LeBlanc and World War II 353
1942–1945: Higgins Industries 361
1943: Governor Sam H. Jones's "Report to the People" 365
1947: Willie Francis's First Trip to the Chair 371
1948–1960: A. P. Tureaud, Governor Jimmie Davis, and the Desegregation of Orleans Parish Schools 381

1948–1970: Representative F. Edward Hébert on Civil Rights....................389
1959: Russell Long on Governor Earl Long's Breakdown...........................395
1960: Testimony of John Scott on Voter Registration Requirements........401
1961: Report on the New Orleans School Crisis..411
1963: Ernest "Dutch" Morial, the NAACP, and the
Citizens Committee Push for Civil Rights..421
1963/1964: Negro Voter Education Project..429
1964: CORE in Louisiana..435
1971: Barbara Scott, Candidate for Representative District 96..................441
1973: Going "Behind the Cane Curtain"..445
1977: New Orleans's Gay Rights Community
Protests Anita Bryant's Appearance..451
1987–1990: The Oil Slump and Resulting Gambling Legislation..............455
1991: The Race from Hell: Edwards and Duke Debate..............................461
1992: Dorothy Mae Taylor and the
Public Accommodations Ordinance..469
1998: Petrochemical Industries vs. the People...477
2005: Mary Gehman Survives Hurricane Katrina..485
2005/2010: Governor Blanco's Response to Hurricane Katrina................491
2017: Mayor Mitch Landrieu on the Removal of
Confederate Monuments...499
For Further Reading...509

Introduction

We are university professors who, almost daily, teach classes on, research, write about, and otherwise engage with the history of Louisiana. We also run into each other on a regular basis at conferences or other scholarly get-togethers. It was at one of those conferences that we broached the idea of putting together a collection of primary sources for use in our classrooms. We recognized a need, and this book is our attempt to satisfy that need. Of course, our needs as professors are not unique, and we know that this collection will also appeal to our colleagues who teach Louisiana History on a regular basis, students at our own and other institutions, and even members of the general-interest population.

Why a collection of primary sources? Primary sources provide firsthand accounts of the events—some obviously important, others seemingly mundane—that historians use to construct narratives of the past. They are the building blocks of history. Examining primary sources can be challenging, but they allow the reader a view to the thoughts of people long deceased, people they might not agree with, people who most often think differently from them. Beyond that, and perhaps more importantly, such firsthand accounts encourage critical thinking, causing the reader to question inherited knowledge and assess biases—both the writer's and their own. Louisiana historians and their students, many of whom will teach future generations the history of our state, benefit from such independent, critical thinking and deep analysis of voices not their own.

Clearly there are benefits of such a book as this for academic historians and their students, but what of the general reader? For those who consider themselves history "buffs," who are fascinated by the histories portrayed in museums and at historic sites, and who enjoy reading accessible and popular histories that often show up on best-seller lists, delving into primary sources gives one a sense of where those portrayals and places get their own information from. Perhaps, given the firsthand account, readers might interpret a history differently than they previously have. Perhaps they won't. But either way, they will have evidence to support their understanding of the past—in this instance, Louisiana's past.

There is much information contained in this book, yet it is by no means comprehensive. The sources are too numerous, and the space too short, to include every relevant primary source pertaining to Louisiana's history. Instead, we have chosen sources that illuminate significant turning points, historical periods, and individual perspectives for inclusion.

The book is broken down into three parts. The first covers the colonial era from 1682 until 1803, a period when Europeans, Africans, and American Indians first encountered each other and then came to terms with the implications of such encounters. Because of the relatively few extant sources (compared to later centuries) for the colonial period, the documents necessarily tend to be what historians refer to as "top-down," meaning the writings of government officials, expedition leaders, literary figures, and the like. Yet there are examples of "bottom-up" sources in the form of individuals' letters, typically to family members back home in France. Much can be learned about the peoples of Louisiana and their lives from both perspectives.

Part Two covers the years from the Louisiana Purchase through the New Orleans Race Riot in 1900. Nineteenth-century Louisiana witnessed not just the shift from colony to state but also a growing Americanization process that brought more and more English speakers, Protestants, and fortune-seekers to the state. The clash of cultures played out in politics, culture, education, and commerce. Ultimately, the sources presented here depict a deeply divided Louisiana, especially on matters of race. Events of the 1890s, including the *Plessy v. Ferguson* decision and the 1898 constitution, effectively ended any discussion of race until well into the twentieth century.

Finally, Part Three provides perspectives from the increasingly complicated historical landscape of Louisiana in the twentieth and twenty-first centuries. As the state's population grew and Americanization continued apace, Louisianians, even those of French or African ancestry, began to increasingly think of themselves as Americans. This was nothing new, of course, but it became the defining element of a state that played a major role in Allied efforts during World Wars I and II, that became a driving force in the petrochemical industry, and that emerged as a frontrunner in cultural and eco-tourism. Of course, Louisianians, especially white Louisianians, stuck with their fellow southerners when it came to matter of racial progress; conversely, black Louisianians engaged in protests and direct-action campaigns just like those in other areas of the South. By the 2000s, Louisianians on all sides squared off with the vestiges of their shared past, from the environmental and health devastation that resulted from certain petrochemical industries to the debate over the removal of Confederate statues in prominent locations around New Orleans.

Louisiana's history, like that of anywhere else, is difficult to piece together and, if anything, even more exasperating to understand. It is our hope that the readers of the book will come to their own conclusions about that history on the basis of the primary sources presented here.

A final note: standards of spelling and grammar have evolved over time, as has access to education. Many of the documents included in this collection therefore contain what we today would see as errors. Because of the frequency of these "mistakes," the traditional notation [*sic*] (meaning "in this manner") has been largely omitted, except in instances that may cause misunderstanding.

We would like to thank our student assistants: Emily Wright, August McQueen, and Mary-Kate Core of McNeese State University; Andrew Cerisse of Tulane; and Lindsey Delaughter of the University of Louisiana at Lafayette, all of whom diligently tracked down, transcribed, and uncovered new primary sources for us to include. This book would not exist without their help. We also wish to acknowledge the current and former staff members of the University of Louisiana at Lafayette Press—Joshua Caffery, Devon Lord, James Wilson, and Mary Duhé—whose comments, edits, and creativity made our jobs easier and the results a better book. We also thank them for their patience. Of course, without our families, none of this would matter. So, we are grateful to Amy, Sam, and Alex Martin; David L. Edwards; and J.R. and Betty Keeling and Clara Keeling-Ware. They have been supportive, encouraging, and, when necessary, prodding.

We also wish to acknowledge the assistance of archivists and historians who provided both documents and ideas for research: Pati Threatt, McNeese; Laura McLemore, Noel Memorial Library, LSU-S; Lori Schexnayder, Leon Miller, and Kevin Williams at Louisiana Research Collection, Tulane; Jason Theriot; the staff at UNO; Pamela Arceneaux and the staff at the Historic New Orleans Collection; the staff at the New Orleans Public Library; Michael Powers, Angelo State University; John M. Sacher, Central Florida University;

and Heaven Smith, Louisiana State Archives in Baton Rouge. We would also like to thank Billy and Kay Blake and the rest of the family of Juliet Hardtner. Without the Juliet Hardtner endowment funds, we would not have been able to complete this project.

Janet Allured, Professor of History and Director of Women's Studies, McNeese State University

John Keeling, Assistant Professor, McNeese State University

Michael S. Martin, Cheryl Courrégé Burguières/Board of Regents Professor in History, University of Louisiana at Lafayette

Part I

Colonized Louisiana 1682–1803

1682:
La Salle Reaches the Mouth of the Mississippi River

In 1682, Frenchman René-Robert Cavelier, sieur de La Salle (1643–1687), a former member of the Jesuit Order and an experienced explorer, led an expedition of about forty Frenchmen and American Indians down the Mississippi River to its mouth. There, on April 9, 1682, he claimed the river and its tributaries for France. Unbeknownst to La Salle and his men, this claim covered about one-third of the modern United States, stretching from Canada to the Gulf of Mexico and from the Rocky Mountains to the Appalachians. La Salle named the place *La Louisiane*, honoring King Louis XIV. The following excerpts, taken from a memoir by La Salle's trusted lieutenant, Henri de Tonti, relate important views of the French explorers on the environment they found, the American Indians they encountered, and the discovery of the Mississippi's mouth.

Description of Louisiana

That large Country is now called by the name of Louisiana, since the French took possession thereof in the Name of Lewis the Great. The Soil is, generally speaking, so fertile, that it produces Naturally without any Culture, those Fruits that Nature and Art together have much ado to bring forth in Europe: They have two Crops every Year without any great fatigue; the Vines bring extraordinary Grapes, without the Care of the Husbandmen; and the Fruit-Trees need no Gardiners to look after them;

the Air is everywhere temperate; the Country is watered with Navigable Rivers and delicious Brooks and Rivulets, and diversified with Forests and Meadows; it is stockt with all sorts of Beasts, as Bulls, Orignacs, Wolves, Lines, Wild Asses, Stags, Goats, Sheep, Foxes, Hares, Beavers, Otters, Dogs, and sorts of Fowls, which afford a plentiful Game for the Inhabitants. They have discovered Mines of Lead and iron, and 'tis not doubted that there are also Mines of Gold and Silver, if they would give themselves the trouble to look for them, but the Inhabitants of those Countries valuing things only as far as they are necessary for Life, are yet unacquainted with the Fanciful Value we put upon those Metals, and have not dig'd up the Earth to look for them. . . .

Description of American Indians

Those Inhabitants have nothing of Man but the Shape and the Name; they live without any Laws, Religion, Superiority, and Subordination, Independency and Liberty being their *Summum Bonum*[1], or the ultimate end they propose to themselves. Their Life is always wandering, having no settled Possessions; they take several Wives, if they please, whom they quit when they will, and leave them to others, just as they do their Habitations, for after having for some time cultivated a piece of Ground, they quit it without any occasion to Cultivate another and the first comer takes possession thereof, so that they are perpetually changing their Habitations, and by this continual motion, everything becomes in a manner common amongst them: they know no Superiority, and this the World is made only for them.

I said they have no Religion, tho' it seems they have an obscure Idea of God, because they live as if they thought there was none. They believe in general that there is a God, but who does not concern himself in what they do. Some Worship the Sun, and others fancy that the World is full of certain Spirits, who preside over their Actions, and they are so extravagant as to believe, that everything in the World has a Spirit, and that they are Good or Hurtful, according to the *Caprice* of that Spirit. 'Tis upon this Principle that are grounded all the foolish Superstitions of their Jugglers or Monitous, who are their Priests or Magicians.

1. Latin for "supreme good."

I don't believe that they have carried their Reflections so far, as to think on the Nature of their Souls; tho' 'tis true, they seem to believe their Immortality, and a kind of *Metempsychosis*, or Transmigration of Souls; but they have so many extravagant fancies upon this Subject, that it is in a manner impossible to discover their true Opinion. I may say in general, that they are so stupid in matters of Religion, that they are not convinced of their own Belief, nor of what others believe, and therefore Laugh at the Instructions of our Missionaries.

However, notwithstanding that brutish temper, they have as good a Sense as the rest of Mankind, to know their true Interests, and therefore are capable of Negotiations, Commerce, and Counsel. They know how to weigh and consider the Consequences of an Enterprize, and take Just Measures to compass it. When they meet together to consult about some great Design, they sit in a private place, in a profound Silence, smoking Tobacco, and every one speaks gravely in his turn. It is to be observed by the by, that they never make any Treaty, Convention or Agreement with anybody, till they have first of all, mutually exchanged Presents. They give commonly Collars as the Symbol of Union; they have a particular Kettle for Peace, and another for War. They proclaim Peace with the Calumet, and War by great Outcries, or rather dreadful Howlings. . . .

One may observe in Men a great Gravity and Authority, and in Women an extraordinary Complaisance for their Husbands, and as they follow their Natural Instinct in everything they do, their Behaviour is always sincere and without any affectation; and one may truly say, That the conjugal Union between them, is the effect of a Natural Inclination, which is common to Men and to Brutes, and not founded upon any true Friendship. . . .

Reaching the Mouth of Mississippi River

Twelve Leagues from the Quinipissa's, we fell to the Right on the Village Call'd Tangibao; we found it pillag'd, sack'd, and a great Heap of dead Bodies one upon another. This sight struck a mighty horror in us, and concluding that it was not good staying there, we went on; and about Ten Leagues further, we begun to find the Water brackish; the Shore seemed somewhat more extended, and all strewed with Shells of different shape and figure, Some like drinking Cups, some like Snails ending in a spiral point, and all of a most agreeable variety of Colours. We kept on still, and after an Hours sailing, we put ourselves into a Canoo, and kept along the Coast, the better to take our observation of the Shore, and so came back to land at the River Mouth.

This was on the Seventh of April, 1683 [1682]. The first thing we then took care to do, was to return our humble thanks to Almighty God, for our good Success, and for that he had carried us safely to the end of our Voyage, after more than Eight Hundred Leagues sailing and rowing with so small a handful of Men, and so little Ammunition; and that through so many barbarous Nations, which we had not only discover'd, but in some measure made subject to us. We Sung the *Te Deum*; after which, taking our Canoos, and our Equipage upon Sledges, we went and planted our Huts a little above the Shore, to be out of the reach of the Sea, which wholly overflows it, after six Hours Ebb, during which it's left quite dry.

Having pitched here our New Camp, we fastened a Cross to the top of a large Tree, and set up the Arms of *France*: After which we raised three or four Huts more, and Entrenched ourselves there. Then M. *de la Salle* took the Altitude, to know where the Mouth of the *Mississippi* was. The Spaniards, who had attempted to find it out, tho' in vain, had already given it the Name of *Del Rio Ascondido*. According to M. *de la Salle*'s Calculation, it is between the Twenty second and Twenty third Degree of Latitude; that it throws itself into the Gulph of Mexico, with a large Channel which is Twenty leagues wide, and very deep and navigable.

Questions to Consider:

1. *Do you think Tonti embellished his description of the natural resources of Louisiana? If so, why?*
2. *Did Tonti view the American Indians encountered by the La Salle expedition as "noble savages" or "brutal savages"?*

Source:

An Account of Monsieur de La Salle's last expedition and discoveries in North America : presented to the French king, and published by the Chevalier Tonti, governour of Fort St. Louis, in the province of the Illinois : made English from the Paris original: also the adventures of the Sieur de Montauban, captain of the French buccaneers on the coast of Guinea, in the year 1695. (London: J. Tonson, 1698), 5–6, 6–9, 13–14, 103–5, https://archive.org/details/accountofmonsieu00unkn/page/n8.

1699:
Excerpts from Iberville's Diary

Seventeen years after La Salle's claim, Canadian soldier and explorer Pierre le Moyne d'Iberville led an expedition of explorers, colonizers, and Royal Marines to the Gulf Coast to establish a permanent French settlement. That settlement would protect the entry to the Mississippi River. In order to know where to build, Iberville and his men had to first locate the river and then confirm that it was the correct one. On Mardi Gras day (March 3) 1700, Iberville and his explorers entered the river. The following excerpt from Iberville's diary begins at that point and follows his voyage up the Mississippi to an American Indian village marked by poles "reddened by the attached sacrificial offerings of fish and bear heads," a place the French would call Baton Rouge.

March 3. *Mardi Gras.* Today the northeasterly winds were such that I was unable to sound in that particular direction, where, in any case, I doubt any [additional mouths] exist. I ascended the river, finding it to be very deep, twenty feet of water at a longboat's length from the banks, and forty-eight and fifty feet of water at the center. Two and a half leagues[1] above the mouth, the waterway divides into three branches. The center channel is as large as the one through which I entered the river, three hundred and fifty to four hundred *toises*[2] wide; the other which extends to the southwestern shore, is smaller. This entire region is blanketed by reeds, brambles, and ex-

1. A league equates to almost three and a half miles.
2. A *toise* is a bit longer than two yards.

tremely tall grass. Above these forks, the river, which could be five hundred and fifty toises wide, slowly tapers to a maximum width of a hundred toises. The low-lying countryside is covered by reeds and some alder trees, which are not very tall and are occasionally as large as one's thigh. Six leagues upriver, one first encounters woods, especially on the left bank, where there are alder trees, thirty to forty feet tall and as large as a human torso. Above the fork, the waterway's course is quite straight for a distance of six leagues, running to the northwest, five degrees north; it then meanders two leagues to the west and again ranges to the northwest. I camped at the western bend, twelve leagues from the river's mouth, on a point on the right bank, which we have christened *Mardi Gras*. I fired two shots from a swivel gun in order to notify any Indians in the vicinity of our presence. None seem to have come to our camp. I scaled a hazel tree as large as myself; I saw only canes and shrubs. During floods, this region is inundated by four feet of water. I have resolved to ascend the river as far as the Bayogoula village, seeking news of the Quinipissa, depicted by [La Salle's] narratives, which place them twenty-five leagues from the sea.

The fourth. Easterly winds are blowing across the land. We have continued to ascend [the Mississippi] and have traveled approximately eight leagues, finding several bends where the river turns to the west-northwest, the direction in which we utilized the favorable winds. The river has maintained its usual width. From both our campsite and our present position, we see the sea or lake, two or three leagues away, paralleling the waterway's west-northwesterly course. The [Mississippi] is separated from this lake by a strip of land one-fourth of a league wide. The land rises slightly, but discovered by flood waters, one and a half feet deep. We see trees of every variety along the left bank of the river. In several places, there is a border of woodland one-fourth of a league wide; behind it are prairies and groves of trees. I have noticed the channel is swollen, as it is teeming with driftwood. It is only two-and-a-half feet below floodstage. I camped on the right bank.

The fifth. The river was shrouded in fog until nine o'clock. The winds are calm. We broke camp at six-thirty, sailing along the shore aided by favorable winds at the river's curvatures. An unfavorable wind has blown quite briskly above a point twelve leagues from the sea; as a consequence, it has required considerable time for the boats to ascend the river, especially as they required the assistance of the wind at each bend, which, today, has been from the west to the southwest, to the northwest, and to the north. At midday, we discovered a campfire on the left bank, in the prairie, and we know that an Indian had been there. The land continued to rise in elevation and is inundated to the depth of one-and-one-half feet. It could be that the area one league inland is not subject to flooding. Today, we traveled six or seven leagues.

The sixth. It was foggy and calm throughout the morning. We continued our journey with considerable difficulty; the abundance of driftwood in the river is evidence of the current's velocity. We have encountered difficulty in making headway against the surging tide at the oxbows. My brother [Jean-Baptiste le Moyne, Sieur de Bienville], with two canoes, always sails along one of the river's banks and keeps watch for traces of the Indians. At noon, I took my bearings with an astrolabe, which I had made specially for this mission, and I found that I was in the latitude of thirty degrees north.

These sightings were taken at the first east-northeasterly bend in the river. In one instance, it curves to the east; there I camped on the right bank. Today I traveled six and one-half leagues. The woods and the meadows rise and fall from eight to ten inches in elevation. I have still not seen any fruit trees or walnut trees; along the seashore, the blackberries are almost ripe. The trees have dense foliage. We see several vines which have ceased blooming. I have fired two shots from the swivel guns.

The seventh. It was calm through the day. We continue to ascend the river and find that it meanders considerably to the northeast and southwest. To the north and west, in the space of two leagues distance, it forms two or three oxbows. Two leagues from the campsite, I encountered six canoes filled with Indians who immediately put ashore. I disembarked below them and advanced overland towards them. One remained aboard his canoe the others having fled. We saluted one another in their customary manner, which I have previously described. He told me that he was an Annochy and that the Bayogoula and the Annochy, whom I had seen near the vessels at Annochy Bay and with whom I had exchanged presents and smoked the peace pipe, had returned to the Bayogoula village. I gave him and his comrades, whom he had summoned, some presents, including knives, beads, and hatchets; they gave us smoked buffalo and bear meat. I asked them to provide a guide to conduct me to the Bayogoula, and they acceded to my request. According to the [Annochy's] calculations, it is a three-and-a-half-day journey to their [the Bayogoula] village. It could be eighty leagues distant. On that day, I camped near one of their huts, six-and-a-half leagues from my last campsite; here, there are ten huts covered with palmetto fronds. In addition, there is a small redoubt nearby. Located on a point in the river's right bank, its walls are as tall as a man, and are made of canes in the form of an oval, twenty-five paces wide and fifty-five paces' long; it contains several huts. They told us that some of their men had recently been killed by the Chicacha and Napyosa, but I subsequently learned that they were no longer at war. The Quinipissa and the Bayogoula have severed relations with one another because of some quarrel between their chiefs. This is what they [the Indians] call war, according to the Ouma. This entire area floods to a depth of one foot as far as one-half league into the woods. From the sea to my present location, both riverbanks are almost without exception, so densely lined with cane of all sizes, one, two, three, four, five and six inches in circumference, that it is impossible to walk along the riverside. It is an untractable country, which will be easy to clear. Most of the foliage is dry; setting it afire, it burns easily and makes noise while aflame as a pistol shot. A person who was ignorant of this and did not them burnings would think that it was a skirmish. These canes, which resemble bamboo, have roots extending three-to-four feet underground.

The eighth. The winds are north-northwesterly, impeding our ascent considerably at the turns and propelling the water with force that the current exceeded one-fourth of a league per hour; we managed to advance only four-and-a-half leagues and spent the night in a hut which we built on the right bank. My men were exhausted.

The ninth. The winds are northwesterly, which greatly retarded our progress. Two leagues from the campsite, the Indian who accompanied me revealed a terminus of the portage from the southern shore of the bay, where the Indian boats land in order to descend to this river. They drag their canoes along a fine path, where we found the baggage of people who are either leaving or returning by way of this portage. This Indian, our guide, took a parcel there. He remarked that the distance between one end of the trail and the other is indeed inconsiderable. Furthermore, he told me that we were two days distant from the [Bayogoula] village. Today, we traveled five-and-a-half leagues. There could be fifty leagues distance between our present position and the mouth of the river. I camped on the left bank.

March 10. We have had calm weather throughout the day. Today, the river meandered considerably from the north to the southwest, on quarter northwest. I traveled at least five leagues, and I camped on the right riverbank. The entire region floods to a depth of one foot; the trees are large and beautiful. There are many canes.

The eleventh. It rained throughout the day. I remained in camp. At nightfall two [Breton] sailors from the *Marin* went to shoot two ducks along the river-bank within cannon range of our campsite. They have not returned and have apparently gone astray. I have fired shots from muskets and the swivel guns.

The twelfth. I have dispatched eight men, who periodically fired their muskets to different points above and below the camp and into the interior without finding them. They found their footprints among the canes and followed them for a considerable distance into the virgin forest, where they lost their trail. The forests along the river contain a dense undergrowth, and this prevents one from walking more than one-half league into the interior. The land does not flood beyond three-quarters of a league from the river. Throughout the day, I awaited the return of the two sailors from the *Marin*. The longboat, which I had sent two leagues upriver to retrieve the men who had searched for their missing comrades, took soundings in the middle of the river and consistently found ninety, one hundred, and one hundred and twenty feet of water.

The thirteenth. Calm. On the left bank, four leagues from the campsite, I discovered a river, two hundred paces wide, emanating from the west. The Indian who accompanied me called it the Ouacha River. One and a half leagues from there, I found two Indian canoes: one was a Ouacha boat, which carried five men and a woman who were returning home; the other, a Bayogoula dugout with three men and a woman aboard. I negotiated with them for some corn to replenish our dwindling supplies. The Ouacha canoe maintained its course for its village, which is two days journey from here, and the other returned to the Bayogoula village nearby to inform them of our impending arrival. The twilight hours were rent by thunder, a common occurrence here during the winter.

The fourteenth. I broke camp at six a.m. Three leagues from the campsite and one league from the landing at the Bayogoula village. I encountered a wooden canoe or pirogue, as they are called in the West Indies, in which there were four men of the Mougoulacha tribe. They came, bringing me the pipe and chanting in their customary manner. Having joined them, they offered to smoke the calumet with me on behalf of their tribes. Afterwards, the envoy bearing the peace pipe boarded my longboat and we traveled to the village's landing, arriving there at noon. The Mougoulacha aboard my longboat sang as we approached the landing, lifting his calumet at arm's length as a sign of our joy and peaceful intentions.

On approaching the landing, the Bayogoula and the Mougoulacha, which are amalgamated tribes living in the same village, lined the riverbank and sang in celebration of our arrival. While I disembarked, two chiefs, representing each tribe came before me, greeted me in their customary manner, which I have previously described, took my arms to aid me in walking, and conducted me to the bear pelts, placed at the center of their assembled people. While seated there, the chieftains circulated the peace pipe among myself and my men, whom they warmly embraced. The calumet, which I gave to the Bayogoula, was placed at the center of the convocation, on two, two-foot forks. There, one man from each of the two tribes stood in constant vigil. They then brought sagamité[3], made of corn, and their variety of bread to feed me and my men. The afternoon was devoted to singing and dancing. The Mougoulacha chief wore a blue serge coat of Poitou cloth, which, he told me, Tonty[4] had given him as a present when he visited the village. In addition, he spoke of several things, relating part of the narrative by sign language. I understood many of their words, which I had written down the first time that I saw them [the Indians]; at any rate, my brother has a fair knowledge of the language, having grown very attached to our guide, whom I had engaged on the river and who had accompanied him [Bienville] in his canoe.

We spoke at length about Tonty's activities during his stopover, the route which he took, and the Quinipissa, of which, I am told, there are seven villages, eight days distant by land, to the east-northeast of this Indian community. I could not obtain any information concerning the fork, described in the travelogs. I hope to descend that branch to the sea in order to be acquainted with both branches. The Indians tell me that the Malbanchia does not divide and that Tonty traveled exclusively by way of the channel near their village while both ascending and descending the river. I have been unable to reconcile this with the travel accounts, especially the Recollet's narrative, which I think more trustworthy. They [the Indians] drew maps of the entire region, indicating that Tonty traveled to the Ouma village after departing their own. All of this places me in the most embarrassing circumstances, the season compelling me to return, being ninety leagues from the ships, and having yet to construct a [military] establishment and to select an appropriate site. Furthermore, the *Marin* lacks supplies. Upon departing,

3. Sagamité is a sort of stew, usually made by mixing corn and animal fat and sometimes including other available ingredients.

4. Here, Iberville refers to the same Henri de Tonti from the first reading.

Surgères requested that I issue an order authorizing him to depart within six weeks if I had not returned. My soldiers submitted to rowing, wearying of consistently rowing against a strong current. I kept referring to the Recollet Father's narrative about this river, and could not believe that he had been wretched enough to mislead all of France, although I was fully cognizant of the fact that he lied on numerous occasions in his journal, especially in the passages treating Canada and Hudson Bay, where he lied impudently. Believing that these Indians, who are not dear friends of the Quinipissa, would be driven by jealousy to conceal the truth in order to prevent me from going there, I resolved to locate the Quinipissa thirty leagues from the sea as well as the Tangiboa, described by the explorers, who found them plundered and murdered. The Bayogoula told me that the Ouma were responsible for the destruction of the Tangiboa village, which was one of seven Quinipissa communities and that, at present, only six remain, the surviving Tangiboa families having been forcibly seized and conducted to the Ouma village, where they remain and where I shall observe them. They also told me that their village had never been along the banks of the Mississippi. At eight p.m., all of the Indians retired to their village, which is one-fourth league distance from the riverbank on a site which is not subject to inundations. The interjacent area floods to a depth of one foot during the high-water period. Four of these Indians remained in camp with us.

The fifteenth. At daybreak, three men came, bearing my calumet for the ceremonial smoking. They subsequently returned it to the forks, where one man remained to guard it. Accompanied by Sieur de Sauvolle, the Recollet priest, my brother, and two of my Canadians. I went to their village. I found this community to be one-fourth league from the river; a small brook, the source of their drinking water, runs behind it. The village is enclosed by a cane pallisade, one inch thick and ten feet high, which lacks a door that could be secured [against their enemies]. They greeted me at the entrance to the village and conducted me before the Mougoulacha but, where we were made to sit in the sweltering heat on cane wattles. There, I gave them presents, including hatchets, knives, mirrors, needles, blouses, and blankets, which are prized among them. They, in turn, gave me one of their most valuable possessions, a dozen very large deer hides, most of which had been pierced [by arrows]. I gave them to my men for use as shoe leather. They [the Indians] regaled us with bread sagamite. While they divided their presents, I toured the village with the Bayogoula chief, who conducted me to their temple, upon which were placed numerous animal figures, including a rooster painted red. At the entrance, there is a small lean-to, eight feet wide and twelve feet long, supported by two large pillars, with a transom which serves as a girder. Near the temple door, there are several animal figures, such as bears, wolves, and birds; alongside of them lies one which call *choucoüiacha* [opposum]. Its head is shaped like that of a suckling pig and is as large. In addition, it has grey and white fur like a badger, a tail like a rat, and paws like a monkey. It has a bag below its abdomen, in which it engenders and nourishes its offspring. I have killed eight of these animals and carefully examined them. The temple door is eight feet high and two and a half feet wide. The chief directed a man to open it and entered first. The temple was a hut constructed in the same manner as those which serve as lodgings. Thirty feet wide, they consist of mud-plastered staves, the height of a man. Two dried, worm-eaten piles, joined to one another, were ablaze at the center of the structure; at the rear, there was a platform, upon which were placed several bundles of deer, bear, and buffalo hides, which were presents offered to their god, represented by the *choucoüiacha*, portions of which were painted red and black. Finally, there was a glass bottle which Tonty gave to these people. That is all that I saw in the temple.

After departing the temple, I went to the village and inspected the huts which are like the temple, except for the lean-to. Some are larger, some are smaller [than the temple]. These crude dwellings are covered with split canes, which are properly bound together, without windows. These cabins derive their light from an aperture in the roof, two feet in diameter. Due to the absence of wood and stone flooring, the huts have only sand or dirt floors. The beds are supported by four posts, elevated two feet above the ground by red cypress cross bars, approximately as large as one's arm and are covered by a mat. The Indians attach the mats to the posts with small canes, so that they are very straight but not very soft. With regard to mannerisms, they are very righteous people; but they are slightly indolent. Their household goods consist only of clay pottery, which are sufficiently well constructed, delicate, and well designed. All of the men are naked, without being self-conscious. The women wear only a sash of bark, most of which are red and white. The sash is made of several woven bark fibers. The upper part, which is worn on their loins, is eight inches long; the lower part consists of one-foot-long strands of this material, which descend to a point above the knee caps. They [the women] are sufficiently concealed by the garment, the strands being in continuous motion. Many girls six to seven years of age do not wear sashes; they conceal their nakedness with a small bundle of moss, held by a string which runs between the thighs and is fastened to a waistband. I have not seen any of them [the women] who were pretty. Their hair is coiled about the head. This village is complex of 107 huts and 2 temples, and there could be as many as 200 to 250 male residents. There are a few women. Smallpox which continues to ravage the population has exterminated one-fourth of the village. They place their dead on scaffolds near the village. The remains, lifted seven feet above the ground level, are wrapped in cane mats, and are covered by another mat in the form of a roof. The mouldering bodies reek and attract numerous vultures. These are the most destitute Indians that I have ever encountered, having neither conveniences nor works of art. Some wear clothing made from woven bark fibers, similar to French bleached hemp. The men are universally alert, well proportioned, and agile. I do not think that they are hardened for war. Their hair is short and they tattoo their faces and bodies. The women beautify themselves by blackening their teeth with dyes made from ground herbs. They remain black temporarily and eventually become white again. The young girls take great pains to decorate their teeth in this manner, but they keep their faces clean. Some of them have tattoos on their faces and breasts. There are a few roosters and chickens in their villages. The clearings in which the villages are located are small in proportion to the size of the tribes. The surrounding area is quite flat. The beautiful countryside is blanketed by woods, containing all varieties of trees, except pines. I have seen a few wild apple trees and a few peach trees; there are neither strawberries, raspberries, nor mulberries. I returned to camp to join my men. Singing, the entire village escorted me. They devoted the remainder of the day to entertaining one another, singing and dancing, I fired the swivel guns for them, which filled them with wonder. I could not obtain the information which I was seeking. I observed that the latitude of this village, which, while ascending the river is on the left bank, was thirty-one degrees, two minutes north.

The sixteenth. At eight a.m., I set out for the Ouma village in search of information pertaining to the fork in the river, which Tonty, in his account, claims existed. The Bayogoula chief embarked with me and ordered a canoe manned by eight men to accompany us as guides. Today, I traveled seven and a half leagues. Three leagues from their village, on the left while ascending the river, there is a stream by which they travel by canoe to the Outimacha and Magenesito, three days journey from here, to the west. Six and a half leagues above the [Bayogoula] village, on the waterway's right bank, they showed me the river by which they travel to the Annochy [tribe], *whom they call Bilocchy*. They named this river Ascantia, and it flows to the sea, into the bay where the ships are anchored. The Mississippi drains into it. That is the only fork known to them. The river meanders considerably above their village. The more I ascend the Mississippi, the more I notice the acclivity of the land. The grapes, which are abundant along the riverbanks, are as large as snip shot. The land fronting on the river floods to a depth of one foot; I do not know if this is the case with the interior.

The seventeenth. We encountered a rivulet on the right riverbank, five and a half leagues above the campsite. They [the Bayogoula] informed us that these were very fertile fishing grounds. I set several fishing lines, but caught only two catfish, which, they say, are found there in large quantities. The Indians stopped two leagues downstream to hunt bear. My brother remained with them. This waterway marks the boundary between the Bayogoula and Oum hunting grounds. Along the shore, there were several huts, covered with palmetto fronds, and a branchless maypole, which is reddened by the attached sacrificial offerings of fish and bear heads. The countryside is absolutely beautiful.

Questions to Consider:

1. *What difficulties did Iberville and his men encounter as they ascended the Mississippi River?*

2. *How does Iberville's description of Louisiana's natural resources differ from Henri de Tonti's?*

3. *How does Iberville's description of Louisiana's American Indians differ from Henri de Tonti's?*

4. *What does Iberville's diary tell us about American Indians' relationships with each other?*

Source:

Carl Brasseaux, trans. and ed., *A Comparative View of French Louisiana, 1699 and 1762: The Journals of Pierre Le Moyne d'Iberville and Jean-Jacques-Blaise d'Abbadie*, USL History Series, no. 13 (Lafayette, LA: Center for Louisiana Studies, University of Southwestern Louisiana, 1979), 40–52.

1721:
Administrative Ordinances of the Company of the Indies

Almost from the time of Louisiana's establishment, the French government perceived the colony as a failure. As a result, in 1712, the government handed rule over to Antoine Crozat, a wealthy Frenchman and advisor to King Louis XIV, who became the colony's first proprietor. When Crozat asked to be relieved of his proprietorship in 1717, the colony reverted to the government's control. Still unwilling to continue to invest its wealth into what seemed to be a losing venture, the government gave Louisiana to a joint-stock company, the Company of the West (soon renamed the Company of the Indies), overseen by Scottish financier John Law, who planned to use Louisiana to improve the French economy. The scheme failed, and, following the busting of the "Mississippi Bubble" in 1720, Law fled France. Control of Louisiana remained with the Company of the Indies, however, and the French government established a council to oversee its continued operation. The following document presents the earliest laws passed by the council regarding the Louisiana colony.

Ordinance of the Council of State appointed by the King of France to administer the Company of the Indies September 2, 1721

Article I
Negroes will be sold to the inhabitants at 660 livres in currency of the Indies, according to the regulations of the company. Bills will be payable in tobacco or rice, according to the decision of the directors, in relation to the quality of the crops.

If, at the end of the second year, the colonist who will have purchased Negroes is in debt, the Negroes will be sold for the profit of the company after a single order of payment. If the result of the sale of the Negroes is not sufficient for the payment of the company, the debtor will be responsible for the payment of the remainder and will be put in prison in the residence of the commander to remain there until payment is complete.

Article II
For good leaf tobacco or *manoques* (Brazilian tobacco) the inhabitants will be paid at twenty-five livres a hundredweight, less two per cent of the good weight; the inhabitants will be free to supply it in casks or cases, as they wish. . . .

Article III
Tobacco and rice will be delivered by the colonists to the pay-stations of New Biloxi, New Orleans, Mobile, and not elsewhere. The tobacco will be received at the same rate at twenty-five pounds a hundredweight.

Article IV
Rice will be paid for at twelve livres a hundredweight, less two percent of good weight, and the same provision for the depreciation of the barrels as for the tobacco cases. The inhabitants may use canvas bales. . . .

Article V
We exhort the inhabitants not to neglect the making of silk, and to replant mulberry bushes so that they may multiply while waiting for enough people to work on the silk, which must be considered a noteworthy goal.

Article VI
The surplus of other merchandise, of the vineyards, and of the crops of the colony, and that of trading hare skins, beavers, and other skins will be sold . . . at the ordinary price granted by the tariff of the Company of the Indies.

Article VII
Merchandise from France will be sold to the inhabitants at the rate listed below.

At Biloxi, Mobile and New Orleans at five per cent profit; to the Natchez and the Yazoos at seventy per cent profit, to the Natchitoches and the Arkansas at eighty per cent, to the Illinois at one hundred per cent, and to the Alibamons at fifty per cent.

Article VIII
Wine will be sold at 120 livres a keg, and a quarter of brandy at 120 livres, half-quarters, etc. proportionally.

We have been informed that some employees of the company have previously set aside the most sought-after merchandise to offer it to the inhabitants at much higher prices than those regulated by the company for personal profit. We have forbidden employees to carry on any commerce even indirectly during the time that they are in the service of the company; and in case anyone acts against these prohibitions we order the inhabitants to denounce them to the directors who will confiscate the merchandise and inform us.

Article IX
In order that the inhabitants be informed of the supplies in the warehouses of the company, we have ordered that on the first days of each month a list be attached to the door of the companies in New Biloxi, New Orleans, and Mobile, and, aware that there might be in New Biloxi merchandise which would not be found at New Orleans or Mobile, the list of merchandise at New Biloxi will be sent to Mobile and New Orleans.

Article X
There will be sent copper to pay the salaries of the troops and the daily fixed expenses of the company. . . . The inhabitants must not cause any trouble on receiving the copper from the troops and others in payment for merchandise, because this copper will be received in the treasuries of the company in payment for all kinds of merchandise at the same value as gold and silver.

Article XI
We sent orders to divide the colony in nine parts which will be New Orleans, Biloxi, Mobile, Alibamons, the Natchez, Yazoos, the Natchitoches, the Arkansas, and the Illinois.

The colonists will be informed by the Council of Louisiana to which region they belong.

There will be in the main settlement of each region a commander and a judge, who will determine which appeals will be taken to a Superior Council established in Biloxi.

The above order is established so that the inhabitants may easily ask the commanders of their region for protection, and need not leave their homes to seek justice. We urge them to avoid legal proceedings as much as possible, and to live in peace and harmony and help each other.

Article XII
We likewise exhort them to be more regular in fulfilling their duties as Christians than they have been up to the present. To enable them to do so, we order that a sufficient number of chapels and churches be built so that the inhabitants may be easily able to attend Mass and receive the sacraments.

Given at Paris, September 17, 1721
Signed: Dodun, Ferrand, and Maraut

Questions to Consider:

1. *Based on your reading of this document, what would you say were the top priorities of the Company of the Indies?*
2. *What does the document tell you about how the Company of the Indies viewed enslaved people and slavery?*
3. *Do you think the council of the Company of the Indies set itself up for failure by creating some of these rules? How so?*

Source:

Jean-Baptiste Bèrnard de La Harpe, *The Historical Journal of the Establishment of the French in Louisiana*, USL History Series, no. 3, ed. and annot. Glenn R. Conrad, trans. Joan Cain and Virginia Koenig (Lafayette, LA: Center for Louisiana Studies, University of Southwestern Louisiana, 1971), 137–40.

1721:
Le Gac on "the Situation in Louisiana"

Charles Le Gac, named director-general of Louisiana by the Company of the Indies in 1719, documented the colony from an on-the-ground perspective. The following report, dated March 5, 1721, provides an overview of Louisiana's demographic and economic situation of the time.

At Alabamons there is a stockade called Fort Toulouse. Stationed there are sixty to seventy soldiers, a captain, three officers, two sergeants and one clerk who pays the soldiers and conducts trade with the Indians and settlers.

At Mobile there is a similar fort which has been rebuilt. In command is M. de Chateauguay, the king's lieutenant. There are two hundred soldiers, a head clerk, a storekeeper, and some clerks who distribute food and supplies to the two hundred and fifty to three hundred persons who are there. Some of these people have settled on the river to grow rice, tobacco and to saw planks for houses.

There are not more than ten farms in the vicinity of Mobile. . . . The majority of the inhabitants are engaged in trade. There are about eighty houses belonging to the company and to the settlers. There is a mill to saw planks.

With regard to animals, there are not more than one hundred head of cattle because those belonging to the settlers have been moved onto farms along the river or have been transported inland or have been eaten.

At Dauphin Island there are only two officers, a sergeant, two corporals and twelve soldiers. There is but a single settler, one named Arnaud, who has a garden, some sandy land cleared of trees, some Indian and negro slaves, and some cows. There might be three or four other families there, but they are awaiting the completion of work at Biloxi before moving.

At Pensacola there is only a garrison—no settlers.

At the Pascagoula River there is Graveline's farm which is the best in the colony for the number of animals. He has about seventy beasts. In addition, he has begun to farm with the help of Indian and Negro slaves. There are five other small farms in the vicinity but because of the lack of assistance, very little can be done and their owners live from hand to mouth.

In February 1721 M. de Reveillon established a farm. It is one of the best stocked farms in Louisiana and there are about fifty-five to sixty persons, black and white, living on it. The Reveillon farm is only eighteen miles by land from Old Biloxi; by water, however, it is fifteen miles by sea to the entrance of the river and forty-five miles up the river to the farm.

At Biloxi, the Old and New, is to be found the commander of the province, Bienville, along with the major officers and subalterns, two hundred and fifty soldiers, and the Swiss company of M. de Merveilleux. Also at Biloxi is the director-general of the Company, the head storekeeper, some clerks and other employees. The four engineers, their families and their workers also live at Biloxi.

In addition, there are the girls from La Salpêtrière of Paris, but eight or ten of them have already married. There are about two hundred prisoners and other persons of both sexes who are incapable of working because of illness, injuries or age. There are four carpenters and caulkers employed by the Company. Finally, there are about one hundred and fifty men who serve on the transport boats between Ship Island and Biloxi.

The following groups of colonists are present at Biloxi awaiting transportation to their lands.

1. The Groups being conducted by M. [Jean-Baptiste] Faucon-Dumanoir, who has come to take his people and their belongings to Natchez.

2. The group being conducted by Elias Stultheus [Louis-Elias Stutheus] (M. Law's group) who will take his people to the Arkansas River.

3. The group being conducted by M. de Guiche, who is to go with M. Stultheus.

4. The group being conducted by M. du Rost who will take these people to the Yazoo. They will be joined by a company of soldiers being sent to M. LeBlance under the command of M. Bizard.

5. That group conducted by M. Ceard. No plans for this group can be made now because of the illness among his people.

6. Also that of M. d'Artaguiette and L'Epinay.

Thus we count that there are at Old and New Biloxi more than twenty-five hundred people on Company rations.

Questions to Consider:

1. *From this brief report, what can you determine about the European population of Louisiana in 1721?*
2. *Based on what Le Gac discusses, what were the most pressing needs for the colony?*

Source:

Glenn R. Conrad, trans., ed., and annot., *Immigration and War, Louisiana: 1718–1721, from the Memoir of Charles Le Gac*, USL History Series, no. 1 (Lafayette, LA: Center for Louisiana Studies, University of Southwestern Louisiana, 1970), 49–51.

1722:
Charlevoix's Louisiana

The following letter, written by Jesuit priest and educator Pierre François Xavier de Charlevoix to "Madam," gives a glimpse of how observers could see both the contemporary scene and also the future importance of the Mississippi River and its gateway, New Orleans.

New Orleans, January 10, 1722
Madam,

I am now at last arrived at this famous city of *Nouvelle Orleans*, New Orleans. Those who have given it this name, must have imagined Orleans was of the feminine gender. But of what consequence is this? Custom, which is superior to all the laws of grammar, has fixed it so.

This is the first city, which one of the greatest rivers in the world has seen erected on its banks. If the eight fine houses and the five parishes, which our *Mercury* bestowed upon it two years ago, are at present reduced to a hundred barracks, placed in no very good order; to a large ware-house built of timber; to two or three houses which would be no ornament to a village in France; to one half of a sorry ware-house, formerly set apart for divine service, and was scarce appropriated for that purpose when it was removed to a tent: what pleasure on the other hand, must it give to see this future capital of an immense and beautiful country increasing insensibly, and to be able, not with a sigh like Virgil's hero, when speaking of his native country consumed by the flames *et campus ubi Trojæ fuit*, but full of the best grounded hopes to say, that this wild and desart [*sic*] place, at present almost entirely covered over with canes and trees, shall one day, and perhaps that day is not very far off, become the capital of a large and rich colony.

Your Grace will, perhaps, ask me upon what these hopes are founded? They are founded on the situation of this city on the banks of a navigable river, at the distance of thirty-three leagues from the sea, from which a vessel may come up in twenty-four hours; on the fertility of its soil; on the mildness and wholesomeness of the climate, in thirty degrees north latitude; on the industry of the inhabitants; on its neighbourhood to Mexico, the Havana, the finest islands of America, and lastly, to the English colonies. Can there be any thing more requisite to render a city flourishing? Rome and Paris had not such considerable beginnings, were not built under such happy auspices, and their founders met not with those advantages on the Seine and the Tiber, which we have found on the Mississippi, in comparison of which, these two rivers are no more than brooks. . . .

Questions to Consider:

1. *What was the city of New Orleans like when Charlevoix wrote in 1722?*
2. *Was Charlevoix's optimism for the future of New Orleans warranted?*

Source:

Pierre F. X. de Charlevoix, *Charlevoix's Louisiana: Selections from the History and the Journal*, ed. Charles E. O'Neill (Baton Rouge: Louisiana State University Press, 1977), 155–56.

1724:
Excerpts from the *Code Noir*

As made explicit by its title, "The Black Code" in English, Louisiana's *Code Noir* governed Africans, both free and slave, in the colony. Modeled on the 1685 *Code Noir* of the French colony of Saint-Domingue (later called Haiti), the code went well beyond simply applying rules to the enslaved and their "owners," however. It established rules for religious practice in the colony, sexual relations between races, and activities of the *gens de couleur libres* (free people of color).

I. Decrees the expulsion of Jews from the colony.

II. Makes it imperative on masters to impart religious instruction to their slaves.

III. Permits the exercise of the Roman Catholic creed only. Every other mode of worship is prohibited.

IV. Negroes placed under the direction or supervision of any other person than a Catholic, are liable to confiscation.

V. Sundays and holidays are to be strictly observed. All negroes found at work on these days are to be confiscated.

VI. We forbid our white subjects, of both sexes, to marry with the blacks, under the penalty of being fined and subjected to some other arbitrary punishment. We forbid all curates, priests, or missionaries of our secular or regular clergy, and even our chaplains in our navy to sanction such marriages. We also forbid all our white subjects, and even the manumitted or free-born blacks, to live in a state of concubinage with blacks. Should there be any issue from this kind of intercourse, it is our will that the person so offending, and the master of the slave, should pay each a fine of three hundred livres. Should said issue be the result of the concubinage of the master with his slave, said master shall not only pay the fine, but be deprived of the slave and of the children, who shall be adjudged to the hospital of the locality, and said slaves shall be forever incapable of being set free. But should this illicit intercourse have existed between a free black and his slave, when said free black had no legitimate wife, and should said black marry said slave according to the forms prescribed by the church, said slave shall be thereby set free, and the children shall also become free and legitimate; and in such a case, there shall be no application of the penalties mentioned in the present article.

VII. The ceremonies and forms prescribed by the ordinance of Blois, and by the edict of 1639, for marriages, shall be observed both with regard to free persons and to slaves. But the consent of the father and mother of the slave is not necessary; that of the master shall be the only one required.

VIII. We forbid all curates to proceed to effect marriages between slaves without proof of the consent of their masters; and we also forbid all masters to force their slaves into any marriage against their will.

IX. Children, issued from the marriage of slaves, shall follow the condition of their parents, and shall belong to the master of the wife and not of the husband, if the husband and wife have different masters.

X. If the husband be a slave, and the wife a free woman, it is our will that their children, of whatever sex they may be, shall share the condition of their mother, and be as free as she, notwithstanding the servitude of their father; and if the father be free and the mother a slave, the children shall all be slaves.

XI. Masters shall have their Christian slaves buried in consecrated ground.

XII. We forbid slaves to carry offensive weapons or heavy sticks, under the penalty of being whipped, and of having said weapons confiscated for the benefit of the person seizing the same. An exception is made in favor of those slaves who are sent a hunting or a shooting by their masters, and who carry with them a written permission to that effect, or are designated by some known mark or badge.

XIII. We forbid slaves belonging to different masters to gather in crowds either by day or by night, under the pretext of a wedding, or for any other cause, either at the dwelling or on the grounds of one of their masters, or elsewhere, and much less on the highways or in secluded places, under the penalty of corporal punishment, which shall not be less than the whip. In case of frequent offences of the kind, the offenders shall be branded with the mark of the fleur-de-lis, and should there be aggravating circumstances, capital punishment may be applied, at the discretion of our judges. We command all our subjects, be they officers or not, to seize all such offenders, to arrest and conduct them to prison, although there should be no judgment against them.

XIV. Masters who shall be convicted of having permitted or tolerated such gatherings as aforesaid, composed of other slaves than their own, shall be sentenced, individually, to indemnify their neighbors for the damages occasioned by said gatherings, and to pay, for the first time, a fine of thirty livres, and double that sum on the repetition of the offence.

XV. We forbid negroes to sell any commodities, provisions, or produce of any kind, without the written permission of their masters, or without wearing their known marks or badges, and any persons purchasing anything from negroes in violence of this article, shall be sentenced to pay a fine of 1500 livres. . . .

XX. Slaves who shall not be properly fed, clad, and provided for by their masters, may give information thereof to the attorney-general of the Superior Council, or to all the other officers of justice of an inferior jurisdiction, and may put the written exposition of their wrongs into their hands; upon which information, and even ex officio, should the information come from another quarter, the attorney-general shall prosecute said masters without charging any costs to the complainants. It is our will that this regulation be observed in all accusations for crimes or barbarous and inhuman treatment brought by slaves against their masters.

XXI. Slaves who are disabled from working, either by old age, disease, or otherwise, be the disease incurable or not, shall be fed and provided for by their masters; and in case they should have been abandoned by said masters, said slaves shall be adjudged to the nearest hospital, to which said masters shall be obliged to pay eight cents a day for the food and maintenance of each one of these slaves; and for the payment of this sum, said hospital shall have a lien on the plantations of the master.

XXII. We declare that slaves can have no right to any kind of property, and that all that they acquire, either by their own industry or by the liberality of others, or by any other means or title whatever, shall be the full property of their masters; and the children of said slaves, their fathers and mothers, their kindred or other relations, either free or slaves, shall have no pretensions or claims thereto, either through testamentary dispositions or donations inter vivos; which dispositions and donations we declare null and void, and also whatever promises they may have made, or whatever obligations they may have subscribed to, as having been entered into by persons incapable of disposing of anything, and of participating to any contract.

XXIII. Masters shall be responsible for what their slaves have done by their command, and also for what transactions they have permitted their slaves to do in their shops, in the particular line of commerce with which they were entrusted; and in case said slaves should have acted without the order or authorization of their masters, said masters shall be responsible only for so much as has turned to their profit; and if said masters have not profited by the doing or transaction of their slaves, the peculium which the masters have permitted the slaves to own, shall be subjected to all claims against said slaves, after deduction made by the masters of what may be due to them; and if said peculium should consist, in whole or in part, of merchandises in which the slaves had permission to traffic, the masters shall only come in for their share in common with the other creditors.

XXIV. Slaves shall be incapable of all public functions, and of being constituted agents for any other person than their own masters, with powers to manage or conduct any kind of trade; nor can they serve as arbitrators or experts; nor shall they be called to give their testimony either in civil or in criminal cases, except when it shall be a matter of necessity, and only in default of white people; but in no case shall they be permitted to serve as witnesses either for or against their masters.

XXV. Slaves shall never be parties to civil suits, either as plaintiffs or defendants, nor shall they be allowed to appear as complainants in criminal cases, but their masters shall have the right to act for them in civil matters, and in criminal ones, to demand punishment and reparation for such outrages and excesses as their slaves may have suffered from.

XXVI. Slaves may be prosecuted criminally, without their masters being made parties to the trial, except they should be indicted as accomplices; and said slaves shall be tried, at first, by the judges of ordinary jurisdiction, if there be any, and on appeal, by the Superior Council, with the same rules, formalities, and proceedings observed for free persons, save the exceptions mentioned hereafter.

XXVII. The slave who, having struck his master, his mistress, or the husband of his mistress, or their children, shall have produced a bruise, or the shedding of blood in the face, shall suffer capital punishment.

XXVIII. With regard to outrages or acts of violence committed by slaves against free persons, it is our will that they be punished with severity, and even with death, should the case require it.

XXIX. Thefts of importance, and even the stealing of horses, mares, mules, oxen, or cows, when executed by slaves or manumitted persons, shall make the offender liable to corporal, and even to capital punishment. . . .

XXX. The stealing of sheep, goats, hogs, poultry, grain, fodder, peas, beans, or other vegetables, produce, or provisions, when committed by slaves, shall be punished according to the circumstances of the case; and the judges may sentence them, if necessary, to be whipped by the public executioner, and branded with the mark of the fleur-de-lis.

XXXI. In cases of thefts committed or damages done by their slaves, masters, besides the corporal punishment inflicted on their slaves, shall be bound to make amends for the injuries resulting from the acts of said slaves, unless they prefer abandoning them to the sufferer. They shall be bound so to make their choice, in three days from the time of the conviction of the negroes; if not, this privilege shall be forever forfeited.

XXXII. The runaway slave, who shall continue to be so for one month from the day of his being denounced to the officers of justice, shall have his ears cut off, and shall be branded with the fleur-de-lis on the shoulder, and on a second offence of the same nature, persisted in during one month from the day of his being denounced, he shall be hamstrung, and be marked with the fleur-de-lis on the other shoulder. On the third offence, he shall suffer death.

XXXIII. Slaves, who shall have made themselves liable to the penalty of the whip, the fleur-de-lis brand, and ear cutting, shall be tried, in the last resort, by the ordinary judges of the inferior courts, and shall undergo the sentence passed upon them without there being an appeal to the Superior Council, in confirmation or reversal of judgment, notwithstanding the article 26th of the present code, which shall be applicable only to those judgments in which the slave convicted is sentenced to be hamstrung or suffer death.

XXXIV. Freed or free-born negroes, who shall have afforded refuge in their houses to fugitive slaves, shall be sentenced to pay to the masters of said slaves, the sum of thirty livres a day for every day during which they shall have concealed said fugitives; and all other free persons, guilty of the same offence, shall pay a fine of ten livres a day as aforesaid; and should the freed or free-born negroes not be able to pay the fine herein specified, they shall be reduced to the condition of slaves, and be sold as such. Should the price of the sale exceed the sum mentioned in the judgment, the surplus shall be delivered to the hospital.

XXXV. We permit our subjects in this colony, who may have slaves concealed in any place whatever, to have them sought after by such persons and in such a way as they may deem proper, or to proceed themselves to such researches, as they may think best.

XXXVI. The slave who is sentenced to suffer death on the denunciation of his master, shall, when that master is not an accomplice to his crime, be appraised before his execution by two of the principal inhabitants of the locality, who shall be especially appointed by the judge, and the amount of said appraisement shall be paid to the master. To raise this sum, a proportional tax shall be laid on every slave, and shall be collected by the persons invested with that authority.

XXXVII. We forbid all the officers of the Superior Council, and all our other officers of justice in this colony, to take any fees or receive any perquisites in criminal suits against slaves, under the penalty, in so doing, of being dealt with as guilty of extortion.

XXXVIII. We also forbid all our subjects in this colony, whatever their condition or rank may be, to apply, on their own private authority, the rack to their slaves, under any pretense whatever, and to mutilate said slaves in any one of their limbs, or in any part of their bodies, under the penalty of the confiscation of said slaves; and said masters, so offending, shall be liable to a criminal prosecution. We only permit masters, when they shall think that the case requires it, to put their slaves in irons, and to have them whipped with rods or ropes.

XXXIX. We command our officers of justice in this colony to institute criminal process against masters and overseers who shall have killed or mutilated their slaves, when in their power and under their supervision, and to punish said murder according to the atrocity of the circumstances; and in case the offence shall be a pardonable one, we permit them to pardon said masters and overseers without its being necessary to obtain from us letters patent of pardon.

XL. Slaves shall he held in law as movables, and as such, they shall be part of the community of assets between husband and wife; they shall not be liable to be seized under any mortgage whatever; and they shall be equally divided among the co-heirs. . . .

XLIII. Husbands and wives shall not be seized and sold separately when belonging to the same master, and their children, when under fourteen years of age, shall not be separated from their parents, and such seizures and sales shall be null and void. The present article shall apply to voluntary sales, and in case such sales should take place in violation of the law, the seller shall be deprived of the slave he has illegally retained, and said slave shall be adjudged to the purchaser without any additional price being required.

XLIV. Slaves, fourteen years old, and from this age up to sixty, who are settled on lands and plantations, and are at present working on them, shall not be liable to seizure for debt, except for what may be due out of the purchase money agreed to be paid for them, unless said grounds or plantations should also be distressed, and any seizure and judicial sale of a real estate, without including the slaves of the aforesaid age, who are part of said estate, shall be deemed null and void. . . .

L. Masters, when twenty-five years old, shall have the power to manumit their slaves, either by testamentary dispositions, or by acts inter vivos. But, as there may be mercenary masters disposed to set a price on the liberation of their slaves; and whereas slaves, with a view to acquire the necessary means to purchase their freedom, may be tempted to commit theft or deeds of plunder, no person, whatever may be his rank and condition, shall be permitted to set free his slaves, without obtaining from the Superior Council a decree of permission to that effect; which permission shall be granted without costs, when the motives for the setting free of said slaves, as specified in the petition of the master, shall appear legitimate to the tribunal. All acts for the emancipation of slaves, which, for the future, shall be made without this permission, shall be null; and the slaves, so freed, shall not be entitled to their freedom; they shall, on the contrary, continue to be held as slaves; but they shall be taken away from their former masters, and confiscated for the benefit of the India Company.

LI. However, should slaves be appointed by their masters tutors to their children, said slaves shall be held and regarded as being thereby set free to all intents and purposes.

LII. We declare that the acts for the enfranchisement of slaves, passed according to the forms above described, shall be equivalent to an act of naturalization, when said slaves are not born in our colony of Louisiana, and they shall enjoy all the rights and privileges inherent to our subjects born in our kingdom or in any land or country under our dominion. We declare, therefore, that all manumitted slaves, and all freeborn negroes, are incapable of receiving donations, either by testamentary dispositions, or by acts inter vivos from the whites. Said donations shall be null and void, and the objects so donated shall be applied to the benefit of the nearest hospital.

LIII. We command all manumitted slaves to show the profoundest respect to their former masters, to their widows and children, and any injury or insult offered by said manumitted slaves to their former masters, their widows or children shall be punished with more severity than if it had been offered to any other person. We, however, declare them exempt from the discharge of all duties or services, and from the payment of all taxes or fees, or anything else which their former masters might, in their quality of patrons, claim either in relation to their persons, or to their personal or real estate, either during the life or after the death of said manumitted slaves.

LIV. We grant to manumitted slaves the same rights, privileges, and immunities which are enjoyed by freeborn persons. It is our pleasure that their merit in having acquired their freedom, shall produce in their favor, not only with regard to their persons, but also to their property, the same effects which our other subjects derive from the happy circumstance of their having been born free.

In the name of the King,
Bienville, De la Chaise.
Fazende, Buslé, Perry, March, 1724.

Questions to Consider:

1. *Does the code presume that slaves are humans with souls, or does it presume they are chattel? Explain.*

2. *How does the Code Noir's restrictions and rules for the enslaved and their "owners" differ from your preconceived notions about American slavery? Be specific.*

3. *Besides the enslaved and their owners, what can you learn about other colonial populations from the Code Noir?*

Source:

B. F. French, *Historical Collections of Louisiana: Embracing Translations of Many Rare and Valuable Documents Relating to the Natural, Civil, and Political History of that State* (New York: D. Appleton, 1851).

1728:
Marie-Madeleine Hachard's View of New Orleans

Although New Orleans had become colonial Louisiana's capitol and largest population center by the late 1720s, very few extant sources describe life in the city. Marie-Madeleine Hachard was among the earliest of the Ursuline Order of religious who came to New Orleans beginning in 1727. The Ursulines established a convent, a school, and an orphanage within a decade of their arrival. Meanwhile, Hachard wrote letters to her father from New Orleans that provide some of our earliest glimpses into what its inhabitants' lives were like.

January 1, 1728
Hachard to "Dear Father"
New Orleans

I believe that I told you that our city, named New Orleans, capital of all Louisiana is situated on the shore of the Mississippi River, on the east side. It is, in this place larger than the River Seine in Rouen. On our side of this river is a well-constructed levee to prevent the overflowing of the river into the city. And along this embankment, at the side of the city, is a big ditch to collect the water that might overflow it, with palisades of wood to close it.

On the other side of this river are wild woods in which there are some little cabins where the slaves of the Company of the Indies live. You see by this that the map of the state of Louisiana, which you told me you had bought, in which the city of New Orleans is represented as being situated on the shore of a lake named Pontchartrain, a distance of six leagues from the Mississippi River, is not correct. Our city is not situated on the shore of a lake, but rather on the shore of the Mississippi River. It is true that all the force of the river does not flow by here, for above our city the river separates to form three branches of the river that join below and empty themselves rapidly into the Gulf of Mexico.

Our city is very beautiful, well constructed and regularly built, as much as I am able to know of it from what I saw the day of our arrival in this land. Since that day, we have always remained in our cloister. Before our arrival we were given a very bad idea of the city. It is true that those who spoke to us of this had not been here for several years. They have worked, and they continue to work, to improve the city.

The streets are very wide and laid out in lines. The main street measures a league in length. The houses are very well constructed in *collombage* and mortar, whitewashed, paneled, and sunlit. The roofs of the houses are covered with little flat plates made of wood cut in the form of slate. One must know this, in order to believe it, for this covering has all the appearance and beauty of slate. It is enough to tell you that here one publicly sings a song in which there is only this city which resembles the city of Paris. This tells you everything.

In effect, it is a very beautiful city. If I do not have enough eloquence to describe to you the beauty expressed in the song it is because I find a difference between this city and the city of Paris. One could persuade people who have never seen the capitol of France, but I saw it, and the song will not persuade me to the contrary of what I think. It is true that the city grows every day and could become as beautiful and large as the principal cities of France, if workers come again and the population grows in proportion to its size.

The women are ignorant of their welfare, but not of their vanity. The luxury in this city makes no distinctions of person; all are of equal magnificence. Most of them, along with their family, are reduced to living on nothing but *sagamité*, which is a kind of gruel. They are dressed in velvet and satin cloth or damasks full of ribbons, in spite of the cost, for these fabrics sell regularly in this country for three times more than in France. The women here, as women everywhere, wear white powder and rouge to hide the wrinkles on their faces, and beauty spots. In the end, the devil has a great empire here, but this does not take away from us the hope of destroying him, with God's love. There is an infinity of examples to make his strength show through our weakness. The more powerful the enemy is, the more we are encouraged to fight him. What pleases us is the docility of the children, whom one forms as one wants. The blacks are also easy to instruct once they learn to speak French. It is not the same for the savages, whom one does not baptize without trembling because of the tendency they have to sin, especially the women, who, under a modest air, the passion of beasts.

Since our arrival, our [temporary] residence has been the most beautiful house in the city. . . . It is situated at the end of the city. We have a courtyard and a garden, which adjoin each other on one side, and at the end are wild trees of prodigious height and girth. This makes us among the first for an infinite number of visits from mosquitoes and the *Frappes d'abord* [deerflies], and a type of flies or gnats whose species I still do not know. I know them neither by their first nor last names. I only see them, for at this moment, there are several flying around me that would like to attack me. These bad insects sting without mercy. We are assaulted by them at night. Happily, they appear only in the evening after sunset until the next morning, when they return to the woods. This obliges us to close our doors and windows securely at night, otherwise, they will not fail to come to see us in our beds. Whatever precautions we take, we are unable to escape carrying their marks. . . .

During Lent, we eat meat four days a week, as permitted by the Church. Other than during Lent, we fast only on Fridays. We drink beer. Our most common food is rice with milk, little wild beans, meat, and fish. But in the summer we eat little meat. They slaughter only twice a week. It is not easy to preserve. Hunting lasts all winter, which begins in the month of October. It is done ten miles from our city. They hunt wild cattle in great number, which they bring here and to the surrounding area. We buy the meat, such as venison, for three sols[1] per pound. This meat is better than beef or mutton that you eat in Rouen.

The wild ducks are very cheap here. Teals, waterfowl, geese, and other fowl and game are very common. We hardly buy any, for we do not want to indulge ourselves. Finally, it is a charming country all during winter, and in the summer, fish is very abundant and very good. There are oysters and carp of prodigious size which are delicious. In regard to other fish, there are

1. A *sol* was a coin, equivalent to 1/20 of a French livre.

none of this kind in France. There are large monstrous fish that are good enough. We also eat watermelons and French melons, and potatoes, which are large roots that one cooks in the ashes like chestnuts. These taste good, but sweeter, softer, and very good. All of this my dear Father, is just as I report it to you, I do not tell you anything of which I have not had experience. Here they eat many other kinds of meat, fish, and vegetables that I have not yet tasted, and I cannot tell you of their goodness.

As for the fruits of the country, there are many that we do not find very excellent, except the peaches and the figs, which are here in abundance. They send us such great quantities of these from the habitations that we have made preserves, and the jelly of the blackberries is very good. Reverend Father de Beaubois has the most beautiful garden in the city. It is full of orange trees, which bear oranges as beautiful and sweet as the ones in Cap Français. He gave us three hundred sour ones that we preserved. Thank God, we are not in need of anything. Our Reverend Father takes care to furnish us with our food. We fare much better than we believed we would, but that is neither our wish nor the intention of our enterprise. Our principal aim is to gain souls for the Lord, and He gives us the grace to succeed. Our Reverend Father aids us well in this. He says Holy Mass for us every day and gives us public talks. If we had the misfortune to lose him, through sickness or otherwise, we would be very saddened and most pitiable. . . .

Our little community grows from day to day. We have twenty boarders, of whom eight today made their first communion, three ladies also board, and three orphans that we took through charity. We also have seven slave boarders to instruct for baptism and first communion, besides a great number of day students, female blacks and female savages who come for two hours a day for instruction. The custom here is to marry the girls from age twelve to fourteen. Before our arrival, many married before they even knew how many Gods there are. Judge the rest. But since we have been here, none of them have been married without having come to receive our instructions.

We are accustomed to seeing people who are completely black. A few days ago, they gave us two black boarders aged six and seventeen to instruct in our religion, and they will remain here to serve us. If it were the fashion here, black women would wear beauty marks on their faces. They would be given white ones, which would create quite a funny effect.

You see, my dear Father, the sorts of things upon which we can exercise our zeal. I cannot tell you the pleasure that we get from instructing all these young people. It is enough for us to consider the needs that they have. The boarders, ranging from twelve to fifteen years of age, have never been to Confession or even to Mass. They were raised on their habitations, five to six leagues from this city, and in consequence without any spiritual succor. They had never heard anyone speak of God. When we tell them the most common things, for them they are oracles that come out of our mouths. We have the consolation to find in them great docility and a strong desire to be instructed. All would like to be nuns, which is not to the liking of Reverend de Beaubois, our very worthy superior. He finds it more proper for them to become Christian mothers who, by their good example, will finally establish religion in the country.

Questions to Consider:

1. *Is Hachard's description of New Orleans believable? Does any of it seem embellished or understated?*
2. *What was life like for New Orleanians of the late 1720s?*
3. *What does the letter tell us about Hachard as its writer?*

Source:

Emily Clark, ed., *Voices from an Early American Convent: Marie Madeleine Hachard and the New Orleans Ursulines, 1727–1760* (Baton Rouge: Louisiana State University Press, 2007), 76–84.

1729/1751:
Bossu on the Natchez Revolt

Jean Bernard Bossu, a French naval captain and explorer, wrote a series of letters during three separate trips to North America from the 1750s through the 1770s. Two of his voyages took him to Louisiana, where he traveled extensively and reported his views of Europeans, Africans, and American Indians. The below passage describes the Natchez Revolt of 1729, including the internal deliberations of the Natchez leadership in response to French aggressions. Bossu wrote the letter in 1751, well after the event.

In all fairness to the Indians, it must be said that their plan to kill all the French was not the result of treachery or instability. It was the bad conduct of an officer who insulted and infuriated the very people he should have been handling gently. Free and peaceful people, who were living in a land settled by their ancestors, could not permit themselves to be tyrannized by foreigners whom they had welcomed. Monsieur de Chepar, commander of Natchez post, did not win the friendship of either the French or the Indians in his care. He mistreated everyone who was unwilling to go along with his criminal ideas, and he gave important posts to sergeants and corporals who were personally devoted to him. You can easily understand, sir, that such favoritism would subvert all military discipline.

Monsieur Dupont, the second in command, registered official complaints which were not heeded. The only answer he received was to be thrown into irons. As soon as he was freed, he went down to the capital to bring his charges before Monsieur Perrier, the governor of Louisiana. Monsieur de Chepar was recalled to explain his conduct. He was to be broken in irons, but his intrigues and his influence saved him. He was reinstated and sent back to his post.

This humiliating experience had no influence on him. He behaved in exactly the same way that he always had and was equally detested by the French and the Indians, whom he irritated to such a degree that they were forced to take extreme and terrible measures. Monsieur de Chepar, who was eager to make a fortune as quickly as possible, ordered the Sun [chief] of a village called Pomme to move out with all his people. The land, which Chepar was to turn into a plantation would bring him a handsome profit. The Chief explained that the bones of his ancestors were buried there, but his arguments were useless. The French commander ordered the Chief Sun to evacuate the village and even threatened to send him to New Orleans in chains if he did not obey promptly. Perhaps the officer thought that he could treat this chief like a slave. It never occurred to him that he was speaking to a man who was accustomed to giving commands and whose authority over his subjects was absolute.

The Chief Sun listened to him and went off without becoming angry. He assembled his council, and they decided to inform Monsieur de Chepar that, before Pomme could be abandoned, plans for a new village would have to be drawn up. That would take two moons.

The decision was made known to the Commander, who rebuked the messengers and threatened them with the severest punishment if Pomme were not turned over to him within a very short time. When this answer was delivered to the council, the elders concluded that the best policy was to try to gain enough time so that they could think of a way to get rid of these disagreeable guests who were becoming tyrannical. Since they knew that Monsieur de Chepar was very greedy, they thought up a scheme whereby he would grant them a delay of several moons, during which period each cabin would pay him in corn, fowl, and skins. The Commander fell into the trap because of his greed. He accepted the proposition, pretending that he was doing it only to oblige this nation which he loved because of its long-standing friendship for France.

The Sun, who was not taken in by this false altruism, assembled his council once more and announced that the time requested had been granted. During this period of grace, they were to think of a way to end the burdensome tribute they were paying and, especially, to put a stop to the domination of the tyrannical French. He pointed out to them that this enterprise required the profoundest secrecy, well-founded plans, and especially, a great deal of strategy. He advised them, in the meantime, to redouble all their outward signs of friendship and confidence in dealing with the French, while thinking of what had to be done. They were to come back to the council as soon as they had thought of some plan whose success could be assured.

For five or six days the noble elders conferred with each other, and they concluded once again unanimously to destroy all the French. After having greeted his chief, the oldest member of the council reported the decision in this manner:

> We have noticed for a long time that having the French as neighbors has done us more harm than good. We old men see it, but the young men do not. The supplies from Europe please them, but of what use are they? To seduce our women, to corrupt our nation, to lead our daughters astray, to make them proud and lazy. Our boys are the same. Young married men must work themselves to death to keep their wives in luxury. Before the French came into our lands, we were happy with what we had, we walked boldly upon all our paths, because then we were our own masters. But today we tread gropingly, fearing thorns. We walk like the slaves which we will soon be, since they already treat us as though we were. When they are strong enough, they will no longer treat us with consideration. They will put us in chains. Has not their chief already threatened ours with this affront? Is not death preferable to slavery?

The orator paused to catch his breath and then went on:

> What are we waiting for? Are we to let the French grow in numbers until we can no longer resist them? What will the other nations say? We are considered the wisest of all the red men. They will rightly say that we have less intelligence than the other peoples. Why wait longer? Let us free ourselves and prove that we are real men. Let us start this very day to get ready for it. Let us have the women prepare food without telling them why. Let us carry the peace pipe to all the nations of this country and tell them that the French hope to dominate our continent. Since they are stronger in our region than any place else, we shall be the first to wear their chains. When they are powerful enough, they will do the same to all the tribes. Let us convince the others that it is in their interest to prevent this

> misfortune. This can be done only by exterminating the French. Let all the nation join us in the task of wiping out the French, wherever they may be, in the same hours of the same day. Let the massacre take place at the end of the period of time granted us by their chief. In that way we will be free of the burden of our self-imposed tribute and we will get back the products which we have given him. On that great day of freedom, our warriors will carry their firearms. The Natchez will go among the French, and, in each house, we shall outnumber them three or four to one. Our warriors, pretending to go out on a hunt in preparation of a great feast, will borrow firearms and ammunition and will promise to bring back game. The shots fired at the Commander's home will be the signal for attacking the French. The other nations must help us by carrying out similar massacres in their territories at the same time. To succeed in this, we shall have to prepare bundles consisting of equal numbers of twigs, one bundle to be given to each nation. Each morning of the waiting period, one twig will be cut up and thrown into the fire. When there is only one left, they will know that the time for the slaughter has come. It will begin at the first quarter of the day [at nine o'clock in the morning], and we shall all attack the tyrants at the same time from all directions. Once these are destroyed, it will be easy to keep others who may come from the Old World across the great lake from settling among us. It is extremely important that one twig be removed every day without fail. The slightest error can bring dangerous consequences. We shall give this duty to a wise man and shall ask our neighbors to do likewise.

When the orator had finished, the elders gave their approval.

The Sun of Pomme was particularly pleased with this suggestion; since he was the one most hurt by Monsieur de Chepar's injustice, he considered this a matter of personal vengeance. He was so eager to this scheme succeed that he warned the council to be indiscreet and even made the members promise not to reveal it to the female Suns. As much as he wanted to get rid of the French, the Chief Sun, who had to give his approval, felt that the plan called for too much violence. The Sun of Pomme, considered a just and intelligent man by his people, determined to win the Chief Sun over to the plan. He did this by making the Chief realize that his very own safety depended upon this course of action. The French commander had, after all, threatened to chase him from his village. The Chief Sun was weak because of his youth; the man speaking to him was clever; the plan was approved. The next day, when the Suns came to greet their chief, they were told for one reason or another to go to the village of Pomme and did not suspect that they were under specific orders to do so. Everything went according to plan. Charmed by the Sun of Pomme's engaging wit, they all agreed to take part in the conspiracy. They immediately formed a council of Suns and noble elders, which accepted the plan unanimously after it had once again been explained. The elders, accompanied by warriors, were sent out as envoys to the other nations. They were forbidden, under pain of death, to speak to anyone about their mission. Without the French knowing it, all these groups immediately set out together.

Although the secret of the Natchez was well guarded, the meeting of the council of Suns and noble elders worried the people. It is a well-known fact that the people of every country manage to learn court secrets. In this case, however, their curiosity was not satisfied. Only the female Suns, or princesses, had the right to ask why something was being kept secret from them. The Chief Sun's wife was only eighteen years old and was not too much concerned, but Stung Arm, the Chief Sun's mother, a woman well-aware of her intelligence, was not pleased that a secret was being kept from her. When she complained to her son, he told her that the envoys were sent out to renew friendly relations with the other nations, who thought that they were being scorned because the peace pipe had not been smoked with them for so long a time. This excuse seemed to calm Stung Arm, but she was really still troubled. Her worries were increased when she saw the Suns meet secretly with the returned envoys to find out how they were received by the other nations. Such meetings were usually public.

The Princess was furious at the idea that they were hiding from the nation and even from her what they had a right to know. It was only prudence that kept her from breaking out in anger. It was fortunate for the French that she thought she was being treated with contempt. She was right in thinking that the secret would be more loosely guarded and she would find out nothing if she showed her anger. She slyly thought of a sure way to satisfy her curiosity. She got her son to visit a sick relative who lived in the village of Pomme. She took him the long way by telling him it was more beautiful than the other. Her true reason was that they would meet fewer people on the path. She very shrewdly thought that this mystery concerned some sinister plot against the French. The coming and going of the Sun of Pomme supported her belief. When she and her some came to a lonely spot, she spoke to him.

"Let us sit down here. I am tired, and I also have something to say to you." When they were seated, she added, "Open your ears and listen to me, I have always taught you not to lie. I have always told you that a liar is not worthy of being considered a man and that a lying Sun deserves even the contempt of women. I think that you will tell me the truth. Tell me, are not all the Suns brothers? Yet all the Suns are keeping something from me as though my lips were cut and could not keep a secret. Have you ever known me to speak in my sleep? I am deeply hurt by my brothers' contempt for me, but even more by yours. Did I not feed you at my breast? Did I not give you the best blood I had? Does not that same blood flow in your veins? Would you be a Sun if you were not my child? Have you already forgotten that, without the care I gave you, you would have died a long time ago? I have told you, and so has everyone else, that you are the son of a Frenchman; but my own blood is dearer to me that that of stranger. Today I walk beside you like a dog, without being looked at. I am amazed that you do not shove me aside with your foot. I am not surprised that the others avoid me, but can you, who are my son? Have you ever seen a son distrust his mother in our nation? You alone behave this way. There is all this activity in the nation, and yet I do not know the reason for it, I who am the Chief Sun's mother. Are you afraid that I shall oppose you and make you the slave of the French, against whom you plan to take action? How tired I am of being scorned and of dealing with ungrateful men!"

The Chief Sun was deeply touched by the words he had just heard. He wept and listened to these reproaches with the usual calm of the Americans and with the respect due a mother and a princess.

Then he answered her, "Your reproaches are like arrows which pierce my heart. I do not think that I have ever rebuffed you or scorned you. Have you never heard that the decisions of the council elders are not to be revealed? Is not the keeping of a secret the duty of every man, and should I not, as chief, set the example? This was kept from my wife just as it was from you. Even though everyone knows that I am the son of a Frenchman, I have been trusted. We all knew that with your intelligence you would discover the secret, but since it was kept from my wife, was it right to tell you of it? Since you have guessed it all, what do you want me to tell you? You know as much as I do. Just keep your mouth closed."

She replied, "It was not very difficult for me to figure out against whom you were taking all these precautions. Since the French are involved, I am afraid that the measures you have taken to surprise them are not good enough. I know that they are very intelligent, even though their commander seems to have lost his mind. They have enough wealth to turn the warriors of the other nations against us. If your quarrel was with red men, I would sleep more peacefully. I am no longer young, and an old woman's life is not worth much, but yours is dear to me. If the elders think that it is as easy to surprise the French as it is the red men, they have made a serious mistake. The French have resources that we do not have. You know that they have cloth that speaks [paper]."

Her son told her that she had nothing to worry about as far as the plans were concerned. After he had told her everything that I have reported, he informed her that the bundle of sticks was in the temple on the flat wood (table).

When the Princess felt that she had learned enough, she pretended approval of all that had been done, and then leaving her son alone, she set about trying to find a way to thwart this barbarous plan. Time was short; the day for the massacre was not far off.

Unwilling to see the Natchez carry out their plan to kill all the French in a single day, the Princess decided to warn them. For this purpose, she used Indian girls who had French lovers, but she cautioned them never to reveal under whose orders they were working.

Ensign Mace, stationed at Fort Natchez, was advised of the plot by an Indian girl who loved him. She cried when she told him that her people were going to kill all the French. Astonished by this information, Monsieur Mace questioned his mistress. Her frightened, straightforward, and naïve answers convinced him that she was telling the truth. He went to report this immediately to Monsieur de Chepar, who had him arrested for spreading a false alarm. Seven colonists who found out about the plot the way as the ensign asked Chepar for arms to forestall a surprise attack. The Commander threw them in irons and called them cowards for trying to stir up trouble against a nation which had proven itself so friendly to him. The promptness with which the Indians paid their tribute gave him a feeling of security. Blinded by his contempt for them, he did not suspect them of subterfuge. He did not think that men of that kind were capable of being so shrewd.

When Stung Arm sadly realized that all her measures to save the French were useless, she decided to help them in spite of themselves. Since she could not save them all, she tried to find a way to reduce the number of victims. She sneaked into the temple and, without the knowledge of the priests, she pulled some of the twigs out of the fatal bundle. In that way, the day set for carrying out the plot would be advanced. She felt that the news of the massacre which would occur in Natchez territory would spread rapidly. The French who lived among the other nations would thus be warned and would prepare against attack. This was the only things she could possibly do, and she succeeded. When the Natchez, not realizing that they had been tricked, saw that they were down to the last twig, they began the slaughter according to plan, persuaded that their allies were acting at the same moment.

On December 28, 1729, at 8:00 A.M., shots were fired in front of Monsieur de Chepar's residence, giving the signal to the Indians who had infiltrated among the French. The attack began everywhere at once. The Kollys, chief clerks of the India Company, were the first to be killed. Monsieur de la Loire des Ursins' household was the only one that offered any resistance; his servant killed 8 Natchez before they were overcome. Monsieur des Ursins, who had just ridden out on his horse, started to turn back as soon as he heard the first shot, but he was stopped by a band of Indians. He defended himself courageously and killed 4 of them before he died. That is about all the casualties the Indians had in this surprise attack. They slaughtered about 2,000 men; only 20 of them and about 5 or 6 Negroes escaped, most of whom were wounded. About 150 children, 90 women, and as many Negroes were taken as slaves, in the hope that they could be sold to the English in the Carolinas.

During the massacre, the Chief Sun was seated in one of the sheds of the India Company. First he was brought the commanding officer's head, and around it were placed the heads of the most important Frenchmen. The other were heaped up in a pile. The unburied bodes were eaten by the vultures. Pregnant women were disemboweled, and almost all those who were nursing children were killed because of their annoying cries and tears. The others were all made slaves and were treated with the greatest indignity.

Some claim that Monsieur de Chepar, being unfortunate enough to die last, witnessed this horrible slaughter and realized too late that the advice given him had been wise. The Indians told him that those such as he were unworthy of dying at the hands of warriors. He was turned over to the "Stinkers," who killed him with arrows and then chopped off his head.

That was the end of the man who was guided only by his own decisions, cruelty, greed, and ambition. Since none of the French escaped alive, we cannot know how this officer really died. It is enough to know that he was dealing with naturally barbarous people and that he had antagonized them. Under a decent administration these people would have become the allies of the French and would have been very useful. This is how one man's faults can sometimes cause a whole colony to be lost. The greatest of caution must be used when we choose a commanding officer for these territories. Regardless of what we think of the Indians, they are not always easy to manage. Strategy and wisdom are needed to gain their good will. This story proves that you cannot insult them without suffering the consequences. Nothing could have been better carried out than this Natchez conspiracy. How much worse the situation would have been without the help of Providence! The French owed Princess Stung Arm a great deal. I do not know how this debt was paid.

The nations who were in the plot with the Natchez thought they had been betrayed, since they were not aware of the trick which had prematurely touched off the attack. The Choctaws thought that the Natchez did not want them to share in the booty. To prove to the French that they had nothing to do with the plot, they joined the punitive expedition against the Natchez. The French women and the Negroes taken as slaves were returned by the Natchez, whose fortified camps were attacked. The Natchez escaped during a storm and left the territory. About one thousand of them were captured, taken to New Orleans, and sold as slaves on the island of Santo Domingo. Among the prisoners were the Chief Sun, his wife, and his mother. The Chief Sun denied that the massacre was his idea. He said that his nation had taken advantage of his youth, that he had always like the French, and that it was really Monsieur de Chepar's outrageous behavior toward a free born people which had caused them to act in desperation. The French, satisfied that he was not guilty, treated him, his wife, and his mother with consideration. They soon died of grief, however, because they could not return to their people. The territory has been uninhabited since that time. The Natchez, too weak to resist the pursuing French, have found refuge among the Chickasaws.

Questions to Consider:

1. *Does Bossu describe the Natchez as "noble savages" or "brutal savages"?*
2. *Where do Bossu's sympathies lie?*
3. *How might Bossu have learned of the internal debates among the Natchez decades after the events actually took place?*

Source:

Seymour Feiler, trans. and ed., *Jean-Bernard Bossu's Travels in the Interior of North America, 1751–1762* (Norman, OK: University of Oklahoma Press, 1962), 37–47.

1758:
Le Page Du Pratz on "the Negroes of Louisiana"

Le Page du Pratz published his enormous, three-volume *Histoire de la Louisiane* in France in 1758. Du Pratz lived in Louisiana from 1718 until 1734, a crucial time in the French colony's development: the Company of the Indies became its governing authority, New Orleans became the colony's capital, John Law's "Mississippi Bubble" burst, the population increased rapidly, and by the end of his time there, the royal government reclaimed direct governance of the colony. The population growth reflected the arrival of Europeans from France and what is now Germany, but it also resulted from the forced immigration of enslaved Africans. Du Pratz held and managed concessions from the Company of the Indies—first along Bayou St. John, then at Natchez, and finally in New Orleans. At each of these locations, he likely oversaw the work of enslaved Africans.

The *Histoire de la Louisiane*, although usually recognized for its insightful depictions of American Indians, provided what Du Pratz thought would be useful advice for Europeans considering a move to the colony. In the excerpt below, taken from a very early English translation of Du Pratz's book, he shares his opinions on the characteristics of enslaved Africans and how best to manage them. All spellings within this text are from the original.

Book Three
CHAPTER IV.
Of the Negroes of Louisiana.

SECTION I.

Of the Choice of Negroes; of their Distemper, and the Manner of curing them.

Having finished my account of the natives of Louisiana, I shall conclude this treatise with some observations relating to the negroes; who, in the lower part of the province especially, perform all the labours of agriculture. On that account I have thought proper to give some instructions concerning them, for the benefit of those who are inclined to settle in that province.

The negroes must be governed differently from the Europeans; not because they are black, nor because they are slaves; but because they think differently from the white men.

First, they imbibe a prejudice from their infancy, that the white men buy them for no other purpose but to drink their blood; which is owing to this, that when the first negroes saw the Europeans drink claret, they imagined it was blood, as that wine is of a deep red colour; so that nothing but the actual experience of the contrary can eradicate the false opinion. But as none of those slaves who have had that experience ever return to their own country, the same prejudice continues to subsist on the coast of Guinea where we purchase them. Some who are strangers to the manner of thinking that prevails among the negroes, may perhaps think that the above remark is of no consequence, in respect to those slaves who are already sold to the French. There have been instances however of bad consequences flowing from this prejudice; especially if the negroes found no old slave of their own country upon their first arrival in our colonies. Some of them have killed or drowned themselves, several of them have deserted (which they call making themselves Marons) and all this from an apprehension that the white men were going to drink their blood. When they desert they believe they can get back to their own country by going round the sea, and may live in the woods upon the fruits, which they imagine are as common everywhere as with them.

They are very superstitious, and are much attached to their prejudices, and little toys which they call *gris, gris*. It would be improper therefore to take them from them, or even speak of them to them; for they would believe themselves undone, if they were stripped of those trinkets. The old negroes soon make them lose conceit of them.

The first thing you ought to do when you purchase negroes, is to cause them to be examined by a skilful surgeon and an honest man, to discover if they have the venereal or any other distemper. When they are viewed, both men and women are stripped naked as the hand, and are carefully examined from the crown of the head to the sole of the feet, then between the toes and between the fingers, in the mouth, in the ears, not excepting even the parts naturally concealed, though then exposed to view. You must ask your examining surgeon if he is acquainted with the distemper of the yaws, which is the virus of Guinea, and incurable by a great many French surgeons, though very skilful in the management of European distempers. Be careful not to be deceived in this point; for your surgeon may be deceived himself; therefore attend at the examination yourself, and observe carefully over all the body of the negro, whether you can discover any parts of the skin, which though black like the rest, are however as smooth as a looking-glass, without any tumor or rising. Such spots may be easily discovered; for the skin of a person who goes naked is usually all over wrinkles. Wherefore if you see such marks you must reject the negro, whether man or woman. There are always experienced surgeons at the sale of new negroes, who purchase them; and many of those surgeons have made fortunes by that means; but they generally keep their secret to themselves.

Another mortal distemper with which many negroes from Guinea are attacked, is the scurvy. It discovers itself by the gums, but sometimes it is so inveterate as to appear outwardly, in which case it is generally fatal. If any of my readers shall have the misfortune to have a negro attacked with one of those distempers, I will now teach him how to save him, by putting him in a way of being radically cured by the surgeons; for I have no inclination to fall out with those gentlemen. I learned this secret from a negro physician, who was upon the king's plantation, when I took the superintendence of it.

You must never put an iron instrument into the yaw; such an application would be certain death. In order to open the yaw, you take iron rust reduced to an impalpable powder, and passed through a fine search; you afterwards mix that powder with citron juice till it be of the consistence of an ointment, which you spread upon a linen cloth greased with hog's grease, or fresh lard without salt, for want of a better. You lay the plaster upon the yaw, and renew it evening and morning, which will open the yaw in a very short time without any incision.

The opening being once made, you take about the bulk of a goose's egg of hog's lard without salt, in which you incorporate about an ounce of good terebinthine; after which take a quantity of powdered verdigris, and soak it half a day in good vinegar, which you must then pour off gently with all the scum that floats at top. Drop a cloth all over with the verdigris that remains, and upon that apply your last ointment. All these operations are performed without the assistance of fire. The whole ointment being well mixed with a spatula, you dress the yaw with it; after that put your negro into a copious sweat, and he will be cured. Take special care that your surgeon uses no mercurial medicine, as I have seen; for that will occasion the death of the patient.

The scurvy is no less to be dreaded than the yaws; nevertheless you may get the better of it, by adhering exactly to the following prescription: take some scurvy-grass, if you have any plants of it, some ground-ivy, called by some St. John's wort, water-cresses from a spring or brook, and for want of that, wild cresses; take these three herbs, or the two last, if you have no scurvy-grass; pound them, and mix them with citron-juice, to make of them a soft paste, which the patient must keep upon both his gums till they be clean, at all times but when he is eating. In the mean while he must be suffered to drink nothing but an infusion of the herbs above named. You pound two handfuls of them, roots and all, after washing off any earth that may be upon the roots or leaves; to these you join a fresh citron, cut into slices. Having pounded all together, you then steep them in an earthen pan in a pint of pure water of the measure of Paris; after that you add about the size of a walnut of powdered and purified saltpetre, and to make it a little relishing to the negro, you add some powder sugar. After the water has stood one night, you squeeze out the herbs pretty strongly. The whole is performed cold, or without fire. Such is the dose for a bottle of water Paris measure; but as the patient ought to drink two pints a day, you may make several pints at a time in the above proportion.

In these two distempers the patients must be supported with good nourishment, and made to sweat copiously. It would be a mistake to think that they ought to be kept to a spare diet; you must give them nourishing food, but a little at a time. A negro can no more than any other person support remedies upon bad food, and still less upon a spare diet; but the quantity must be proportioned to the state of the patient, and the nature of the distemper. Besides, good food makes the best part of the remedy to those who in common are but poorly fed. The negro who taught me these two remedies, observing the great care I took of both the negro men and negro women, taught me likewise the cure of all the distempers to which the women are subject; for the negro women are as liable to diseases as the white women.

SECTION II.

Of the Manner of governing the Negroes.

When a negro man or woman comes home to you, it is proper to caress them, to give them something good to eat, with a glass of brandy; it is best to dress them the same day, to give them something to sleep on, and a covering. I suppose the others have been treated in the same manner; for those marks of humanity flatter them, and attach them to their masters. If they are fatigued or weakened by a journey, or by any distempers, make them work little; but keep them always busy as long as they are able to do anything, never suffering them to be idle, but when they are at their meals. Take care of them when they are sick, and give attention both to their remedies and their food, which last ought then to be more nourishing than what they usually subsist upon. It is your interest so to do, both for their preservation, and to attach them more closely to you; for though many Frenchmen say that negroes are ungrateful, I have experienced that it is very easy to render them much attached to you by good treatment, and by doing them justice, as I shall mention afterwards.

If a negro woman lies-in, cause her to be taken care of in everything that her condition makes necessary, and let your wife, if you have one, not disdain to take the immediate care of her herself, or at least have an eye over her.

A Christian ought to take care that the children be baptised and instructed, since they have an immortal soul. The mother ought then to receive half a ration more than usual, and a quart of milk a day, to assist her to nurse her child.

Prudence requires that your negroes be lodged at a proper distance, to prevent them from being troublesome or offensive; but at the same time near enough for your conveniently observing what passes among them. When I say that they ought not to be placed so near your habitation as to be offensive, I mean by that the smell which is natural to some nations of negroes, such as the Congos, the Angolas, the Aradas, and others. On this account it is proper to have in their camp a bathing place formed by thick planks, buried in the earth about a foot or a foot and a half at most, and never more water in it than about that depth, for fear lest the children should drown themselves in it; it ought likewise to have an edge, that the little children may not have access to it, and there ought to be a pond without the camp to supply it with water and keep fish. The negro camp ought to be inclosed all round with palisades, and to have a door to shut with a lock and key. The huts ought to be detached from each other, for fear of fire, and to be built in direct lines, both for the sake of neatness, and in order to know easily the hut of each negro. But that you may be as little incommoded as possible with their natural smell, you must have the precaution to place the negro camp to the north or north-east of your house, as the winds that blow from these quarters are not so warm as the others, and it is only when the negroes are warm that they send forth a disagreeable smell.

The negroes that have the worst smell are those that are the least black; and what I have said of their bad smell, ought to warn you to keep always on the windward side of them when you visit them at their work; never to suffer them to come near your children, who, exclusive of the bad smell, can learn nothing good from them, either as to morals, education, or language.

From what I have said, I conclude that a French father and his wife are great enemies to their posterity when they give their children such nurses. For the milk being the purest blood of the woman, one must be a stepmother indeed to give her child to a negro nurse in such a country as Louisiana, where the mother has all conveniences of being served, of accommodating and carrying their children, who by that means may be always under their eyes. The mother then has nothing else to do but to give the breast to her child.

I have no inclination to employ my pen in censuring the over-delicacy and selfishness of the women, who thus sacrifice their children; it may, without further illustration, be easily perceived how much society is interested in this affair. I shall only say, that for any kind of service whatever about the house, I would advise no other kind of negroes, either young or old, but Senegals, called among themselves Diolaufs, because of all the negroes I have known, these have the purest blood; they have more fidelity and a better understanding than the rest, and are consequently fitter for learning a trade, or for menial services. It is true they are not so strong as the others for the labours of the field, and for bearing the great heats.

The Senegals however are the blackest, and I never saw any who had a bad smell. They are very grateful; and when one knows how to attach them to him, they have been found to sacrifice their own life to save that of their master. They are good commanders over other negroes, both on account of their fidelity and gratitude, and because they seem to be born for commanding. As they are high-minded, they may be easily encouraged to learn a trade, or to serve in the house, by the distinction they will thereby acquire over the other negroes, and the neatness of dress which that condition will entitle them to.

When a settler wants to make a fortune, and manage his plantation with economy, he ought to prefer his interest to his pleasure, and only take the last by snatches. He ought to be the first up and the last a-bed, that he may have an eye over everything that passes in his plantation. It is certainly his interest that his negroes labour a good deal: but it ought to be an equal and moderate labour, for violent and continual labours would soon exhaust and ruin them; whereas by keeping them always moderately employed, they neither exhaust their strength nor ruin their constitution. By this they are kept in good health, and labour longer, and with more good will: besides it must be allowed that the day is long enough for an assiduous labourer to deserve the repose of the evening.

To accustom them to labour in this manner I observed the following method: I took care to provide one piece of work for them before another was done, and I informed their commander or driver in their presence, that they might not lose time, some in coming to ask what they were to do, and others in waiting for an answer. Besides I went several times a day to view them, by roads which they did not expect, pretending to be going a hunting or coming from it. If I observed them idle, I reprimanded them, and if when they saw me coming, they wrought too hard, I told them that they fatigued themselves, and that they could not continue at such hard labour during the whole day, without being harassed, which I did not want.

When I surprised them singing at their work, and perceived that they had discovered me, I said to them chearfully, Courage, my boys, I love to see you merry at your work; but do not sing so loud, that you may not fatigue yourselves, and at night you shall have a cup of Tafia (or rum) to give you strength and spirits. One cannot believe the effect such a discourse would have upon their spirits, which was easily discernible from the chearfulness upon their countenances, and their ardour at work.

If it be necessary not to pass over any essential fault in the negroes, it is no less necessary never to punish them but when they have deserved it, after a serious enquiry and examination supported by an absolute certainty, unless you happen to catch them in the fact. But when you are fully convinced of the crime, by no means pardon them upon any assurances or protestations of theirs, or upon the solicitations of others; but punish them in proportion to the fault they have done, yet always with humanity, that they may themselves be brought to confess that they have deserved the punishment they have received. A Christian is unworthy of that name when he punishes with cruelty, as is done to my knowledge in a certain colony, to such a degree that they entertain their guests with such spectacles, which have more of barbarity than humanity in them. When a negro comes from being whipped, cause the sore parts to be washed with vinegar mixed with salt, Jamaica pepper, which grows in the garden, and even a little gun-powder.

As we know from experience that most men of a low extraction, and without education, are subject to thieving in their necessities, it is not at all surprising to see negroes thieves, when they are in want of everything, as I have seen many badly fed, badly cloathed, and having nothing to lie upon but the ground. I shall make but one reflection. If they are slaves, it is also true that they are men, and capable of becoming Christians: besides, it is your intention to draw advantage from them, is it not therefore reasonable to take all the care of them that you can? We see all those who understand the government of horses give an extraordinary attention to them, whether they be intended for the saddle or the draught. In the cold season they are well covered and kept in warm stables. In the summer they have a cloth thrown over them, to keep them from the dust, and at all times good litter to lie upon. Every morning their dung is carried away, and they are well curried and combed. If you ask those masters, why they bestow so much pains upon beasts? they will tell you, that, to make a horse serviceable to you, you must take a good deal of care of him, and that it is for the interest of the person to whom a horse belongs, so to do. After this example, can one hope for labour from negroes, who very often are in want of necessaries? Can one expect fidelity from a man, who is denied what he stands most in need of? When one sees a negro, who labours hard and with much assiduity, it is common to say to him, by way of encouragement, that they are well pleased with him, and that he is a good negro. But when any of them, who understand our language, are so complimented, they very properly reply, *Masser, when negre be much fed, negre work much; when negre has good masser, negre be good.*

If I advise the planters to take great care of their negroes, I at the same time shew them that their interest is connected in that with their humanity. But I do no less advise them always to distrust them, without seeming to fear them, because it is as dangerous to shew a concealed enemy that you fear him, as to do him an injury.

Therefore make it your constant custom to shut your doors securely, and not to suffer any negro to sleep in the house with you, and have it in their power to open your door. Visit your negroes from time to time, at night and on days and hours when they least expect you, in order to keep them always in fear of being found absent from their huts. Endeavour to assign each of them a wife, to keep clear of debauchery and its bad consequences. It is necessary that the negroes have wives, and you ought to know that nothing attaches them so much to a plantation as children. But above all do not suffer any of them to abandon his wife, when he has once made choice of one in your presence. Prohibit all fighting under pain of the lash, otherwise the women will often raise squabbles among the men.

Do not suffer your negroes to carry their children to the field with them, when they begin to walk, as they only spoil the plants and take off the mothers from their work. If you have a few negro children, it is better to employ an old negro woman to keep them in the camp, with whom the mothers may leave something for their children to eat. This you will find to be the most profitable way. Above all do not suffer the mothers ever to carry them to the edge of the water, where there is too much to be feared.

For the better subsistence of your negroes, you ought every week to give them a small quantity of salt and of herbs of your garden, to give a better relish to their Couscou, which is a dish made of the meal of rice or maiz soaked in broth.

If you have any old negro, or one in weak health, employ him in fishing both for yourself and your negroes. His labour will be well worth his subsistence.

It is moreover for your own interest to give your negroes a small piece of waste ground to improve at the end of your own, and to engage them to cultivate it for their own profit, that they may be able to dress a little better, by selling the produce of it, which you ought to buy from them upon fair and just terms. It were better that they should employ themselves in cultivating that field on Sundays, when they are not Christians, than do worse. In a word, nothing is more to be dreaded than to see the negroes assemble together on Sundays, since, under pretence of Calinda or the dance, they sometimes get together to the number of three or four hundred, and make a kind of Sabbath, which it is always prudent to avoid; for it is in those tumultuous meetings that they sell what they have stolen to one another, and commit many crimes. In these likewise they plot their rebellions.

To conclude, one may, by attention and humanity, easily manage negroes; and, as an inducement, one has the satisfaction to draw great advantage from their labours.

Questions to Consider:

1. *Does Du Pratz consider people of African origin or descent to be inherently inferior to Europeans? What proof does he present, one way or the other?*
2. *To what end does Du Pratz encourage "good treatment" of enslaved Africans? Why does he suggest "doing them justice" to potential slaveowners?*
3. *How does Du Pratz compare to common stereotypes of a slaveowner?*

Source:

The History of Louisiana, Or of the Western Parts of Virginia And Carolina: Containing a Description of the Countries That Lie on Both Sides of the River Missisippi: With an Account of the Settlements, Inhabitants, Soil, Climate, and Products. Translated From the French of M. Le Page Du Pratz; With some Notes and Observations relating to our Colonies. A New Edition (London: T. Becket, 1764).

1764:
Jean-Jacques-Blaise d'Abbadie on the Indian Response to the Peace of Paris

The end of the Seven Years' War (the French and Indian War for Anglo-Americans) brought tremendous change to the Louisiana colony. That change affected all people living within the area, notably the American Indians. In the excerpts below, Jean-Jacques-Blaise d'Abbadie, director-general of Louisiana between 1763 and 1765, records in his journal interactions with representatives from a number of American Indian tribes.

July 6. Sieur Cabaret, commandant of the Arkansas Post, arrived here with a deputation of thirty-seven Indians of that tribe [the Arkansas tribe] as I had requested.

July 7. They chanted the calumet for me, and I delivered my speech.

> My children, my heart is ever responsible to the pleasure of seeing you. I have told your father, Mr. de Cabaret, to bring you here. You have come. Listen to the speech which I am going to present to you. Your remoteness from the French and the deplorable state of the post which the inundation has nearly destroyed, place me in the state of seeking a place to re-establish you closer to us. That way, my children, I shall be more capable of providing for your needs. Therefore, see if you can find a site in the Natchitoches district or near the Red River which will suit your intentions. I warn you, however, that I shall not execute this project in the near future, as I

> have not received the necessary orders from the great emperor, and eight or ten moons will pass before that time. Thus, you will remain where you are presently established by the French until at least winter. The Great Spirit has inspired in the French and English the sentiments of peace which unites us, and today, they are our brothers. You know that the two great emperors have resolved to partition their lands, such as the French possessions on the right bank. When the English had desired to ascend the great river in order to take possession of the lands which had been ceded to them, the redmen—the Tunica, Avoyelle and others—had struck against our friends, the English. My heart bleeds from this blow because these redmen have rejected my word. Listen more attentively and heed these words which I give you. Be peaceful and conduct yourselves only according to the advice of your father who loves you.

The Indians asked to respond to these words. On the following day, they assembled at my house and told me:

> My father, the roads have always been white for you to come and see us. When I have found them red, I have whitened them. You are surrounded by tribes who do not observe the world for the French. It is not the same with us. We have always listened, and have never reddened our hands with the blood of the French. Here, you see several warriors who please you. They will deliver your message to the village. I shall espouse it in the village, and we shall desire only to follow your advice. If it depended only upon me, I tell you that I am ready to go and establish myself where you will want, but there are other chiefs and warriors at the village, and I do not know their thoughts on this matter. When I shall be in the village, I shall relate your speech to them, and I am convinced that they will comply with your wishes. I will instruct Mr. Cabaret to notify you of their intentions. My father, I recommend to you the warriors and young men who have come to see you.

My response was practically a repetition of what I had told them on the preceding day. I did not urge them to change post. I told them that they will have time to think about it at least through winter. I urged them to be peaceful, to hear my speech, and to follow my advice. I spoke to them of the peace treaty which had united us with the English, and that if they would want to reascend the Mississippi to Illinois, they must allow them to pass without harassing them, as this was the desire of the great emperor.

July 9. I ordered their presents, and they departed. . . .

July 14. During the morning I received a deputation of twelve Choctaw who bore witness to me of their extreme regret at no longer seeing the French in their village. I received them in the presence of Mr. Pittman, an English officer. I tried everything to calm them, assuring them that the British would provide for their needs. They would also give marks of their friendship.

The same day, I received a deputation of Tunica whom I had summoned from Pointe Coupée. The chiefs, Perruquier, Latanache, and Bride les Bouef were accompanied by thirty warriors. Here is what I told them, and what they replied in the presence of Mr. Pittman:

> My children, I have told your father, Mr. de Mazelière, to bring you here. I would have seen you sooner, but you had reddened the land, and my heart burns because you have rejected my word. Why have you struck against our friends, the English, who had not harmed you? They were going to take possession of the lands which the great emperor had given them.

Perruequier responded:

> My father, the British have always corrupted the ways among all the tribes. They have given them [the Indians] liquor to drink which has killed them. When I learned that they would come to our lands, I said: "They will put us to death; kill them!" I well know that you had forbidden it. But, as I know in my heart that they would enslave us, I could not refrain from attacking them. If they had put their garrison ashore, we would have killed them all. But they fled, and they did the right thing. Finally, my father, I come to you as an embarrassed child. Chastise me if you if you wish, but have pity on us.

> My children, [D'Abbadi replied], today I carry you within my heart. But if you do not observe my counsels, and if you reject my word, no longer count upon my favor. I reiterate that the intention of the great emperor is that the roads be white throughout the world for the happiness of redmen and whites.

Perruquier responded: "Since you ordain it, my father, we shall remain peaceful, and the English can come, but let them not be ungrateful and give us a present."

Response: "I am very relieved to see you in this disposition. You lighten my heart. You must keep your word of honor. Do you see this English chief? He is my friend. I shake his hand. The English will do the same every time that they will meet you."

All of the Indian chiefs offered their hand to Sieur Pittman, who promised them, on the part of the English, the same good will and the same friendship as the French.

The Indians sang the calumet for me and then withdrew.

July 18. I gave the Tunica their annual present, and they departed....

Questions to Consider:

1. *How did American Indians in Louisiana respond to the division of the colony and its cession to England and Spain as a result of the Peace of Paris (1763)?*
2. *What do the responses of D'Abbadie tell us about how the French viewed the American Indians?*
3. *What do you think was the chief concern for American Indians in the aftermath of the Seven Years' War?*

Source:

Carl A. Brasseaux, trans., ed., and annot., *A Comparative View of French Louisiana, 1699 and 1762: The Journals of Pierre Le Moyne d'Iberville and Jean-Jacques-Blaise d'Abbadie*, rev. ed. (Lafayette, LA: Center for Louisiana Studies, University of Southwestern Louisiana, 1981).

1764–1766: Correspondence Regarding the Acadians

The Acadians, who began arriving in Louisiana in the mid-1760s, went years without a place to call home. Scattered around the Atlantic World during and after the Seven Years' War, these former inhabitants of *Acadie* (today's Nova Scotia) came to Louisiana at an opportune moment. The administrators of the colony, desperate to shore up its defenses and increase its agricultural and commercial productivity, needed to grow Louisiana's population quickly. They therefore placed the Acadians in strategic locations, including along the Mississippi River and in the Attakapas District in the southwestern section of modern Louisiana.

The following sources include several official documents and one personal letter. The first official document, issued by then-governor of Nova Scotia Montague Wilmot, established the terms by which the Acadians who were not expelled could remain in their ancestral home following the Seven Years' War. The second, a series of very detailed instructions regarding the establishment of Acadians in the Attakapas District, was directed to Lieutenant Louis Andry by Louisiana Commandant Charles Phillipe Aubry and Commissaire-Ordonnateur Denis-Nicolas Foucalt. The third official document is a letter from Aubry to the French foreign minister requesting aid for the Acadians arriving in Louisiana. (Note that, although the letter is dated 1766, "the Spaniards" had not yet arrived.) The last governmental document shows that the lack of money for establishing the Acadians in Louisiana did not diminish when the first Spanish Governor, Antonio de Ulloa, arrived.

The final document, a letter written by Jean-Baptiste Semer, an Acadian in Louisiana, to his father Germain in Le Havre, France, is the earliest known letter describing what the Acadians encountered in Louisiana. It provides a firsthand account of the difficulties the earliest arrivals faced, but it also shows the promise of a better future many Acadians foresaw.

Proclamation by Montague Wilmot November 7, 1764

By [command of] His Excellency, Montague Wilmot, captain-general, governor, and vice-admiral of the Province of New England and its dependencies, and colonel of the 80th Regiment, etc., etc., etc., commandant of His Majesty's troops in said province, A PROCLAMATION

Inasmuch as it has pleased His Majesty to notify me that he readily and gladly permits the French Acadians to remain in this province, and to establish themselves there, provided that they take an oath of allegiance to his government, all French Acadians wishing to accept the benefits and advantages so graciously offered to them must presently take an oath of allegiance, both to the person of His Majesty and to his government, in the following terms:

> To swear and solemnly and sincerely promise before God that I shall be faithful to His Britannic Majesty, King Geroge III, and that I shall defend him with all my might against all of his enemies, and against all assaults upon his person, his government, and his dignity. In addition, I shall make every effort to discover and to inform His Majesty and his successors of every treasonous conspiracy, or any attack against him or against them, the princes of the royal house.
>
> I promise to do all of these things sincerely and in good faith, adhering to all of the oaths declared by me without equivocal mental restrictions or secret reservations whatsoever. I take this oath, and promise with all my heart, without duress, and in all sincerity, upon the Christian faith, so help me God and the Holy Gospel.

I have found it proper to publish this proclamation as a means of effectively notifying the said Acadians of the condition under which they can remain and establishing themselves in this province. . . . Long live the king!

By command of His Excellency [Wilmot].

Copy of the Instructions to be Followed by Sieur Andry, Half-Pay Lieutenant and Engineer, Regarding the Settlement of Acadian Families in the Attakapas Area Louisiana, April 17, 1765

These instructions [are] to be attached to Commandant Aubry's letter, dated April 15, 1765.

Charles Philippe Aubry, royal and military chevalier of the Order of St. Louis, king's commandant of the province of Louisiana, and Denis-Nicolas Foucault, *commissaire-ordonnateur* of the same province.

We have ordered Mister Andry to leave this city with the Acadian families and go to the district of the Attakapas, and in agreement with them choose the most suitable site for the establishment of a village where these new colonists wish to be reunited.

It is extremely important to choose a salubrious place and avoid the miasma of stagnant water and marshes. If at all possible, it would be desirable to build the said village along a navigable river, checking carefully the high water level so that flooding can be avoided.

The surrounding area within a radius of at least a league, should be properly evaluated with regard to its fertility. Soil that is mineral, sandy, or not well drained should be avoided as much as possible.

Mister Andry will keep a record of the type of forests which exist around the area. He will note whether there is rock and of what type and also whether springs exist and carefully examine the water.

We are relying on Mister Andry's judgment to choose land that will present all the advantages and the fewest inconveniences.

The above statements notwithstanding, he will make his choice in concert with said Acadians. However, Mister Andry's decision will always prevail in cases of conflicting opinions. Furthermore, we bid Mister Beausoleil and all the Acadians to defer to the judgment of Mister Andry, whom we know to be zealous and talented. We are ordering all the said Acadians to assist him in whatever capacity they can, and we are forbidding them to oppose any of his actions.

Mister Andry's decision relative to the shape of the village, whether round, octogonal [*sic*], or square, will be determined by the configuration of the land. He will take special care that each farmer will cultivate his land as closely as possible to the center of the village. Whatever shape is given to the village, it must be laid out as uniformly as possible with a large square of 100 fathoms in diameter in the center, for eight large streets 10 fathoms wide. There should be approximately 12 fathoms between the bank of the river and the inhabited areas. The tracts of land of the said village will be of 80 fathoms square, each of these tracts capable of being divided into four lots. There, lots will be distributed to one, two, or three families proportionally to the number of children in each family. This should be done so that when the children marry, they will have the satisfaction of being close to their father and mother.

At a distance of 12 fathoms from the river, Mister Andry will designate, on the square an area on which to locate a parochial church, the rectory, the yard, and the garden. The area specified for this purpose should be of a size befitting the dignity and the needs of the past. The cemetery will be approximately 40 fathoms from the public square, but not beyond the village limits. On the other side of the square, directly opposite the church, on the upper bank, parallel to the river at a distance of 12 fathoms from the said river, he [Andry] will leave a vacant lot sufficiently large, marked by a series of stakes. This lot will be for the commandant's lodging, whenever, in the future, the king will deem it necessary to name one. When these two principal places will be marked off; Mister Beausoleil, as leader of the settlement, will choose a piece of land, which, in his estimation, would be most suitable for him and his family. In fact, he will be given a parcel of land proportionately larger by one-half than the ones provided the other individuals. The other two eldest and most esteemed heads of families will be given the same choice, in consideration of their virtues and their wisdom. If god should dispose of the said Beausoleil, they would be in a position to replace him. Each of these then would receive a fourth more than their alloted [*sic*, portion of] land and always in proportion to the number of their children. It is our intention that each family should receive sufficient land to create an appropriate and useful settlement, in which each and every one should be able to monitor the poultry yard, the slave he may acquire, the cattle barns, cow sheds, stables, and vegetable garden, all of this being contingent upon its feasibility.

Beyond the precincts of the village and surrounding it within at least a 100 yard radius, an area should be left vacant to serve as a common grazing land for milk cows and other cattle. Under no circumstances can anyone encroach upon this common land. (The settlers will eventually be able to mark and set out the boundaries by way of two good ditches, one inside and one outside the common land.) The arable land which will lie beyond the common land will be distributed as follows: For a man and his wife, a parcel of land with a surface area of 20 arpents; that is to say, a surface area of 12 arpents for each male child and 6 arpents of surface area for each daughter. These combined pieces of land rounded off as well as possible will constitute a family tract, and this should apply to all the others. Mister Beausoleil, as the leader will have 30 superficial arpents, and the other two persons considered [as his possible successors] because of their qualifications will have a surface area of 25 arpents, all this independently of their children's share. If within the precincts of these lands or in the neighboring area there are forests to be exploited, they should be distributed equally [among the settlers]. We appeal to the spirit of justice and prudence of Mister Beausoleil and the other persons selected to distribute the land wisely and equitably, in agreement with, and in the presence of Mister Andry. It is understood, however, that the wooded area allotted to each individual will be in excess of the arpents earmarked for cultivation. It will also be advisable to build large roads of 5 or 6 fathoms [wide] between the tracts.

In the event that the topography will not allow Mister Andry to carry out our instructions to the letter, knowing his zeal and his talents, we trust him implicitly and approve all changes he is likely to make.

Mister Andry will prepare a detailed plan of the said village at the scale of 4 inches per 100 fathoms, as well as a map of the cultivated land at the scale of 2 inches per 100 fathoms. He will keep an accurate record of the families to be settled as well as the land alloted [*sic*] to them in the village and in the country. He will be particularly careful that each and every one is well acquainted with his respective land allotment. In order to prevent the occurrence of later difficulties and discord, he will maintain for each individual a page in his register, which will be signed by Misters Andry, Beausoleil, the two notables, and the landowner. In this way, everyone will know that systematic order will safeguard each grantee.

Since very little is known about the location of the lakes, rivers, bayous and the land which are included in the western area of the king's domain, we bid Mister Andry to investigate them as much as possible and to draw a map of the areas he explores. Since he will not have the necessary means nor the time to draw up a geometric map of the territory, he will merely do it with the aid of a compass and by estimating distances. He will start these proceedings by leaving the right bank of the river. Travelling as slowly as necessary, he will estimate distances with the naked eye and observe the currents of the wind. He will keep an accurate record of all the things he will deem interesting during his voyage.

Upon arrival at the location intended for the settlement of the Acadian families, he will take whatever time is necessary to formulate plans and draw maps of the residential and farming areas, as well as the surrounding territory. He will also establish a meridian line for the said village, which he will verify on different days by means of 2 or 3 different operations. This will be done for the purpose of checking these findings against the compass and all variations or deviations will be noted.

He will do his best to inform himself of the shortest and most convenient routes connecting New Orleans with this settlement. He will make a note of the land elevation of the proposed settlement, its surroundings, as well as of the water content of the river along which they [the Acadians] will settle. Upon completion of all the proceedings regarding the village settlement, it would be most desirable to have Mister Beausoleil appoint 2 intelligent young men to accompany Mister Andry and with him become acquainted with the above river. If for some reason this plan could not be executed, Mister Andry will go [alone] along the river all the way to the sea, making notes and comments. It will be advisable when he reaches the sea to plan to remain there long enough to acquaint himself with the exact and geometric outline of the port of the bay or cove formed by the mouth of the river. We consider such information as being of vital importance to the colony.

If at all possible he will attempt to determine whether a sand bar exists off the coast and at what distance and at what depth. If the sandbar is not too distant, it will be easy for him to place a buoy or noticeable objects, and to measure the distance accurately from base on the banks in order to determine its trigonometric distance.

After having recorded all essential data and observations which could afford valuable information concerning the mouth of the river, he will return by way of the shortest and most convenient route leading to the river.

We have already informed the court of Mister Andry's planned departure and mission and have not neglected to acquaint the court with this officer's merit, talents, and zeal. Upon his return we will send to the minister an accurate record of his operations, and we have no doubt that he will discharge his duties in a reputable manner, worthy of the mission entrusted to his care.

Aubry to Choiseul-Stainville
New Orleans, May 14, 1765

My Lord,

When I first had the honor of informing you of the arrival of the sixty Acadian families from St. Domingue and their subsequent departure for the Attakapas with Mister Andry for the purpose of establishing a village, I did not anticipate that they would be followed by so many others. This uninterrupted influx of new families will soon turn Louisiana into a New Acadia. At this moment, I am informed that 300 men, women and children are on the lower river. Rumors presently indicate that we are no longer dealing with hundreds [of Acadian immigrants], but thousands. It appears that there are approximately 4,000 who would like to put an end to their long years of exile by settling in Louisiana.

The unexpected events have thrust Mister Foucault and myself onto the horns of a serious dilemma. No arrangements have been made to receive such a large number of people, and the circumstances in which we find ourselves are the most critical. Never has the colony been so lacking in provisions as it is today. Foreigners travelling continuously through the colony keep us very busy. The English established at Mobile and at Pensacola have removed large quantities of corn from the colony for shipment to the Indians and thus improved their relations with them. Conditions are such that in three months hence, we will be faced with a most distressing situation. To make matters worse, the Acadians have smallpox, and will inflict a new calamity upon the colony. However, under present circumstances, we are duty bound to assist them. Even though we have been ordered to postpone all expenses until the Spaniards' arrival, I dare flatter myself that your Lordship will not disapprove of the assistance we intend to give them. This aid will keep them alive until they are in a position to help themselves. Mister Foucault and I shall ensure that all expenses are handled economically and cautiously. We will give them only what is absolutely necessary for survival and ultimate self-sufficiency. They need provisions, tools, arms and ammunition. These last two items are indispensable in a colony such as ours where people live by means of their guns, and [where they] are threatened by Indian raids. Our magazine lacks the necessary muskets and ammunition. I believe that our country's honor and sense of humanity demands that some consideration be given these poor people, whose wretchedness is only the result of their sacred attachment to their homeland and to their religion. I feel certain, My Lord, that our conduct in this matter can only have the approval of a minister, whose actions have always had as an objective the welfare and glory of France.

Despite what is happening there, may I add, at the most inopportune time, one cannot help but think that the colony will someday benefit from it. The Acadians are hard-working, courageous and devoted beyond words to their prince and homeland.

I became acquainted with the Acadians in New England. They never spoke of anything but their religion and their king. They have always refused the advantageous English offers to remain there. Born in a cold clime transported after untold hardships to Saint-Domingue, where they suffered greatly from its torrid climate, unaccustomed as they were to this heat, they became unable to work. They are now being reborn in Louisiana, and, if they are helped a little, they will accomplish wonders. As unlikely as it may seem, their situation will improve soon, thanks to the fertile land they are going to cultivate. With a fine and brave militia, the country will flourish. If the need should arise, with a few troops, ammunition and good leaders, we will be in a position to repulse our enemies. Notwithstanding the cession of this country to Spain, a reciprocity of interest will result from the close ties between the two crowns. It will be to the Spaniards' advantage, when they take possession of the country, to have loyal subjects administer the Mexican posts. I am firmly convinced that, at the first hostilities, the English will attack these posts if they are not well defended. Since I have had the honor, at different times, to acquaint you, My Lord, with all the interesting events in the colony, I shall forego at this time any additional details. Therefore I am informing you only of the Acadians' arrival, of which I am just now being advised. I have the honor to send this letter by way of Saint-Domingue.

I have the honor to be, with the deepest respect, your most humble and obedient servant,

Aubry.

Ulloa to [Spanish Secretary of State] Grimaldi New Orleans, September 29, 1766

My Dear Sir:

An English sloop carrying the French Acadian families arrived here on the twenty-eighth. After a voyage of three months—since June 26, when it departed Maryland, New England—it brought 224 men, women, and children, 150 in the last two categories. During the voyage fourteen died and three [more perished] after they had spoken to the [customs] inspector [at Balise] and had obtained some provisions. Three of them were born during the trip and two more have died since their arrival, [while their ship navigated] the river. Because these people arrived in misery and in great need [of assistance], they were helped immediately, by order of the French general [Aubry] and myself, being given drinks and biscuits which had been reserved for the first needy [Acadians] who might arrive; I also gave them a bull and a calf, which I had brought from up-river for consumption by myself and my companions. I did so the same night in which the boat carrying them was discovered. The shipmaster assured me that as soon as they [the Acadians] received the animals, they killed them and ate the meat raw. The sloop continued upstream until it joined the boats that had been summoned when we were first apprised [of its arrival], so that they could be transferred and then taken to New Orleans.

The arrival of these people, together with those of the same nationality who are already here and with those who may come, is a source of great embarrassment for me, as it would be for any other ruler, because as soon as they arrive, we must spend money on them, given them what they need, and continue doing so until they have a way to support themselves, which requires at least two years. To settle them we must provide them with arms and ammunition, tools, etc. Widows and orphans have to be furnished everything, and all of them need a physician, medicines, and food. In the first two years after their arrival, many fall sick and the number of deaths is large, as is the case now, and, having no orders from His Majesty, we do not know what to do: On one hand, we are motivated [to help them] by charity and [a host's] obligation to [offer] hospitality, because if they are not helped, they will inevitably die; and, on the other, we are duty-bound not to use money for ends that are not authorized by royal decree, so we are uncertain about what course to take.

My thoughts on this matter always lead to the conclusion that I previously explained to Your Excellency: If it is His Majesty's desire to preserve the colony as a buffer for the kingdoms of New Spain, because he considers it advantageous or the surest means of safeguarding them, without expecting any kind of profit [from Louisiana], now or later, then it should be populated, and, to do this, it is necessary to spend large sums and to do so immediately. If His Majesty believes that the colony may be commercially valuable to his royal treasury or to his vassals in the future, then, of course, it [the expense] should be reconsidered. Save the money that would be spent without ever obtaining this goal, because its [Louisiana's] productivity will never be greater than now, and the increasing number of Acadians that may come, once settled, will get by if they are helped, but that is all, since they are not capable of cultivating indigo or tobacco unless they have sufficient Negroes to do so. Thus, they are reduced to having a few head of cattle and to cultivating grain and roots for their own consumption with which they will enrich themselves, but [their property] will not enrich the colony or expand its trade, which will never be anything but wood, indigo of the worst quality, and tobacco in small quantities and of mediocre quality. The increasing number of ships that have come here from France and that have traded with Saint-Domingue and Martinique have carried back nothing but this and what the illicit commerce with our ports has produced. I have not been able to ascertain its origin, but they assure that the *duro* was more common before than after my arrival, and I do not doubt it, since it is the coin that is used in the colonies of Pensacola and Mobile. Your Excellency can use this information to explain [the situation] to His Majesty and, according to his wishes, inform me of the policy to be implemented regarding the Acadians that are already here and the others that may come of their own accord.

I offer my devoted obedience to Your Excellency's commands, and I pray to God to preserve your life for many years. Balis, September 29, 1766.

Jean-Baptist Semer to Germain Semer
April 20, 1766

My very dear father, at the time of my departure for Attakapas, I had the honor of receiving yours in New Orleans, where I had gone with about thirty of our Acadians who went there to return the king's boats which had been loaned to us to take our goods and our families. We had left last year in April from here [from New Orleans] to go there [Attakapas] and illnesses having overcome us this past summer, we were in no state to row them until now, but we were once again given others to add to those we prepared up there, and we are leaving again with our supplies and munitions and other provisions we have made. I gave your letter to the hospitaller, Mother Ste. Madeleine, who has rendered all of us a thousand acts of kindness and who again has the kindness to reply to you, which she does while assuring you, my very dear father, that it is not for want of natural [affection] for you and my very dear mother that I have not had the honour of telling you our news. The Attakapas [District is] sixty leagues from here, and our letter-writers are dead. I shall forget myself sooner than [I shall] forget you both; the kindnesses that you have rendered me are always in my thoughts, and I never miss offering them to God in my prayers for your dear preservation and ask of you also to do the same in return and to continue your friendship to both of us and to please me by giving me your precious news as often as possible. I will tell you then my very dear father that I arrived here in the month of February 1765 with 202 Acadian persons, including Joseph Brossard, called Beauplaisir [*sic*], and all of his family, La Greze, and Catalan, all coming from Halifax and having passed by the Cape. Beausoleil led [the group] and paid the passage for those who didn't have the means. After us, there arrived yet another 105 in another ship and then eighty, forty, [and] some twenty or thirty, in three or four others. I believe there are about 500–600 of us Acadians, counting women and children. We the first ones have been sent seven or eight men to look over the land and locations in order to find a suitable site, and we were told that at Attakapas there were magnificent grasslands with the finest soil in the world.

M. Aubry, who commanded [the colony] as a result of Mr. D'Abbadie's death, assisted us as much as he was able, but he has not been in complete control [of the government], not having the support of the finance ministries. Finally, while we were here [New Orleans] they gave us a pound and a half of bread and meat for women who were pregnant or nursing as well as the disabled and sick persons at the king's hospital. Upon departure, [they gave us] bread, that is to say, flour for the men and an equal amount of rice and corn for the women and children. We went to Attakapas with guns, powder, and shot, but as it was already the month of May, the heat being so intense, we started to work in too harsh conditions. There were six plows that worked; we had to break in the oxen [and] travel fifteen leagues to get horses. Finally, we had the finest harvest, and everybody contracted fevers at the same time and, nobody being in a state to help anyone else, thirty-three or thirty-four died, including the children. Those who started again wanted to go and work on their wilderness properties, and they fell ill again, but we came down in the month of February 1766 of this year and here we all are, thank God, very well and hoping for a very fine harvest this year, with God's help, having cleared a great deal [of land]. We have only to sow, and we already have oxen, cows, sheep, horses and the finest hunting in the world, deer, such fat turkey, bears and ducks and all kinds of game. We saw them from the sights of our guns. There are several since Beausoleil's death who came down from Attakapas, among others those of the Riviere de Saint-Jean, and settled along the Mississippi River along the German Coast, where the latter [Germans] have already started a settlement.

We lack only good missionaries like we had in Acadia for here there are only a very few Capuchin fathers. There was a gouty one here who had gone up with us, but he was forced to return. There is a Spanish governor [Ulloa] who likes us very much, who has just arrived with two very zealous Capuchin fathers, but they know only Spanish. We are awaiting others. The land here brings forth a good yield of everything anyone wants to sow. Wheat from France, corn and rice, sweet potatoes, giraumont, pistachios, all kinds of vegetables, flax, cotton. We lack only people to cultivate it. We produce indigo, sugar, oranges, and peaches here grow like apples in France. They have granted us six arpents to married people and four and five [arpents] to young men, so we have the advantage, my dear father, of being sure of our land [ownership], and of saying I have a place of my own. Wood is very common here, and we do a good trade in it, for construction and for the building of houses at the Cape and other islands. A person who wants to devote himself to property and make an effort will be comfortably off in a few years. It is an immense country; you can come here boldly with my dear mother and all the other Acadian families. They will always be better off than in France. There are neither duties nor taxes to pay and the more one works, the more one earns without doing harm to anyone. The religious from here who are Ursulines and who, although they teach the young girls at home, are also responsible for the care of troops at the hospital, have done a great deal of good for all of our Acadians; the girls go there to be taught, and they do about an hour of catechism every day at the hospital for the boys of whom they have gotten more than forty at various times to make their first communion. This is, dear father, a detailed account of the advantages that we have here and which everyone is very happy about. They promise us missionaries very shortly. There are around sixty families fifteen leagues from us, settled at Appellonsa; they are very happy there. The new governor is coming up to do a tour of all the posts, to build churches and fortify the forts because at the last peace treaty, we ceded to the English a large part of the country, and we are expecting Spanish troops soon to fortify all the places that France has given away to the Spanish; thus we have a good country. The governor is a man of great distinction, of great piety, a bachelor, who is supremely talented and who understands all sorts of languages. We hope for a great deal from his disinterested administration which is coming from Peru and has given to poor communities and to shamefully poor people all that it had, having an annual budget here of thirty thousand piastres.[1] He was forced to borrow in Havana while coming here. He is a man of rare merit in every respect.

Lacking paper, I can only assure you of the profound and obedient respect with which I am, my very dear father and mother, your very humble, etc. . . .

Signed Jean-Baptiste Semer

1. A piastre was a rough equivalent to a peso.

Questions to Consider:

1. *How did the governments' views of the Acadians evolve over the first couple of years after their arrival in Louisiana?*
2. *Semer presents two seemingly contradictory versions of life in Louisiana for the Acadians. What are they?*
3. *How important was the Roman Catholic faith to the Acadians?*

Sources:

1. Carl Brasseux, ed., Brasseaux, et al. trans., Brasseaux and Jacqueline K. Voorhies, annot., *Quest for the Promised Land: Official Correspondence Relating to the First Acadian Migration to Louisiana, 1764–1769* (Lafayette, LA: Center for Louisiana Studies, University of Southwestern Louisiana, 1989), 23–24, 33–37, 49–51, 77–79.

2. Jean-François Mouhot and Bey Grieve, "Letter by Jean-Baptiste Semer, an Acadian in New Orleans, to His Father in Le Havre, April 20, 1766," *Louisiana History: The Journal of the Louisiana Historical Association* 48, no. 2 (2007): 222–26.

1768:
Governor Ulloa and the Creole Revolt

When the first Spanish governor of Louisiana, Antonio de Ulloa, arrived at the Mississippi River, he took great pains to not alienate the mostly French population of the newly Spanish colony. Ulloa did not assert Spanish authority—symbolically or practically—spending most of his time at Fort Balize, down the Mississippi from New Orleans, and he governed through a French intermediary, Charles Philippe Aubry, whom even Ulloa referred to as "governor-general." This lack of command on Ulloa's part led to friction with the French Creole merchants and planters in Louisiana, especially those who would have been affected by his attempt to implement Spanish mercantilist trade rules. As a result, the Superior Council, led by Attorney General Nicolas Chauvin de Lafrénière and a bastion of these French Creoles, launched a revolt against Ulloa. On October 29, 1768, the council voted to expel Ulloa. Three days later, on November 1, Ulloa fled Louisiana. The following document describes from Governor Ulloa's perspective the events leading up to the Insurrection of 1768.

Ulloa to Grimaldi
October 26, 1768

MY VERY DEAR SIR: Yesterday, the 25th, at eleven o'clock M. Maxent came to inform me of what had been learned about the present disturbances, and a little later the engineer, Don Ypolito Amelot brought me the same information. This leaves no doubt that there is already a general conspiracy of the whole colony to refuse submission to the dominion of His Majesty.

Their plan is to present a manifesto full of complaints against me, because it is necessary to have some pretext to excuse their report to the council. They claim that, as my government is harsh even before possession has been taken, it will be much more so after this is done. The conspirators will ask, according to what has been learned, that the council intimate to me that I should depart from the province with all the Spaniards, leaving the colony under the dominion of France, as it formerly was. In order to make it appear that they are forcing the council to accede to this decision, they have drawn up a memorial and have been gathering the signatures of the citizens here, and the outsiders, of whom there are a large number, as well as the Germans and Acadians, whom they have won over by pointing out to them the injuries which are being done to them by me and the Spanish government. They vary their talk according to the class and situation of each kind of people, and do many other things which even the people who have given me this information cannot explain.

On receipt of this news, which I immediately communicated to the governor general, Don Carlos Aubry, we met and he assured me that he had heard nothing of this up to that time. He said that only two days before it had come to his knowledge that the people wished to make representations on a matter of commerce, but that he had never suspected that it was of the nature which had been discovered, nor that the decision would be forced by violence. We discussed what should be done to extinguish this conflagration. By means of the steps which he took with M. Lafreniere, the attorney general of the council, as well as my own, we learned that next Friday the city will be full of people, the Germans and Acadians coming to it, together with the people here, armed to carry out the coup. We also found out that in the city they have in a certain house (which one has not been learned) a large store of guns and ammunition to arm those who lack them.

When the governor tried to persuade the attorney general to exert himself to put down this uprising, the latter replied that he could not do so, because things were so far advanced that was impossible. He assured him that the manifesto or representation to the council was in very proper and respectful terms, and that everything would be done in the best of order without trouble or noise. This confirms, even if there were no other proofs, that he and his friends have instigated this sedition. I should call your Excellency's attention to the fact that no one in the colony but myself knows anything on His Majesty's decisions about the council and form of government.

One of the arguments which has been used to win over the Germans and Acadians to the uprising is that they have not been paid for the grain which they supplied for the support of the other, and that is because I and the Spanish ministers plan to swindle them and divide this sum up among ourselves.

I immediately ordered that, of the less than 6000 pesos, comprising all the funds there were in the treasury yesterday, M. Maxent should be given 1500, which is the most that can be owed them, and that he should pay them and try to see if he can quiet them with the assistance of the commandants, Messrs. De Arensburg, Judice, and Veret. Three thousand were sent them last year also in payment for the same. This pretext is as unfounded as all the others they have used, because if anyone owes them, it is the French commissariat for grain they furnished in the year '66 to supply this city. They were made to sell this in the market place, but were not paid for it. But on such occasions when they desire to escape the obligations of fealty, they disguise their real reasons with specious arguments, and this is what has happened in this case.

My informants tell me that the ones who are collecting the signatures, which is like enlisting under a flag for sedition are one Cares and the Milhet brothers, all foreigners engaged in business here. The first named is the man who was refused entry for a party of negroes which he brought from Martinique on account of their having been vicious characters there. Regarding this, I made a report to Your Excellency. There are also M. De Bienville, ensign-of-ship in France, brother of M. de Noyan, and Villere, a relative of Lafreniere, together with some others of the same group.

The French governor is of the opinion that this uprising has been plotted among Lafreniere, *Comisario* Foucault, and Noyan, the son-in-law of the former, who is associated with Foucaut in a plantation. He has not been named to me as an accomplice by my informants, but in view of the part he played in the uprising in the year '66, I am not loathe to believe what the governor says.

The French governor is determined to leave and abandon the province in case I am compelled to do so, because he knows the gravity of this, and that the court of France can not regard it favorably. He has called his officers together and exhorted them to follow his example and to conduct themselves with honor on this occasion, reminding them of all that they and their families will lose if they do not do so. He hopes that the few troops here will remain faithful. Today he has called up the militia, but does not expect much of them. It has been learned that they have had some rather improper notions, among them being the uncalled-for action of having discarded the Spanish uniform which they adopted of their own free will last year without the slightest suggestion on my part.

What these people want is, as I have told Your Excellency on other occasion, military or political employment according to the fancy of each, highly comfortable and lucrative at the expense of the King. They desire liberty in everything, and that the Sovereign be so only in expenditures but not in authority with the country said to belong to Spain, and the people to France. The want to have plenty of money here, but in order that it may go to France and not to Spain, and finally under the term full liberty, all that is understood by it.

They make imputations against me because in this business I am, as the executor of His Majesty's orders, the one who must bear the burden of their fault finding. One of them results from my reports to His Majesty and his subsequent command to publish in these realms and thus provide the project of commerce, which excludes that of France.

With the withdrawal of the English, I thought, in view of the tranquility which was reigning up to that time, that half of the troops would be sufficient for the protection of the country. Now, in view of what is being experienced, I see that more are necessary in order to conquer it, because when there was the least reason and excuse for it, this news has come to light. I have not done the least thing with respect to the vessels going to and coming from Santo Domingo, for the reason that, as Your Excellency had not given me any orders to the contrary, I had nothing on which to base action.

The beginning and origin of everything was Noyan's decision to sell his plantation and go to Cayenne with his negroes.

This man recently married the only daughter of Lafreniere. There was great grief and tears over the separation, and the way they were assuaged was by deciding at a dinner that the whole family and their friends should join the same party. They knew that this threat had not disturbed me, but that on the contrary I, with considerable severity, had told those who spoke to me about it that they could leave the colony as honored citizens, but that His Majesty did not desire subjects who were not content and could better themselves elsewhere, and that he would never regard as good subjects those who were so only for Bordeaux wine. I mentioned this since they were giving as one of the causes of their displeasure with the new commercial regulation, that they would not have this wine but would have to use that of Catalonia, which did not suit their palates.

They saw that I was not moved by all this and perhaps reflected on the uncertainties of the Cayenne project and their regret at leaving their country and the estates they had in it. Consequently they decided in their meetings and parties to take off their masks altogether, and to take as a pretext the harshness of my actions and government, citing the measures I have taken, but without making mention of the gravity of the causes which gave rise to them. Up to now these measures have been only in matters pertaining to the royal exchequer and expenditures. They argued that as formal possession had not yet been taken and they were still subjects of the Most Christian King, it was not wrong to try to continue being so and to have the country again as it was before the cession.

I have given Your Excellency this long account before the trouble breaks out. By means of Don Manuel Felix Riesck who is going there I shall give you information of what transpires, so that subsequent events may not be confused, if the living voice can make more comprehensible the facility with which these uprising are provoked here, together with the character and propensities of these people, than can the muteness of the pen. Your Excellency can inform yourself from him about all the deceptions I have suffered here since my arrival and the way I have overlooked the liberties they have taken, although sometimes my tolerance was overstrained, despite its being considerable.

I place myself with all respect at Your Excellency's orders and pray God to preserve your life many years.

NEW ORLEANS, *October 26, 1768.*

Your most sincere and devoted servant kisses Your Excellency's hand.
DON ANTONIO DE ULLOA

Questions to Consider:

1. *Who did Ulloa blame for the insurrection?*

2. *The phrase "They desire liberty in everything" would seem to indicate a positive response to most modern readers. Why does it seem like an insult the way Ulloa writes it?*

Source:

Lawrence Kinnaird, ed., *Annual Report of the American Historical Association for the Year 1945*, vol. 2: *Spain in the Mississippi Valley, 1765–1794*, pt. 1: *The Revolutionary Period, 1765–1781* (Washington, DC: United States Government Printing Office, 1945), 77–81.

1769:
O'Reilly Brings Order to Louisiana

For decades prior to the 1760s, Louisiana had been largely ignored by the French government. The lack of outside regulation or interference led to what historical archaeologist Shannon Dawdy has termed "rogue colonialism," in which the inhabitants of Louisiana created social, economic, and governmental structures on their own. By no means would Louisiana have been considered an "ideal" colony. When Louisiana's first Spanish governor, Antonio de Ulloa, attempted to implement firmer regulations on the colony, the roguish nature of the colonists emerged in the Insurrection of 1768. Ulloa fled Louisiana, and the Spanish sent Governor-General Don Alejandro O'Reilly to reclaim the colony and exert Spanish authority. The following documents show a two-pronged approach on behalf of O'Reilly and the Spanish government: first, assure the people of Louisiana that the many will not be punished for the actions of the few, and second, deal swiftly with the leaders of the insurrection.

Proclamation by O'Reilly
August 21, 1769

By Order of the King

DON ALEXANDRE O'REILLY, Commander of Benfayan in the Order of Alcántara, Lieutenant General and Inspector General of His Catholic Majesty's Armies, Captain General and Governor of the Province of Louisiana.

By virtue of the orders and powers invested in me by His Catholic Majesty, we declare to all the inhabitants of the province of Louisiana that, although past events have fully justified His Majesty in expressing to them his displeasure, he is willing to be moved solely by clemency toward the public at this point in the belief that it has sinned only because it allowed itself to be led astray by the intrigues of ambitious, fanatical, and ill-intentioned people, who have rashly taken advantage of its ignorance and great credulity. The latter alone shall be responsible for their crimes and shall be judged according to the laws.

So generous an action should assure His Majesty that his new subjects will endeavor each day of their lives by their fidelity, zeal, and obedience to deserve the mercy he grants them, and the protection which he henceforth accords them.

Done at New Orleans, August 21, 1769.
O'Reilly (Rubric)

O'Reilly to Arriaga
October 27, 1769

No. 9

Most Excellent Sir.

MY VERY DEAR SIR: The case that was being prosecuted against the twelve leaders, instigators, and principal accomplices of the recent uprising in the province has been concluded. The merits of the case resulted in the penalty of the gallows for six of them, but as one of them had already died in prison, and as there is not hangman here, five of them were shot on the 25th instant, at three o'clock in the afternoon. The other six were sentenced to imprisonment in a castle, one for life, two for ten years, and three for six, and all twelve to confiscation of their property.

The six sentenced to prison in a castle are being sent on this date to one of the fortresses of Havana to the captain general of which I am sending a copy of the sentence for compliance therewith in that post. The property of these prisoners had been sequestered from the beginning, and I have now given special directions for its prompt liquidation, according to law, so that the part that belongs to the exchequer may be applied thereto, and the widows and creditors may receive theirs.

Full satisfaction has now been given for the offense committed against due respect for the sovereign authority of the King in this province and the bad examples set for his subjects. Everyone recognized the necessity, justice, and clemency of the proceedings, and this example will remain eternally graven on the hearts of all. Respect for the authority of the King is greatly augmented by the strict justice and great celerity with which it has been carried out.

Henceforth, I shall receive without discrimination those who were seduced and signed the first representation to the council, and it will be the greatest consolation to the public to know that I shall not leave in the province any memory of that ill-considered act. I shall reconcile and calm their minds by all means possible, and not is more effective than to let them know that there is and always will be entire forgetfulness of the past, and that everyone will find in the government the protection and favor of which he is deserving.

The attached certified copy of the accusation by the prosecuting attorney, the sentence, and its execution will inform His Majesty in detail of all these grave proceedings.

I hope that I have carried out his royal instructions, and if I have attained this happiness, my satisfaction will be complete.

May Our Lord preserve Your Excellency's valuable life many years.

New Orleans, *October 27, 1769.*
Most Excellent Sir, your most attentive servant kisses Your Excellency's hand.

Alejandro O'Reilly

Questions to Consider:

1. *Do you think it was wise of O'Reilly and his superiors to offer an olive branch to the people of Louisiana? Why or why not?*

2. *Why did the Spanish want to put the Insurrection of 1768 behind them and the Louisiana colonists so quickly?*

Source:

Lawrence Kinnaird, ed., *Annual Report of the American Historical Association for the Year 1945*, vol. 2: *Spain in the Mississippi Valley, 1765–1794*, pt. 1: *The Revolutionary Period, 1765–1781* (Washington, DC: United States Government Printing Office, 1945), 89, 105–6.

1770:
An Outsider's Perspective on Louisiana

In the following brief description of agriculture along the lower Mississippi River, English Captain Philip Pittman lays out the commercial prospects for Louisiana in the early years of Spanish rule. Writing just two years following the Creole revolt, Pittman notes that the Louisiana colonists, using mainly enslaved labor, have developed some commercially viable products, especially indigo, but the two cash crops with the largest potential for developing wealth—cotton and sugarcane—have not proven to be feasible.

Having now gone through the richest and most cultivated plantations on the Mississippi, it is necessary to say something of their produce, which form the greatest part of the commerce of Louisiana. The different articles are indigo, cotton, rice, maiz [*sic*], beans, myrtle wax-candles, and lumber. The indigo of this country is much esteemed for its beautiful colour and good quality; the colour is brighter than that which is fabricated at St. Domingo. The cotton, though of a most perfect white, is of a very short staple, and is therefore not in great request. The maiz [*sic*], different sorts of beans, rich, myrtle candles, are articles in constant demand at St. Domingo.

Some of the richest planters, since the year 1762, have begun the cultivation of sugar, and have erected mills for squeezing the canes; the sugar produced in this country is of a very fine quality, and some of the crops have been very large; but no dependance can be had on this, as some years the winters are too cold, and kill the canes in the ground.

In the autumn the planters employ their slaves in cutting down and squaring timber, for sawing into boards and scantling; the carriage of this timber is very easy, for those who cut it at the back of their plantations make a ditch, which is supplied with water from the back swamps, and by that means conduct their timber to the river side without labour. Others send their slaves up to the cypress swamps, of which there are great many betwixt New Orleans and Pointe Coupee; there they make rafts of the timber they cut, and float them down to New Orleans.

Many of the planters have saw-mills, which are worked by the waters of the Mississippi in the time of floods, and then they are kept going night and day till the waters fall. The quantity of lumber sent from the Mississippi to the West Indian islands is prodigious, and it generally goes to a good market.

Question to Consider:

1. *Based on Pittman's report, what commercial activities seem most likely to produce profit in 1770 Louisiana?*

Source:

Philip Pittman, *The Present State of the European Settlements on the Missisippi [sic]: With a Geographical Description of that River* (London: J. Nourse, 1770), 23–24.

1779:
José de Gálvez on Military Plans

When the American Revolution began in the mid-1770s, most European observers expected the colonists to lose in their war for independence. Despite this, American envoys urged England's traditional enemies, especially France, to join up on the colonists' side. Following the Battle of Saratoga (1777), which saw an American army defeat a British one for the first time, France reconsidered its stance and formed an alliance with the Americans in 1778. The following year, Spain allied itself with France as the fighting spread to Europe.

Across the ocean, the Spanish colony of Louisiana lay at a strategic place—controlling the Mississippi River and within striking distance of the so-called Keys to the Gulf. The following secret correspondence from José de Gálvez (of the Spanish Council of the Indies) to Diego José Navarro (capitane-general of Cuba), provides instructions on how the Spanish military should proceed under the leadership of Bernardo de Gálvez, governor of Louisiana and José's nephew.

Gálvez to Navarro
August 29, 1779

(Confidential copy)

The King has decided that the principal objective of his arms in America during the war with the English is to drive them from the Gulf of Mexico and the banks of the Mississippi, where their settlements are so prejudicial to our commerce, as well as to the security of our richest possessions. The present conditions in Europe favor the success of this important enterprise. Great Britain, weakened by her enormous losses, pressed by superior forces in both hemispheres, abandoned by other nations, who for a long time have been irritated by her odious dominance, and on the point of having her own island invaded by a French army of more than forty thousand men, will find herself unable to resist our efforts if we act with prudence and energy. To await aid from Spain would endanger the success of an operation in which speed is so essential, and perhaps the delay would lose the propitious moment for executing it. Therefore, His Majesty desires that an expedition be organized without delay, composed of whatever land and sea forces it is possible to assemble in those dominions, and that an attack be made on Mobile and Pensacola, the keys to the Gulf of Mexico, sending detachments before or afterwards to attack and clear the English from the banks of the Mississippi, which should be considered as the bulwark of the vast empire of New Spain.

For this purpose Your Excellency will send all the troops you can spare from the garrison of your island, and the same will be done by the viceroy of Mexico. Both of you shall agree on the number of men each is to contribute and conform with the plan and opinion of the governor of Louisiana, who is informed of the position and forces of the enemy. In any event, it will be necessary to assemble four or five thousand men, including three hundred dragoons, or an even larger number of troops, in order not to fail in a stroke of such importance. Although the English have no strong fortifications at Pensacola, but only some wooden batteries, it is probable that they have greatly reinforced the garrison of that post, knowing its importance and fearing our attacks.

The troops sent by Your Excellency should be of selected men as far as possible, commanded by officers of talent and energy, of which none shall be above the rank of colonel. Each battalion will take with it two bronze campaign guns and a full supply of proper stores, munitions, and provisions, so that they will lack nothing they need to operate effectively. The King desires that the commander-in-chief of this expedition shall be Brigadier Don Bernardo de Gálvez, proprietary governor of Louisiana. He has had the foresight to map the area and acquire a practical knowledge of that country. He maintains agents among the enemy, if informed of the diversion which are to be made at the same time in Georgia by the troops of the United States of America, and has gained the friendship of the Choctaws and other tribes of Indians, who would side with the English if they saw at the head of this enterprise another and unknown leader. Finally the effective measures, plus perhaps a happy combination of events, have won him credit among the members of the American Congress and have spread respect for his name among the English settlements in the vicinity of Louisiana. His great knowledge of war and his reputation among the enemy has determined His Majesty to select the said governor, giving him preference over other officials of greater experience and doubtless more suitable for any other enterprise than this one.

The operations of the land troops will be supported by a squadron of a strength proportionate to the important object to which it is destined. On this matter, the Señor Marqués Gonzales de Castejón is giving the proper orders to the commandant of that department, and Your Excellency, together with the viceroy of New Spain and the governor of Louisiana will agree with him and with the chief who goes in command of the squadron, on the number of warships to be taken, the method of transporting the troop with safety, the point of meeting of the convoy from your island with the one from Vera Cruz, the place where the landing is to be made, the timing of the attacks, and all else conducive to the success of the enterprise.

At the same time that the land and sea attacks on Pensacola and Mobile are made, troops of the United States to the number of three thousand men will invest St. Augustine, Florida, and perhaps they will make another diversion along the upper reaches of the Mississippi to be given them as payment for their expenses. Don Juan de Miralles, who resides in those states, upon receipt of the advice which I am sending him through Your Excellency, will arrange the manner, time and places for making their attacks, so that the expedition may be well co-ordinated.

I inform Your Excellency that the court of France has just repeated to the governors of its islands and to the chiefs of its squadrons in those seas order to co-operate in the defense of our possessions and assist with their land and seas forces any enterprises we may undertake against the English settlements. In view of this, if the troops which can be assembled from your island and from New Spain without leaving either placed undefended are not sufficient for the conquest of Pensacola and Mobile, Your Excellency will ask the governor of the French part of the island of Santo Domingo for the number of men necessary, and these will go to complete the expedition or be left to garrison your island, whichever Your Excellency thinks most advisable.

The success of this enterprise depends in a great measure upon the enemy's being unaware of it until the moment of its execution. So, Your Excellency shall preserve profound secrecy about this, and take effective measures for the embarkation of the troops and equipment, pretending an objective other than the real one, for example, that of attacking Jamaica. You shall come to an agreement with your chief of navy, the viceroy of Mexico, and the governor of Louisiana and send to the latter all the aid he needs that you can spare him. The King trusts that you will make all the efforts, inspired in you by your love for the royal service and your country, to assure the splendor of the Spanish arms in an enterprise which is of the greatest importance.

May God protect Your Excellency many years.

San Ildefonso, August 29, 1779.
JOSÉ DE GÁLVEZ

Questions to Consider:

1. *What were the Keys to the Gulf, and why were they called that?*
2. *How had Governor Gálvez prepared for the military activities he was ordered to undertake?*

Source:

Lawrence Kinnaird, ed., *Annual Report of the American Historical Association for the Year 1945*, vol. 2: *Spain in the Mississippi Valley, 1765–1794*, pt. 1: *The Revolutionary Period, 1765–1781* (Washington, DC: United States Government Printing Office, 1945), 355–57.

1792:
Governor Carondelet on Slaves in Louisiana

Like the French *Code Noir*, the regulations governing enslaved persons under Spanish rule differed dramatically from those that would come following the Louisiana Purchase. In the letter below, Governor Francisco Luis Héctor, barón de Carondelet, provides instructions for the Spanish rules regarding slavery.

Carondelet to De Blanc
July 11, 1792

Having received from the court the most precise orders as to the treatment which the inhabitants must give to their Negroes so that they may get a suitable usefulness out of them without infringing with impunity the laws of humanity, I enjoin the inhabitants observe the following articles under penalty of a fine of a hundred piastres for whomsoever shall infringe them, as well as the sale of the negro who shall have been unjustly maltreated or used beyond measure.

1. Each Negro shall receive, as a minimum, the barrel of corn customary in the colony, for his nourishment.

2. Sundays will be given to him for his free rest or for his private work, except in extraordinary cases for which he shall be paid, or compensated for at another time.

3. On work days they shall begin work at daybreak at the earliest, and they shall end at nightfall at the latest.

4. They shall have a half-hour's rest for lunch, and two hours for dinner.

5. They shall be given a shirt and trousers of cloth for the summer time; a blanket cape, a large pair of woolen trousers, and one shirt for the winter, and two ordinary handkerchiefs.

6. No master shall have the power to have more than thirty blows of the whip dealt to his slave; should he deserve more, he shall leave at least one day's interval between one punishment and the other. The majordomo who shall exceed the limit in this respect shall be punished with two month's imprisonment, without his being able to offer any excuse.

7. In order that this regulation may be brought to the attention of all the inhabitants, without which the slaves would not be able to avail themselves of it through failure of having heard it, an authentic copy of it shall be remitted to each commandant and syndic, who shall read it especially to the inhabitants, whose general and particular safety is involved in the exact observation of these regulations to a much greater extent than they imagine; they shall be allowed to make a copy of it for their own enlightenment.

At New Orleans, July 11, 1792

Questions to Consider:

1. *Based on this document what would life have been like for an enslaved person?*

2. *Why would there be a need for regulations dealing with the punishment of slaves?*

Source:

Lawrence Kinnaird, ed., *Annual Report of the American Historical Association for the Year 1945*, vol. 2: *Spain in the Mississippi Valley, 1765–1794*, pt. 3: *Problems of Frontier Defense, 1792–1794* (Washington, DC: United States Government Printing Office, 1945), 58–59.

1792:
Seeking Refuge from Saint-Domingue

In 1791, a slave revolt began on the French sugar island of Saint-Domingue. By the time the fighting ended, a revolution had occurred and a new nation had been created: Haiti. Although the enslaved achieved their dreams of independence, for the sugar planters and others who claimed to own those slaves, the situation was a nightmare. Facing execution or exile, those who could chose the latter, fleeing to Cuba or Louisiana. The below letter from a former infantry lieutenant who had served in Louisiana before returning to France and then retiring to Saint-Domingue describes a desire to return to Louisiana—and more pressing needs.

Count of Montault to Livaudais
March 2, 1792

To my friends and compatriots in Louisiana,

My unlimited attachment for my country, for my best friends, and my former comrades is known to them and to everyone. Fleuriau, Reggio, Saint-Cyr, Marigny, Macarty, Foucher, Trudeau, Le Blanc, Robert, and you, my dear Livaudsais, have seen more closely than the others the extreme regret which I manifested the first time I left Louisiana with the intention of returning there to die after having reunited my friends and a large family which I cite lastly, certain I am that they know the place they hold in my heart. My brother never had any other way of thinking, [or] plans other than mine. He and I would have preferred remaining and working in Louisiana to continuing our service in France, thereby avoiding the catastrophe that we foresaw for our compatriots. An enlightened father, whose loss is etched at this very moment upon my mind by fresh pangs of grief, preserved from the mistake which claimed many as victims. We awaited receipt of our retirement pensions in order to ask for the permission that we should surely have obtained to enjoy it amongst our relatives and friends. We fortunately escaped a revolution that we always abhorred and that we now justifiably disdain because of the rabble's blind ingratitude and injustice. We are now back among you, my dear friends and compatriots, a little sooner than we had planned. Such, as you will see for yourselves, are our intentions, which are as ardent and pure as our very souls. We do not doubt that you will do for us what we would do for you if our situations were reversed. I find myself with my wife six months pregnant, feeding a son not yet eight months old; my brother is more unfortunate than I, for he is without his wife and his child who were compelled by poor health to remain temporarily at Saint-Domingue. We were constrained to abandon our possessions and our Negroes, who have shown us fidelity and attachment, which did not permit us at the last minute to hide from them our route and our plans. "What is going to become of us," these poor unfortunates said to us, "if you abandon us in this lost and ruined country? Take us with you, any place you want to go; we will follow you anywhere. As long as we die with you, we will be happy." Moved by this speech that each of them expressed in his own way, and all in a manner that appeared natural to us, how could have we conceal[ed] from them the uncertainty clouding the attempt which we, acting out of gratitude, must make to bring them to Louisiana. We could only promise to request permission.

My dear friends, we confidently anticipate that motivated by your friendship, your zeal, and your humanity, you will solicit support for our cause in your dealings with, and petitions to, Louisiana's governor.

In receiving the passports we dare hope that the governor would well accord us, for us and for the families who are allied to us and who have the greatest desire to withdraw with us to Louisiana, the ships travelling between the Leeward and Windward islands and New Orleans being for the most part too small to contain us all together, we ask you, my dear friends, to try and obtain for us two separate passports, one for Madame de Montault, my sister-in-law, M. and Mme. De Bruhier, Monsieur and Madame Pradines, his brothers and sisters, brothers-in-law and sisters-in-law and their children, *negres bossales*,[1]

1. Refers to recently arrived African-born slaves on Saint-Domingue.

related subjects and their belongings in Saint-Domingue; and another passport permission for my brother-in-law, my wife, and myself. Address the first of these passports to Madame de Montault in Aux Cayes; send the other to me here in care of M. MacLean, a businessman. Our gratitude will be equal to the very sincere and inviolable attachment to you that my brother shares. We ask you, dear friends and dear compatriots, to extend our reassurances to all those who are still fortunately interested in our country. No one will be able to disapprove the fact that, I addressed my letter to you because of your proximity to the city and asked you, my dear friend to communicate it to all the others, whether or not they are named in this letter, so that you may all act, as I am sure you will, in such a manner as to rejoin friends who were unable to control the circumstances that drove them away. . . .

In addition, kindly extend our respectful regards to your ladies and to assure them of the earnest desire ours have to make their acquaintance and to deserve from them [the Livaudais women] the same friendship for them [the Montault women] that they [the Livaudais women] now feel from the bottom of their hearts.

I reiterate to you with pleasure, my dear Livaudais, assurances of my faithful attachment.

Montault, Chevalier de Saint-Louis,

retired infantry lieutenant

P. S. The exportation of cash from Saint-Domingue being forbidden, we will be obligated to take whatever one will be willing to offer us in exchange for our belongings. Consequently, do us the pleasure of letting us know the colonial commodities and the merchandise . . . [available] in Louisiana.

Question to Consider:

1. *The letter is clearly one of desperation. Based on the text, what can you tell about the writer and his circumstances?*

Source:

Carl A. Brasseux and Glenn R. Conrad, eds., David Cheramie, trans., *The Road to Louisiana: The Saint-Domingue Refugees, 1792–1809* (Lafayette, LA: Center for Louisiana Studies, University of Southwestern Louisiana, 1992), 142–45.

1793: Governor Carondelet on the French Revolution

Governor Francisco Luis Héctor, barón de Carondelet, faced numerous difficulties as governor of Louisiana. Among the most pressing, and potentially the most dangerous, were Louisianians of French descent, or worse in the view of free people, Louisianians of African descent, embracing the ideals of the French Revolution. He thus attempted to suppress any rumored or real threats from Louisianians inspired by "the new ideas of equality and independence." The below letters and government decrees show the lengths to which he would go in these efforts.

Carondelet to Las Casas
February 15, 1793

Copy. No. 67
Confidential.

Most excellent Señor,

As a result of a letter written by a certain Girod, a citizen of this city, but residing at present in yours, I am greatly concerned. He reports the news, doubtless apocryphal, of the cession of Louisiana to France in exchange for the French part of the island of Santo Domingo. The minds of these people, already excited by the news brought by some vessels of the great advantage secured by the Republic, have been disturbed. Moreover, a revenue guard assured me that some of the French had talked of surprising the redoubt of San Carlos by night, and of hoisting the national flag, which would certainly cause an insurrection.

I have also learned that some thirty individuals, partisans of the French revolution, had assembled to enjoy a dinner, after having toasted the victories and progress of the French arms, they drink to the reunion of Louisiana with France.

An officer of the regiment of Louisiana advised me positively that at a party held behind closed doors, at which a certain Bujac was present, the guests cut up a ribbon of the colors of the French federation and distributed it, each one placing a piece in the button-hole of his coat.

Finally, I was informed that a certain Sauve, a merchant established here, and one of the richest, had received some barrels of wine that had been sent to him from Bordeaux by his friends to be drunk with the good patriots.

Convinced of the rapidity with which the new ideas of equality and independence are spreading, which, if not stopped immediately, will cause a general insurrection and the loss of the province, I decided to publish a proclamation, a copy of which I enclose [see Proclamation of Carondelet, below]. At the same time I also ordered the arrest of the Frenchman, Bujac, who is the most fanatical of all the partisans on the lookout for the most dangerous news and went about spreading it in the most public places, talking with the greatest brazenness against monarchial government. He did this despite the prohibitions repeated several times by the government on this matter, and the example I made some months ago of three French troublemakers, whom I expelled from the colony, which was enough to restrain the others up to the time mentioned.

I know all those who are fomenting sedition in this city. Their number does not exceed some ten individuals, all merchants, who came from France some years ago to engage in trade. Two of them are men of astute minds, and the wealthiest in the capital. I was wondering whether it would not be more advisable to arrest them all suddenly and send them to Your Excellency, so that, holding them incommunicado in El Morro, not only would they serve as a warning to the rest but also, without their assistance, those who are trying to inflame the colony from France will not be able to pursue their secret plots for some time. I was convinced that the creoles would not take their part. Even though they feel an inclination toward France, their former fatherland, I did not consider them yet sufficiently instructed in the new ideas to take so daring a step. I was, therefore, not deterred by any fear of sedition on their part. However I was deterred by the fear that they would afterwards ask me for some judicial proofs, difficult and perhaps impossible to obtain under such circumstances, on account of the dangers to which those, who would testify, fear to expose themselves, in case there should be an uprising in the province, or should it be returned to France, according to the almost general idea or hope prevailing at the present time.

Torn between these and other doubts, I have taken the most tactful course of sending to Your Excellency only the aforesaid Bujac. Public opinion and my conscence [*sic*] condemn him. If this is not enough, Your Excellency should set him free, because written proofs are not to be had at present; but the results of such benignity will be the insurrection of the province, which is being held by no more than a thread, and it will be very difficult to preserve it without an additional battalion.

I figure that, as his offense is so public and notorious, no one will accuse me of an excess of severity or of injustice in this city. The said Bujac should be kept secure in El Morro, without permitting him paper or ink, until affairs in France become settled, and the province emerges from the imminent peril in which anyone who has the least knowledge considers it to be. What has been found in his house consists only of a cap of the federation, the French constitution, hymns to liberty and other trifles that show his fanaticism.

It has also come to my notice that in the house of Don Pablo Segond, one of the merchants abovementioned, where Bujac was accustomed to go and even to write, there has been made a cap that they call Liberty, to whose health they drink. The individual who told this to one of the adjutants of the post will not testify to the fact for the reasons already explained. Furthermore he is not a man to whom entire credence can be given. I shall try to ascertain the truth of everything, and report the results to Your Excellency, sending the cap that was found in Bujac's house. Among all these fanatics I consider the said Segond the most dangerous, not only on account of his acquaintances and fortune, but also his taciturn and acrimonious spirit. As this last characteristic has made him disliked by the other merchants, I am convinced that none of them will regret his expulsion from the province.

It seems to me that it will be very advisable for Your Excellency to reprimand or punish the said Girod, who is to a great extent the cause of these things, on account of the imprudence with which he wrote the news abovementioned. I do not doubt that this is some machination on the part of some Frenchmen in Bordeaux who have relations with this province, and are seeking some means of inflaming it; but Your Excellency will be able to verify this easily by the testimony of that man.

May God guard Your Excellency many years.
New Orleans, *February 15, 1795.*
El Baron de Carondelet

Proclamation by Carondelet February 15, 1793

Don Francisco Luis Hector de Carondelet, Baron de Carondelet, Knight of the Order of St. John, Colonel of the Royal Armies, Governor, Intendant General, Vice-Patron of the Provinces of Louisiana and West Florida and Inspector of their troops, etc.

Being informed that some discontented spirits, jealous of the tranquility being enjoyed by these provinces (of which they are aliens), are endeavoring, for their own particular purposes, to spread rumors and statements with the sole object of disturbing the good understanding and harmony existing between Spain and France; and desiring to prevent the disturbances and fatal consequences that necessarily must result from the divergence of opinion between the inhabitants and aliens indicated, I have resolved to have published and observed the following articles:

1. It is absolutely prohibited to peruse or read aloud in public writings, printed matter or papers relating to the political affairs of France, whether pro or contra, under the penalty of the offenders' being transported to El Morro of Havana, where they will suffer the punishment of which their offense is considered deserving, according to the merit shown by the reports that will be submitted to the superior government.

2. Anyone who permits meetings, gatherings, or conversations of this nature to be held in his home, or who, not having been able to prevent same, does not report this to the government within the time of twenty-four hours, shall suffer the fine of two hundred pesos, applica-

ble in the ordinary form, without prejudice to the penalty prescribed in the foregoing article.

3. In order that aliens and seamen arriving at this capital may not allege ignorance of this order, a certified copy shall be given to the commercial representatives so that all owners of vessels at present in the roadstead may inform their respective crews of its contents. Another similar one shall be sent to the commandant of the post of Plaquemine with the express order that it be read now and henceforth to all and every one of the crews of the vessels that enter the river, giving those who do not wish to conform thereto the choice of withdrawing.

4. Anyone who finds the observance of this order too rigorous may withdraw from the colony with all his effects to where he pleases, as the government does not care to admit or retain any subjects other than those who come to enjoy the peace, union, immunities, and advantages that form the basis of its prosperity, and which before long must make it the goals of other nations.

Given in New Orleans, *February 15, 1793.*
El Baron de Carondelet (Rubric)

Warning Against Revolution February 12, 1794

Circular Addressed by the Government to all the Inhabitants of Louisiana.

Inhabitants of Louisiana, ready to fall into the trap which infamous seducers spread amongst you, have been setting for you for a year, learn the danger which is threatening you. Open at last your eyes to the most evident truth, and be warned by the murders, the fires, the devastation of France and of its colonies. Prevent by your firmness the same fate, which is being prepared for you by rascals who have been chased out of the Island of Santo Domingo whose ruin they have caused and who were sent to the Ohio by the so-called minister of the Convention, Genet, to repeat the same scenes of horror amongst you.

Nothing is more false than the news that a body of French troops has arrived on the Ohio. Three rascals, escaped from the Cape, left New York in October with despatches [*sic*] from Genet to gather at the Ohio Falls a band of vagabonds but they are without money because the letters of exchange of which they were bearers were protested in Kentucky. In January, they were barely able to gather a certain number of American brigands and French refugees by promising them to sack Louisiana and to give to each one of them the choice of one thousand acres of land in that province.

Having no artillery, they are counting upon that of New Madrid in order to attack Nogales, but even if they should seize the Fort of New Madrid (which would not be surprising because it is guarded by only thirty men) they will not be able to take Nogales with four pieces of four and two pieces of eight. Already the United States is publishing a proclamation expressly forbidding their inhabitants to take part in that expedition either directly or indirectly. Already Major Hamilton and Mr. Drayton, Secretary of the Government of Charleston, have been arrested and tried by order of the Congress for having favored the views of Genet, who himself has fallen into disrepute and has been forced to return to France.

Will you let ourselves be deceived by the false hopes of a liberty, an equality which they have been unable to set up in France or in its colonies, despite the torrents of blood which have been flowing for the last four years, because they can exist nowhere on earth?

In the first year for the revolution, one-fourth of each individual's income was taken away from him and in the third year, one-half. Every Frenchman, without exception, under penalty of death was sundered from his family, and made to march under arms.

The freedom of the press, a fundamental law of the constitution, was infamously violated and pitilessly bloodstained through the massacre of those who wrote against the acts of the members of the Convention or against the republican principles.

The king and the queen were iniquitously condemned and executed without being able to enjoy the six weeks' respite granted to the lowest scoundrel by the new criminal code.

The immunity of the members of the Convention, decreed by the constitution, has been violated by the execution of twenty-one of its members in one single day. All France is divided into enemy parties and is nothing but the scene of massacre and horrors; and if Santo Domingo is beginning to enjoy some respite, it is due to the fact that the inhabitants have injured their first principles and have submitted to the English and Spanish governments, to which they themselves have appealed. The Negroes themselves, after being alternately tossed about by rival parties, victims of the made hopes of freedom which they had entertained and which was secured by the massacre of a great number of their bravest men, have voluntarily submitted to the Spanish government, and have returned to their duty.

The looting and loss of your property, the massacre of your families, the renewal of all the calamities which have devastated Santo Domingo, those are the things which are being planned for you by the monsters who have escaped from the Cape, and who are gathering on the Ohio. They are raising before you the ghost of liberty in order to set you in opposition to one another, and to profit surely from the remains of your fortunes. The scenes of horror which they are preparing will doubtless surpass all those which they have perpetrated at Santo Domingo since, instead of national troops, they will be able to employ only unpaid, insubordinate, and undisciplined vagabonds.

Ready to lead you if you remain united and if you proceed to the place I shall tell you, I guarantee you on my head, brave inhabitants, that the enemy shall not pass Nogales. If, on the contrary, I notice amongst you nothing but discord, distrust of the government and lack of enthusiasm for the common cause, I shall limit myself to defending the places entrusted to me by the King. I shall proclaim to the whole world that I shall remain blameless for the calamities that you will have brought down upon yourselves and for the anger of a sovereign who has constantly heaped his benefactions upon you in the twenty-three years that you have been living under his laws; for it is useless to deceive yourselves.

The extremity at which the so-called Republic finds itself will never permit it to make an advantageous peace, even if it should succeed in having itself recognized by the enemies of France. Louisiana, having by then become pacified (assuming against all appearances that it would have been conquered through the fault of its inhabitants), could no longer expect the advantages and exceptions which she enjoys, and which render her the happiest and most peaceful province of America.

The statement, based solely on the most precise truth and on the great interest which I take in your happiness, will, I hope, dispel the doubts which they are trying to inspire in you; but, should someone desire even more convincing proof of its veracity, I shall be pleased to show him the incontestable proofs on which it is founded.

In our government mansion at New Orleans. *February 12, 1794.*
Le Baron de Carondelet (Rubric)

Questions to Consider:

1. *Why was the French Revolution so terrifying to the Spanish government of Louisiana?*
2. *Do you think Carondelet's efforts against pro-Revolution sentiment were the wisest course of action? Might some other tactic have worked better to reach his goals?*

Source:

Lawrence Kinnaird, ed., *Annual Report of the American Historical Association for the Year 1945*, vol. 2: *Spain in the Mississippi Valley, 1765–1794*, pt. 3: *Problems of Frontier Defense, 1792–1794* (Washington, DC: United States Government Printing Office, 1945), 137–41, 255–57.

1795:
Treaty of San Lorenzo

The Treaty of San Lorenzo, known to Americans as Pinckney's Treaty after US negotiator Thomas Pinckney, resolved a number of issues. Of particular interest to Pinckney, the treaty guaranteed that, for a specific term, American farmers in what was then the western United States would be able to use the Mississippi River and the port of New Orleans without fear of being harassed, or worse, shut out. Those farmers relied on the Mississippi and its connecting waterways to get their produce to markets. If they could not use those rivers, their economic security would be dashed. The treaty also clearly demarcated the southern boundaries of the United States and the northern ones of Spanish East and West Florida.

Treaty of Friendship, Limits, and Navigation, signed at San Lorenzo el Real October 27, 1795. Original in English and Spanish Submitted to the Senate February 26, 1796. Resolution of advice and consent March 5,1796. Ratified by the United States March 7,1796. Ratified by Spain April 25, 1796. Ratifications exchanged at Aranjuez April 25, 1796. Proclaimed August 2, 1796.

His Catholic Majesty and the United States of America desiring to consolidate on a permanent basis the Friendship and good correspondence which happily prevails between the two Parties, have determined to establish by a convention several points, the settlement whereof will be productive of general advantage and reciprocal utility to both Nations. . . .

ART. I.

There shall be a firm and inviolable Peace and sincere Friendship between His Catholic Majesty his successors and subjects, and the United States and their Citizens without exception of persons or places.

ART. II.

To prevent all disputes on the subject of the boundaries which separate the territories of the two High contracting Parties, it is hereby declared and agreed as follows: to wit: The Southern boundary of the United States which divides their territory from the Spanish Colonies of East and West Florida, shall be designated by a line beginning on the River Mississipi at the Northernmost part of the thirty first degree of latitude North of the Equator, which from thence shall be drawn due East to the middle of the River Apalachicola or Catahouche, thence along the middle thereof to its junction with the Flint, thence straight to the head of St Mary's River, and thence down the middle there of to the Atlantic Ocean. And it is agreed that if there should be any troops, Garrisons or settlements of either Party in the territory of the other according to the above mentioned boundaries, they shall be withdrawn from the said territory within the term of six months after the ratification of this treaty or sooner if it be possible and that they shall be permitted to take with them all the goods and effects which they possess. . . .

ART. IV.

It is likewise agreed that the Western boundary of the United States which separates them from the Spanish Colony of Louisiana, is in the middle of the channel or bed of the River Mississippi from the Northern boundary of the said States to the completion of the thirty first degree of latitude North of the Equator; and his Catholic Majesty has likewise agreed that the navigation of the said River in its whole breadth from its source to the Ocean shall be free only to his Subjects, and the Citizens of the United States, unless he should extend this privilege to the Subjects of other Powers by special convention.

ART. V.

The two High contracting Parties shall by all the means in their power maintain peace and harmony among the several Indian Nations who inhabit the country adjacent to the lines and Rivers which by the proceeding Articles form the boundaries of the two Floridas. . . . And whereas several treaties of Friendship exist between the two contracting Parties and the said Nations of Indians, it is hereby agreed that in future no treaty of alliance or other whatever (except treaties of Peace) shall be made by either Party with the Indians living within the boundary of the other; but both Parties will endeavour to make the advantages of the Indian trade common and mutually beneficial to their respective Subjects and Citizens observing in all things the most complete reciprocity: so that both Parties may obtain the advantages arising from a good understanding with the said Nations, without being subject to the expense which they have hitherto occasioned.

ART. VI.

Each Party shall endeavour by all means in their power to protect and defend all Vessels and other effects belonging to the Citizens or Subjects of the other, which shall be within the extent of their jurisdiction by sea or by land, and shall use all their efforts to recover and cause to be restored to the right owners their Vessels and effects which may have been taken from them within the extent of their said jurisdiction whether they are at war or not with the Power whose Subjects have taken possession of the said effects.

ART. VII.

And it is agreed that the Subjects or Citizens of each of the contracting Parties, their Vessels, or effects shall not be liable to any embargo or detention on the part of the other for any military expedition or other public or private purpose whatever; and in all cases of seizure, detention, or arrest for debts contracted or offences committed by any Citizen or Subject of the one Party within the jurisdiction of the other, the same shall be made and prosecuted by order and authority of law only, and according to the regular course of proceedings usual in such cases. The Citizens and Subjects of both Parties shall be allowed to employ such Advocates, Solicitors, Notaries, Agents, and Factors, as they may judge proper in all their affairs and in all their trials at law in which they may be concerned before the tribunals of the other Party, and such Agents shall have free access to be present at the proceedings in such causes, and at the taking of all examinations and evidence which may be exhibited in the said trials.

ART. VIII.

In case the Subjects and inhabitants of either Party with their shipping whether public and of war or private and of merchants be forced through stress of weather, pursuit of Pirates, or Enemies, or any other urgent necessity for seeking of shelter and harbor to retreat and enter into any of the Rivers, Bays, Roads, or Ports belonging to the other Party, they shall be received and treated with all humanity, and enjoy all favor, protection and help, and they shall be permitted to refresh and provide themselves at reasonable rates with victuals and all things needful for the sustenance of their persons or reparation of their Ships, and prosecution of their voyage; and they shall no ways be hindered from returning out of the said Ports, or Roads, but may remove and depart when and whither they please without any let or hindrance.

ART. IX.

All Ships and merchandise of what nature soever which shall be rescued out of the hands of any Pirates or Robbers on the high seas shall be brought into some Port of either State and shall be delivered to the custody of the Officers of that Port in order to be taken care of and restored entire to the true proprietor as soon as due and sufficient proof shall be made concerning the property there of.

ART. X.

When any Vessel of either Party shall be wrecked, foundered, or otherwise damaged on the coasts or within the dominion of the other, their respective Subjects or Citizens shall receive as well for themselves as for their Vessels and effects the same assistance which would be due to the inhabitants of the Country where the damage happens, and shall pay the same charges and dues only as the said inhabitants.

ART. XI.

The Citizens and Subjects of each Party shall have power to dispose of their personal goods within the jurisdiction of the other by testament, donation, or otherwise; and their representatives being Subjects or Citizens of the other Party shall succeed to their said personal goods, whether by testament or *ab intestate* and they may take possession thereof either by themselves or others acting for them, and dispose of the same at their will paying such dues only as the inhabitants of the Country wherein the said goods are shall be subject to pay in like cases, and in case of the absence of the representatives, such care shall be taken of the said goods as would be taken of the goods of a native in like case, until the lawful owner may take measures for receiving them.

ART. XII.

The merchant Ships of either of the Parties which shall be making into a Port belonging to the enemy of the other Party and concerning whose voyage and the species of goods on board her there shall be just grounds of suspicion shall be obliged to exhibit as well upon the high seas as in the Ports and havens not only her passports but likewise certificates expressly strewing that her goods are not of the number of those which have been prohibited as contraband.

ART. XIII.

For the better promoting of commerce on both sides, it is agreed that if a war shall break out between the said two Nations one year after the proclamation of war shall be allowed to the merchants in the Cities and Towns where they shall live for collecting and transporting their goods and merchandises, and if any thing be taken from them, or any injury be done them within that term by either Party, or the People or Subjects of either, full satisfaction shall be made for the same by the Government.

ART. XIV.

No subject of his Catholic Majesty shall apply for or take any commission or letters of marque for arming any Ship or Ships to act as Privateers against the said United States or against the Citizens, People, or inhabitants of the said United States, or against the property of any of the inhabitants of any of them, from any Prince or State with which the said United States shall be at war.

Nor shall any Citizen, Subject, or Inhabitant of the said United States apply for or take any commission or letters of marque for arming any Ship or

Ships to act as Privateers against the subjects of his Catholic Majesty or the property of any of them from any Prince or State with which the said King shall be at war. And if any person of either Nation shall take such commissions or letters of marque he shall be punished as a Pirate.

ART. XV.

It shall be lawful for all and singular the Subjects of his Catholic Majesty, and the Citizens People, and inhabitants of the said United States to sail with their Ships with all manner of liberty and security, no distinction being made who are the proprietors of the merchandises laden thereon from any Port to the Places of those who now are or hereafter shall be at enmity with his Catholic Majesty or the United States. It shall be likewise lawful for the Subjects and inhabitants aforesaid to sail with the Ships and merchandises aforementioned, and to trade with the same liberty and security from the Places, Ports, and Havens of those who are Enemies of both or either Party without any opposition or disturbance whatsoever, not only directly from the Places of the Enemy aforementioned to neutral Places but also from one Place belonging to an Enemy to another Place belonging to an Enemy, whether they be under the jurisdiction of the same Prince or under several, and it is hereby stipulated that Free Ships shall also give freedom to goods, and that every thing shall be deemed free and exempt which shall be found on board the Ships belonging to the Subjects of either of the contracting Parties although the whole lading or any part thereof should appertain to the Enemies of either; contraband goods being always excepted. It is also agreed that the same liberty be extended to persons who are on board a free Ship, so that, although they be Enemies to either Party they shall not be made Prisoners or taken out of that free Ship unless they are Soldiers and in actual service of the Enemies.

ART. XVI.

This liberty of navigation and commerce shall extend to all kinds of merchandises excepting those only which are distinguished by the name of contraband; and under this name of contraband or prohibited goods shall be comprehended arms, great guns, bombs, with the fuses, and other things belonging to them, cannon ball, gun powder, match, pikes, swords, lances, spears, halberds, mortars, petards, grenades, saltpetre, muskets, musket ball bucklers, helmets, breast plates, coats of mail, and the like kind of arms proper for arming soldiers, musket rests, belts, horses with their furniture and all other warlike instruments whatever. These merchandises which follows shall not be reckoned among contraband or prohibited goods; that is to say, all sorts of cloths and all other manufactures woven of any wool, flax, silk, cotton, or any other materials whatever, all kinds of wearing apparel together with all species whereof they are used to be made, gold and silver as well coined as uncoined, tin, iron, latton, copper, brass, coals, as also wheat, barley, oats, and any other kind of corn and pulse: tobacco and likewise all manner of spices, salted and smoked fish, salted fish, cheese and butter, beer, oils, wines, sugars, and all sorts of salts, and in general all provisions which serve for the sustenance of life. Furthermore all kinds of cotton, hemp, flax, tar, pitch, ropes, cables, sails, sail cloths, anchors, and any parts of anchors, also ships masts, planks, wood of all kind, and all other things proper either for building or repairing ships, and all other goods whatever which have not been worked into the form of any instrument prepared for war by land or by sea, shall not be reputed contraband, much less such as have been already wrought and made up for any other use: all which shall be wholly reckoned among free goods, as likewise all other merchandises and things which are not comprehended and particularly mentioned in the foregoing enumeration of contraband goods: so that they may be transported and carried in the freest manner by the subjects of both parties, even to Places belonging to an Enemy, such towns or Places being only excepted as are at that time besieged, blocked up, or invested. And except the cases in which any Ship of war or Squadron shall in consequence of storms or other accidents at sea be under the necessity of taking the cargo of any trading Vessel or Vessels, in which case they may stop the said Vessel or Vessels and furnish themselves with necessaries, giving a receipt in order that the Power to whom the said ship of war belongs may pay for the articles so taken according to the price thereof at the Port to which they may appear to have been destined by the Ship's papers: and the two contracting Parties engage that the Vessels shall not be detained longer than may be absolutely necessary for their said Ships to supply themselves with necessaries: that they will immediately pay the value of the receipts: and indemnify the proprietor for all losses which he may have sustained in consequence of such transaction.

ART. XVII.

To the end that all manner of dissensions and quarrels may be avoided and prevented on one side and the other, it is agreed that in case either of the

Parties hereto should be engaged in a war, the ships and Vessels belonging to the Subjects or People of the other Party must be furnished with sea letters or passports expressing the name, property, and bulk of the Ship, as also the name and place of habitation of the master or commander of the said Ship, that it may appear thereby that the Ship really and truly belongs to the Subjects of one of the Parties. . . .

ART. XVIII.

If the Ships of the said subjects, People or inhabitants of either of the Parties shall be met with either sailing along the coasts on the high Seas by any Ship of war of the other or by any Privateer, the said Ship of war or Privateer for the avoiding of any disorder shall remain out of cannon shot, and may send their boats aboard the merchant Ship which they shall so meet with, and may enter her to number of two or three men only to whom the master or Commander of such ship or vessel shall exhibit his passports concerning the property of the ship made out according to the form inserted in this present Treaty: and the ship when she shall have showed such passports shall be free and at liberty to pursue her voyage, so as it shall not be lawful to molest or give her chase in any manner or force her to quit her intended course.

ART. XIX.

Consuls shall be reciprocally established with the privileges and powers which those of the most favoured Nations enjoy in the Ports where their consuls reside, or are permitted to be.

ART. XX.

It is also agreed that the inhabitants of the territories of each Party shall respectively have free access to the Courts of Justice of the other, and they shall be permitted to prosecute suits for the recovery of their properties, the payment of their debts, and for obtaining satisfaction for the damages which they may have sustained, whether the persons whom they may sue be subjects or Citizens of the Country in which they may be found, or any other persons whatsoever who may have taken refuge therein; and the proceedings and sentences of the said Court shall be the same as if the contending parties had been subjects or Citizens of the said Country.

ART. XXI.

In order to terminate all differences on account of the losses sustained by the Citizens of the United States in consequence of their vessels and cargoes having been taken by the Subjects of his Catholic Majesty during the late war between Spain and France, it is agreed that all such cases shall be referred to the final decision of Commissioners to be appointed in the following manner. His Catholic Majesty shall name one Commissioner, and the President of the United States by and with the advice and consent of their Senate shall appoint another, and the said two Commissioners shall agree on the choice of a third, or if they cannot agree so they shall each propose one person, and of the two names so proposed one shall be drawn by lot in the presence of the two original Commissioners, and the person whose name shall be so drawn shall be the third Commissioner, and the three Commissioners so appointed shall be sworn impartially to examine and decide the claims in question according to the merits of the several cases, and to justice, equity, and the laws of Nations. . . .

ART. XXII.

The two high contracting Parties hoping that the good correspondence and friendship which happily reigns between them will be further increased by this Treaty, and that it will contribute to augment their prosperity and opulence, will in future give to their mutual commerce all the extension and favor which the advantage of both Countries may require; and in consequence of the stipulations contained in the IV. article his Catholic Majesty will permit the Citizens of the United States for the space of three years from this time to deposit their merchandise and effects in the Port of New Orleans, and to export them from thence without paying any other duty than a fair price for the hire of the stores, and his Majesty promises either to continue this permission if he finds during that time that it is not prejudicial to the interests of Spain, or if he should not agree to continue it there, he will assign to them on another part of the banks of the Mississippi an equivalent establishment.

ART. XXIII.

The present Treaty shall not be in force until ratified by the Contracting Parties, and the ratifications shall be exchanged in six months from this time, or sooner if possible.

In Witness whereof We the underwritten Plenipotentiaries of His Catholic Majesty and of the United States of America have signed this present Treaty of Friendship, Limits and Navigation and have hereunto affixed our seals respectively.

Done at San Lorenzo el Real this seven and twenty day of October one thousand seven hundred and ninety five.

THOMAS PINCKNEY
[Seal]
EL PRINCIPE DE LA PAZ
[Seal]

Questions to Consider:

1. *This very extensive and detailed treaty deals with a relatively short period of time and covers a rather small and seemingly insignificant place. What does it tell you about the significance of the Mississippi River and water-borne commerce at the time?*

2. *Based on your reading, did Spain or the United States get the better terms?*

Source:

Hunter Miller, ed., *Treaties and Other International Acts of the United States of America*, vol. 2, *Documents 1–40: 1776–1818* (Washington, DC: United States Government Printing Office, 1931). https://avalon.law.yale.edu/18th_century/sp1795.asp.

1796–1802:
James Pitot on Louisiana Commerce and Sugar

James Pitot, a native of France and a citizen of the United States, offered the following observations on the eve of the Louisiana Purchase. Pitot, who would later become mayor of New Orleans, describes Louisiana and its capital city as bustling commercial locales, places that soon will be even more lucrative due to the burgeoning sugarcane industry.

Commerce, such as I have described it at the time of my arrival, has thus expanded itself as a result of these initial advantages, in a rapid enough progression to have considerably increased its exports. In 1796, it had perhaps not received from the western territory of the United State more than 1,200 barrels of flour, and this same country shipped supplies to the colony by sea; while in 1801, it exported to Louisiana, from Kentucky and the back countries of Pennsylvania, more than 50,000 barrels of flour, making up the deficit in the colony's requirements. Tobacco and rope have increased almost in the same proportion; and from the banks of the Mississippi and several of its branches in the same year, Louisiana offered the United States in exchange more than 15,000 bales of cotton, more than 1,000 boxes of raw sugar, some indigo, pelts, and so on. Such then would have been the progress if the war, hampering all operations had not prevented the speculator in Kentucky, and in other territories equally fertile from finding a market at New Orleans as ready as it was advantageous for commodities, in the cultivation of which the planters, if encouraged, might have been more persevering and daring. What an increase in wealth would not New Orleans have derived from the land under control is of its government in shipping to the tropical colonies its lumber, tar, rosin, masts, and other products, and in selling to its advantage in the European markets the old indigo that commerce and its planters were holding back for the advent of peace, as well as the plug tobacco which Spain had discontinued importing.

It is possible to visualize the colony's growth by the experience of this year [1802], which already feels the advantages of a peace which the hero of France [Napoleon Bonaparte] seems to want to assure to Europe and America. The waterways of the Mississippi have brought to the New Orleans market 30,000 more barrels of flour than in the preceding year; they will provide there, in addition, 12,000 to 15,000 bales of cotton and at least 3 million pounds of raw sugar. The receipts of the pelts in actual fact have been negligible because of corrupt supervision, on which I shall elaborate when discussing trade with the Indians. New harvests of indigo have also been insignificant for many years. The low price of tobacco has reduced its export. The production of cordage has not been sufficient to meet the demands of government and individuals, and especially to supply the large consumption which the baling of cotton has required. Salt pork and salt beef, which they had not yet offered for export, have finally been produced in considerable quantities; and as a unique result of the peace preliminaries, all these matters have avoided the ruinous effects of the deposit and the protracted warehousing to which an uncertain shipping situation previously forced them. Starting in January and February [1802], the port of New Orleans, filled with three rows of ships, presented the spectacle of a forest of masts, unheard-of up to now, that reduced in April and May only in assuring the end of the colony's stagnation and the certainty of its future prosperity. And newly arrived vessels, loaded in ballast, have generally taken the place of others, and have assured that every spring and summer the New Orleans warehouses will have numerous cargoes either to exchange for imports or to load as freight for Europe and the Antilles.

The other domestic resources of Lower Louisiana have not yet been able to be made profitable by the benefits of pacification in Europe, nor to increase the amount of exports this year. Rosin and tar, lumber of every kind, Natchitoches tobacco, rice, and other items would soon complete the assortment of products; and I can repeat there the prophecy that I made regarding the advantages and wealth of the New Orleans market in my memoir of 1798. There, as I said with some admiration, one will see the coming together of all the products of the Temperate Zones with the much larger number from the Torrid Zones. Ships in great numbers will discharge simultaneously on her fortunate shores cargoes of sugar, flour, indigo, salt provisions, cotton, hemp, rope, pelts, lead, lumber of every kind, iron, rice, and tobacco.

The list of commercial imports has not been any less astonishing. Rich and varied cargoes have replaced the small number and mediocrity of those that it received, for which the land produced almost nothing in exchange. In that same year, 1796, the consumption of imported goods could have been at the most a million piastres, and commerce had then, as a pledge for its credit and encouragement of its operations only the misery of the planter. Now it has imported not less than three million piastres, which agriculture, as I will prove shortly in much greater detail, can already pay for with its products. Finally, the businessmen, storekeepers, and peddlers have increased in numbers. Some important business houses of the United States have already become silent partners in local firms, with guarantees of the greatest security. Several from Europe, in fact, will rival them in success, and one sees prevailing everywhere the affluence that comes to a country which enriches itself, and the expectation of wealth that it promises. . . .

In 1795, an active and enterprising planter—who had exhausted all the means of continuing the cultivation of indigo, and had suffered more from this crop than anyone else—resolved to establish and undertake on a large scale the cultivation of sugarcane. The year before, another planter with little means and aided by day laborers had realized a modest income by making syrup and converting it into tafia; and this feeble attempt, by reason of the prejudice against such cultivation, might have languished many more years and perhaps even died out. For sugar to turn to the great advantage of the colony, it was necessary that a daring man undertake its production; and the person about whom I want to speak—despite the new financing that he had to take on for the equipment, and despite his family protests, the advice of his friends, and even the observations of numerous acquaintances whom the loyalty of his character has always attracted to him—planned early in that year a large establishment; he planted 100 arpents of cane to be harvested into sugar in 1796, paid a high price to be certain of having a sugarmaker, built the grinding shed, sugar mill, drying house, and sheds, and to the astonishment of the entire province made, with about thirty Negroes, 100,000 pounds of raw sugar. The first attempts of the previous year had already encouraged some others who also made a little money, but in 1797 there was [an] increase in sugar mills, and if establishments of this type have been limited to about fifty, it is because there is a lack of workers due to the ban on the importation of Negroes.

Before summarizing the advantages which the colony has gained from that cultivation, I think that I should speak about the quality of sugar they have produced up to this time; five years of experience not having irrevocably fixed the opinion of commerce in its favor, and not having been able then to encourage the planter could undertake but nevertheless, has not yet undertaken, and establishment of that nature. If I am permitted to give my opinion based upon the knowledge which ten years of residence on sugar plantations in Saint-Domingue placed me in the position of acquiring, I shall affirm that one can make fine and good sugar in this colony, barring (as can also happen in the tropics) an excess of rain or a dry spell, and barring also a freeze which in unusual years can damage the uncut cane. And if I do not doubt that a good sugar producer can grow sugar in Louisiana less subject to decomposition than is that of the Torrid Zones. I must acknowledge that by the nature of the soil and climate, the cane, having an early maturity more apparent than real, cannot stand the carelessness in production which was often permitted in other countries—especially in sugar mills producing only raw sugar. Because of that situation I am convinced that all the defective sugars which are produced and which, to the temporary disadvantage of the colony have been exported, are in that condition only through lack of care in production, or because a planter, by laziness or want of foresight, allowed the standing cane to freeze and has persisted in making sugar out of it rather than turning it only into syrup.

The first buyers in the United States contributed not a little to the planters' mistakes by demanding sugar of them, deluded into thinking that the cane would live up to expectations. From another angle, pride has blinded many persons, who, at the sight of a product favored by the weather in its thickening rather than in its crystallization, thought that they had made fine merchandise. They had in fact barreled only a molasses thickened in appearance, but filled with foreign particles which turns it sour as a result of fermentation when warm. Thus, the buyer, who as an expert has a sugarmaker's pride, is completely deceived in his speculation. Neglecting to skim the juice, which, because of the cane's richness in very hot climates, does not have as many foreign particles, can, in itself and even with a good sugarmaker, cause a sort of decomposition in the sugar of this country during warm weather. For that reason, the sugarmaker needs to take greater pains here, as the cane juice requires close attention and cautious handling.

He should not spoil, by a deficiency of lime, a cane juice too weak in its maturity to be able to tolerate a residue of acid or gum without danger; he should handle the skimming with the same attention as if he were making white sugar, that is to say to be bleached and dried. But he should also guard against making it too thin by an excess of alkali, too thick by over-cooking, or separating, by too little cooking, the texture of a sugar of fine and good quality which he can produce by his carefulness, and in which the raw material does not acquire enough richness so that one can handle it with the negligence common in climates more adapted to the cultivation of sugarcane.

Questions to Consider:

1. *How do Pitot's views of the commercial potential of Louisiana differ from those of earlier observers in this book?*
2. *How does Pitot's description of New Orleans differ from Marie-Madeleine Hachard's?*

Source:

James Pitot, *Observations on the Colony of Louisiana from 1796 to 1802*, ed. Robert D. Bush, trans. Henry C. Pitot (Baton Rouge: Louisiana State University Press for the Historic New Orleans Collection, 1979), 59–62, 73–75.

For Further Reading

Brasseaux, Carl A. *Denis-Nicolas Foucault and the New Orleans Rebellion of 1768.* Ruston, LA: McGinty Publications, 1987.

———. *The Founding of New Acadia: The Beginnings of Acadian Life in Louisiana, 1765–1803.* Baton Rouge: Louisiana State University Press, 1987.

Brasseaux, Carl A., and Glenn R. Conrad. *The Road to Louisiana: The Saint-Domingue Refugees, 1792–1809.* Lafayette, LA: Center for Louisiana Studies, University of Southwestern Louisiana, 1992.

Brown, R.F., ed., *Coastal Encounters: The Transformation of the Gulf South in the Eighteenth Century.* Lincoln, NE: University of Nebraska Press, 2008.

Burton, H. Sophie, and F. Todd Smith. *Colonial Natchitoches: A Creole Community on the Louisiana-Texas Frontier.* College Station, TX: Texas A&M Press, 2008.

Clark, Emily. *Masterless Mistresses: The New Orleans Ursulines and the Development of a New World Society, 1727–1834.* Chapel Hill, NC: University of North Carolina Press, 2007.

———. *The Strange History of the American Quadroon: Free Women of Color in the Revolutionary Atlantic World.* Chapel Hill, NC: University of North Carolina Press, 2013.

———, ed. *Voices from an Early American Convent: Marie Madeleine Hachard and the New Orleans Ursulines 1727–1760.* Baton Rouge: Louisiana State University Press, 2009.

Cowan, Walter Grieves and Jack McGuire. *Louisiana Governors: Rulers, Rascals, and Reformers.* Jackson, MS: University Press of Mississippi, 2008.

Crouse, Nellis M. *Lemoyne d'Iberville: Soldier of New France.* Baton Rouge: Louisiana State University Press, 2001.

Dawdy, Shannon. *Building the Devil's Empire: French Colonial New Orleans.* Chicago: University of Chicago Press, 2008.

Dessens, Nathalie. *From Saint-Domingue to New Orleans: Migration and Influences.* Gainesville, FL: University Press of Florida, 2007.

Din, Gilbert. *The Canary Islanders of Louisiana.* Baton Rouge: Louisiana State University Press, 1999.

———. *Populating the Barrera: Spanish Immigration Efforts in Colonial Louisiana.* Lafayette, LA: University of Louisiana at Lafayette Press, 2014.

———. *Spaniards, Planters, and Slaves: The Spanish Regulation of Slavery in Louisiana, 1763–1803.* College Station, TX: Texas A&M Press, 1999.

Din, Gilbert C., and John E. Harkins. *The New Orleans Cabildo: Colonial Louisiana's First City Government, 1769–1803.* Baton Rouge: Louisiana State University Press, 1996.

Ethridge, Robbie, and Sherri M. Shuck Hall, eds. *Mapping the Mississippian Shatter Zone: The Colonial Indian Slave Trade and Regional Instability in the American South.* Lincoln, NE: University of Nebraska Press, 2009.

Evans, Freddi Williams. *Congo Square: African Roots in New Orleans.* Lafayette, LA: University of Louisiana at Lafayette Press, 2011.

Foster, William, and Johanna S. Warren. *The La Salle Expedition on the Mississippi River: A Lost Manuscript of Nicolas de La Salle.* Austin, TX: University of Texas Press, 2003.

Galloway, Patricia K., ed. *La Salle and His Legacy: Frenchmen and Indians in the Lower Mississippi Valley.* Jackson, MS: University Press of Mississippi, 1982.

Greenwald, Erin. *Marc-Antoine Caillot and the Company of the Indies in Louisiana: Trade in the French Atlantic World.* Baton Rouge: Louisiana State University Press, 2016.

Guenin-Lelle, Dianne. *The Story of French New Orleans: History of a Creole City.* Jackson, MS: University Press of Mississippi, 2016.

Hall, Gwendolyn Midlo. *Africans in Colonial Louisiana: The Development of Afro-Creole Culture in the Eighteenth-Century.* Baton Rouge: Louisiana State University Press, 1992.

Hanger, Kimberly S., *Bounded Lives, Bounded Places: Free Black Society in Colonial New Orleans, 1769–1803.* Durham, NC: Duke University Press, 1997.

Hodson, Christopher. *The Acadian Diaspora an Eighteenth-Century History.* Oxford, UK: Oxford University Press, 2012.

Ingersoll, Thomas N. *Mammon and Manon in Early New Orleans: The First Slave Society in the Deep South, 1718–1819.* Knoxville, TN: University of Tennessee Press, 1999.

Lee, Jacob F. *Masters of the Middle Waters: Indian Nations and Colonial Ambitions along the Mississippi.* Cambridge, MA: Harvard University Press, 2019.

Milne, George. *Natchez Country: Indians, Colonists, and the Landscapes of Race in French Louisiana.* Athens, GA: University of Georgia Press, 2015.

Narrett, David. *Adventurism and Empire: The Struggle for Mastery in the Louisiana-Florida Borderlands, 1762–1803.* Chapel Hill, NC: University of North Carolina Press, 2017.

Palmer, Vernon Valentine. *Through the Codes Darkly: Slave Law and Civil Law in Colonial Louisiana.* Clark, NJ: The Lawbook Exchange, Ltd., 2012.

Powell, Lawrence N. *Accidental City: Improvising New Orleans.* Cambridge, MA: Harvard University Press, 2012.

Sayre, Gordon M., Carla Zecher, eds. *The Memoir of Lieutenant Dumont, 1715–1747: A Sojourner in the French Atlantic.* Chapel Hill, NC: University of North Carolina Press, 2013.

Spear, Jennifer M. *Race, Sex, and Social Order in Early New Orleans.* Baltimore, MD: The Johns Hopkins University Press, 2009.

Usner, Daniel H., Jr. *American Indians in Early New Orleans: From Calumet to Raquette.* Baton Rouge: Louisiana State University Press, 2018.

———. *American Indians in the Lower Mississippi Valley: Social and Economic Histories.* Lincoln, NE: University of Nebraska Press, 2003.

———. *Indians, Settlers, and Slaves in a Frontier Exchange Economy: The Lower Mississippi Valley before 1783.* Chapel Hill, NC: University of North Carolina Press, 1992.

Vidal, Cécile. *Caribbean New Orleans: Empire, Race, and the Making of a Slave Society.* Chapel Hill, NC: University of North Carolina Press, 2019.

———, ed. *Louisiana: Crossroads of the Atlantic World.* Philadelphia: University of Pennsylvania Press, 2014.

White, Sophie. *Voices of the Enslaved: Love, Labor, and Longing in French Louisiana.* Chapel Hill, NC: University of North Carolina Press, 2019.

———. *Wild Frenchmen and Frenchified Indians: Material Culture and Race in Colonial Louisiana.* Philadelphia: University of Pennsylvania Press, 2014.

Part II

The Nineteenth Century 1803–1900

1802/1803: Letters from President Jefferson about the Louisiana Purchase

By the turn of the nineteenth century, Napoleon Bonaparte had consolidated his control over the French government and set his sights on re-establishing France's empire in North America. To advance this goal, he pressured the weak Spanish monarch to cede the Louisiana territory back to France with the Third Treaty of San Ildefonso, agreed to in secret in 1800. Spain continued to administer Louisiana while Napoleon's attempted to re-establish control over the rebellious colony of Saint-Domingue in the Caribbean.

In Washington, DC, notwithstanding his usual French sympathies, President Thomas Jefferson viewed the cession of Louisiana as a potential security threat to the United States. When the final Spanish governor of Louisiana, Juan Manuel de Salcedo, revoked the right of deposit in New Orleans for American traders in 1802, Jefferson instructed the American minister to France, Robert Livingston, to engage the French government in negotiations for the purchase of New Orleans. Discussions quickly reached an impasse, and Jefferson asked James Monroe to travel to France to assist in the effort. The second document below contains his explanation for why this had become urgent and his request to Monroe.

Thomas Jefferson to Robert R. Livingston April 18, 1802

The cession of Louisiana & the Floridas by Spain to France works most sorely on the US. On this subject the Secretary of State has written to you fully. Yet I cannot forbear recurring to it personally, so deep is the impression it makes in my mind. It completely reverses all the political relations of the US and will form a new epoch in our political course. Of all nations of any consideration France is the one which hitherto has offered the fewest points on which we could have any conflict of right, and the most points of a communion of interests. From these causes we have ever looked to her as our *natural friend*, as one with which we never could have an occasion of difference. Her growth therefore we viewed as our own, her misfortunes ours. There is on the globe one single spot, the possessor of which is our natural & habitual enemy. It is New Orleans, through which the produce of three eighths of our territory must pass to market, and from its fertility it will ere long yield more than half of our whole produce and contain more than half our inhabitants. France placing herself in that door assumes to us the attitude of defiance. Spain might have retained it quietly for years. Her pacific dispositions, her feeble state, would induce her to increase our facilities there, so that her possession of the place would be hardly felt by us, and it would not perhaps be very long before some circumstance might arise which might make the cession of it to us the price of something of more worth to her. Not so can it ever be in the hands of France. The impetuosity of her temper, the energy & restlessness of her character, placed in a point of eternal friction with us, and our character, which though quiet, & loving peace & the pursuit of wealth, is high minded, despising wealth in competition with insult or injury, enterprizing & energetic as any nation on earth, these circumstances render it impossible that France and the US can continue long friends when they meet in so irritable a position. They as well as we must be blind if they do not see this; and we must be very improvident if we do not begin to make arrangements on that hypothesis. The day that France takes possession of N. Orleans fixes the sentence which is to restrain her forever within her low water mark. It seals the union of two nations who in conjunction can maintain exclusive possession of the ocean. From that moment we must marry ourselves to the British fleet & nation. We must turn all our attentions to a maritime force, for which our resources place us on very high ground: and having formed and cemented together a power which may render reinforcement of her settlements here impossible to France, make the first cannon which shall be fired in Europe the signal for tearing up any settlement she may have made, and for holding the two continents of America in sequestration for the common purposes of the United British & American nations. This is not a state of things we seek or desire. It is one which this measure, if adopted by France, forces on us, as necessarily as any other cause, by the laws of nature, brings on its necessary effect. It is not from a fear of France that we deprecate this measure proposed by her. For however greater her force is than ours compared in the abstract, it is nothing in comparison of ours when to be exerted on our soil. But it is from a sincere love of peace, and a firm persuasion that bound to France by the interests and the strong sympathies still existing in the minds of our citizens, and holding relative positions which ensure their continuance we are secure of a long course of peace. Whereas the change of friends, which will be rendered necessary if France changes that position, embarks us necessarily as a belligerent power in the first war of Europe. In that case France will have held possession of New Orleans during the interval of a peace, long or short, at the end of which it will be wrested from her. Will this short-lived possession have been an equivalent to her for the transfer of such a weight into the scale of her enemy? Will not the amalgamation of a young, thriving, nation continue to that enemy the health & force which are at present so evidently on the decline? And will a few years possession of N. Orleans add equally to the strength of France? She may say she needs Louisiana for the supply of her West Indies. She does not need it in time of peace, and in war she could not depend on them because they would be so easily intercepted. I should suppose that all these considerations might in some proper form be brought into view of the government of France. Tho' stated by us, it ought not to give offence; because we do not bring them forward as a menace, but as consequences not controllable by us, but inevitable from the course of things. We mention them not as things which we desire by any means, but as things we deprecate; and we beseech a friend to look forward and to prevent them for our common interests.

Thomas Jefferson to James Monroe January 13, 1803

DEAR SIR:

I dropped you a line on the 10th informing you of a nomination I had made of you to the Senate, and yesterday I inclosed [*sic*] you their approbation not then having time to write. The agitation of the public mind on occasion of the late suspension of our right of deposit at N. Orleans is extreme. In the Western country it is natural and grounded on honest motives. In the seaports it proceeds from a desire for war which increases the mercantile lottery; in the federalists generally & especially those of Congress the object is to force us into war if possible, in order to derange our finances, or if this cannot be done, to attach the Western country to them, as their best friends, and thus get again into power. Remonstrances, [*sic*] memorials &c. are now circulating thro' the whole of the Western country & signing by the body of the people. The measures we have been pursuing being invisible, do not satisfy their minds. Something sensible therefore was become necessary; and indeed our object of purchasing N. Orleans & the Floridas is a measure liable to assume so many shapes, that no instructions could be squared to fit them. It was essential then to send a Minister extraordinary, to be joined with the ordinary one, with discretionary powers, first however well impressed with all our views and therefore qualified to meet and modify to these every form of proposition which could come from the other party. This could be done only in full & frequent oral communications. Having determined on this, there could not be two opinions among the republicans as to the person. You possessed the unlimited confidence of the administration & of the Western people; & generally of the republicans every where; and were you to refuse to go, no other man can be found who does this. The measure has already silenced the feds here. Congress will no longer be agitated by them: and the country will become calm as fast as the information extends over it. All eyes, all hopes are now fixed on you; and were you to decline, the chagrin would be universal, and would shake under your feet the high ground on which you stand with the public. Indeed I know nothing which would produce such a shock. For on the event of this mission depends the future destinies of this republic. If we cannot by a purchase of the country ensure to ourselves a course of perpetual peace & friendship with all nations, then as war cannot be distant, it behooves us immediately to be preparing for that course, without however hastening it, and it may be necessary (on your failure on the continent) to cross the channel. We shall get entangled in European politics, and figuring more, be much less happy & prosperous. This can only be prevented by a successful issue to your present mission. I am sensible after the measures you have taken for getting into a different line of business, that it will be a great sacrifice on your part, and presents from the season & other circumstances serious difficulties. But some men are born for the public. Nature by fitting them for the service of the human race on a broad scale, has stamped them with the evidences of her destination & their duty.

Questions to Consider:

1. *Why was the cession of Louisiana to France a major worry for President Jefferson?*

2. *Why would Jefferson, normally a Francophone who had little regard for the British, believe that under certain circumstances, "we must marry ourselves to the British fleet & nation"? What were those circumstances?*

3. *Why was the suspension of the right of deposit in New Orleans of great concern to Jefferson and to many Americans?*

Sources:

1. Thomas Jefferson to Robert R. Livingston, 18 April 1802. The Thomas Jefferson Papers, Manuscript Division, Library of Congress. https://www.loc.gov/item/mtjbib011277/.

2. Thomas Jefferson to James Monroe, 13 January 1803. The Thomas Jefferson Papers, Manuscript Division, Library of Congress. https://www.loc.gov/item/mtjbib012071/.

1804:
The War of the Quadrilles

Establishing American sovereignty over Louisiana in the wake of the Purchase was fraught with problems and tensions. The cultural divide between the region's native-born population and the American newcomers was substantial. Louisiana Creoles spoke French, attended Catholic Mass (if at all), were part of a Latin cultural tradition, and followed a continental-inspired civil law system. Americans, by contrast, spoke English, attended Protestant services, were part of an Anglo cultural tradition, and followed a common law tradition derived from England. Most Creoles would have preferred to remain part of the French empire, while American officials had grave doubts about the ability of the Creoles to master the art of republican governance. The United States was still a young nation, with a relatively weak administrative structure and a national identity still emerging. The previous time lower Louisiana changed owners, from the French to the Spanish in the 1760s, the populace staged a revolt. The person charged by Jefferson and Madison to take the reins of power in New Orleans was twenty-eight-year-old William C. C. Claiborne, previously the governor of the Mississippi territory. Due to the slowness of communication in early nineteenth-century North America, he would have to handle problems as they emerged with little opportunity to turn to the Jefferson administration for guidance. Moreover, the French prefect who handed Louisiana over to Claiborne, Pierre de Laussat, along with French soldiers and even the previous Spanish governor, stayed in New Orleans through the winter of 1804, and were in positions to cause trouble for Claiborne. The first problem to emerge for Claiborne was a series of incidents that broke out over the choice of dance at the many balls held during the city's winter social season.

W. C. C. Claiborne to James Madison
New Orleans, January 10, 1804

The more I become acquainted with the inhabitants of this Province, the more I am convinced of their unfitness for a representative Government. The Credulity of the People is indeed great, and a virtuous Magistrate resting entirely for Support on the Suffrages and good will of his fellow Citizens in this quarter, would often be exposed to immediate ruin by the Machinations of a few base individuals who with some exertion and address, might make many of the people think against their will, and act against their Interests.

I know indeed that Misrepresentation throughout America has had its effects in respect to the worthiest men and best measures; but here it would have an unlimited field for Mischief. Until therefore the progress of information shall in some degree remove that mental darkness which at present so unhappily prevails, and a general knowledge of the American Language, laws and customs be understood, I do fear that a representative Government in Louisiana, would be a dangerous experiment.

God forbid that I should recommend for this people Political provisions under which oppression of any kind could be practiced with impunity, by persons in power, but I do think that their own happiness renders it advisable that they remain for some years under the immediate Guardianship of Congress, and that for the present a local and temporary Government for Louisiana upon principles somewhat Similar to our Territorial Government in their first grade, be established.

I have discovered with regret that a strong partiality for the French Government still exists among many of the inhabitants of this City, and it appears to me, that Mr. Laussat is greatly Solicitous to increase that partiality. With what views I know not, but I have learned that in some circles a Sentiment is cherished, that at the close of the War between England and France, the great Bonaparte will again raise his standard in this country. For my part, I attach no importance to this little Political Speculation,—It is directed more by the wishes of those who busy themselves on the subject, than by any reasonable ground of expectation. . . .

A *Fracas* also took place at a Public Ball, on Thursday last, which altho' it arose from trifling causes, has occasioned some warmth. It originated in a contest between some young Americans and Frenchmen, whether the American or French Dances should have a preference. I believe this affair is at an end, but being desirous at the present juncture of communicating every circumstance which might have a political tendency, I have deemed it worthy of mentioning.

Claiborne to James Madison
New Orleans, January 31, 1804

I am sorry to inform you that a few of the French Officers and Citizens who are here, continue to evidence a disorderly disposition; they are mortified at the loss of this delightful Country and seem to foster great hatred to the *Americans* who are here;— Among *these* (the Americans) there are also some warm and imprudent young Men, and I can assure you Sir, that it requires much address and prudence to preserve the Harmony of the City.

Some unpleasant Diplomatic Letters have passed between M. Laussat and the American Commissioners, upon the disorderly conduct of some of the French Officers which he denies, and charges it to the Americans. Copies of these Letters will be transmitted to you. . . .

The Public Ball room has been the Theatre of all this Disorder. During the Winter Season, there has for many years been a Ball twice a week. Every white Male Visits it who will pay at the door 50 cents, and the Ladies of every Rank attend these assemblies in great numbers. The Consequence is that the company is generally composed of a very heterogenous Mass. To keep order at these Balls (under the Spanish Government) a Strong guard was Stationed at the Ball room, and on the first appearance of disorder the persons concerned were committed.

On my arrival at New Orleans, I found the people very Solicitous to maintain their Public Ball establishment, and to convince them that the American Government felt to disposition to break in upon their amusements (as had been reported by some mischievous persons) General Wilkinson and myself occasionally attended these assemblies.

Under the Spanish Government, the Governor General was the Regulator of the Balls, but this Gallant duty I have cheerfully surrendered to the Municipality of the City. I fear you will suppose that I am wanting in respect in calling your attention to the Balls of New Orleans, but I do assure you Sir, that they occupy much of the Public mind, and from them have proceeded the greatest embarrassments which have heretofore attended my administration.

Claiborne and General James Wilkinson to Madison New Orleans, February 7, 1804

A Difference, of a rather a serious Nature, has sprung up, Apparently from a very trivial Source, between the American and French Citizens (in which, hitherto, the Creoles or Natives of the Province, have taken no Open Part, though we suppose them to favor decidedly the French Interest) of which this is the Origin. That Species of Country Dance, which is best known & practiced in the United States, passes here by the name of Contra Danse, Anglaise, against which (as great Importance is often Attached to mere Words) the Officers and Citizens of France, Strangers & not permanent Residents here, have manifested a decided Disapprobation, and pretended, that the Taste of the Americans, for this Dance, indicated a partiality, to the English, their Enemies: of Consequence, they undertook, not in a very open way at first, to prevent the Americans from practicing [this Danse, at the Public Ball Room, which Occasioned a trifling Disturbance there, not long after our taking Possession of the Town; To prevent the like in future, the Municipality decreed, that Managers should be Appointed on these Occasions, with ample Powers to preserve order &c. Notwithstanding which, at a public Ball, which took place on the 22nd ultimo, at which we were both present, a great Riot and Disturbance happened, on the Grounds above Stated. Some French Officers & troublesome young Men from Bordeaux, were the Aggressors: much Confusion ensued, Swords were drawn; and it Required, the greatest Exertions, to prevent the Spilling of Blood, finally two Frenchmen, one a Shopkeeper in this Town, and the Other, as it afterwards appeared, a Surgeon in the French service, were Arrested, the latter on giving his parole d'honour to appear and Answer in the Morning, was released, and the former Committed to the Guard; they were tried the next Morning before a Tribunal of the City, chiefly French, and acquitted; notwithstanding it was fully proved, that they had been principally, Concerned in Commencing & Promoting the disturbance, and interrupting the Amusement, of the Company.

Laussat Remembers

During the night of the eighth of January, an unfortunate potential for trouble broke out between the French and Anglo-Americans at the regular public ball. Two quadrilles, one French, the other English, formed at the same time. An American, taking offense at something, raised his walking stick at one of the fiddlers. Bedlam ensued. Claiborne remained quiet until [Daniel] Clark roused him. Unable to explain himself in French, Claiborne appeared embarrassed and weak; he yielded at first, then endeavored to reassert his authority. In the end, he resorted to persuasion rather than to rigorous measures in order to silence the American, who was a simple surgeon attached to the troops. The French quadrille resumed. The American interrupted it again with an English quadrille and took his place to dance. Someone cried, "If the women have a drop of French blood in their veins, they will not dance." Within minutes, the hall was completely deserted by the women. The Marquis de Casacalvo, who was present, continued to play cards, laughing up his sleeve. He had gumbo served to two or three women who came to him for protection, and he maliciously played his hand.

Claiborne spoke to me of the incident. "There you have a picture of the feelings that stir up people." I replied, "See to it that they do not clash over things more serious and more important." He retorted, "The people of Louisiana love France dearly; I get proofs of it all the time." There is no doubt that they loved France. It would take the ablest of American statesmen to erase this fond predilection and a great display of kindness on the part of the new government.

The following Sunday there was no ball; but there was one again on the 22nd of January. . . .

The ball began in a generally bad atmosphere. The city officials had ruled that one should dance successively two rounds of French quadrilles, one round of English quadrilles in groups of twelve partners, and one round of waltzes. This order was being observed, uninterrupted by an English quadrille into which fourteen or fifteen dancers had slipped. However, another group with only twelve partners, one of whom was General Wilkinson, had finished its round. Suddenly protests were raised; immediately, one of the municipal officers charged with keeping order, called out, "French quadrille"! It began and apparently order was restored when all of a sudden, as if planned, remarks and murmurings were heard.

General Wilkinson was then seen, with a friendly look, leading a French citizen by the name of Gauthier toward the guard. The rumor spread that the young man had been arrested. The uproar redoubled. General Wilkinson got up on a bench and interspersed a few words of bad French with his English statements. Claiborne got up beside the general. He pointed to an individual, Labalch, a health officer of the 110th Demibrigade [Regiment], just arrived from Saint-Domingue, whom I placed on the brig *Argo*. General Wilkinson asked, "What do you want?" Labalch answered, "The posted rules be complied with." At these words, the general began to conduct Labalch, as he had Gauthier, to the guardhouse. His release was demanded because he was a French officer. . . . Saint-Abit [Saint-Avid] then pledged his word of honor for him. Labalch left. While Saint-Abit was still speaking with the general, a United States officer presented himself to speak to the general. Saint-Abit unintentionally pushed this officer aside with a brusque movement. This was taken as an insult. Thirty Americans and Frenchmen scuffled with each other. The guard of regular troops came in. Saint-Abit escaped death by a miracle. He was unarmed and had been beaten and wounded.

Teihl, who was lodging nearby, arrived armed with his saber, and he spoke to General Wilkinson. . . . Lafitte, another Frenchman, joined him. . . . The Americans fell on Teihl, who reached a nearby closet, and the quarrel ended. . . . The women had left at the beginning of the quarrel. Only twelve or fifteen ladies stayed on. Other than these, there were only men present. . . . An infernal brawl [broke out]. After this cabaret scene, Claiborne and Wilkinson, escorted by Americans and the band, returned to their homes.

Clark had not appeared on the night of the ball, although customarily he never missed any of them. He was generally regarded as the instigator of these disorders. Saint-Abit boldly challenged those who had attacked him, but in vain; no one showed up. Finally, the influential and right-minded Americans believed that the best thing to do was to invite the French to a reconciliation banquet. The French had to be coaxed a great deal and finally accepted. So this war of esteem came to an end.

The principal responsibility for the fracas belonged to the American leaders. They played a role in it, encouraged it, participated in it. Claiborne kept repeating, "To bring these folks to their senses, we'll have to aim cannons at them and knock down the walls of the city from top to bottom." Clark, their interpreter, let it be rumored around that "until two or three Frenchmen have been hanged, we will not rule over this country [Louisiana]." . . .

Proud of this country, which he praised to the skies, the Creole also cherished France. He never mentioned O'Reilly without hate and horror, and he despised the Spanish government, whose depravity he related at length. Yet, he showed an even greater antipathy toward the Americans. On the other hand, devoid of energy, organization, and public spirit, he would allow himself to be subjugated without complaining, except when beside his fireplace or while strolling up and down his galleries.

Louisianians preserved the spirit of adventure from their forebears and were enterprising in their efforts to amass a fortune. They bought and sold on long-term credit—a practice that derived from that custom of arriving and starting with nothing, prospering, and facing up to debts contracted on one's word alone. From this practice derived also their general laxity in keeping engagements, while maintaining an admirable tolerance in conceding to others delay after delay.

The Americans, in contrast, introduced the strictness of their laws and exactness of their customs. For two months they had been apprehending and imprisoning debtors. The Louisianians found this unbearable, and everything was in confusion. Their leaders were blind enough not to grasp the unwise policy of so swift a change; however, it was hopeless. The poor Louisianians would have to adjust.

The customs of the city differed strangely from those of the country. The city resident was often reckless; the man who lived there without incurring huge debts was rare. I was thinking of him especially when I spoke of the uncertainty of payments.

The women were drowned in luxury. Inside and out, they were glutted with superfluous things, but often lacked necessities. They had taste, elegance, coquetry, and a precocious frivolity; but they could not be counted on either for intellectual resources or for conversational charm. Generally, there prevailed a great deal of idle gossip in their society. They knew even the shadiest stories about other women and kept the secret badly. Some mothers of families were good managers; however, most of them were noted for the indolence which seemed to constitute the dominant tendency in their character.

Nowhere as in the city were there so many single women. The burdens of family life frightened men. The mulatto women were in great demand and were much cheaper. Even one kept at great expense had no qualms of conscience about her infidelity to the lover she ruined or betrayed.

Questions to Consider:

1. *Compare Laussat's and Claiborne's accounts of the problems between the French and the Americans during the winter of 1804. For each, how did the problem at the balls originate, and who did each blame?*

2. *In what ways did their views of the Creole population of New Orleans correspond?*

Sources:

1. Dunbar Rowland, ed., *Official Letter Books of W.C.C. Claiborne, 1801–1816* (Jackson, MS: State Department of Archives and History, 1917), 329–33.

2. Rowland, *Official Letter Books*, 352–55.

3. Clarence Edwin Carter, ed., *The Territorial Papers of the United States*, vol. 9, *The Territory of Orleans, 1803–1812* (Washington, DC: United States Government Printing Office, 1934), 178–79.

4. Pierre Clement de Laussat, *Memoirs of My Life*, ed. Robert D. Bush (Baton Rouge: Louisiana State University Press, 1978), 92–96, 100–1.

1812–1862:
The Slave Trade in New Orleans

In 1808, acting on a provision in the Constitution, Congress ended the international slave trade to the United States. To meet the expanding labor demands of cotton producers throughout the South and sugar planters in Louisiana, an interregional southern slave trade developed. Slave owners in the upper South had transitioned to less labor-intensive crops by the early 1800s, and the region's more salutary weather led to less disease, fewer childhood deaths, and more slaves living to adulthood. Upper South planters realized they could earn substantial profits by selling their excess slaves to those in the lower South. Some slave traders marched their slaves overland bound in coffles, others transported them aboard steam vessels leaving from Virginia and Maryland. New Orleans, the lower South's commercial hub, was a prime destination. Historians still debate how many people fell victim to the interregional trade, but one estimate suggests there were as many as 750,000. Total sales in New Orleans likely surpassed a half a million. The best description of the slave markets in the city is found in John Brown's slave narrative *Slave Life in Georgia.* The slave trading depot he describes was operated by Theophilus Freeman, best known as the trader who handled Solomon Northup's sale in 1841. Freeman's firm operated at a location off Esplanade Avenue, on the east side of the French Quarter, when Northup was sold. In this account, by the mid-1840s, Freeman had moved his depot to St. Charles Avenue, in the commercial heart of the city. Born in Georgia and later sold in New Orleans, Brown managed to escape to the North from a plantation in Mississippi and later moved to England, where he dictated his story.

"The Slave-Pen in New Orleans."

I have stated that the slave-pen to which I was taken, stood facing the St. Charles Hotel. It had formerly been an old Bank. It consisted of a block of houses forming a square, and covering perhaps an acre of ground. The center of this square had been filled quite up with rubbish and stones, as high as the back of the first floor of the houses, so as to form a solid foundation for the yard of the pen, which, it will be understood, was level with the first floor, and nicely graveled for the slaves to take exercise in. The houses themselves were built upon brick pillars of piers, the spaces between which had been converted into stores. Of these there were a great number, one of them being used as the negro auction-room.

The accommodations for the negroes consisted of three tiers of rooms, one above the other, the yard I have spoken of being common to all. There were two entrances to the pen, one for the "niggers," the other for visitors and buyers. The windows in front, which overlooked the street, were heavily barred, as were those which overlooked the yard. It was an awfully gloomy place, notwithstanding the bustle that was always going on with it. . . .

A mulatto named Bob Freeman, and who was called the Steward, had charge of the arrangements that concerned the slaves. He had a great deal of power of a particular kind, and did very nearly what he liked in the way of making them comfortable or otherwise; shutting them up if he disliked them, or they displeased him: according as they were favorites with him or not. The pen would contain about five hundred, and was usually full. The men were separated from the women, and the children from both; but the youngest and handsomest females were set apart as the concubines of the masters, who generally changed mistresses every week.

. . . I think it only right, however, to mention the above fact, that people may get a glimpse of the dreadful fate which awaits the young slave women who are sold away South, where the slave-pen is only another name for a brothel.

As may be imagined, the slaves are brought from all parts, are of all sorts, sizes, and ages, and arrive in various states of fatigue and condition; but they soon improve in their looks, as they are regularly fed, and have plenty to eat. As soon as we were roused in the morning, there was a general washing, and combing, and shaving, pulling out of grey hairs, and dyeing the hair of those who were too grey to be plucked without making them bald. When this was over—and it was no light business—we used to breakfast, getting bread, and bacon, and coffee, of which a sufficiency was given to us, that we might plump up and become sleek. Bob would then proceed to instruct us how to show ourselves off, and afterwards form us into companies, according to our size; those who were nearly of the same height and make being put into separate lots; the men, the women, and the children of both sexes, being divided off all alike. In consequence of this arrangement, the various members of a family were of necessity separated, and would often see the last of one another in that dreadful show-room. The buying commenced at about ten in the morning, and lasted till one, during which time we were obliged to be sitting about in our respective companies, ready for inspection. At one we used to go to dinner, our usual food being a repetition of the morning meal, varied with vegetables, and a little fruit sometimes. After dinner we were compelled to walk, and dance, and kick about in the yard, for exercise; and Bob, who had a fiddle, used to play up jigs for us to dance to. If we did not dance to his fiddle, we used to have to do so to his whip, so no wonder we used our legs handsomely, though the music was none of the best. When our exercises were over, we used to be "sized out" again, ready for the afternoon sale, which commenced at three, and ended at six. This over, we had tea, and were then free to do what we liked in the pen, until Bob rang us off to bed at ten. . . .

At the top of the building there was an attic called the "flogging-room." It was quite empty. Screwed into the floor were several rows of wooden cleets [*sic*], for the purpose of reaving [*sic*] cords through. The name of the room tells what used to be done here. Every day there was flogging going on. It is a rule amongst "nigger dealers," not to flog with any instrument that will cut the skin, because this would depreciate the value of the "property;" therefore the punishment is inflicted with what is called a "flopping paddle." The "flop" is of leather, about a foot-and-a-half long, and as broad as the palm of the hand; perhaps a little broader: the handle is of wood, and about two feet long. Men, women, and girls are all punished alike. They are brought in and stripped stark naked, and laid flat on the floor with their face downwards, their hands being made fast to the cleets [*sic*] by means of the cords. Sometimes their feet are bound in the same manner, but usually a negro, who is called in for the purpose, holds the victim's feet down by main force, whilst the whipper lays on, "flop, flop, flop," for half an hour, which is the usual time the flogging lasts. The punishment is dreadfully severe, for all no blood is drawn. I have frequently been forced to come in and hold the feet of women and girls, and sometimes to "flop" them, as well as men; but I was never myself punished in this manner. "Flopping" was inflicted for various offences, especially the unpardonable one of "not speaking up and looking bright and smart" when buyers were choosing.

As the importance of "looking bright" under such circumstances may not be readily understood by the ordinary run of readers, I may as well explain that the price a slave fetches depends, in great measure, upon the general appearance he or she presents to the intending buyer. A man or a woman may be well made, and physically faultless in every respect, yet their value be impaired by a sour look, or a dull, vacant stare, or a general dullness of demeanor. For this reason the poor wretches who are about to be sold, are instructed to look "spry and smart:" to hold themselves well up, and put on a smiling, cheerful countenance. They are also told to speak up for, and recommend themselves; to conceal any defect they may have, and especially not to tell their age when they are getting past the active period of life. It is quite a truism that " a nigger never knows when he was born," for though he may be quite certain of the year, and might swear to it blindfold, he must say he is just as old as his master chooses to bid him do, or he will have to take the consequences. It may be conceived that "nigger trading" is as much a calling as any other, and that there is an enormous amount of cheating and roguery in it. There are "nigger jockeys" as well as horse jockeys, and as many tricks are played off to sell a ban or an unsound "nigger," as there are to palm off a diseased horse; and the man who succeeds in "shoving off a used up nigger," as one sound in the wind and limb, takes as much pride in boasting of it, as the horse dealer does who has taken in a green-horn with a wall-eyed pony. Of course these "tricks of the trade" are known, and every means are employed to defeat attempt at dishonest sales. I dare not—for decency's sake—detail the various expedients that are resorted to by dealers to test the soundness of a male or a female slave. When I say that they are handled in the grossest manner, and inspected with the most elaborate and disgusting minuteness, I have said enough for the most understanding to fill up the outline of the horrible picture. What passes behind the screen in the auction-room, or in the room where the dealer is left alone with the "chattels" offered to him to buy, only those who have gone through the ordeal can tell. But God has recorded the wickedness that is done there, and punishment will assuredly fall upon the guilty.

I do not think any pen could describe the scene that takes place at a negro auction. The companies, regularly "sized out," are forced to stand up, as the buyers come up to them, and to straighten themselves as stiffly as they can. When spoken to, they must reply quickly, with a smile on their lips, though agony is in their heart, and the tear trembling in their eye. They must answer every question, and do as they are bid, to show themselves off; dance, jump, walk, leap, squat, tumble, and twist about, that the buyer may see they have no still joints, or other physical defect. Here may be seen husbands separated from their wives, only by the width of the room, and children from their parents, one or both, witnessing the driving of the bargain that is to tear them asunder forever, yet not a word of lamentation or anguish must escape from them; nor when the deed is consummated, dare they bid one another good-bye, or take one last embrace. Even the poor, dear, little children, who are crying and wringing their hands after "daddy and mammy," are not allowed to exchange with them a parting caress. Nature, however, will not be thus controlled, and in spite of the terrors of the paddle and the cow-hide, the most fearful scenes of anguish and confusion too often take place, converting the auction-room into a perfect Bedlam of despair. I cannot think of it without a cold shiver. I often dream of it, and as often dwell upon it in the day-time.

Question to Consider:

1. *How did Brown's depiction of the New Orleans slave market provide ammunition for the arguments abolitionists made against slavery?*

Source:

John Brown, *Slave Life in Georgia: A Narrative of the Life, Sufferings, and Escape of John Brown, A Fugitive Slave*, ed. Louis Alexis Chamerovzow (London: 1855), 94–100.

1814:
Prelude to the Battle of New Orleans

During the War of 1812, the military operations on the Gulf Coast that climaxed with the Battle of New Orleans in January 1815 began the previous summer. The original British strategy called for an invasion directed at Spanish Florida and Mobile, followed by a march westward to New Orleans. With consent of the Spanish authorities, Lieutenant Colonel Edward Nicholls of the British Marines arrived with a small force in Pensacola in August 1814. Though his primary task was the organization of American Indians and the recruitment of enslaved people to serve as allies in the upcoming campaign, he also initiated contact with privateer Jean Laffite to gauge his interest in assisting the British cause. In an attempt to rally Louisianians and Americans in the Mississippi Valley to support his side, he also issued the proclamation excerpted below. The following month, Nicholls was wounded while leading his men in an unsuccessful attack on Fort Bowyer, which guarded the entrance to Mobile Bay. After his forces repulsed the attack, Major General Andrew Jackson sent his own proclamation to unite the citizens of Louisiana. Realizing the need for additional manpower for his army, Jackson also issued a proclamation to the free people of color in the New Orleans to attract volunteers for its defense. During the Spanish colonial era, a militia composed of free people of color played a prominent role in the life of the city. However, in the territorial era, Governor Claiborne began to downsize its numbers, only to call it back into service once the war began. In November, Jackson led American forces into Spanish Florida and forced the British out of Pensacola. With their initial plan now a failure, the British decided to launch their attack directly on New Orleans. On December 1, Jackson and his troops arrived in New Orleans, and chain of events that led to the historic battle in Chalmette began.

Proclamation by Lieutenant Colonel Edward Nicholls Pensacola, August 29, 1814

Natives of Louisiana! On you the first call is made to assist in liberating from a faithless, imbecile government, your paternal soil: Spaniards, Frenchmen, Italians, and British, whether settled or residing for a time, in Louisiana, on you, also, I call to aid me in this just cause: the American usurpation in this country must be abolished, and the lawful owners of the soil put in possession. I am at the head of a large body of Indians, well-armed, disciplined, and commanded by British officers—a good train of artillery with every requisite, seconded by the powerful aid of numerous British and Spanish squadron of ships and vessels of war. Be not alarmed, inhabitants of the country, at our approach; the same good faith and disinterestedness which has distinguished the conduct of Britons in Europe, accompanies them here; you will have no fear of litigious taxes imposed on you for the purpose of carrying on an unnatural and unjust war; your property, your laws, the peace and tranquility of your country, will be guaranteed to you by men who will suffer no infringement of theirs; rest assured that these brave red men only burn with an ardent desire of satisfaction, for the wrongs they have suffered from the Americans, to join you in liberating these southern provinces from their yoke, and drive them into those limits formerly prescribed by my sovereign. The Indians have pledged themselves, in the most solemn manner, not to injure, in the slightest degree, the persons or properties of any but enemies; to their Spanish or English fathers, a flag over any door, whether Spanish, French, or British, will be a certain protection, nor dare any Indian put his foot on the threshold thereof, under penalty of death from his own countrymen; not even an enemy will an Indian put to death, except resisting in arms, and as for injuring helpless women and children, the red men, by their good conduct and treatment to them, will (if it be possible) make the Americans blush for their more inhuman conduct lately on the Escambia, and within a neutral territory.

Inhabitants of Kentucky, you have too long borne with grievous impositions—the whole brunt of the war has fallen on your brave sons; be imposed on no longer, but either range yourselves under the standard of your forefathers, or observe a strict neutrality; if you comply with either of these offers, whatever provisions you send down, will be paid for in dollars, and the safety of the persons bringing it, as well as the free navigation of the Mississippi, guaranteed to you.

Men of Kentucky, let me call to your view (and I trust to your abhorrence) the conduct of those factions, which hurried you into this civil, unjust and unnatural war, at a time when Great Britain was straining every nerve in defense of her own and the liberties of the world—when the bravest of her sons were fighting and bleeding in so sacred a cause—when she was spending millions of her treasure in endeavoring to pull down one of the most formidable and dangerous tyrants that ever disgraced the form of men—when groaning Europe was almost in her last gasp—when Britons alone showed an undaunted front—basely did those assassins endeavor to stab her from the rear; she has turned on them, renovated from the bloody but successful struggle—Europe is happy and free, and she now hastens justly to avenge the unprovoked insult. Show them that you are not collectively unjust; leave that contemptible to shift for themselves; let those slaves of the tyrant send an embassy to Elba, and implore his aid; but let every honest, upright American, spurn them with united contempt. After the experience of twenty-one years, can you any longer support those brawlers for liberty, who call it freedom, when themselves are free; be no longer their dupes—accept of my offers—everything I have promised in this paper I guarantee to you, on the sacred honor of a British officer.

Proclamation by Major General Andrew Jackson Mobile, September 21, 1814

LOUISIANIANS!

The base, the perfidious Britons have attempted to invade your country—they had the temerity to attack Fort Bowyer with their incongruous horde of Indians and negro assassins—they seemed to have forgotten that this fort was defended by freemen—they were not long indulged in their error—the gallant [American major William] Lawrence, with his little spartan band, has given them a lecture that will last for ages; he has taught them what men can do when fighting for their liberty, when contending against slaves. He has convinced Sir W. H. Percy [the British naval commander] that his companions in arms are not to be conquered by proclamations; that the strongest British bark is not invulnerable to the force of American artillery, directed by the steady nervous arm of a freeman.

Louisianians!—The proud Briton, the natural and sworn enemies of all Frenchmen, has called upon you, by proclamation, to aid him in his tyranny, and to prostrate the holy temple of our liberty. Can Louisianians, can Frenchmen, can Americans, ever stoop to be the slaves or allies of Britain.

The proud, vain-glorious boaster colonel Nicholls, when he addressed you, Louisianians and Kentuckians, had forgotten that you were the votaries of freedom, or he would never have pledged the honor of a British officer for the faithful performance of his promise, to lure you from your fidelity to the government of your choice. I ask you, Louisianans, can we place any confidence in the honor of men who have courted an alliance with pirates and robbers? Have not these noble Britons, these honorable men, colonel Nicholls and the honorable captain W. H. Percy, the true representatives of their royal master, done this? Have they not made offers to the pirates of Barataria to join them, and their holy cause? And have they not dared to insult you by calling on you to associate, as brethren with them, and this hellish banditti.

Louisianians!—The government of your choice are engaged in a just and honorable contest for the security of your individual and her national rights—on you, a part of America, the only country on earth where every man enjoys freedom, where its blessings are alike extended to the poor and the rich, calls to protect these rights from the invading usurpation of Britain; and she calls not in vain. I well know that every man whose soul beats high at the proud title of freeman; that every Louisianan, either by birth or adoption, will promptly obey the voice of his country; will rally round the eagle of Columbia, secure it from the pending danger, or nobly die in the last ditch in its defense.

The individual who refuses to defend his rights, when called upon by his government, deserves to be a slave, and must be punished as an enemy to his country, and a friend to her foe. The undersigned has been entrusted with the defense of your country—on you he relies to aid him in this important duty; in this reliance he hopes not to be mistaken. He trusts in the justice of his cause and the patriotism of his countrymen—confident that any future attempt to invade our soil will be repelled as the last, he calls not upon either pirates or robbers to join him in the glorious cause. Your governor has been fully authorized by me to organize any volunteer company, battalion, or regiment which may proffer its services under this call, and is informed of their probable destination.

Proclamation by Major General Andrew Jackson Mobile, September 21, 1814

To the free colored inhabitants of Louisiana.

Through a mistaken policy you have heretofore been deprived of a participation in the glorious struggle for national rights in which our country is engaged. This no longer shall exist.

As sons of freedom, you are now called upon to defend our most inestimable blessing. As Americans, your country looks with confidence to her adopted children, for a valorous support, as a faithful return for the advantages enjoyed under her mild and equitable government. As fathers, husbands, and brothers, you are summoned to rally round the standard of the eagle, to defend all which is dear in existence.

Your country, although calling for your exertions, does not wish you to engage in her cause, without amply remunerating you for the services rendered. Your intelligent minds are not to be led away by false representations.—Your love of honor would cause you to despise the man who should attempt to deceive you. In the sincerity of a soldier, and the language of truth I address you.

To every noble-hearted, generous freeman of color, volunteering to serve during the present contest with Great Britain, and no longer, there will be paid the same bounty in money and lands, now received by the white soldiers of the United States, viz. one hundred and twenty-four dollars in money, and one hundred and sixty acres of land. The non-commissioned officers and privates will also be entitled to the same monthly pay and daily rations, and clothes furnished to any American soldier.

On enrolling yourselves in companies, the major-general commanding will select officers for your government, from your white fellow citizens. Your non-commissioned officers will be appointed from among yourselves.

Due regard will be paid to the feelings of freemen and soldiers. You will not, by being associated with white men in the same corps, be exposed to improper comparisons or unjust sarcasm. As a distinct, independent battalion or regiment, pursuing the path of glory, you will, undivided, receive the applause and gratitude of your countrymen.

To assure you of the sincerity of my intentions and my anxiety to engage your invaluable services to our country, I have communicated my wishes to the governor of Louisiana, who is fully informed as to the manner of enrollment, and will give you every necessary information on the subject of this address.

Questions to Consider:

1. *How could one describe Nicholls's proclamation as politically inept?*
2. *What language does Jackson use to rally the citizens of New Orleans to its defense?*
3. *Do you think that Jackson's promises to the free persons of color are sincere?*

Source:

Arsène Lacarrière Latour, *Historical Memoir of the War in West Florida and Louisiana in 1814–15, with an Atlas*, ed. Jane Lucas de Grummond (Gainesville, FL: University Press of Florida, 1964), vii–viii, xxix–xxxii. Reprinted with permission of the University Press of Florida.

1835–1841:

Antebellum Politics and the Second Party System

In the wake of John Quincy Adams's controversial victory over Andrew Jackson in the election of 1824, the Republican Party of Thomas Jefferson divided into two new national political organizations. The National Republicans, later known as the Whigs, inherited the Federalist idea of a stronger federal government that was active in promoting the nation's economic growth. The Democratic Republicans, later shortened to the Democrats, believed that too much federal power was a threat to individual liberty and preferred that more power should reside in the states. The new party system created political battles that had a profound effect on Louisiana politics. Henry Clay's American System called for tariffs to protect nascent American manufacturing from foreign competitors, but included in his program were tariffs for domestically produced sugar. Louisiana sugar planters needed tariff assistance to ward off competition from Caribbean producers, and as a result they were in the Whig camp. For Democrats uneasy with economic change caused by the emerging market economy, the nation's banking system was a concern, and the defeat of the re-charter of the monopolistic Bank of the United States in the 1830s was a crusade. The commercial hub that was antebellum New Orleans was also a center of American finance, and its commercial interests often were aligned with the Whigs. The devastating depression brought on by the Panic of 1837 was in part a product of unregulated and profligate policies of banks, and they became a prime target of the state's Democrats.

Senator Josiah Stoddard Johnston on the Sugar Tariff

When Louisiana was acquired by the United States, there was a duty on brown sugar of two and a half cents a pound, levied for revenue. The people of that State, who had already made some experiments in the culture of the cane, saw that the duty afforded them some protection from foreign competition, and secured the benefit of the home market, which was then of considerable extent, and rapidly increasing. This induced them within the region then considered adapted to the cane, to turn their attention to the production of sugar. They embarked their whole fortunes, and for a long time struggled, under very discouraging circumstances, against the effects of the climate, the vicissitudes of seasons, the deficiency of capital, the want of skill, and all the difficulties incident to the commencement of such an enterprise. It was for many years a doubtful experiment and hazardous undertaking, but they persevered . . .

The increase of capital, the introduction of machinery, the diversion of labor from other less profitable pursuits, the acquisition of skill, and, above all, the confidence of the people in the protection of the Government, have vastly augmented the means of production. It now promises an ample supply for the consumption of the country, and a steady but moderate profit. . . .

Under the faith of the laws, they have embarked their capital in the production of one of the great necessaries of life, and in support of a national system, which they [sugar planters] understood it was the object of the Government to establish. They have opened a new and extensive field of agricultural industry; directed labor to more profitable employment; maintained the value of slaves; and increased the internal commerce of the country. They have contributed their full share to all the duties paid on other articles. . . .

The value of lands and slaves, which constitute a sugar establishment, is predicated upon the value of sugar; and that depends on the rate of duty established by the laws. A reduction of duty which will change the price of sugar, will at the same time reduce the value of the labor employed in making it; and by that means the value of land and slaves, and the standard of value of everything depending on it. A reduction of duty would produce a corresponding reduction, not only on all capital invested in Louisiana in sugar estates, but upon the value of slaves everywhere in the Southern States.

The cultivation of sugar, which has diverted the labor of so large a number of slaves, has sustained their value at the present high rates; and the demand which this article creates for this labor, will continue to maintain the price, while the article maintains its price. Whatever cause, whether over-production or reductions of duties, diminishes the value of sugar, will equally affect the value of slaves everywhere in this country. . . .

The present price of slaves is fixed by sugar at 5 ½ cents per pound; of this the expenses are equal to 3 ½ cents per pound, leaving 2 cents profit; and this 2 cents constitutes the standard value of the slaves. Whatever, therefore, diminishes this sum, diminishes the value of slaves by the same rule. Thus a reduction of 1 cent profit would diminish the profit one-half; and, therefore, the rate of interest on the investment one-half; and, therefore, the value of slaves one-half. A reduction, therefore, of 1 cent a pound on sugar would take away 1 cent from the profit, and that is equal to half of the profit, which would reduce the value of the slaves one-half: but if the profit produced was less than the general average of profit, there would be no motive to invest capital in it; and they would cease to buy at any price; and the whole of the slave labor would be directed into other channels. There are as many slaves now engaged in cotton and tobacco as supply the general market of the world. The natural increase of those employed in these objects will supply the increase of consumption. There will be no demand, therefore, for more labor for these purposes. These articles are now very low, and leave only a small profit, and would not afford half the present price of slaves, if, indeed, there could be any demand for them. And if the surplus slaves, with their increase, were thrown upon these two staple articles, which now constitute the chief dependence of the South, and the principal export of the United States, the quantity would be greatly increased, and the price greatly reduced below its present reduced price, and the whole value of the slave property would be sunk. It is, therefore, easy for each of the Southern States to calculate the value of the property they have at stake.

Inaugural Address of Governor Alexandre Mouton January 30, 1843

I learn with deep mortification and regret from the Treasurer's reports and otherwise, that there is now due by the State to our banks, in round numbers, one million two hundred thousand dollars, that there is due for salaries, interest and other ordinary expenses, about two hundred thousand dollars; that there are State bonds, for the payment of which the State has no guarantee, to the amount of one million two hundred and seventy-three thousand dollars, on which the interest is unpaid; that there are State bonds to a large amount, for which the State has the guarantee of the stockholders of the Citizens' Bank and Consolidated Association of Planters [bank], now in liquidation, on which the interest will probably not be paid; that the ordinary expenses of the Government exceed, and has for several years exceeded its ordinary income by more than two hundred thousand dollars; that there is nothing in our exhausted Treasury that the State can no longer borrow a dollar from her own banks, and that the people are taxed as heavily as they can bear. This is indeed a deplorable situation of our affairs. Having within our limits the greatest commercial metropolis in the Union, a luxuriant climate and the richest and most inexhaustible soil in the world, we are forced to ask what has produced this disastrous result . . .

In justice to ourselves, I think this course ought to be adopted. We should not be held responsible for the acts of those who have preceded us, to which I allude in no spirit of unkindness. When the condition of the State is ascertained, we will strive to administer its affairs so as to retrieve prosperity. To arrest the falling fortunes of our State, to contribute in any manner to the restoration of that prosperity for which the God of Nature has destined her, to enable her to maintain her position in our glorious Union, are objects worthy of the ambition of all her sons.

I am opposed to the creation of any corporation or monopoly which may give exclusive or undue advantages to a portion of the community over the mass of the people, holding such legislation unjust and oppressive; as taking rights and privileges from the many to be conferred upon the few who are thus favored.

Among the many causes which now afflict our State, and a large portion of our citizens, it must be admitted, none has more directly or powerfully contributed to the evil, than the unrestrained creation of Banks with charters not guarded by prudent legislation. Under the pretense that borrowed capital was wanted, and a circulation for commercial and agricultural purposes for which the Gold and Silver of the world was inadequate, sixteen Banks were incorporated with a nominal capital of fifty-five millions of dollars. Many of them commenced operations without any real capital, or at best with money borrowed upon onerous conditions. With but few exceptions they have been shamefully administered. Palaces were erected at enormous cost as Banking houses; the most extravagant expenses were incurred in salaries and prerequisites to Presidents, Cashiers, Clerks, Lawyers and other officers and persons employed by them, amounting in the aggregate to more than the sum necessary for the economical support of the whole administration of the State Government, and operating as a ruinous burden upon the Institutions themselves, and an oppressive indirect tax upon the whole people; and yet these extravagancies form but a small item when compared with the vast sums squandered upon their favorites and parasites, which have been lost to the Institutions, and which, so far from benefitting the community, led to unbounded individual extravagance, and stimulated wild speculations of the most reckless and ruinous character. The abuses and frauds already detected and exposed, have convinced all of the pernicious effects of those institutions, thus organized, upon the morals of the community, and their powerful influence in destroying a sound monetary system. The slavish opinion that a Northern Institution should furnish a currency for New Orleans and the South West, is rejected as the most artful means ever devised of imperceptibly abstracting our wealth and resources, without any return but paper. Even in the North, a National Bank is regarded as an obsolete idea.

And yet the time has barely passed when it was held most sacrilegious to arraign the conduct of these institutions, whose abuses have brought destruction on themselves and distress upon the people. It is not surprising that a system so cunningly devised, and so universally operative as the paper money system, should be defended to the last by those who are interested in the continuance of its abuses. But it must now share the fate of other ephemeral fallacies which have, from time to time, caused much mischief in human affairs, but which the great and conservative instinct of the people eventually exploded. The Banking system, as heretofore organized, has been tried and it has fallen by its own inherent corruption.

There are but few, and the number of them is daily diminishing, who would wish to see it revived. Had it been controlled in its organization or progress, it might have been more harmless. The evils under which we labor are to be attributed to the ascendency, the supremacy, this interest attained in our

State. Had Banks been held to the responsibilities of individuals; had they at all times been kept in a sphere subordinate to the government itself; had the supremacy of the laws been asserted and maintained, things would not have come to the present stage of discredit and disaster. What citizen who feels for the honor of his State, would wish to see the late state of things renewed? Our policy, our duty, then is obvious. We must prevent, by all possible means, all tendency in our legislation to a renewal of the banking system, as heretofore organized.

Questions to Consider:

1. *How does Senator Johnston relate the market for Louisiana sugar with the market for the South's slaves?*

2. *Could Governor Mouton's criticism of the state's banks be described as demagogic?*

Sources:

1. Josiah Stoddard Johnston, "Letter of Mr. Johnston, of Louisiana, to the Secretary of the Treasury, in reply to his circular of the 1st of July, 1830, relative to the culture of the sugar cane" (Washington, DC: Gales and Seaton, 1831), 3–5.

2. Sidney J. Romero, ed., *"My Fellow Citizens. . .": The Inaugural Addresses of Louisiana's Governors* (Lafayette, LA: Center for Louisiana Studies, University of Southwestern Louisiana, 1980), 84–86.

1841–1845:
Expansion of Suffrage and the Constitution of 1845

A central theme of nineteenth-century American political history was the expansion of suffrage for adult white men. Of the twenty-six states in 1840, only seven still had property requirements for voting, one of these states being Louisiana. Sentiment for a more democratic electorate grew in the state during the 1830s, championed by the state's Democrats; and Whig resistance began to wane by the early 1840s. A constitutional convention had to be called because the state's 1812 constitution had no provision for simple amendments. The provisions included in the 1845 constitution were far-reaching. Its most notable feature was the elimination of property qualifications for voting. Other provisions included the creation of the office of lieutenant governor and a system of public education. To satisfy citizens who wanted the state capital moved from New Orleans, a provision called for a new capital to be located at least sixty miles outside the city, which the legislature later decided to be Baton Rouge. After much wrangling, the delegates agreed to base representation in the state senate on the entire population of a parish, including enslaved people, which was a substantial benefit to the state's large planters. Also, reflecting the economic crisis of the late 1830s and the Democratic control of the convention, the constitution barred monopolies, state subsidies for business interests, and the incorporation of banks and other corporations. This last feature ultimately led to a new convention seven years later.

Remarks on the Propriety of Calling a Convention to Amend the Constitution

The tendencies of the age are decidedly revolutionary. Change is the order of the day among nations. There is a strong and increasing desire throughout the world to simplify the action and restrain the power of government, to secure effectually the political rights of the mass, and to introduce direct responsibility to the people, on the part of all who are entrusted with power. This movement, we have learned from past experience, it is the height of folly to resist. It will have its way, and work its purpose. Its action is felt by the whole human race; and it is impossible for any people to remain stationary under its influence; particularly for any state in this republic, where the ultimate sovereignty of the people is an article of faith so universally acknowledged . . .

There are many well-meaning persons who are seriously in favor of the property qualification, and there are more who advocate it of whom the most unbounded charity will not permit us to entertain so favorable an opinion. It is to the former only that reason can be successfully addressed, and it is those only whom we wish to convince. For their sakes then let us examine whether there be any, and what are the arguments in favor of the property qualification. Does the possession of wealth make a man more intelligent, more moral, more patriotic? Is the man whom misfortune has reduced to poverty less qualified to discharge faithfully the duties of a good citizen than when he was the owner of thousands, or will the fool or the knave be made wise and honest because a lucky accident or successful fraud has given him the command of riches? Is there in reality any favorable change in a man's feelings towards his country and her institutions brought about by a change in his pecuniary circumstances? . . .

If, then, property produces no favorable alteration in the intellect and feelings of its fortunate holders, on what do they base their claims for the exclusive control of the destinies of the government? It is sometimes, indeed, urged that such a limitation of the right of suffrage is necessary for the security of property, and this assertion which cannot be sustained by any facts or reasoning, has not been without its influence upon many, and the more so as it has been always accompanied by mysterious givings out about agrarianism, and numberless florid allusions to the French revolution. . . . Is there one fact in all past history, or in the present condition of the world which would lead a reasonable man to suppose that the rights of property will be less respected by a government founded on a purely popular suffrage, than by one in which suffrage is restricted? Was property more secure in Europe under the operation of the feudal system, in which all power was vested in the lords of the soil, than it is at this day in the comparatively liberal government of Louisiana; or is a man more safe in the enjoyment of his possessions under the freehold representation of England than under the system of universal suffrage in New York? Away, then, with the pretense that property would be more insecure by extending the right of suffrage to those who have little or none. They could not, if they would, affect its tenure unless the majority were desirous of so doing, and if ever such a majority should exist, it would matter but little whether they had the right of suffrage or not, for we may rest assured that they would not wait to attain their ends by the tardy forms of legislation. But the insinuation that any such result is or would be desired is a base libel on humanity propagated by those only who hate and distrust the people. Never were the rights of property endangered by the laboring portion of mankind. It is only from the would-be great and needy rich that anything is to be feared. The man who toils, respects and supports the law which protects him in the enjoyment of the products of his own labor; but he who lives by his wits, the tax-paying speculator, and respectable bankrupt will always be found to favor a system of legislation which will exonerate him from restoring the property of others. . . .

The history of the past, and observation of the present alike teach the great political truth,—that just in proportion as rights are enjoyed by the mass is the government strong, the nation prosperous, and the people happy . . . Indeed so evident is the fact that the most acute casuists have been unable to determine whether what they call the progress of civilization has been the cause or the effect of the advance to democratic principles of government. And it is but reasonable that democracy and civilization should go hand in hand; for what is the highest state of civilization, but that in which man's powers and virtues are in their highest state of development? And does anything tend to raise the individual to this condition as much as to give him rights to enjoy and duties to perform? Deprive a man of his civil and political rights and you degrade a being of godlike capacities to a brute and a slave—but grant him those, and he will soon assert the dignity of his nature and show himself worthy of their enjoyment. . . .

A popular government is the strongest of all governments. . . . Nowhere are strong governments needed so much as in the southern portions of this Union—not strong, indeed, in the extent of the powers that they wield, but in their ability duly to fulfill the duties which have been entrusted to them, the protection of the person and property of the people. They want that strength which arises from the union, physical force, and cordial support of the millions. The materials of combustion exist—the torch of the incendiary is lighted—and we know not at what instant the train may be fired. If the systematic efforts which are being made in some portions of this country and in England, to excite our servile population, and suddenly abolish our southern system of involuntary labor, should only be partially successful, the day may not be distant when the services of every man in the state will be required. It is a contingency to which all prudent men should look forward, and if the time ever come, how can the privileged voters of Louisiana consistently confide the defense of the state in its extremity to men on whom they looked in days of quietness as unworthy of political existence; and how can we reasonably expect good service from that large portion of our people whom the present constitution places on a par with the free blacks? That in the hour of danger whether from domestic or foreign foes they would not be found wanting is certain—they would, cheerfully, as they always have done, endure the toils of the campaign and be found in the front of the battle. But is it policy—is it wisdom to pursue a course the natural tendency of which is to estrange their affections from the government and destroy all sympathy with the more favored classes; for we must remember that the disfranchised, though they have no potential voice in the government, are men with the same intelligence, the same feelings, and the same keen sense of degradation, as the most exalted among the privileged, and that it is not in their nature tamely to submit to a wrong, much less to support a system which subjects them to that wrong forever. The necessity of our position compels us to have two classes in the community, the white and the black; common sense dictates that every means should be used to unite the former by common interests and common feelings, in the support of the government, and yet the very contrary seems to have been the settled policy of the state. But this is a point which it is delicate to discuss; and enough, it is hoped, has already been said, to secure for it the attention which it deserves. . . .

Then let us discard the property qualification as unreasonable, illiberal, and inconsistent with the great principles of modern politics; as a relic of ancient barbarism, and an insult to the intellect and moral feelings of mankind.

Letter to the *Baton-Rouge Gazette* July 2, 1842

LOUISIANIANS!—On the 4th of July inst. you will be called on to pronounce the decree of your future destiny, in voting for or against a convention for the purpose of amending your Constitution.

Never has a more weighty and important question merited such serious reflection. Mistrust those zealous apostles of a convention, who mask their ambitious views under the show of republicanism. Listen not to their fallacious protestations. Do not believe that it is for the welfare and prosperity of the country that they desire to make amendments to your Constitution. If, unfortunately, by the vote you are about to give, you permit them, with a sacrilegious hand, to profane the palladium of your rights, your fortunes, and your peace; you will henceforward be at the mercy of a parcel of intriguers, who will flock from all nations to give laws to you, and afterwards divide your spoils.

Have they not already unmasked themselves, these self-dubbed defenders of the rights of the people? Have they not openly declared that, if they succeeded, they would wholly overthrow the constitutional edifice, and substitute another more in harmony with the wicked designs that actuate them?

Give them this power, and you will soon see amongst their first Machiavelical [*sic*] deeds, universal suffrage, that deceitful lure, thrown to the avidity of the multitude, the better to seduce them, and which would give to the greatest vagabond the right of voting at your elections, and to be himself elected the representative of a country in which he would have no interest, but that of profiting by the disorders that such scum as himself would not fail to create under the aegis of their monstrous constitution.

Then would you see the nomination of judiciary officers, and others left exclusively to the people. Thence would flow the denial of justice, the non-performance of the laws, crimes, and misdemeanors, committee with impunity, which if not encouraged would at least be tolerated by officers who would endeavor more to preserve their popularity than to fulfil the duties of their stations.

The State of Mississippi has made the sad experiment; let us be more prudent, and learn to profit by her unfortunate condition.

Is it not easily to be seen that this universal suffrage, vaunted so highly, those pretended rights of the sovereign people, claimed with so much warmth, are but vain pretexts used to attain other results?

Is it then so difficult to obtain the right of suffrage in Louisiana? No! any industrious honest man can easily acquire it by his labor and perseverance, and thus become a useful member of our great family. To extend, without distinction, this sacred right to a horde of vagabonds, that Europe and other parts of our confederation, vomit forth upon our shores, is to desire the destruction of the wise institutions that have shielded us unto this day. It is to annihilate all spirit of nationality amongst the children of the soil. It is, in short, to make us strangers in our own country.

Away! vile anarchists! furious democrats! away! your wicked projects are discovered, the mine is countermined.

Louisianians of every origin, and you who are become so by choice—rally yourselves! your enemy is before you. The 4th July will be the day of battle. Let it be for us the day of triumph. Let your vote be unanimous. Let it be NO CONVENTION.

UN CREOLE

Questions to Consider:

1. *Though the anonymous author of the pamphlet makes an idealistic argument for an expansion of suffrage, how does the issue of slavery factor into his thinking?*

2. *As alluded to by the author of the first selection, how does the Creole who wrote the second selection invoke the specter of revolution to argue against suffrage expansion?*

Sources:

1. Anonymous, *Remarks on the Propriety of Calling a Convention to amend the Constitution of the State of Louisiana* (New Orleans: D. W. Noble, 1841), 4, 18–22.

2. *Baton-Rouge Gazette*, July 2, 1842, English Edition. From Louisiana State University Libraries Special Collections.

1840–1860:
Antebellum Women in Politics and Reform

Though denied the right to vote during the antebellum era, women not only displayed an interest in politics but also sometimes participated in an auxiliary role. The Whig Party in particular believed that government had a role in ensuring the nation's moral well-being, so the visible support of women—viewed as the "guardians of the hearth" in antebellum society—served that goal. In addition, the party thought that the attendance of women at conventions and rallies could temper the intense passions that inflamed the masculine world of politics. At the 1844 state convention, the Whig Ladies of East and West Baton Rouge presented to the Iberville Parish delegation a banner, which the New Orleans *Bee* described as follows: "It is of white satin, supported by a gilded bow and arrow, with a bust of CLAY in the center surrounded by thirteen gold stars. Surmounting it is a wreath of gold. Motto—'We love our country and will support her Clay.' Reverse—Portrait of the Genius of Liberty, holding in her hand the national shield with 'Liberty' inscribed upon a gold wreath. Motto—'Ladies of East and West Baton Rouge, we have won your offering.'" Although the urban North was the center of moral and social reform movements in antebellum America, these efforts had a southern component that has often been overlooked. Temperance societies had chapters in Louisiana, and women in New Orleans sought to spread Protestant Christianity in their ethnically diverse city by distributing Bibles, as described in the second excerpt.

Mary Gayle, Presentation of the Prize Banner, Whig State Convention, Baton Rouge, 1844

In the name and on behalf of the Whig Ladies of East and West Baton Rouge, I have the honor to present you this beautiful *Prize Banner*, made after their own minds and emblazoned with the mottoes of their own hearts.

It was offered as a pledge of the devotion of the fair donors to the great Whig cause in which you are so nobly struggling, and being proudly won by the Whigs of your Parish, is now given as a reward of their gallantly and patriotic spirit manifested on this occasion.

They believe the principles and policy of the Whig party to be the true principles and policy of the Federal Constitution: the faithful observance of which has never failed to bless—the neglect or contempt of which has never failed to blight and blast the best interests of our country.

And they also believe that their own welfare, as well as that of their beloved country, social, civil and religious, depends essentially on the speedy triumph and ultimate prevalence of those well tried principles and doctrines.

Disfranchised by the organic law, their moral power is the only political armor of the American fair: And the Whig Ladies of East and West Baton Rouge therefore feel that so long as Christian woman's smile shall cheer the heart of her country's friends, or her frown shall chill the heart of her country's foe, it is as much her duty as it is her privilege to exert all her influence on that country's side.

Animated by a lofty spirit of devotion to the happiness and well-being of their beloved country, and believing the great Whig party throughout the Union—at this moment engaged in a sacred revolutionary struggle, as eventful as the Revolution of 1776—they feel assured by their heads as well as their hearts that in this momentous contest they may, without overstepping the becoming modesty of their sex, thus publicly make this civic offering to testify their confidence in your fidelity, and to cheer you on as honest champions in the cause of civil and religious liberty and light.

Such, sir, is their purpose, and such their offering.—And, in presenting it, I am charged to express their hope that none of you will ever prove unworthy of the confidence this day manifested—that not one of you will ever by recreance or apathy dishonor woman's flag; and that should any one of you ever doubt or falter in the path of patriotic duty, he will look on the VOTIVE BANNER, and remember the hands that made, and the hearts that gave it!

Thus, and thus only, you may continue to deserve their approving smiles, and all enjoy their united blessings!

Then take it!— The gift of beauty to manly patriotism! You have gallantry won it, and may you long and proudly wear it! Bear it with you to your homes, and as the contest brightens, amid the heat and strife of battle, *remember* that the Ladies of East and West Baton Rouge expect the Whigs of your Parish to come out of the contest with your Honor waving in triumph, and with the sunlight of victory glittering upon every fold!

Report of the Ladies Bible Society, of the First and Third Municipalities—now the Second and Third Districts

At a meeting of the Committee, the field of our operations was, as far as practicable, marked off into districts, of which one was assigned to each member of the Committee, who was expected to call upon the various families resident therein for contributions to the funds of this Society. Some of those elected as managers at the last annual meeting have declined to act in that capacity, and the districts assigned to them have thus remained unvisited. Other members of the Committee have, owing to various causes, but partially explored their portions of the field; and in those districts, which have been most faithfully visited, but few have been found disposed to contribute pecuniary aid to the furtherance of the objects of our Society. Only $82.95 have been received into the Treasury since the last annual meeting.

But whilst, in the review of their own efforts, the Committee can only regret that no more efficient service has been rendered, and that no more important results have been produced, they discover a brighter side to the picture as they listen to the reports of those who have been engaged in the distribution of those invaluable treasures, which the funds of our Association have provided.

One colporteur[1] informs us that he has supplied more than sixty families, in our midst, with Bibles during the past year. At one time he gave a Bible to a Spaniard, who was ignorant of its contents, and who, actuated by curiosity,

1. An agent who distributes religious tracts

desired to examine the revealed will of God. The perusal of the Scriptures awakened a desire to receive religious books, which was gratified. He was thus led to renounce the errors of Romanism, and to yield his belief to the doctrines of a pure Christianity, and we trust, that having given an intellectual assent to the truth, he may be led to possess that faith, without which "it is impossible to please God."

A German woman expressed a wish to receive a copy of the Bible in her own language. Her daughter, having obtained one of the English version at the Sabbath School, had related to her mother some of the interesting narratives contained in the Holy Book, and the parent desired to read, in her own tongue, the wonderful words which the child could but imperfectly translate to her.

Two German colporteurs have been employed in the work of distributing Bibles, within our limits, for some time past. One of them is conversant with the various languages of Northern Europe, and can thus accompany his proffer of the Book of Life, with words of counsel, and expressions of sympathy, which may reach the understanding and heart of the stranger from a distant land.

Through the efforts of these laborers three hundred and forty families have been supplied with the Word of God. More than forty persons in one neighborhood have, through their instrumentality, been led earnestly to search the Scriptures, and now assemble together for the purpose of learning the will, and imploring the guidance of Him of whom these Scriptures "testify."

The agent of the S. W. Bible Society says that the good work among the German Catholics, in the Second District, "still continues and spreads silently. Many seem willing to receive the truth; some attend prayer meetings; and we hope God by his Spirit is working a saving change in their hearts." He adds: "Some foreigners, from Roman Catholic countries, have received Bibles with great joy." . . .

While the Committee feel that their feeble efforts have not been without some encouraging results, they cannot but express the hope that the history of the coming year may give evidence of greater zeal and more efficient action in the part of those who may be called to engage in this work.

The peculiar character of the field we occupy, furnishes a strong motive for activity and perseverance in the prosecution of the objects of this Society.

We have among our population the representatives of all European countries. Led by various motives, there have come among us the hardy sons of the rough climes of the North, and those whose early years have been spent beneath the kinder skies of France and Italy, or among the "vine-clad hills" of Spain. Though born amidst such different scenes, and educated under such various influences, they are all fellow travelers to the grave and to eternity; all have sinned, and for all has one atoning sacrifice been made. But most of these have never listened to the story of Redemption, or if they have heard of Bethlehem and Calvary, the reality has been so blended with fable, that their minds have failed to discern the truth. Shall we not, then, be more diligent in our endeavors to furnish them with that volume, which will tell them of "the Lamb of God, which taketh away the sin of the world?"

And may He, who can control all hearts, dispose many more of those who reside in these districts to contribute personal effort, and pecuniary aid, to this work.

Questions to Consider:

1. *How did the Whigs ladies understand their role in antebellum politics?*

2. *How the Bible Society view the recipients of their Bibles? Did they consider their efforts successful?*

Sources:

1. *New Orleans Bee*, October 9, 1844. Louisiana State University Libraries Special Collections.

2. *New Orleans Christian Advocate*, February 12, 1853. Archives of the Louisiana Conference of the United Methodist Church, Centenary College of Louisiana Archives and Special Collections.

1841–1842:
The Brig *Creole* Revolt

In the antebellum interregional slave trade, one route used by traders to bring slaves from the upper to the lower South followed coastal shipping lanes from Virginia to New Orleans. The persistent danger, though, in shipping large numbers of enslaved people on coastal vessels was revolt. In 1841, on the brig *Creole*, such an insurrection did get off the ground, and it is arguably the most successful slave revolt in American history. The *Creole* had 135 enslaved people on board when a group of nineteen initiated the revolt on November 7. The rebels swiftly took control of the vessel, killing one slave trader and wounding the ship's captain. The rebels then forced the ship to sail for the British Bahamas. As slavery was by then abolished in the British Empire, enslaved persons aboard American slave ships that had run aground in British territories had previously secured their freedom, a fact known to one of the rebels on the *Creole*. Once in Nassau, British officials detained the nineteen who instigated the revolt while telling the others that they were now free. All but five decided to remain in the Bahamas. After an investigation, in April 1842, British officials released the rebels that were held in custody. The *Creole* incident became a sticking point in relations between Great Britain and the United States for the remainder of the decade. A claims commission set up by the two nations in the 1850s later determined compensation paid by the British government to the owners of the *Creole* slaves.

The meaning and significance of the *Creole* mutiny became the subject of debate soon after it occurred. Once the brig arrived in New Orleans from Nassau, with only five slaves out of the original group, a member of the ship's crew recounted before a notary a version of the revolt favorable to his employers in a "sea protest," a legal statement given to protect the owners of a ship from liability in case of cargo loss or damage. Abolitionists, on the other hand, celebrated the rebels as heroes in the fight against slavery. Later, as the alleged owners of the lost slave property pressed their claims against insurance companies in the courts of New Orleans, lawyers representing the insurance firms offered their own construction of the motivations of the rebels.

Protest of the Brig *Creole*, Given by Acting Master Zephaniah C. Gifford, Before Notary William Y. Lewis New Orleans, December 2, 1841

Sunday, the seventh day of November, eighteen hundred forty [one], at about nine o'clock, P. M. . . . there being a fresh breeze, and the sky a little hazy. . . . Mr. Gifford was then on watch, and was told by Elijah Morris, one of the slaves of Thomas McCargo, that one of the men had gone down aft among the women; that Mr. Gifford then called Mr. Merritt, who was in the cabin, and informed him of it; that Mr. Merritt came up, and went to the main hatch, which was the entrance to the afterhold, and asked two or three slaves which were near, if any of the men were down in the hold, and was informed that there were. Mr. Merritt then waited until Mr. Gifford procured a match, and then Mr. Merritt went down into the hold with a match and a lamp, and lighted the lamp; Mr. Gifford remained over the hatchway. On striking a light, Mr. Merritt found Madison Washington, a very large and strong slave belonging to Thomas McCargo, standing at his back: Mr. Merritt then said, "Madison, is it possible that you are down here! [y]ou are the last man on board of the brig I expected to find here." Madison replied, "Yes, sir, it is me;" and instantly jumped to the hatchway, and got on deck, saying, "I am going up, I cannot stay here:" he did so, in spite of the resistance of Gifford and Merritt, who both tried to keep him back, and laid hold of him for that purpose. Madison then ran forward, and Elijah Morris fired a pistol, the ball of which grazed the back part of Mr. Gifford's head. Madison then shouted, "We have commenced, and must go through; rush, boys, rush aft; we have got them now:" calling to the slaves below, he said, "Come up, every damned one of you; if you don't, and lend a hand, I will kill you all and throw you overboard." Mr. Gifford then ran to the cabin, and aroused the captain and others, who were asleep, and the passengers. . . . The slaves rushed aft, and surrounded the cabin. Mr. Merritt heard the report of the pistol, and blew out the light; he came on deck from the hold, and was caught by one of the negroes, who exclaimed, "Kill him, God damn him, he is one of them;" and the other negroes immediately laid hold of him: one of them attempted to strike Mr. Merritt with a handspike, but missed his aim, and knocked down the negro who was holding Merritt. Mr. Merritt then escaped to the cabin. [John R.] Hewell got out of his birth, seized a musket, ran to the companionway of the cabin, and after some struggling, fired it; the negroes instantly wrenched the musket from him; he then seized a handspike, and defended the cabin from the negroes who pursued him; they thought he had another musket, and retreated a little; he advanced, and they fell on him with clubs, handspikes, and knives; they knocked him down, and stabbed him in not less than twenty places; he got away from them, and staggered back to the cabin, and exclaimed, "I am dead—the negroes have killed me." It is believed that not more than four or five of the negroes had knives. . . . Merritt then hid himself in one of the births, and three of the female house servants covered him with blankets, and sat on the edge of the birth, crying and praying. Theophilus McCargo dressed himself, on the alarm being given; Hewell, after being wounded, staggered into McCargo's state-room, where he fell and expired in about half an hour; his body was thrown overboard by order of Madison, Ben Blacksmith, and Elijah Morris. . . . The helmsman was a Frenchman. Elijah Morris and Pompey Garrison were going to kill him, when Madison told them, they should not kill him, because he was a Frenchman, and could not speak English; so they spared his life.

The *Liberator*, "The Hero Mutineers"
January 7, 1942

In publishing the Protest of the officers and the crew of the *Creole*, we have wished to place an important providential event in such a manner before our readers, as to enable them to give it the most thorough consideration. Like the death of Lovejoy and the case of the Amistad captives, it forms a part of that train of high providences by which God is developing to this nation the nature of American slavery—its deleterious influence, and the absolute necessity of its abolition. The Protest . . . cannot be supposed to represent in too favorable colors the conduct of the mutineers. . . .

We read it with surprise and admiration. Whether we consider the force and presence of mind displayed, the clemency exercised, the unsleeping vigilance maintained, or the sublime reliance on the justice of their cause, as they approached Nassau, we confess that we can think of nothing in the long range of history which gives a nobler impression. . . .

It does not appear whether the mutineers had previously digested their plan, or not. If they had, they betrayed remarkable fidelity and efficiency in bringing it to an issue. If not, the leaders, and especially Madison Washington, manifested astonishing presence of mind and decision of character, in his movement. His reply to Merritt, when found in the hold where the women were kept—his escape to the deck, in spite of the united resistance of Merritt and Gifford—his commanding attitude and daring orders, when he stood a freeman on the slaver's deck, and his perfect preparation for the grand alternative of liberty or death, which stood before him, are splendid exemplifications of the true heroic.

His generous leniency towards his prisoners, his oppressors—men who were carrying him and 134 others, from a condition of slavery already intolerable, to one which threatened still more galling chains, is another remarkable feature. He spared the life of the poor Frenchman, because he could not speak English. . . . All his movements show that malice and revenge formed no part of his motives.

Yet this leniency was accompanied with the most vigorous and efficient measures. . . . To heighten the moral grandeur of the scene, remember that he did not know how many of the remaining slaves might side against him; and even feared he should have to quell an insurrection against the new authority. The 19 consulted together, kept their counsels to themselves—and, so far as we can learn, exercised complete self-control over their passions, and maintained uninterrupted harmony of purpose and action.

Judah P. Benjamin [attributed], Brief for Defendants, *Edward Lockett v. The Merchants' Insurance Company*, The Supreme Court of Louisiana

What is a slave? He is a human being. He has feelings and passions and intellect. His heart, like the white man's, swells with love, burns with jealousy, aches with sorrow, pines under restraint and discomfort, boils with revenge, and ever cherishes the desire of liberty.

His passions and feelings in some respects may not be as fervid and as delicate as those of the white man, nor his intellect as acute; but passions and feelings he has, and in some respects they are more violent, and consequently more dangerous, from the very circumstance that his mind is comparatively weak, and unenlightened. Considering the character of the slave, and the peculiar passions which, generated by nature, are strengthened and stimulated by his condition, he is prone to revolt in the very nature of things, and ever ready to conquer his liberty where a probable chance presents itself. Hence the profound attention which the penal codes of all slave holding countries give to the police of the servile population. In our legislation, we find the most minute and careful details upon this subject, establishing a discipline rigorous indeed, but which no prudent citizen would desire to relax. With what reason can we distinguish this subject matter of insurance, and abstract it from the operation of the well established general principle which we have just invoked? Will any one deny that the bloody and disastrous insurrection of the *Creole* was the result of the inherent qualities of the slaves themselves, roused, not only by their condition of servitude, but stimulated by the removal from their friends and homes, for the purpose of sale by their owners in an unknown land, and encouraged by the lax discipline of the vessel, the numerical weakness of the whites, and the proximity of a British province?

Questions to Consider:

1. *The main version of what happened aboard the* Creole *comes from the crew and other white passengers on the ship. How would the rebels have justified and described their actions, in your opinion? Would their account resemble the views of abolitionists?*

2. *Judah P. Benjamin was a prominent Louisiana lawyer and slaveholder who later served in the US Senate and then in the Confederate government during the Civil War. What would account for his argument about the motivations of the* Creole *rebels?*

Sources:

1. Message from the President of the United States, Communicating in Compliance with a Resolution of the Senate Copies of Correspondence in Relation to the Mutiny on Board the Brig *Creole*, and the Liberation of the Slaves Who Were Passengers in the Said Vessel, S. Doc. 27-51, at 46 (1842).

2. "The Hero Mutineers," *Liberator* (Boston, MA), January 7, 1842.

3. Slidell, Benjamin & Conrad. *Edward Lockett versus the Merchants' Insurance Company. Brief for Defendants.* Special Collections, Howard-Tilton Memorial Library, Tulane University.

1839–1856:
Nativism in Antebellum Louisiana

Immigration has been a recurrent issue in American history, and in antebellum Louisiana politics, this issue was particularly salient. New Orleans was one of the most ethnically diverse cities in the United States and was an important port of entry for immigrants before the Civil War. Nativism first emerged in New Orleans in the mid-1830s as a consequence of the city's complex politics. Simmering tensions between the city's established Creole population and a rising wave of American newcomers intensified, and added to the mix were controversies over prominent foreign-born politicians and a growing immigrant population. A group of Americans attempted to further stoke these tensions by forming the Louisiana Native American Association in 1835 and publishing a newspaper, the *True American.* Immigration to New Orleans, and the United States in general, expanded dramatically by the 1850s due to the Irish potato famine and political unrest in Europe. The 1850 Census revealed that one-fourth of the white population of the city was foreign-born. The anxieties of native-born Protestants in the United States to this foreign and largely Catholic influx led to the creation of the nativist American, or Know-Nothing, Party in the middle of the decade. The rise of the Know-Nothings also coincided with national political turmoil brought on by increased sectional tensions over slavery and the collapse of the Whig Party. Some former Louisiana Whigs, looking for a new political home and still resentful of Democratic co-option of the city's immigrant vote, gravitated to the anti-immigrant party. However, the party was also anti-Catholic, which became a problem for anti-immigrant Creoles like Charles Gayarré (a former Democrat) when the party refused to seat him at the national convention because of his faith.

Address of the Louisiana Native American Association, 1839

If our apprehensions of the dangers from foreign influence in the United States, be founded in sound reason;—and the wise, the just and the good, of every political party, are daily becoming more and more convinced of its correctness, and our opinion is rapidly becoming universal throughout our country; then, not only *our* posterity, and the posterity of naturalized citizens, but even foreigners who may desire to emigrate to our happy land, to the end of time, are interested in the accomplishment of our wishes, viz, the repeal of the naturalization laws. For if it be admitted that the participation in our political privileges of the ignorant, the corrupt, the perfidious, the vile, the seditious, and the hostile foreigner, may eventually warp, distort, or overthrow our republican form of Government, then those benign features which at present characterize our institutions, being destroyed. Anarchy, confusion, and eventually despotism must inevitably ensue, hence, the beneficent peculiarities of our country will become extinct, and thus this last asylum of the oppressed and afflicted for relief and happiness, will be cut off forever.

Thus it appears that the future happiness of succeeding generations . . . may be secured by the accomplishment of the great object which we have in view: the withholding political power from the hordes of foreigners, who are now crowding into our country, by the repeal of the naturalization laws. . . . The object of the present undertaking is to aid in arousing our countrymen to a keen perception of the dangers which threaten them from foreign influence through the suicidal process of indiscriminate foreign naturalization.

. . . We are determined in conjunction with the fearless and patriotic spirits, who are now employed in the same great cause, to sound the alarm far and wide, until the American people have been aroused from their lethargy and induced to think deeply and solemnly on this momentous subject, until every city, town, village and hamlet, throughout our country shall respond to our warning cry, and shall lend their aid in the correction of this great and incalculable evil. . . .

When we sometimes converse with our countrymen, who never reflected on the momentous subject of foreign influence, they sometimes reply to our expressions of apprehension, "Oh! what can a few foreigners more or less, do to injure the United States." . . .

When we tell them that among these paupers and vagrants, are the vicious,—the illiterate and the insubordinate,—the felon,—the incendiary and the alibiist, who have fled or been transported to our young, pure and beautiful republic, reeking with the perfected and finished proficiency in vice, —graduates in the school of crimes, which have been maturing in degree for many centuries in their own native lands, and that this transportation of paupers, vagrants, and convicts to the United States is rapidly becoming an established system of policy by foreign governments. . . .

When we tell our countrymen, that such as these are the very elements with which civil commotions are effected in their own lands, or as they have been not inaptly termed "the blood lappers of revolutions," who having no congeniality of feelings, interests, or aspirations with ourselves—destitute of principles, —educated from their earliest infancy in feuds—brawls—tumults and insurrections, and who are liable at any time to be wielded by artful demagogues, menaced by ecclesiastical fulminations, or bought with money to strike their daggers deep into the institutions of the countries which gave them birth, but how much, oh! how much more readily and willingly into ours, for which they have no sympathies, and which they despise and abhor. . . .

When we tell our countrymen, that such are the hordes of foreign mechanics, and artisans, now congregating hither from other lands, who by underbidding the native American mechanic, have almost monopolized the whole mechanical business of the United States, —that hosts of foreign merchants have congregated in our cities, and obtained the control of almost all our commercial and banking interests, and operations, —that every department of Law, Science, and even Divinity is being rapidly overrun, and absorbed by foreigners, and foreign influence—that two thirds of the teachers in our schools, seminaries, and institutions for the education of our youth, and the instruction of the rising generation, consist of foreigners, who have themselves been brought up in distant lands, —imbued with feelings, prejudices and aspirations alien to our own, —and who cannot with the patriotic fire which burns in the heart of a native American. . . .

When we tell our countrymen, that many of the professors in our Colleges and Universities are foreigners, and that the Press, the great moral lever of nations, has almost been absolutely monopolized by foreigners . . . that presses whose whole object, aim and end, is the establishment of a foreign tone and feeling among the multifarious hosts of foreigners now in our country, have been quietly permitted to erect themselves throughout every part of the United States. Presses which . . . shout paeans of praise and adulation to all foreigners and every circumstance of foreign origin. . . .

When we tell our countrymen, that in the private and social circles, where foreigners congregate unobserved by the eye of the native American, that jibes, taunts, and insulting sarcasms are heaped upon our country, and her institutions, and comparisons the most opprobrious and degrading to us, are made between *our* habits, manners and capacities, and those of the countries from which they have been transported or escaped for refuge to our happy land.

Charles Gayarré's Address to the General Assembly of the Know-Nothing Party, May 1855

If you retain, as one of the fundamental principles of the American party, the clause introduced in your constitution in relation to a particular religious creed, you are attempting to do *de facto*, what you cannot do *de jure*—to do by party enactment what you cannot do by legislative enactment—to do by party legislation what Congress cannot do by national legislation. As a party, in direct violation of a special provision of the constitution, you prohibit *the free exercise of an establishment of religion*, by inflicting disabilities on those who profess it. This is what the American party does, and what Congress cannot do. The Federal Government cannot require a religious test as a qualification to any office of trust or profit under the United States. The American party requires that test. It is only by a miserable quibble, unworthy of the dignity of the American character, and not by any sound argument, that we can endeavor to establish that this is not a violation of the Constitution of the United States. . . . The Constitution of the United States being the highest law of the land, every evasion of it is illegal, and ought to be carefully checked. . . .

But if you really think that Catholicism thus debases mankind, you ought to take more vigorous measures against it. If Catholicism makes bad citizens, it is not enough to inflict disabilities on those citizens when they are made. You ought to prevent their being made at all. You ought as statesmen, as lovers of your country, to punish those who teach Catholicism—you ought to prevent the propagation of Catholicism, as you prevent the propagation of a crime. . . . Why hang a man who kills another—and not burn the Catholic priest who will degrade and sink to a state of Helotism all those to whom he may communicate his doctrines? The same reasons which are given to exclude Catholics from office would be equally as strong to fine and imprison them, and even to drive them away—so as to have done with them at once. Nay, if Catholics are to remain such an inferior race among you, I think that you are not consistent if you do not prevent the increase of that population by immigration, or by birth. . . . It is far more humane to forbid a man to come to this country, than to permit him to come and have children who are to constitute an inferior race. There is no evil more sedulously to be guarded against than the introduction of an inferior race of citizens in any state. . . . Do not stop half way. If Catholics deserve to be maimed and crippled, off with their heads. They will do less mischief when dead, than when half alive. . . .

[The Know-Nothings claim that] Catholicism contracts the intellect and depraves the heart. Protestantism refines the soul, and expands the mind. Catholics, from their very creed, are necessarily slavish in their dispositions. Protestants, for the same reason, are essentially freemen. Therefore, in a free country, Catholics must be excluded from all participation in the government. They must be the governed, and Protestants the rulers. . . . And what do you do, men of the North, who wish to abolish slavery in the South—the slavery of the Blacks? You proceed to establish the worst kind of slavery among the Whites—the servitude of the mind—the servitude of the soul—the yielding of man to man, not of his labor and sweat, but the yielding of what he owes to his God—the surrender not of his time, his field, or the fruits of his toil, but the delivering over of his conscience into the hands of another—the relinquishment of his religion, which is dearer to an honest man than life and property—a servitude of the heart, infinitely more odious than the servitude of the limb. See what weapons you give to the advocates of the slavery of the Blacks. What are your reasons for degrading Catholics to a state of inferiority? It is that their moral and religious training is incompatible with Republican institutions. . . . Catholics are an inferior race of beings on account of their defective education, and ought to be kept in political servitude. . . . Millions of Protestants in the South say also, Negroes are an inferior race of beings from physical and intellectual organization, and therefore they must be kept in political and civil servitude. . . .

By this solemn consecration of the most hateful of all narrow-minded and bigoted prejudices, you will have enlisted against you, not only a considerable number of your Protestant fellow-citizens, but also the remainder of the civilized world. For Great Britain has abandoned the religious test to which she clung so long; all other Protestant countries have adopted or are adopting the same liberal course of policy. All Catholic countries, swayed by the force of public opinion, have done, are doing, or will do the same in relation to Protestants. . . . Shall America alone retrograde in the march of philanthropy and Christian liberality? No religious test!—no religious proscription!—is the cry—the absolute want of the civilized world. If that is the case, and you cannot deny it, you are in the position in which you place the slaveholder and with which you taunt him so exultingly. If your argument is good against them in relation to Negroes, mine is conclusive against you in relation to Catholics. It is from your own arsenal that I take the weapon which strikes you to the heart.

Questions to Consider:

1. *How could one describe the concerns of the Native American Association as paranoid?*
2. *Do you think that Gayarré's argument could convince a Know-Nothing to change his mind about Catholicism?*

Sources:

1. Louisiana Native American Association, *Address of the Louisiana Native American Association: to the Citizens of Louisiana And the Inhabitants of the United States* (New Orleans: D. Felt & co., 1839).

2. Charles Gayarré, *Mr. Gayarré's Address to the General Assembly of the Know Nothing Committee in Philadelphia, 1855.* (n.p.: 1855).

1860: Rev. Benjamin Palmer's Thanksgiving Sermon

In the tense atmosphere in Louisiana after Abraham Lincoln's victory in the 1860 presidential election, Governor Thomas Moore proclaimed Thursday, November 29, as a day of Thanksgiving. On that day the movement for secession received a significant boost from a sermon read by Reverend Benjamin M. Palmer. One of the most prominent ministers in the South, Palmer was the pastor of the First Presbyterian Church in New Orleans. Having avoided political pronouncements in the past, Palmer unambiguously declared his support for secession in his sermon. The city's pro-secession newspapers quickly printed it in their pages, and as many as fifty thousand copies may have been distributed in the city. Also distributed and discussed throughout the South, it influenced public opinion regionally in favor of secession.

Reverend Palmer's Thanksgiving Sermon November 29, 1860

In determining our duty in this emergency it is necessary that we should first ascertain the nature of the trust providentially committed to us. . . . The particular trust assigned to such a people becomes the pledge of the divine protection; and their fidelity to it determines the fate by which it is finally overtaken. What that trust is must be ascertained from the necessities of their position, the institutions which are the outgrowth of their principles and the conflicts through which they preserve their identity and independence. If then the South is such a people, what, at this juncture, is their providential trust? I answer, that it is *to conserve and to perpetuate the institution of domestic slavery as now existing.* It is not necessary here to inquire whether this is precisely the best relation in which the hewer of wood and drawer of water can stand to his employer; although this proposition may perhaps be successfully sustained by those who choose to defend it. Still less are we required, dogmatically, to affirm that it will subsist through all time. Baffled as our wisdom may now be in finding a solution of this intricate social problem, it would nevertheless be the height of arrogance to pronounce what changes may or may not occur in the distant future. In the grand march of events Providence may work out a solution undiscoverable by us. What modifications of soil and climate may hereafter be produced, what consequent changes in the products on which we depend, what political revolutions may occur among the races which are now enacting the great drama of history: all such inquiries are totally irrelevant because no prophetic vision can pierce the darkness of that future. If this question should ever arise, the generation to whom it is remitted will doubtless have the wisdom to meet it, and Providence will furnish the lights in which it is to be resolved. All that we claim for them, for ourselves, is liberty to work out this problem, guided by nature and God, without obtrusive interference from abroad. These great questions of Providence and history must have free scope for their solution; and the race whose fortunes are distinctly implicated in the same is alone authorized, as it is alone competent, to determine them. It is just this impertinence of human legislation, setting bounds to what God alone can regulate, that the South is called this day to resent and resist. The country is convulsed simply because "the throne of iniquity frameth mischief by a law." Without, therefore, determining the question of duty for future generations, I simply say, that for us, as now situated, the duty is plain of conserving and transmitting the system of slavery, with the freest scope for its natural development and extension. Let us, my brethren, look our duty in the face. With this institution assigned to our keeping, what reply shall we make to those who say that its days are numbered? My own conviction is, that we should at once lift ourselves, intelligently, to the highest moral ground and proclaim to all the world that we hold this trust from God, and in its occupancy we are prepared to stand or fall as God may appoint. If the critical moment has arrived at which the great issue is joined, let us say that, in the sight of all perils, we will stand by our trust; and God be with the right!

. . . This duty is bound upon us again *as the constituted guardians of the slaves themselves.* Our lot is not more implicated in theirs, than their lot in ours; in our mutual relations we survive or perish together. The worst foes of the black race are those who have intermeddled on their behalf. We know better than others that every attribute of their character fits them for dependence and servitude. By nature the most affectionate and loyal of all races beneath the sun, they are also the most helpless; and no calamity can befall them greater than the loss of that protection they enjoy under this patriarchal system. Indeed, the experiment has been grandly tried of precipitating them upon freedom which they know not how to enjoy; and the dismal results are before us in statistics that astonish the world. With the fairest portions of the earth in their possession and with the advantage of a long discipline as cultivators of the soil, their constitutional indolence has converted the most beautiful islands of the sea into a howling waste. It is not too much to say that if the South should, at this moment, surrender every slave, the wisdom of the entire world, united in solemn council, could not solve the question of their disposal. Their transportation to Africa, even if it were feasible, would be but the most refined cruelty; they must perish with starvation before they could have time to relapse into their primitive barbarism. Their residence here, in the presence of the vigorous Saxon race, would be but the signal for their rapid extermination before they had time to waste away through listlessness, filth and vice. Freedom would be their doom; and equally from both they call upon us, their providential guardians, to be protected. I know this argument will be scoffed abroad as the hypocritical cover thrown over our own cupidity and selfishness; but every Southern master knows its truth and feels its power. My servant, whether born in my house or bought with my money, stands to me in the relation of a child. Though providentially owing me service, which, providentially, I am bound to exact, he is, nevertheless, my brother and my friend, and I am to him a guardian and a father. He leans upon me for protection, for counsel, and for blessing; and so long as the relation continues, no power but the power of Almighty God shall come between him and me. Were there no argument but this, it binds upon us the providential duty of preserving the relation that we may save him from a doom worse than death.

. . . Last of all, in this great struggle, *we defend the cause of God and religion.* The abolition spirit is undeniably atheistic. The demon which erected its throne upon the guillotine in the days of Robespierre and Marat, which abolished the Sabbath and worshipped reason in the person of a harlot, yet survives to work other horrors, of which those of the French Revolution are but the type. Among a people so generally religious as the American, a disguise must be worn; but it is the same old threadbare disguise of the advocacy of human rights. From a thousand Jacobin clubs here, as in France, the decree has gone forth which strikes at God by striking at all subordination and law. Availing itself of the morbid and misdirected sympathies of men, it has entrapped weak consciences in the meshes of its treachery; and now, at last, has seated its high priest upon the throne, clad in the black garments of discord and schism, so symbolic of its ends. Under this suspicious cry of reform, it demands that every evil shall be corrected, or society become a wreck—the sun must be stricken from the heavens, if a spot is found upon his disk. The Most High, knowing his own power, which is infinite, and his own wisdom, which is unfathomable, can afford to be patient. But these self-constituted reformers must quicken the activity of Jehovah or compel his abdication. In their furious haste, they trample upon obligations sacred as any which can bind the conscience. It is time to reproduce the obsolete idea that Providence must govern man, and not that man shall control Providence. In the imperfect state of human society, it pleases God to allow evils which check others that are greater. As in the physical world, objects are moved forward, not by a single force, but by the composition of forces; so in his moral administration, there are checks and balances whose intimate relations are comprehended only by himself. But what reck they of this—these fierce zealots who undertake to drive the chariot of the sun? Working out the single and false idea which rides them like a nightmare, they dash athwart the spheres, utterly disregarding the delicate mechanism of Providence, which moves on, wheels within wheels, with pivots and balances and springs, which the great Designer alone can control. This spirit of atheism, which knows no God who tolerates evil, no Bible which sanctions law, and no conscience that can be bound by oaths and covenants, has selected us for its victims, and slavery for its issue. Its banner-cry rings out already upon the air—"liberty, equality, fraternity," which simply interpreted mean bondage, confiscation and massacre. With its tricolor waving in the breeze,—it waits to inaugurate its reign of terror. To the South the high position is assigned of defending, before all nations, the cause of all religion and of all truth. In this trust, we are resisting the power which wars against constitutions and laws and compacts, against Sabbaths and sanctuaries, against the family, the State, and the Church; which blasphemously invades the prerogatives of God, and rebukes the Most High for the errors of his administration; which, if it cannot snatch the reign of empire from his grasp, will lay the universe in ruins at his feet. Is it possible that we shall decline the onset? . . .

This argument, then, which sweeps over the entire circle of our relations, touches the four cardinal points of duty *to ourselves, to our slaves, to the world, and to Almighty God.* It establishes the nature and solemnity of our present trust, to *preserve and transmit our existing system of domestic servitude, with the right, unchallenged by man, to go and root itself wherever Providence and nature may carry it. . . .*

Against this institution a system of aggression has been pursued through the last thirty years. Initiated by a few fanatics, who were at first despised, it has gathered strength from opposition until it has as assumed its present gigantic proportions. No man has thoughtfully watched the progress of this controversy without being convinced that the crisis must at length come. Some few, perhaps, have hoped against hope, that the gathering imposthume might be dispersed, and the poison be eliminated from the body politic by healthful remedies. But the delusion has scarcely been cherished by those who have studied the history of fanaticism in its path of blood and fire through the ages of the past. . . .

It is alleged, for example, that the President-elect has been chosen by a fair majority under prescribed forms. But need I say, to those who have read history, that no despotism is more absolute than that of an unprincipled democracy, and no tyranny more galling than that exercised through constitutional formulas? But the plea is idle, when the very question we debate is the perpetuation of that Constitution now converted into an engine of oppression, and the continuance of that union which is henceforth to be our condition of vassalage. I say it with solemnity and pain, this union of our forefathers is already gone. It existed but in mutual confidence, the bonds of which were ruptured in the late election. Though its form should be preserved, it is, in fact, destroyed. We may possibly entertain the project of reconstructing it; but it will be another union, resting upon other than past guarantees. . . . For myself I say that, under the rule which threatens us, I throw off the yoke of this union as readily as did our ancestors the yoke of King George III, and for causes immeasurably stronger than those pleaded in their celebrated declaration.

It is softly whispered, too, that the successful competitor for the throne [i.e., Lincoln] protests and avers his purpose to administer the government in a conservative and national spirit. Allowing him all credit for personal integrity in these protestations, he is, in this matter, nearly as impotent for good as he is competent for evil. He is nothing more than a figure upon the political chessboard—whether pawn or knight or king, will hereafter appear—but still a silent figure upon the checkered squares, moved by the hands of an unseen player. That player is the party [the Republicans] to which he owes his elevation—a party that has signalized its history by the most unblushing perjuries. . . .

But some quietist whispers, yet further, this majority is accidental and has been swelled by accessions of men simply opposed to the existing administration; the party is utterly heterogeneous and must be shivered into fragments by its own success. I confess, frankly, this suggestion has staggered me more than any other, and I sought to take refuge therein. Why should we not wait and see the effect of success upon a party whose elements might devour each other in the very distribution of the spoil? Two considerations have dissipated the fallacy before me. The first is, that, however mixed the party, abolitionism is clearly its informing and actuating soul; and fanaticism is a bloodhound that never bolts its tracks when it has once lapped blood. The elevation of their candidates is far from being the consummation of their aims. It is only the beginning of that consummation; and, if all history be not a lie, there will be cohesion enough till the end of the beginning is reached, and the dreadful banquet of slaughter and ruin shall glut the appetite. The second consideration is a principle which I cannot blink. It is nowhere denied that the first article in the creed of the now dominant party is the restriction of slavery within its present limits. It is distinctly avowed by their organs and in the name of their elected chieftain. . . .

Thus, with restored confidence, we may be rejoined a united and happy people. But, before God, I believe that nothing will effect this but the line of policy which the South has been compelled in self-preservation to adopt. I confess frankly, I am not sanguine that such an auspicious result will be reached. Partly, because I do not see how new guarantees are to be grafted upon the Constitution, nor how, if grafted, they can be more binding than those which have already been trampled under foot; but chiefly, because I do not see how such guarantees can be elicited from the people at the North. It cannot be disguised that almost to a man they are anti-slavery where they are not abolition. A whole generation has been educated to look upon the system with abhorrence as a national blot. . . .

The position of the South is at this moment sublime. If she has grace given her to know her hour she will save herself, the country, and the world.

It will involve, indeed, temporary prostration and distress; the dykes of Holland must be cut to save her from the troops of Philip. But I warn my countrymen the historic moment once passed, never returns. If she will arise in her majesty, and speak now as with the voice of one man, she will roll back for all time the curse that is upon her. If she succumbs now, she transmits that curse as an heirloom of posterity. We may, for a generation, enjoy comparative ease, gather up our feet in our beds, and die in peace; but our children will go forth beggared from the homes of their fathers. Fishermen will cast their nets where your proud commercial navy now rides at anchor, and dry them upon the shore now covered with your bales of merchandise. Sapped, circumvented, undermined, the institutions of your soil will be overthrown; and within five and twenty years the history of St. Domingo [or Haiti] will be the record of Louisiana. If dead men's bones can tremble, ours will move under the muttered curses of sons and daughters, denouncing the blindness and love of ease which have left them an inheritance of woe.

I have done my duty under as deep a sense of responsibility to God and man as I have ever felt. Under a full conviction that the salvation of the whole country is depending upon the action of the South, I am impelled to deepen the sentiment of resistance in the Southern mind and to strengthen the current now flowing toward a union of the South in defence of her chartered rights. It is a duty which I shall not be called to repeat, for such awful junctures do not occur twice in a century. Bright and happy days are yet before us; and before another political earthquake shall shake the continent, I hope to be "where the wicked cease from troubling and where the weary are at rest."

It only remains to say, that whatever be the fortunes of the South, I accept them for my own. Born upon her soil, of a father thus born before me—from an ancestry that occupied it while yet it was a part of England's possessions—she is in every sense my mother. I shall die upon her bosom—she shall know no peril, but it is my peril—no conflict but it is my conflict—and no abyss of ruin, into which I shall not share her fall. May the Lord God cover her head in this her day battle!

Questions to Consider:

1. *How was the southern ideology of paternalism manifested in Palmer's view of enslaved people?*

2. *Aside from being atheists and fanatics, what problem did Palmer have with abolitionists on theological grounds?*

3. *What were other arguments that Palmer used to support the South's position?*

Source:

B. M. [Benjamin Morgan] Palmer, *Thanksgiving sermon, delivered at the First Presbyterian church, New Orleans, on Thursday, November 29, 1860* (New York: George F. Nesbitt & Co., Printers, 1861), 6–20.

1861:
Louisiana Secedes

In the wake of Lincoln's election in November 1860, momentum decisively broke in favor of Louisiana's secession from the United States. A special session of the state legislature set January 7, 1861, as the date for an election for delegates to a state secession convention, which would meet in Baton Rouge. Candidates for immediate secession received 52.7 percent of the votes and comprised 80 of the 130 delegates. Most of the rest were moderates who favored a meeting of southern states before a decision regarding secession, along with a few who wished for the state to remain in the union. With five states already out of the union when the convention met on January 23, the fate of Louisiana was never in doubt. The final vote was 113 to 17 in favor of immediate secession, and all but seven delegates signed the secession ordinance.

One of convention's few committed unionists was lawyer and newspaper editor James G. Taliaferro of Catahoula Parish. He laid out his argument against secession in his protest, which pro-secession delegates refused to publish in the convention journal. Once the movement for secession began in the winter of 1860–61, some southern states appointed special commissioners to travel to their fellow slaveholding states to build support for leaving the union. George Williamson was Louisiana's commissioner to the Texas secession convention, and his letter to the convention explicitly describes the reasons at the heart of secessionist cause.

Louisiana's Ordinance of Secession

AN ORDINANCE

To dissolve the union between the State of Louisiana and other States united with her under the compact entitled "The Constitution of the United States of America."

We, the people of the State of Louisiana, in convention assembled, do declare and ordain, and it is hereby declared and ordained, That the ordinance passed by us in convention on the November 22, in the year eighteen hundred and eleven, whereby the Constitution of the United States of America and the amendments of the said Constitution were adopted, and all laws and ordinances by which the State of Louisiana became a member of the Federal Union, be, and the same are hereby, repealed and abrogated; and that the union now subsisting between Louisiana and other States under the name of "The United States of America" is hereby dissolved.

We do further declare and ordain, That the State of Louisiana hereby resumes all rights and powers heretofore delegated to the Government of the United States of America; that her citizens are absolved from all allegiance to said Government; and that she is in full possession and exercise of all rights of sovereignty which appertain to a free and independent State.

We do further declare and ordain, That all rights acquired and vested under the Constitution of the United States, or any act of Congress, or treaty, or under any law of this State, and not incompatible with this ordinance, shall remain in force and have the same effect as if this ordinance had not been passed.

Adopted in convention at Baton Rouge this January 26, 1861.

Taliaferro's Protest against the Ordinance of Secession

The delegate from the parish of Catahoula opposes the separate secession of Louisiana from the federal union, and asks leave to place upon the records of the convention his reasons for that opposition. They are as follow:

I oppose the act of secession because, in my deliberate judgment, the wrongs alleged as the cause of the movement might be redressed under the constitution by an energetic execution of the laws of the United States, and that, standing upon the guarantee of the constitution, in the Union, southern rights might be triumphantly maintained under the protection and safeguards which the constitution affords.

Because, in secession I see no remedy for the actual and present evils complained of, and because the *prospective* evils depicted so gloomily may never come; and if they should, the inalienable right to resist tyranny and oppression might then be exercised as well and as successfully as now.

Because I see no certainty that the seceding states will ever be confederated again; none that the border states will secede at all; and if they should, I see no reliable ground for believing that they would incorporate themselves with the gulf or cotton states in a new government. I see no surety either that Texas would unite with them.

Because the gulf or cotton states alone, were they to unite in a separate confederacy, would be without the elements of power, indispensable in the formation of a government to take a respectable rank among the nations of the earth.

Because I believe that peaceable secession is a right unknown to the constitution of the United States; that it is a most dangerous and mischievous principle in the structure of any government, and when carried into the formation of the contemplated confederacy of the gulf states, will render it powerless for good, and complete its incapacity to afford to the people permanent security for their lives, liberties and property.

Because it is my solemn and deliberate conviction that the distraction of the southern states by separate secession will defeat the purpose it is intended to accomplish, and that its certain results will be to impair instead to strengthen the security of southern institutions.

Because the proper status of Louisiana is with the border states, which nature has connected her by the majestic river which flows through her limits; and because an alliance in a weak government with the gulf states east of her, is unnatural and antagonistic to her obvious interests and destiny.

Because by separate secession the state relinquished all its rights within the government; it surrenders its equal rights to the common territories, to the vast public domain of the United States and the public property of every kind belonging to the nation. And for this reason I oppose secession as being emphatically submission.

Because, secession may bring anarchy and war, as it will assuredly bring ruinous exactions upon property in the form of direct taxation, a withering blight upon the property of the state, and a fatal prostration of all its great interests.

Because, the act of dissolving the ties which connect Louisiana with the federal Union is a revolutionary act that this convention is, of itself, without legitmate [*sic*] power to perform. Convened without authority of the people of the state, and refusing to submit its action to them for the sanction in the grave and vital act of changing their government, this convention violates the great fundamental principle of American government, that the will of the people is supreme.

George Williamson, "Letter to President and Gentlemen of the Convention of the People of Texas."

To the Hon. O. M. Roberts, President of the convention of the people of Texas. . . .

Before desirous of obtaining the concurrence of the people of Texas in what she has done, Louisiana invites you to a candid consideration of her acts in resuming the powers delegated to the government of the late United States, and in providing for the formation of a confederacy of "The States which have seceded and may secede." The archives of the Federal Government bear ample testimony to the loyalty of Louisiana to the American Union. Her conservatism has been proverbial in political circle. The character and pursuits of her people, her immense agricultural wealth, her large banking capital, her possession of the great commercial metropolis of the South, . . . present facts sufficient to make "assurance doubly sure" she did not take these grave steps for light or transient causes. She was impelled to this action to preserve her honor, her safety, her property and the free institutions so sacred to her people. She believed the federal agent had betrayed her trust, had become the facile instrument of a hostile people, and was usurping despotic powers. She considered that the present vacillating executive, on the 4th of March next, would be supplanted by a stalwart fanatic of the Northwest, whose energetic will, backed by the frenzied bigotry of unpatriotic masses, would cause him to establish the military despotism already inaugurated.

The people of Louisiana were unwilling to endanger their liberties and property by submission to the despotism of a single tyrant, or the canting tyranny of pharisaical majorities. Insulted by the denial of her constitutional equality by the non-slave-holding States, outraged by their contemptuous rejection of proffered compromises, and convinced that she was illustrating the capacity of her people for self-government by withdrawing from a union that had failed, without fault of hers, to accomplish its purposes, she declared herself a free and independent State on the 26th day of January last. . . . Louisiana looks to the formation of a Southern confederacy to preserve the blessings of African slavery, and of the free institutions of the founders of the Federal Union, bequeathed to their posterity. . . . Louisiana and Texas have the same language, laws, and institutions. They grow the same great staples—sugar and cotton. Between the citizens of each exists the most cordial social and commercial intercourse. The Red river and the Sabine form common highways for the transportation of their produce to the markets of the world. . . . Both States have large areas of fertile, uncultivated lands, peculiarly adapted to slave labor; and they are both so deeply interested in African slavery that it may be said to be absolutely necessary to their existence and is the keystone to the arch of their prosperity. Each of the States has an extended Gulf coast, and must look with equal solicitude to its protection now, and the acquisition of the entire control of the Gulf of Mexico in due time. No two States of this confederacy are so identified in interest, and whose destinies are so closely interwoven with each other. . . . The Mexican yoke could not have been more galling to "the army of heroes" of '36 than the Black republican rule would be to the survivors and sons of that army at the present day.

The people of Louisiana would consider it a most fatal blow to African slavery, if Texas either did not secede or having seceded should not join her destinies to theirs in a Southern Confederacy. If she remains in the union the abolitionists would continue their work of incendiarism and murder. Emigrant aid societies would arm with Sharp's rifles predatory bands to infest her northern borders. . . . The people of the slave-holding States are bound together by the same necessity and determination to preserve African slavery. The isolation of any one of them from the others would make her the theatre for abolition emissaries from the North and from Europe. Her existence would be one of constant peril to herself and of imminent danger to other neighboring slave-holding communities. . . . I am authorized to say to your honorable body that Louisiana does not expect any beneficial result from the peace conference now assembled at

Washington. She is unwilling that her action should depend on the border States. Her interests are identical with Texas and the seceding States. With them she will at present co-operate, hoping and believing in his own good time God will awaken the people of the border States to the vanity of asking for; or depending upon, guarantees or compromises wrung from a people whose consciences are too sublimated to be bound by that sacred compact, the constitution of the late United States. That constitution the Southern States have never violated, and taking it as the basis of our new government we hope to form a slave-holding confederacy that will secure to us and our remotest posterity the great blessings its authors designed in the Federal Union. With the social balance wheel of slavery to regulate its machinery, we may fondly indulge the hope that our Southern government will be perpetual. Geo. Williamson, Commissioner of the State of Louisiana, City of Austin Feby 11th 1861

Questions to Consider:

1. *How prescient was Taliaferro's warning about the consequences of secession?*
2. *What was Williamson's main argument why Texas should join Louisiana and other southern states and leave the Union?*

Sources:

1. *Official Journal of the Proceedings of the Convention of the State of Louisiana* (New Orleans: J. O. Nixon, 1861), 231.

2. James G. Taliaferro, *A protest against the ordinance of secession, passed by the Louisiana convention, on the 26th January, 1861, presented to the Convention on that day, by James G. Taliaferro, the Delegate from the Parish of Catahoula, who asked that it might be entered upon the journal of the Convention, which was refused* (Catahoula, LA: 1861). Library of Congress, Rare Book and Special Collections Division, *Printed Ephemera Collection.* Pdf. https://www.loc.gov/item/rbpe.02402700/.

3. James W. Loewen and Edward H. Sebesta, eds. *The Confederate and Neo-Confederate Reader: The "Great Truth" about the "Lost Cause"* (Jackson, MS: University Press of Mississippi, 2010), 145–48.

1862:
Butler's "Woman Order"

One of the great "villains" of Louisiana history is Union general Benjamin F. Butler. Butler was a prominent lawyer and Democratic politician from Massachusetts. Typical of his party before the war, he exhibited no reservations about slavery, and curiously, in light of what happened during the war, even championed Jefferson Davis for the Democratic nomination in 1860. In the wake of the bombardment of Fort Sumter, Massachusetts quickly mobilized some of its militia units, and as a general in the state's militia, Butler took a leadership role, eager to gain military glory. Placed in charge of Fort Monroe in Virginia in May 1861, Butler arguably initiated the chain of events that led to the end of slavery during the war when he refused to hand over three slaves who escaped to Union lines to their master by declaring them "contraband of war." His experience in working with naval forces in operations along the North Carolina coast led to his appointment as commanding army officer in the assault on New Orleans in 1862. Butler quickly and powerfully enforced Union control of the city by executing gambler William Mumford for taking down the American flag that was hoisted above the city. Mumford then became a martyr for the pro-Confederate citizens of the city. Amid Butler's difficulties in asserting control over New Orleans, though, nothing compared to his "woman order." It not only enraged the Confederates, but it even brought criticism from abroad, as British Prime Minister Lord Palmerston denounced it before the House of Commons. Along with other controversies surrounding his tenure in Louisiana, Lincoln ultimately replaced him with General Nathaniel Banks.

Excerpt from Butler's *Autobiography*

From the second day after we landed, we had the men of New Orleans so completely under our control that our officers and soldiers could go anywhere in the city without being interfered with. . . . One result of our conduct was that any of us, from the highest to the lowest, went where he pleased without insult or hostile act by any man in New Orleans. . . .

But not so with the women of New Orleans. . . . Pretty soon, complaints of treatment from women of all states and conditions and degrees in life came pouring in upon me. When a soldier or an officer was passing along quietly on the sidewalk (these acts seemed rather the more venomous towards the officers) a woman coming the opposite way would turn out in the carriage way, take great pains to hold her skirts aside as if she feared they might be contaminated if they touched the soldier, and accompany this act with every possible gesture of contempt and abhorrence. . . .

There were five or six women leaning over a balcony on one occasion when I was riding along quite near it. . . . Just as we were passing the balcony, with something between a shriek and a sneer, the women all whirled around back to with a flirt which threw out their skirts in a regular circle like the pirouette of a dancer. I turned around to my aid, saying in full voice: "Those women evidently know which end of them looks the best." That closed that exhibition.

. . . How is this course of conduct to be changed? How is this to be stopped? . . . Some of these women desire to exhibit what they call their patriotism, and there are many of them who would be very happy to be arrested for any insult put upon a Yankee officer or soldier and have it so published. Much more will be the danger of riot if Yankee soldiers arrest the women of New Orleans on the streets for the acts which these women think proper to do as their part in carrying on the war. An order for arrests in these cases—simple arrests and transportation of "these ladies"—would be a source of perpetual turmoil at least, and possibly ripen into insurrection.

. . . Colonel Deming went to the levee to meet the flag-officer [Commodore David Farragut] when he landed, and they walked up arm in arm in full uniform. While going along one of the principal streets, there fell upon them what at first they took to be a sudden and heavy shower; but it proved to be the emptying of a vessel of water upon them from the balcony above, and not very clean water at that. Of course the vessel was proof that this was done by one of "the ladies of New Orleans.". . .

On the next day, the Sabbath, one of my officers dressed himself in full uniform, took his prayer-book in his hand, and was on the way to the church to attend divine service. As he as walking quietly along he met two very well dressed and respectable looking women, and, as a gentlemen should, he withdrew to the outer side of the sidewalk to let them pass by. As he did so, one deliberately stepped across in front of the other and spit in his face. . . .

There was no case of aggression after that order was issued, no case of insult by word or look against our officers or soldiers while in New Orleans.

The order executed itself.

No arrests were ever made under it or because of it. All the ladies in New Orleans forebore to insult our troops because they didn't want to be deemed common women, and all the common women forebore to insult our troops because they wanted to be deemed ladies, and of those two classes were all the secessionists of the city.

The "Woman Order"

Headquarters Department of the Gulf
New Orleans, May 15, 1862
General Order No. 28.

As the officers and soldiers of the United States have been subject to repeated insults from the women (calling themselves ladies) of New Orleans, in return for the most scrupulous non-interference and courtesy on our part, it is ordered that hereafter when any female shall, by word, gesture, or movement, insult or show contempt for any officer or soldier of the United States, she shall be regarded and held liable to be treated as a woman of the town plying her avocation.

By command of Major-General Butler
Geo C. Strong
Assistant Adjutant-General and Chief of Staff.

Proclamation of Governor Thomas O. Moore

The annals of warfare between civilized nations of forwarded no similar instance of infamy to this order. It is thus proclaimed to the world that the exhibition of any disgust or repulsiveness by the women of New Orleans to the hated invaders of their home and the slayers of their fathers, brothers, and husbands shall constitute a justification to a brutal soldiery for the indulgence of their lust. The commanding general from his headquarters, announces to his insolent followers that they are at liberty to treat as women of the town the wives, the mothers, and the daughters of our citizens, if by word, gesture, or movement any contempt is indicated for their persons or insult offered to their presents. Of that nature of the movement and meaning of the look these vagabond refuse of the northern states are to be the judges.

What else than contempt and abhorrence can the women of New Orleans feel or exhibit for these officers and soldiers of the United States? The spontaneous impulse of their hearts must appear involuntary upon their countenances and thus constitute the crime for which the general of those soldiers adjudges the punishment of rape and brutalized passion.

History records instances of cities sacked and inhuman atrocities committed upon the women of a conquered town, but in no instance in modern times, at least without the brutal ravishers suffering condign punishment from the hands of their own commanders. It was reserved for a Federal general to invite his soldiers to the perpetration of outrages at the mention of which the blood recoils in horror— to quicken the impulses of their sensual instincts by the suggestion of transparent excuses for their gratification, and to add to an infamy already well merited these crowding titles of a panderer to lust and a desecrator of virtue. . . .

Its inhabitants must arm and strike, or the insolent victors will offer this outrage to your wives, your sisters, and your daughters. . . . Organize, then, quickly and efficiently. If your enemy attempt[s] to proceed into the interior let his pathway be marked by his blood. It is your homes that you have to defend. It is the jewel of your hearths—the chastity of your women—you have to guard. Let that thought animate your breasts, nerve your arms, quicken your energies, and inspire your resolution. Strike home to the heart of your foe the blow that rids your country of his presence. If need be let his blood moisten your own grave. It will rise up before your children as a perpetual memento of a race whom it will teach to hate now and evermore.

British Prime Minister Palmerston before the House of Commons

Sir, having been appealed to as I have been by my hon. Friend, I am quite prepared to say that I think no man could have read the proclamation to which our attention has been drawn without a feeling of the deepest indignation. . . . Sir, an Englishman must blush to think that such an act has been committed by one belonging to the Anglo-Saxon race. If it had come from some man belonging to a barbarous race that was not within the pale of civilization, one might have regretted it, but might not have been surprised; but that such an order should have been promulgated by a soldier —by one who has raised himself to the rank of General—is a subject undoubtedly of not less astonishment than pain. Sir, I cannot bring myself to believe but that the Government of the United States, when they had notice of this order, must of their own accord have stamped it with their censure and condemnation.

Proclamation of Jefferson Davis December 23, 1862

And whereas an addition to the tacit admission resulting from the above refusal to answer, I have received evidence fully establishing the truth of the fact that the said William B. Mumford, a citizen of this Confederacy, was actually and publicly executed in cold blood by hanging after the occupation of the city of New Orleans by the forces under the command of General Benjamin F. Butler, when said Mumford was an unresisting and non-combatant captive . . .

Now, therefore, I Jefferson Davis, President of the Confederate States of America, and in their name, do pronounce and declare the said Benjamin F. Butler to be a felon deserving of capital punishment. I do order that he be no longer considered or treated simply as a public enemy of the Confederate States of America, but as an outlaw and common enemy of mankind, and that in the event of his capture the officer in command of the capturing forces do cause him to be immediately executed by hanging; and I do further order that no commissioned officer of the United States taken captive shall be released on parole before exchange until the said Butler shall have met with due punishment for his crimes.

And whereas the hostilities waged against this Confederacy by the forces of the United States under the command of said Benjamin F. Butler have borne no resemblance to such warfare as is alone permissible by the rules of international law or the usages of civilization, but have been characterized by repeated atrocities and outrages, among the large number of which the following may be cited as examples:

. . . The soldiers of the United States have been invited and encouraged by general orders to insult and outrage the wives, the mothers, and the sisters of our citizens. . . .

Egress from the city has been refused to those whose fortitude withstood the test, even to lone and aged women and to helpless children; and after being ejected from their homes and robbed of their property they have been left to starve in the streets or subsist on charity.

. . . And, finally, the African slaves have not only been excited to insurrection by every license and encouragement, but numbers of them have actually been armed for a servile war—a war in its nature far exceeding in horrors the most merciless atrocities of the savages.

Questions to Consider:

1. *Was Butler justified in issuing his order?*
2. *What did the reaction of Southerners to Butler's order say about the role of women in Southern society?*
3. *In what ways did Butler become a problem for Lincoln, especially diplomatically?*

Sources:

1. Benjamin F. Butler, *Autobiography and Personal Reminiscences of Major-General Benjamin F. Butler: Butler's Book* (Boston: A. M. Thayer & Co., 1892), 414–19.

2. United States War Department, *The War of the Rebellion: A Compilation of the Official Records of the Union and Confederate Armies.* ser. 1, vol. 15 (Washington, DC: 1886), 426.

3. War Department, *The War of the Rebellion*, 743–44.

4. 167 Parl. Deb. (3d ser.) (1862) cols. 611–17. Contains Parliamentary information licensed under the Open Parliament Licence v3.0.

5. War Department, *The War of the Rebellion*, 906–7.

1862–1863:
Sarah Morgan and Baton Rouge during the Civil War

Like many other well-to-do women left behind on the home front while their menfolk went off to fight, Sarah Morgan dealt with stress and frustration—and the break from usual routines—by keeping a diary from 1862 until 1865. Sarah was the seventh child of Judge Thomas Gibbes Morgan and Sarah Hunt Fowler Morgan. The family lived for a time in New Orleans, but in 1850 they moved to Baton Rouge, where Thomas Morgan served as a district attorney and later a district judge. Though her father opposed secession he supported the state once it seceded. Sarah's father died in 1861, but her mother's loyalty to the Confederate cause remained steadfast. Three of the Morgan sons entered the Confederate military, and two died of disease before the war ended. However, the Morgan family was divided in its loyalties, with some relatives siding with the Union. This gave Sarah a more even-handed view of the Union occupying forces in 1862 than most other women who remained on the home front while the men went off to fight.

The Union's capture of both New Orleans and Baton Rouge were uncontested, and the cities remained intact (and generally safe) as a result, which allowed the Morgans and many other families now dominated by women to remain in place, too. The peace was broken, however, in August 1862 when Confederate troops sought to reclaim the capital. The Morgans, like thousands of other women in the Confederacy, became refugees, moving from one place to another. Friends brought them news that federal forces had retaken the city and ransacked their home. In January 1863, they learned that it had been confiscated and had become the residence of a Union colonel and his wife. This was a devastating blow to the Morgan family. Their furniture and family treasures slipped into northern hands, and their slaves headed for Union lines. They never returned to Baton Rouge, and Sarah's hatred of the Yankees lasted for the rest of her life.

Excerpts from Sarah Morgan's Diary

May 9, 1862: Our lawful (?) owners have at last arrived. About sunset, day before yesterday, the *Iroquois* [a ship] anchored here, and a graceful young Federal stepped ashore, carrying a Yankee flag over his shoulder, and asked the way to the Mayor's office. I like the style! If we girls of Baton Rouge had been at the landing instead of the men, that Yankee should never have insulted us by flying his flag in our faces! We would have opposed his landing except under a flag of truce; but the men let him alone . . .

Last evening came the demand: the town must be surrendered immediately: the federal flag Must be raised, they would grant us the same terms they granted to New Orleans. Jolly terms those were! . . .

"All devices, signs, and flags of the Confederacy shall be suppressed." So says Picayune Butler [the commander of federal forces in Louisiana, a derogatory nickname given to him because he was short]. *Good.* I devote all my red, white, and blue silk to the manufacture of Confederate flags. As soon as one is confiscated, I make another, until my ribbon is exhausted, when I will sport a duster emblazoned in high colors, "Hurra! For the Bonny blue flag!" Henceforth, I wear one pinned to my bosom—not a duster, but a little flag—the man who says take it off will have to pull it off for himself; the man who dares attempt it—well! A pistol in my pocket fills up the gap. I am capable, too.

This is a dreadful war to make even the hearts of women so bitter! I hardly know myself these last few weeks. I, who have such a horror of bloodshed, consider even killing in self-defense murder, who cannot wish them the slightest evil, whose only prayer is to have them sent back in peace to their own country,—*I* talk of killing them! For what else do I wear a pistol and carving-knife? I am afraid I *will* try them on the first one who says an insolent word to me. . . . O! if I was only a man! Then I could don the breeches, and slay them with a will! If some few Southern women were in the ranks, they could set the men an example they would not blush to follow. Pshaw! There are *no* women here! We are *all* men! . . .

May 11th . . . I was not ashamed of the flag of my country—I proved that by never attempting to remove it in spite of my mortification—but I was ashamed of my position, for these are evidently gentlemen, not the Billy Wilson's crew we were threatened with. Fine, noble looking men they were, showing refinement and gentlemanly bearing in every motion. One cannot help but admire such foes! They set us an example worthy of our imitation, & one we would be benefitted by following. They come as visitors, without either pretentions to superiority, or the insolence of conquerors; they walk quietly their way, offering no annoyance to the citizens, though they themselves are stared at most unmercifully, and pursued by crowds of ragged little boys, while even men gape at them with open mouths. They prove themselves gentlemen, while many of our citizens have proved themselves boors, and I admire them for their conduct. With a conviction that I had allowed myself to be influenced by bigoted, narrow-minded people, in believing them to be unworthy of respect or regard, I came home wonderfully changed in all my newly acquired sentiments, resolved never more to wound their feelings, who were so careful of ours, by such unnecessary display. And I hung my flag on the parlor mantle there to wave, if it will, in the shades of private life; but to make a show, make me conspicuous and ill at ease, as I was yesterday—Never again! . . .

May 14th . . . was never a secessionist, for I quietly adopted father's views on political subjects, with out meddling with them; but even father went over with his state, and when so many outrages were committed by the fanatical leaders of the North, though he regretted the Union, said "Fight to the death for our liberty." I say so too. I would want to fight until we win the cause so many have died for. I don't believe in Secession, but I do in Liberty. I want the South to conquer, dictate its own terms, and go back to the Union, for I believe that apart, inevitable ruin awaits both. . . .

[Upon arriving back in Baton Rouge after a short flight, they discovered the house in disarray and the servants gone.]

June 1st . . . What a day I have had! Here mother and I are alone, not a servant on the lot. We will sleep here tonight, and I know she will be too nervous to let me sleep. The dirt and confusion was extraordinary in the house. I could not stand it, so I applied myself to making it better. I actually swept two whole rooms! I ruined my hands at gardening, so it made no difference. . . . I discovered I could empty a dirty hearth, dust, move heavy weights, make myself generally useful and dirty, and all this is thanks to the Yankees! . . .

June 8th, Sunday. These people mean to kill us with kindness. There is such a thing as being too kind. Yesterday General Williams sent a barrel of flour to mother accompanied by a note begging her to accept it "in consideration of the present condition of the circulating currency," and the intention was so kind, the way it was done so delicate, that there was no refusing it. I had to write her thanks, and got in a violent fit of the trembles at the idea of writing to a stranger. . . . And to think that it is out of our power to prove them our appreciation of the kindness we have universally met with! . . .

June 16th, Monday. . . . In my opinion, the Southern women, and some few of the men, have disgraced themselves by their rude, ill mannered behavior in many instances. I insist, that if the valor and chivalry of our men cannot save our country, I would rather have it conquered by a brave race, than owe its liberty to the Billingsgate oratory and demonstrations of some of these "ladies." If the women have the upper hand then, as they have now, I would not like to live in a country governed by such tongues.

Do I consider the female who could spit in a gentleman's face merely because he wore United States buttons, as a fit associate for me? Lieut. Biddle assured me he did not pass a street in New Orleans without being most grossly insulted by ladies. It was a friend of his into whose face a lady spit as he walked quietly by without looking at her. . . . "Loud" women, what a contempt I have for you! How I despise your vulgarity!

Some of these Ultra-Secessionists evidently very recently from "down East" who think themselves obliged to "kick up their heels over the Bonny blue flag" as Brother describes female patriotism, shriek out "What! See those vile Northerners pass patiently? No true Southerner could see it without rage!

I could kill them! I hate them with all my soul, the murderers, liars, thieves, rascals! You are no Southerner if you do not hate them as much as I!" Ah ça! A true blue Yankee tell me that I, born and bred here, am no Southerner! . . .

This war has brought out wicked, malignant feelings that I did not believe could dwell in woman's heart. . . .

Sunday, January 4th [1863]. One just from Baton Rouge tells us that my presentiment about our house is verified; Yankees do inhabit it, a Yankee colonel and his wife. . . . And a stranger and a Yankee occupies our father's place at the table where he presided for thirty-one years. "What a fall was there, my country!". . . Give the devil his due. Bless Yankees for one thing; they say they tried hard to save our State House.

Questions to Consider:

1. *Do you see any nascent feminist sentiments in these excerpts? Explain.*
2. *In what ways did the women resist the Yankee occupiers?*
3. *Did Sarah find the new-to-her task of housework empowering, liberating, exhausting, or something else? Explain.*

Source:

Sarah Morgan Dawson, *A Confederate Girl's Diary* (Boston: Houghton Mifflin, 1913).

1865:
A Sugar Planter and the End of the Civil War

One of the best examples of families divided by the Civil War was the Palfrey family. Originally from Massachusetts, John Palfrey (1768–1843) settled in Louisiana during the territorial period with four of his sons and became a sugar planter in St. Mary Parish. His son William became a sugar planter as well. In 1860 he owned 320 enslaved people, making him the twenty-ninth largest slaveholder in the state. The eldest Palfrey son, John Gorham, remained in Boston to continue his education. John Gorham then embarked on a distinguished career as a minister, editor, historian, and dean of the Harvard Divinity School. In the 1840s he served one term in Congress as an anti-slavery Whig, then became a Free Soil Party politician before joining the Republicans. William wrote this letter in response to his brother's offer in May of a $2,000 loan to help him recover financially from the war. William Palfrey died in 1868.

William Palfrey's Letter to his Brother John, June 29, 1865

Bayou Cypre Mort,
Parish of St. Mary, La. June 29, 1865

My dear Brother,

I rec'd. on yesterday your very brief note of the 29th. Ulto., in which you seem to hesitate to "approach me."—Your wife has, I presume, felt the same hesitation, as you abstain from giving any account of her, or conveying any message from her—You also express a doubt as to whether I might be willing "to meet you in friendship," pointing out the course you wish one to pursue, in case your doubts are well founded—namely that of "silence."—

I beg, my dear brother, you will dismiss from your mind, these doubts & misgivings.—My breast was never the abode, for any length of time, of hateful feelings towards any one; and now age & recent severe misfortunes certainly can find no place there.—However antagonistic our positions are in regard to the public topics of the day, however different have been the results of these positions to you & to me, . . . I feel that we are still brothers, & while your abolition principles and chiefly your *public action* upon them, have reflected discredit not only upon my character, but likewise the memory of your father, still, if the expression is admissible, I forgive you with all my heart.—I am convinced that your note is not dictated by the desire to taunt me or that it is the expression of exultation & triumph, but written from a feeling of kindness.—As such I received & reciprocate it.—

I have been one of the severest sufferers by this calamitous war.—A war that I did my utmost in a humble way to prevent.—In 1860 I was an unsuccessful candidate in this Parish for the Convention (which passed the Ordinance of Secession) on the Union or Cooperation Ticket, & did all I could by public speaking & writing & by private persuasion to check the onward course of disunion, for which exertions I was lampooned & abused very bountifully.—My efforts were unavailing & I have suffered with the rest. . . .

In attending upon them [slaves affected by typhoid fever and other diseases during the war], which I did sedulously, I caught the infection of typhoid fever myself, was confined to my bed with it upwards of two months, & was near adding another grave to the number.— In the mean time, I have been spending my means previously acquired, in supplying the wants of these negros and my family, as well as others who needed and were entitled to my assistance, without any revenue worth speaking of—So that I have been going down hill pretty fast, with present prospect of soon reaching the bottom.—And my case is no worse than that of very many others. . . .

And now let me ask, who has been benefitted by all this: The South has been destroyed, but has the North gained any thing?—Have the unfortunate creatures, whose condition it has been the pretext to improve, have they gained by it? Let their present destitute squalid condition answer that question.—Wandering about in rags & starvation, without employment, with idle & vicious habits gaining on them more & more, with no one to look to for care & attention when sick, sustaining a precarious existence in a multitude of cases by theft alone they are disappearing rapidly—In the mean time the soil deprived of its former labor, is returning to the condition of a desert. . . .

They [his former slaves] have remained together & behaved remarkably well, compared to others & considering the temptations that were placed before them.—they are still working along under my direction managing to raise enough to eat, which is all that can be expected under the present circumstances.—From present appearances they will soon be obliged to disperse & seek their own support.— In the dilapidated condition of my plantation, it could not be put in order to produce a revenue under 4 years, (and then a precarious one) & paying wages to these people in the interval & restoring the buildings & fences would be running me deeply in debt.—Such is the effect of the present proposed system.—Instead of giving prosperity, freedom & happiness to these people [his former slaves] it will produce privation & distraction, with a sudden *disruption* of *family ties*, the Banquo's ghost of Abolitionism. . . .

[T]hese ties have subsisted through successive issues or generations under our father & myself since the year 1810, and I have done much & successfully to keep them together.—It has been a matter of pride to me and I believe of much happiness to themselves. . . . Such has been my course towards these people, and it remains to be seen whether their comfort or happiness will be increased by the change which is in progress.—Many times have I, at my old home, without any companion, my children absent for their education or following their own pursuits, sat listening to their noisy mirth, their merry shouts, and "the loud laugh that spoke the jocund mind," while I was endeavoring in vain to obtain entertainment from some book, and envying what really appeared to me their happier social condition. . . .

I am subject to a great deal of fatigue, being obliged to travel back & forth between my family & the place I am cultivating, a distance of about 20 miles & frequently on horseback, exposed to hot sun & heavy showers of rain.— but my physical exertions do not exhaust me so much as the moral discouragement, the constant sinking of the heart which always attends me when I think of what may be the fate of my wife & the little ones when I shall be called away, which event in the ordinary course of nature, cannot now be far off. . . .

It is hard, very hard, my dear brother, now to be reduced to poverty & privation, at a period of life when I might properly look for quiet & tranquility.—

I feel that I am excusable in indulging a disposition to rebuke those mischievous & fanatical theories of abolitionism on the one hand & fire eating secessionism on the other, which combined, have brought all this calamity to my country & myself.—

I thank you sincerely for your considerate offer in relation to a remittance of funds.—but I shall not be under the necessity of availing myself of it.— With our present economical habits & system, I can eke out my resources awhile longer, when perhaps "something may turn up,"—and when it comes to the worst, we will rely in that Friend who suffers not a sparrow to fall to the ground, without his Divine permission.—

And now farewell my brother, —When you sit down to a full & dainty meal or lay your head on your soft & downy pillow, (long may these comforts be yours) do not let your thoughts revert to the condition of those who are reduced to these cruel events to the slender crust and the hard couch of poverty. Shut your eyes & close your recollections to the slow, snake like progress with which these fiendish theories have crept to their final accomplishment, & then you will sleep the sounder, and eat with a better appetite.—

Ever, your affectionate brother,

W. T. Palfrey.—

Question to Consider:

1. *How did the antebellum ideal of paternalism still affect Palfrey's attitudes toward his former slaves after the war?*

Source:

Frank Otto Gattell, "The Slaveholder and the Abolitionist: Binding up a Family's Wounds," *Journal of Southern History* vol. 27, no. 3 (Aug. 1961): pp. 368–391.

1866:
The New Orleans Massacre

The first major incident of violence in Reconstruction-era Louisiana was the New Orleans Massacre on July 30, 1866. Its origins lay in the most contentious issue of Reconstruction, the rights of African Americans in a post-slavery America. The 1864 constitution drafted in Union-controlled New Orleans abolished slavery but did not provide voting rights for former slaves and free persons of color. Though initially opposed to black suffrage, Governor James Madison Wells warmed up to the idea by 1866 to bolster his political fortunes in his battles against the legislature, dominated by ex-Confederates thanks to President Andrew Johnson's lenient policies toward former rebels. Wells gave his support to a plan backed by advocates of black suffrage to call the 1864 constitutional convention back into session to add voting rights to the constitution. Tensions in the city were high. The recently elected mayor had served in the same capacity when it was a Confederate city, and the police force now included many former Confederate soldiers. The state's Democrats also viewed the reconvened convention as illegal. The reconvened convention met at the Mechanics' Institute off Canal Street, the site of the Roosevelt Hotel today, but recessed in the early afternoon for a lack of a quorum. At the same time, a march of African Americans supporting voting rights ended at the Institute, where a mob of whites were waiting. The mob attacked the marchers in the street and followed some of them into the building. Many of the police, instead of restoring order, joined the mob in attacking men inside and outside the Institute, including delegates. General Philip Sheridan, in a message sent three days later to General Grant, called it "an absolute massacre." Though the exact numbers are not certain, officials put the casualty toll as 38 dead, 146 wounded, including 34 African Americans dead and 119 wounded. The political ramifications of the massacre were substantial. Along with an earlier race riot in Memphis, the northern press and public laid blame on President Johnson, and the Radical wing of the Republican Party scored a decisive victory in that fall's midterm elections.

Letter of Cyrus Hamlin to Hannibal Hamlin August 19, 1866

I commenced to write you a letter the day after the Riot here but I felt the effect of it so much that I did not finish it & what I wrote concluded to destroy.

I have seen death on the battlefield but time will erase the effects of that, the wholesale slaughter & the little regard paid to human life I witnessed here on the 30 of July I shall never forget. I done all I could to persuade them not to call this Convention in [the] manner it was done. I tried to have it delayed but to no purpose. I did not agree with them although I wished the same result they were endeavoring to accomplish. . . .

I thought there would be trouble so I did not go near the Institute but remained in the office. . . . I could distinctly hear the firing & see the people run as they came onto Canal St. I saw men & boys walking with pistols & I saw the Police retire after discharging their revolvers. I saw a Policeman trip a Negro up in Canal St. about a square from where I was & shot him twice killing him instantly. I saw a brute then crush his head by throwing a stone on it. This is not more fiendish than other things which have been related to me by those who saw them.

. . . The streets might have been cleared by fifty [policemen] by forming a line & marching to the crowd which would dispersed it but this was not their object. They desired to suppress the Convention therefore they encouraged & aided to get up the Riot, as they were unable to accomplish their desire except in this way.

Mayor Monroe made no secrecy that it was required that men should have served in the Rebel army to obtain a place on the Police force.

The Police were many of them drunk & made their toasts how many they had killed, that they had got their revenge on the d____ Yankee.

Dr. Dostie [one of the convention leaders] was killed by a Policeman after he was in the hands of the Police. Ex-gov Hahn & [former sheriff] Shaw were wounded after the Police had taken charge of them by the good law abiding citizens as the Press here endeavors to explain it.

Testimony of Stephen S. Fish, *Report of the Select Committee on the New Orleans Riots*, 1867

There were but few of us there then, and we felt that there was no use in attempting to drive them out; there were not enough of us, and we were not armed. I thought I would choose the lesser evil; there was a possibility of escaping if I got out, but there was none inside. At the door I met a young man, a stranger to me. . . . I asked him if he would arrest me and secure me from personal violence. I will state here, what I told him at the time, that I had taken no part in the resistance, or in driving the police out of the hall; that I had been perfectly passive, except urging those inside to keep quiet. When I asked this man for protection, to arrest me, he said, with an oath, "No, sir: none of you can get out here alive." He had a club, formed apparently of a rough piece of wood three inches wide, one inch thick, and three feet long. As I attempted to run by him he struck at me with this board, but I dodged him. Going through the door I met a policeman in uniform; I offered myself to him, but he would not arrest me. Going down stairs I passed two other policemen. At the time I passed them they had a Negro in charge, and were knocking him down the stairs with their policemen's clubs, pounding him over the head, he at the same time begging that they would spare him. . . . As I arrived on the second floor, I was seized by two citizens. One of them was a "rough"—one of the low order of Irishmen, I should think; the other was what appeared to be one of the chivalry—a well-dressed person, of middle age. They both seized me by the collar and commenced striking me with their fists in the face. I shook them off without any serious injury, at least to myself, and went on. Going out the door I met on the steps another policeman, I offered myself to him. I had a large white handkerchief in my hand, and held it up. . . . I asked him to arrest me and protect me. His reply was, "Yes, damn you, I will give you protection," drawing out a large revolver, bright and new. . . . He drew that up and knocked me down on the landing, and stunned me for the time being. . . . I gathered myself up as well as I could and staggered to another policeman in the middle of the street, and asked him, as well as I could, being considerably confused by the effects of the blow I had received, but I had not quite got to him, when he drew up his revolver and shot at me. I was not more than three or four feet from him at the time, but his ball did not take effect. I darted from him, and started towards Carondelet Street. There were a great many people, and though my head was whirling all this time I could hear the firing as though it was an irregular musketry firing. . . . I got half way to Common Street before any policeman would arrest me and take me in charge. . . . He told me that he was an extra policeman that came out when the alarm was given. He went a little way, as far as Common Street; the crowd thickened there, and appeared to be very threatening, calling out "Kill the Yankee nigger," "Shoot the nigger son of a bitch," "There goes another nigger," "There goes another damned Yankee." Such expressions as these I heard, and a great many others of like import. This policeman . . . called another to his assistance, and the two together seemed to make great exertions to keep the crowd off till I got to the police station.

"President Johnson's Responsibility"
New York Tribune, August 1, 1866

If any doubt existed as to President Johnson's connection with the massacre in New Orleans, it will be removed by reading his dispatch to Attorney-General Herron of Louisiana. This dispatch, written with the knowledge that loyal citizens of the United States were dying from wounds received by a Rebel mob, assumes the full responsibility of the deed. The policy that prompted Mayor Monroe and his followers found its inspiration in Washington. . . .

This is a small point in our argument, but it shows the tendency of the President. His dispatch recognizes a usurpation, and proceeds to defend the massacre. All "unlawful assemblies" must be suppressed. Well, this particular assembly was suppressed—and very effectually—for its leaders were murdered, and those who escaped murder are either lying in the prison or the hospital. According to the President, this Convention had not "obtained the consent of the people of the State." If it at all entered into our argument we might ask him what right had the President to determine this fact? Gov. Wells thought the Convention was legal, and, as he is Governor, what right has President Johnson with it? Who gives the President of the United States the power to traverse the decision of a State Executive, or to decide upon the competency of a State Convention? . . . According to the President's own theory—the theory that Louisiana is a sovereign State and her officers competent to govern it—he is guilty of the most flagrant assumption of executive power. . . .

It is folly to use soft phrases in speaking of this appalling crime. The policy of Andrew Johnson engendered the demon fury which has shed blood in the streets of the Crescent City. His statesmanship has once more raised Rebel flags in New Orleans. His construction of Presidential duty has led him to commit an act of direct usurpation in Louisiana. His oath to protect and defend the nation finds expression in the unavenged assassination of men whose loyalty was as conspicuous and self-denying and sorely tried as his own. All that we have gained by the war comes to this: that in Louisiana an illustrious General of the Union army is compelled to accept the orders of a notorious punished Rebel. The time has come for the people to speak—and let it be in tones so distinct and unmistakable that even Andrew Johnson will not dare to disobey the warning.

Speech of President Andrew Johnson St. Louis, September 8, 1866

The time has come when it seems to me that all ought to be prepared for peace—the rebellion being suppressed, and the shedding of blood being stopped, the sacrifice of life being suspended and stayed, it seems that the time has arrived when we should have peace; when the bleeding arteries should be tied up. . . .

And if you will go back—if you go back and ascertain the cause of the riot at New Orleans, perhaps you would not be so prompt in calling out New Orleans. If you will take up the riot at New Orleans and trace it back to its source, or to its immediate cause, you will find out who was responsible for the blood that was shed there.

If you will take up the riot at New Orleans and trace it back to the radical Congress you will find that the riot at New Orleans was substantially planned—if you will take up the proceedings in their caucuses you will understand that they know that a convention was to be called which was extinct, by its powers having expired; that it was said, and the intention was, that a new government was to be organized; and in the organization of that government the intention was to enfranchise one portion of the population, called the colored population, who had just been emancipated, and at the same time disfranchise white men. . . .

When you read the speeches that were made, or take up the facts you will there find that speeches were made, incendiary in their character, exciting that portion of the population, the black population, to arm themselves and prepare for the shedding of blood. You will also find that that convention did assemble in violation of law, and the intention of that convention was to supersede the recognized authorities in the State government of Louisiana, which had been recognized by the government of the United States, and every man engaged in that rebellion—in that convention. . . . —I say that he was a traitor to the Constitution of the United States, and hence you will find that another rebellion was commenced, having its origin in the radical Congress. These men were to go there, a government was to be organized, and the one in existence in Louisiana was to be superseded, set aside, and overthrown. You talk to me about New Orleans! And then the question was to come up, when they had established their government—a question of political power—which of the two governments was to be recognized; a new government, inaugurated under this defunct convention, set up in violation of law, and without the consent of the people. And then, when they had established their government, and extended universal or impartial franchise, as they called it, to this colored population, then this radical Congress was to determine that a government established on Negro votes was to be the government of Louisiana.

So much for the New Orleans riot; and there was the cause and the origin of the blood that was shed, and every drop of blood that was shed is upon their skirts, and they are responsible for it. I could trace this thing a little closer, but I will not do it here tonight. But when you talk about New Orleans, and talk about the causes and consequences that resulted from the proceedings of that kind, perhaps, as I have been introduced here, and you have provoked questions of this kind, though it don't provoke me, I will tell you a few wholesome things that have been done by this radical Congress.

Questions to Consider:

1. *How does President Johnson lay blame for the massacre? The northern press?*
2. *What do accounts of the violence say about the bitterness of the pro-Confederate population of New Orleans?*

Sources:

1. Letter of Cyrus Hamlin to Hannibal Hamlin, August 19, 1866, Hamlin Family Papers, SpC MS 0219, Box 1, Folder 17, Raymond H. Fogler Library Special Collections Department, University of Maine, Orono, Maine.

2. Select Comm. on the New Orleans Riots, *Report of the Select Committee On The New Orleans Riots*, H.R. Rep. No. 39–16, at 9 (1867).

3. Daniel Alexander Payne Murray, *The New-Orleans riot: Its official history: the dispatches of Gens. Sheridan, Grant, and Baird -- the President answered* (New York?: New York tribune?, 1866), 9–10. Daniel Murray Pamphlet Collection. Pdf. https://www.loc.gov/item/03004157/.

4. Select Comm., H.R. Rep. No. 39–16, at 24 (1867).

1868:
A Reconstruction Constitution

The Congressional, or Radical, phase of Reconstruction began with the passage of the Military Reconstruction Act in March 1867. For ten of the eleven former Confederate states, this meant ratification of the Fourteenth Amendment and the creation of new state constitutions. These constitutional conventions would include the participation of African Americans and severely restrict the participation of whites who supported the Confederacy. Louisiana's convention met in New Orleans in 1867, with fifty black delegates and forty-eight white. What they produced has been called the most radical, or most progressive, constitution in the state's history.

The Constitution of Louisiana, 1868

TITLE I—BILL OF RIGHTS

Article 1—All men are created free and equal, and have certain inalienable rights; among these are life, liberty and the pursuit of happiness. To secure these rights, governments are instituted among men, deriving their just powers from the consent of the governed.

Art. 2—All persons, without regard to race, color, or previous condition, born or naturalized in the United States, and subject to the jurisdiction thereof, and residents of this State for one year, are citizens of this State. The citizens of this State owe allegiance to the United States; and this allegiance is paramount to that which they owe to the State. They shall enjoy the same civil, political, and public rights and privileges, and be subject to the same pains and penalties.

Art. 3—There shall be neither slavery nor involuntary servitude in this State, otherwise than for the punishment of crime, whereof the party shall have been duly convicted.

Art. 4—The press shall be free; every citizen may freely speak, write and publish his sentiments on all subjects, being responsible for the abuse of this liberty.

Art. 5—The right of the people peaceably to assemble and petition the Government, or any department thereof, shall never be abridged.

Art. 6—Prosecutions shall be by indictment or information. The accused shall be entitled to a speedy public trial by an impartial jury of the parish in which the offence was committed, unless the venue be changed. He shall not be compelled to give evidence against himself; he shall have the right of being heard by himself or counsel; he shall have the right of meeting the witnesses face to face, and shall have compulsory process for obtaining witnesses in his favor. He shall not be tried twice for the same offense.

Art. 7—All persons shall be bailable by sufficient securities, unless for capital offenses where the proof is evident, or the presumption great, or unless after conviction, for any crime or offense punishable with death or imprisonment at hard labor. The privilege of the writ of *habeas corpus* shall not be suspended.

Art. 8—Excessive bail shall not be required; excessive fines shall not be imposed; nor cruel or unusual punishments inflicted.

Art. 9—The right of the people to be secure in their persons, houses, papers and effects, against unreasonable searches and seizures, shall not be violated; and no warrant shall issue but upon probable cause, supported by oath or affirmation, and particularly describing the place to be searched, or the person or things to be seized.

Art. 10—All courts shall be open; and every person for injury done him in his land, goods, persons or reputation, shall have adequate remedy by due process of law, and justice administered without denial or unreasonable delay.

Art. 11—No law shall be passed fixing the price of manual labor.

Art. 12—Every person has the natural right to worship God according to the dictates of his conscience. No religious test shall be required as a qualification for office.

Art. 13—All persons shall enjoy equal rights and privileges upon any conveyance of a public character; and all places of business, or of public resort, or for which a license is required by either State, parish or municipal authority, shall be deemed places of a public character, and shall be opened to the accommodation and patronage of all persons, without distinction or discrimination on account of race or color.

TITLE VI.—GENERAL PROVISIONS . . .

Art. 99—The following persons shall be prohibited from voting and holding any office: All persons who shall have been convicted of treason, perjury, forgery, bribery, or other crimes punishable in the penitentiary, and persons under interdiction. All persons who are estopped from claiming the right of suffrage, by abjuring their allegiance to the United States Government, or by notoriously levying war against it, or adhering to its enemies, giving them aid and comfort, but who have not expatriated themselves, nor have been convicted of any of the crimes mentioned in the first paragraph of this article, are hereby restored to the said right, except the following: Those who held office, civil or military, for one year or more, under the organization styled "the Confederate States of America;" those who registered themselves as enemies of the United States; those who acted as leaders of guerrilla bands during the late rebellion; those who, in advocacy of treason, wrote or published newspaper articles or preached sermons during the late rebellion; and those who voted for and signed an ordinance of secession in any State. No person included in these exceptions shall either vote or hold office until he shall have relieved himself by voluntarily writing and signing a certificate setting forth that he acknowledges the late rebellion to have been morally and politically wrong, and that he regrets any aid and comfort he may have given it; and he shall file the certificate in the office of the Secretary of State, and it shall be published in the official journal. *Provided*, That no person who, prior to the first of January eighteen hundred and sixty-eight, favored the execution of the laws of the United States, popularly known as the Reconstruction Acts of Congress, and openly and actively assisted the loyal men of the State in their efforts to restore Louisiana to her position in the Union, shall be held to be included among those herein excepted. . . .

Art. 100—Members of the General Assembly, and all other officers, before they enter upon the duties of their offices shall take the following oath or affirmation: "I, (A. B.), do solemnly swear (or affirm) that I accept the civil and political equality of all men, and agree not to attempt to deprive any person or persons, on account of race, color, or previous condition, of any political or civil right, privilege, or immunity enjoyed by any other class of men; that I will support the Constitution and laws of the United States, and the Constitution and laws of this State, and that I will faithfully and impartially discharge and perform all the duties incumbent on me as—according to the best of my ability and understanding. So help me God."...

Art. 128—Contracts for the sale of persons are null and void; and shall not be enforced by the courts of this State . . .

TITLE VII—PUBLIC EDUCATION

Art. 135—The General Assembly shall establish at least one free public school in every parish throughout the State, and shall provide for its support by taxation and otherwise. All children of this State between the ages of six (6) and twenty-one (21) shall be admitted to the public schools or other institutions of learning sustained or established by the State in common without distinction of race, color, or previous condition. There shall be no separate schools or institutions of learning established exclusively for any race by the State of Louisiana.

Questions to Consider:

1. *Why was it important for the framers of the 1868 constitution to begin it with a bill of rights?*

2. *Why did the vision for Louisiana laid out in the constitution ultimately prove unattainable?*

Source:

Constitution adopted by the State Constitutional Convention of the State of Louisiana, March 7, 1868 (New Orleans: New Orleans *Republican*, 1868), 3–4, 14–17.

1868:
Elections and Violence

The 1868 elections marked the beginning of a terror campaign by Democrats and former Confederates to wrest political control of the state from the Republicans and to return the freedmen and freedwomen to subordinate status. The instruments of the campaign were a variety of secret terror organizations modeled on the Ku Klux Klan. The state placed the official death toll at 784, but later estimates judged the number to be over 1,000. One of the most brazen acts of violence was the murders in Franklin of Judge Valentine Chase and Sheriff Henry H. Pope of St. Mary Parish. Chase was originally from Ohio but had settled in the parish before the Civil War and was a Unionist. Pope was Lieutenant Colonel of the 33rd Illinois Regiment and remained in Louisiana once the war ended. The extent of the violence in Louisiana in 1868 attracted the attention of the Republican-controlled Congress, and a special House committee investigated. The committee called a wide range of individuals to give testimony while it met in New Orleans in the late spring and early summer of 1868. One of these individuals was John J. Moore. Born a slave in South Carolina and brought to Louisiana as a boy in the 1840s, Moore secured his freedom by running away to Union lines during the war and then became a key Republican organizer in St. Mary Parish.

Testimony of John J. Moore

Q. What was the condition of things in St. Mary's Parish before the last election?

A. We had a very good time at the April election in 1868. I was a supervisor at one of the polls. We had first-rate times. There was no disturbance. At the last election I was not in Franklin. I was run away there before the election came on. I went to Cypremort, to hold a mass meeting, on the 17th of October last, and on that night there was some murdering done in Franklin. The sheriff of the parish and the judge were killed. Their names were Valentine Chase and Henry H. Pope. I was one of the members of the Republican executive committee of the parish, and had to attend to almost all the business of the parish. I went out to fulfill an appointment at Cypremort, and before going I told them that they had better not stay there. I had heard the talk around that there was an intention to kill them, and all the leaders of the Republican party. On the night of the 16th of October I went and told Mr. Pope not to stay there next day, because there was going to be a Democratic procession, and I thought he stood in danger. He said he did not think that there was any danger, but I knew that there was. I said that there could not be so much smoke without some fire. I told him that I would see Mr. Chase, anyhow, because I thought I could make him believe it. I went into the tavern and saw Mr. Chase, and talked with him. He said that he thought there would be no trouble. I told him that there would be, because the people had told me several time that there was an intention to kill these men, that it was intended to kill off all the white Republicans and all the Republican negroes who could read or write, or do any kind of business. I read and write a little—enough to lead them. . . . He told me he didn't think that there was any danger; that these fellows were just blowing around and trying to scare him; but that he didn't come there to be scared, and that he intended to go right forward and attend to his business. I told him that was very good, but that a coward sometimes lived longer than a brave man, and that I was a coward, and was going to get out of that before the day, and that nobody would know where I went. I went to Cypremort on the 17th, to a mass meeting. In the evening some of the party wanted me to return to Franklin, but I declined doing so. That was the day of the murder. They murdered Chase and Pope that night. . . .

Q. Did you go back to Franklin before the election?—

A. I attempted to go back. I got off the boat a few miles from Franklin at Mr. Cleveland's plantation. I wanted to get to Franklin to distribute tickets among my party, but a man told me on the boat that he had heard some white people say that Jack Moore was going to Franklin, and he was sorry for it because they were going to kill him. I therefore got off at Mr. Cleveland's plantation and staid [*sic*] there. I wasn't there more than an hour or an hour and a quarter before three white men, with revolvers, stepped right up the door of the colored man's house where I was stopping, and said, "Fred, ain't Jack Moore here?" I jumped up from beside the door where I was sitting, and had to cross right in front of them to get under the bed. It was at night, and the lamp was burning in the house. The men did not see me; I saw them and their revolvers. . . .

Q. Do you not think it was your dark color that saved you from being seen?—

A. You can see a dark object as well as a white one. I got under the bed, but I was so scared that I could not stay there. One of the men said, "Come here, Fred, we want to talk to you, and we want you to tell the truth." "No massa," said he, "he is not." Said the man, "They tell us at Franklin that they put him off at Cleveland's plantation, and we must get him to-night. He has got up a great excitement, and has got the negroes so that there is no doing anything with them, and so we are going to put him out of the way to-night, God damn him." I was so scared that I thought I wasn't safe under the bed, so I got up over a woman who was lying in front of the bed and got behind her. I broke one bar down, and raised up the mattress and got under the mattress. I asked the woman to get up on top of me, but she was so scared she wouldn't do it. I was too scared to stay there; I thought I looked too big under the mattress, and that they would see me if they came in. They were right behind the house and I heard every word they said. I got out on the floor, jumped up, and caught a joist and got up on the loft right over the bed, and there I lay. Fred was the president of the club on Mr. Cleveland's plantation; I had appointed him president and they knew it very well. I heard one of these white men say to Fred, "Now, Fred, there is but one way that you niggers can live here with us, and that is to let politics die. Leave them alone; you cannot live with us, and live and work and vote against our interests. All that you get and all that you have comes from us and by us; and now if you do not let politics alone you will all get killed here. It is white peoples' business; the business of negroes is to go into the fields and work, and we will pay you. Do we not always pay you?" "Yes, massa," said Fred. "Well," said the other, "we will always pay you, but you niggers are going voting against our interests and sinking the country. We will kill the last one of you if you don't stop it." I thought then that I had a very poor chance there. Then the white man said again, "Now will you not tell me that Jack Moore is here; we must get him to-night. Fred said "No sir, he is not here." "Well," said the other, "where did the boat land?" Fred said "The boat landed at the sugar-house, and I expect that he went right across the sugar-house lot to the public road and from there to his wife's house." He said, "Well, we will go up there and see, but I believe that he is here."... He went out and came back and said "Now they are gone; you can listen and hear them." I was too scared myself to hear them, but I ventured down then off the loft. I had a white coat which I thought was too conspicuous, and I changed it for Fred's dark coat. I went down to the bottom where there was a skiff, and crossed over to the other side of the bayou, where there was not any public road, so that I would be out of danger. . . .

Q. Were there any radical colored clubs in that parish?—

A. We had radical clubs all over the parish. I organized clubs on every third or fourth plantation.

Q. About how many had you in those clubs all over the parish?—

A. Some clubs had about sixty, and some had forty. The club at Franklin had four hundred and twenty-eight members. I was secretary of that club. . . .

Q. About how many colored radicals had you in the whole parish?—

A. Over two thousand. . . .

Q. Do you think they would have all voted the radical ticket if they had been let alone, and if there had been no killing and nothing to scare them?—

A. There was great excitement among the negroes. Some of them put on red shirts and turned democrats. I told them that they must keep perfectly cool; that it did not amount to anything at all. As to their joining the

Democratic party, I thought I knew the nature of the negro, and I thought they weren't going to stick to that party. . . . All the colored men who belonged to democratic clubs belonged to my clubs also. They just said that they would go with the Democratic party until election day, but that they intended to disappoint them on that day all over the parish. Those who did not join the Democratic party of course I depended upon, and I knew that they would vote the republican ticket. . . .

Q. Do you think that there were any Ku-Klux up there?—

A. I never saw any. I saw people in the Democratic processions carrying arms. That was something strange to me.

Q. Did not the colored people have arms too?—

A. The colored radicals had none. I would not allow it. I was at a club meeting one night when a colored man came with a pistol. I quashed him, and told him never to carry a pistol there again. I always cautioned the colored men not to carry pistols.

Q. Do colored people up there believe in the Ku-Klux?—

A. They believe that there are white people around trying to murder and to kill them. They did not believe that they were ghosts. They had too much sense for that. . . .

Q. When the colored men voted in the parish of St. Mary, did they not come to you and ask you for the ticket which you desired them to vote?—

A. Yes, sir; they did.

Q. Would you go to the trouble of explaining to every man who came and asked you for a ticket the reason why he should vote it?—

A. I did so all the time. I just occupied the best part of my time in explaining to them before the election came on, and when the election came on they had that confidence in me as to say to me, "Jack, show me a ticket, and I will vote it," and they would ask no further questions about it. They did not know how to read, and they would ask me to give them a ticket, and whatever ticket I would give them they would vote. All of them knew that they were voting for the constitution. . . .

Q. How many men of your color in the parish of St. Mary knew, when they voted for the constitution [in April 1868], what was the meaning of the word "constitution."[?—]

A. I cannot tell you that, because a good many people would be ignorant if you told them a thousand times. We organized those clubs with the intention of teaching the people what they were to vote for and what the constitution meant. We held those meetings weekly all the time, and we had men of the most influence and intelligence among our people to speak to them, and to tell them what the constitution meant. They all believed that the constitution was something which gave them equal rights before the law. Ignorant as they are, they got that idea. They believed it was something which would give them the right to be equal with all voters, and to be better than they were in former times. . . .

Q. Do the white people of that parish know the position which you occupy among the colored people as a leader?—

A. Yes, sir; they called me "the chieftain."

Questions to Consider:

1. *What was the political atmosphere like in St. Mary Parish in 1868?*
2. *How engaged were former slaves in politics during Reconstruction?*

Source:

"Louisiana Contested Elections," H.R. Miscellaneous Doc. No. 41–154, at 634–38 (1870).

1868–1893:
The Louisiana State Lottery Company

The most powerful entity in Louisiana politics immediately after Reconstruction was the infamous Louisiana State Lottery Company. The brainchild of a New York lottery syndicate, the Louisiana Lottery was a product of Reconstruction-era politics, receiving its charter from the Republican state government in 1868. For a twenty-five-year term of operation, the company would pay the state a mere $40,000 a year. With the end of Reconstruction, lottery officials quickly allied the company with the state's Democrats to ensure its survival. Their effort was so successful that the convention to write a new state constitution in 1879 enshrined the lottery charter in its final product. Despite its charitable activities and the employment of former Confederate generals to give the drawings a veneer of respectability, the lottery became synonymous with the state's Gilded Age corruption. Less than half of its revenues went to prizes; much of the rest went to profit for the syndicate and bribes to state politicians. By the end of the 1880s, reformers mobilized against the lottery and its corrupt political allies, and anti-lottery politician Francis T. Nicholls returned to the governor's mansion in 1888. Facing a steep challenge to get re-chartered in the early 1890s, the lottery offered to increase its payment to the state to over $1 million a year. But the lottery had by this time become a national political issue. Congress passed a bill in 1890 prohibiting the sale of lottery tickets through the US mail, and the US Supreme Court upheld it two years later. With over 90 percent of its tickets sold outside of Louisiana, this was the deathblow to the lottery, and it departed Louisiana to unsuccessfully revive its operations in Honduras.

Coming Relief for the Sick and Destitute

The old saying that charity begins at home is soon to be demonstrated by the fact that the Louisiana State Lottery Company designs to make a magnificent gift to the poor of this city, who are most in need of it. We learn that an agreement was signed yesterday between Gen. Beauregard, of Louisiana, and Early, of Virginia, by which the above mentioned gentlemen are to superintend a grand lottery in June, 1877, for the benefit of the Charity Hospital in New Orleans.

It is well known that of all our charitable institutions, this, as the abode of the suffering, infirm and helpless, appeals first to our feelings. Moreover, the precarious conditions of our city finances prevent those unfortunate persons from obtaining, at present, all the relief that in their distress should be granted to them. Under these circumstances our community cannot but be profoundly grateful to the Louisiana State Lottery Company, which, with its proverbial liberality in everything which tends to the good and benefit of our city, comes generously forward to minister to the wants of our sick poor.

The Louisiana State Lottery has made for itself a record that will endure. We do hope that the sums of money realized by the grand drawing in June next will be such as to make the Charity Hospital a successful and independent institution.

—*The Daily Picayune*, March 6, 1877

President Benjamin Harrison on the Louisiana Lottery July 29, 1890

The recent attempt to secure a charter from the State of North Dakota for a lottery company, the pending effort to obtain from the State of Louisiana a renewal of the charter of the Louisiana State Lottery, and the establishment of one or more lottery companies at Mexican towns near our border, have served the good purpose of calling public attention to an evil of vast proportions. If the baneful effects of lotteries were confined to the States that give the companies corporate powers and a license to conduct the business, the citizens of other States, being powerless to apply legal remedies, might clear themselves of responsibility by the use of such moral agencies as were within their reach. But the case is not so. The people of all the States are debauched and defrauded. The vast sums of money offered to the States for charters are drawn from the people of the United States, and the General Government, through its mail system, is made the effective and profitable medium of intercourse between the lottery company and its victims. . . . It would be practically impossible for these companies to exist if the public mails were once effectively closed against their advertisements and remittances. The use of the mails by these companies is a prostitution of an agency only intended to serve the purposes of a legitimate trade and a decent social intercourse.

It is not necessary, I am sure, for me to attempt to portray the robbery of the poor and the widespread corruption of public and private morals which are necessary incidents of these lottery schemes.

The national Capital has become a sub-headquarters of the Louisiana Lottery Company, and its numerous agents and attorneys are conducting here a business involving probably a larger use of the mails than that of any legitimate business enterprise in the District of Columbia. There seems to be good reason to believe that the corrupting touch of these agents has been felt by the clerks in the postal service and by some of the police officers of the District.

Severe and effective legislation should be promptly enacted to enable the Post Office Department to purge the mails of all letters, newspapers, and circulars relating to the business.

Speech of State Representative Aristide Barbin Regarding His Support of the Lottery, June 24, 1890

First—Because our State in its financial condition is unable to advance the schools as I would like to see them advanced.

Second—Because what the Company offers would help build our levees, and sustain our hospitals, asylums and other charitable institutions, which I fear otherwise would be neglected for want of means. . . .

Fourth—I vote yes because it is not taking one cent from the people of our State forcibly. If any one wishes voluntarily to pay anything towards defraying the expenses of the State by buying lottery tickets it is his own lookout.

And if the people of other States and countries wish to play at this lottery and in a manner help pay the debt of our State which is large, and which was largely contracted without our consent and by the influence of people from other States, backed by federal bayonets, I have no objections.

Another reason why I vote yes, it that most of the money played in this lottery comes not from the people of our State. Where one dollar comes from Louisiana one thousand dollars comes from other parts of the world.

The opponents of the lottery say it is immoral; if so, all those who play at it must be immoral, and I certainly have no objection that the immoral people, whether residing in our State or elsewhere, pay to build our levees, support our schools and sustain our hospitals and asylums and other charitable institution. . . .

On principle, I am opposed to lotteries or any game of chance, and hate to pay a State debt dishonestly contracted; but as we have assumed the payment of it, let us pay it as soon as possible and by all means in our power that are not dishonest. We found in the household of the Republicans who had our State government in hand, this machine by them created. Now, as I say, we have to pay these millions of dollars they have saddled us with; let us keep this wonderful machine, in order to help pay this large debt. I think we had better do that, school our children, take care of our sick, infirm and insane and build our levees, than to put on airs of morality, hand down to our children this large debt bearing interest, neglect the education of our children, abandon our sick, infirm and insane and let the waters of the great Mississippi inundate our rich lands.

We have one consolation which is, that the Republicans cannot blame us for continuing this institution, for it was invented and created by them when they had the full and entire management of our State affairs.

Speech of Murphy J. Foster to the Anti-Lottery Democratic Convention, Baton Rouge, August 7, 1890

Gentlemen of this Convention, it may be that I was in this fight so long, but somehow or other my whole soul is wrapped up in this anti-lottery cause.

I see gathered here to-day the bone and sinew of Louisiana. I see the manhood of my State and the manhood of the Democratic Party here. They have come in the interest of no man and of faction. They . . . are here in the interest of no man nor set of men; but they have come here in the interest of their loved State and in the interest of the Democratic Party of Louisiana. . . .

But, fellow-citizens, we can never do it, we can never march onward and upward, we can never enter the race with our sister States handicapped with this infernal lottery. We can never enter this contest of States unless we do it as a sovereign State, and this proposition means that the sovereignty of the State shall be sold, her political manhood shall be emasculated, the integrity of our party destroyed.

This proposition means that we, the white people of the State, must declare to the civilized and to the Christian world that we are dependent upon the turning of the wheel for the maintenance of our levees, the education of our children and the support of our charitable institutions. These, gentlemen of the convention, are the solemn responsibilities of statehood; . . . these obligations and these responsibilities are what a State should take a pride in executing, but we are asked to publish to the world that the manhood of Louisiana is unable, unwilling and incompetent to perform these sacred and these high duties. . . .

I say, gentlemen, that to me, to my mind, OF ALL THE IGNOBLE ACTS that this company has ever been guilty of, that which it did when it sent this relief boat in the guise of charity to the overflowed parishes, was the most despicable and ignoble, taking advantage of a poor, suffering people, taking advantage of their wants and of their distress, in order to win them from their allegiance to honor, and to win them from the path of rectitude to one of shame, to win them from their loyalty to their State to fealty to this gambling concern.

I say, sir, that there are some things I can forgive them for—the want of principle—getting a man here and there into trouble; getting some poor clerk to steep his soul in everlasting sin, getting some poor market girl to rob her employer, getting some poor, misguided youth to spend his money here and there; all these I might overlook, but, great God, when they strike at the manhood of my people, when they strike at the honor of my State, when they attempt to prostitute honest government to their foul ends, when they attempt to win my people by corrupt gifts, I say that sin is unpardonable.

Knowing no God, knowing no religion, knowing no people, knowing no faith or State, without a habitation, it stalks abroad in our land seeking to destroy that which we all hold dearer than life, the honor of our State, the integrity of our party and the absolute supremacy of our race.

I say to you, my friends, that if there ever be a cause, A JUST AND HOLY CAUSE, almost as holy and just, probably more so, in a moral view, than that which called you to strap on your knapsacks in '61 and face the then unknown hardships and perils of war, it is the one in which we are now engaged. Now is the time, gentlemen of the Convention, to strap on your knapsacks. I don't mean that there is any physical war, but I mean for a warfare against this monster which is seeking to undermine the citizenship of this State, to sap its honor and destroy its future prosperity; not by argument but by the insidious and dangerous workings of the almighty dollar.

Questions to Consider:

1. *What would be a pragmatic argument in favor of keeping the Lottery in operation?*
2. *How did Foster use gendered language to rally opponents of the Lottery?*

Sources:

1. "Coming Relief for the Sick and Destitute," *Daily Picayune* (New Orleans), March 6, 1877. Library of Congress.

2. "Message from the President of the United States, transmitting Letter of the Postmaster-General in regard to the use of the mails by the Louisiana Lottery Company, and Exhibit A, history of the Post-Office Department concerning lotteries." Ex. Doc. No. 51–196 (1890).

3. *Official Journal of the Proceedings of House of Representatives of the State of Louisiana at the Second Regular Session of the Third General Assembly* (Baton Rouge: *The Advocate*, 1890), 441–42.

4. *Official Report of the Proceedings of the Anti-Lottery Democratic Convention held in the hall of the House of Representatives* (New Orleans: 1890), 19–23.

1874: Opposition to Radical Reconstruction

Most white Louisianians vehemently disagreed with the mission of Radical Reconstruction, in which former slaves gained civil and political rights. They viewed Republican state government as illegitimate and considered the federal troop presence in the state as an occupying force. Not content with the clandestine violence of the Knights of the White Camellia and similar vigilante groups, in 1874 they embarked upon a new strategy to overthrow Republican control by forming the paramilitary organization known as the White League. A new wave of violence that began that year climaxed with an attempted coup against the state government in New Orleans in September, the street battle which became known as the Battle of Liberty Place. The Alexandria newspaper the *Caucasian* began publication in March 1874 and served as a catalyst for the white supremacist ethos that resulted in the White League.

From the *Caucasian* (Alexandria, LA) April 25, 1874

OUR POSITION

The almost every day's increase of the subscription list of the *Caucasian* indicates the popularity of its principles; and fearlessness with which it exposes frauds and corruptions whenever and wherever found, meets, we are assured, with public approbation. We are sometimes asked the question if the name and principles will not drive from us a large number of colored men who would vote with us, provided we would pursue a more conciliatory policy toward them. In answer to this we say, that the large mass of colored voters in this parish have been governed entirely in their political action, by a direct appeal to the prejudices of their race, and all of our persuasion, conciliation and concessions have not accomplished the slightest good. We do not propose to interfere with any of the rights of the colored man nor drive him from us. We propose to convince him by the inexorable logic of facts that his race is not capable of self-government, and to tell him truthfully, of the ruin and poverty that has been brought upon the people of both races, by his injudicious use of the ballot, by his election of corrupt white men and ignorant negroes to office, who have deceived the negro voter—plundered and oppressed the property holder and tax-payers to such an extent that there is no prosperity and contentment for either. We propose to tell them plainly that we do not believe the negro equal to the white man, in the science of government, and the offices should be filled by tax-payers, and honest intelligent men of the country who can and will do justice to both races. If Louisiana is still further to be degraded we do not wish the stain of her degradation to rest on our hands. We rely upon the strength of numbers etc., intelligence, the esprit du corps, of the white people of Louisiana for success in the coming campaign, and not on the disintegration of the ranks of the Republican party. It shall be our duty to use every effort to arouse and unite the white men of this parish and state, into a compact political organization, and when this is accomplished, there will be but little need of any political alliance that does not come of its own free will and accord.

We have been asked by some of our liberal friends if the *Caucasian* would not favor the Democratic party. We distinctly stated in our first issue that we believed the campaign this fall should be a fair square, stand up fight of the honest intelligent white people, against negro incompetency and carpetbag rascality. . . .

We have a great work before us that will tax all of our energies and intelligence. The *little prejudices* of the past must be forgotten; as they become insignificant in comparison with the great interest of all, the redemption of Louisiana, and the restoration of her government, in all its branches, to the intelligent and honest masses, and the expulsion of the dishonest and ignorant from rule. The principles of the *Caucasian* have been endorsed almost unanimously by the white people of Rapides. We will continue to advocate them boldly and fearlessly, relying upon the advocacy of these principles entirely for the success of our journalistic enterprise.

From the *Caucasian* May 23, 1874

THE CONFLICT OF RACES

The only objection that we have heard urged against the movement to organize a white man's party for the next campaign, is that it is an effort to array the white race against the black. This is not the fact, and if the whites do organize a party upon that issue, they will not be responsible for arraying of the two races in political conflict. The responsibility will rest upon the negro, alias Republican party who, since 1868 have held the balance of power in this State, upon that issue alone. The strength of that party consists in the fact that it is the *negro* party, the representative of their peculiar ideas, the exponent of their views upon matters of legislation, and the sworn champion of their rights in contra distinction to the rights of the white men. The few white men who belong to that party, have signified their complete transmigration by accepting *social* as well as political equality; by becoming in fact, negroes in all but the complexion of their skins. So jealously has the negro guarded this point that nothing less would satisfy him, in no single particular would he relax the vigor of his insolent demands. . . .

The closest bonds of union among themselves and complete and entire abnegation of every tie that bound a white man to his race, have been the controlling ideas with the negro in his social and political relations with the whites. Legislation has been directed to the securing of the supremacy of the negro, and the law has been made to bow and kneel to this great mogul of their idolatry. Courts have been created and lauded as they have sacrificed every principle of law, and trampled upon every vestige of right in asserting the supremacy of the negro; and justice has been made to tear the bandage from her eyes and bidden to see only the negro: ordered to weigh him and his rights alone in her scales. He has sat in the halls of our legislature and with an insolence that no Russian Czar riding roughly over the prostrate and shrieking form of a bleeding Poland, ever dared assume, and with the grinning consciousness of a power to oppress that never entered into the wildest dream of the Turk, he has bidden to educate his children and we have kept *ours* at home and paid the money for *their* education; commanded us to pay outrageous taxation to support him and his party friends in fat offices with exorbitant salaries and we have toiled and groaned and seen our own families suffer for the common necessaries, that we might run with the sweat of honest toil pouring from our faces, to hand our contributions to his ease and luxury over to his tax collector, before he could have time to put up and sell our property.

He has made our halls of legislature a den of thieves, our courts a mockery upon justice, and the Executive department of our Government a synonym for rascality, a reproach and a bye-word among the honest men of the world. Huge monopolies, under his rule, have reared their hydra heads all around us, and we have been made to pay tribute to them, without mercy and without ceasing. Chaos and confusion have held a high carnival in our public places; crime has been encouraged, murder, rape, and arson have exhibited their hideous forms in broad light of day; and ruin and desolation have marked us for their own in obedience to his behests.

These monstrous things have not come to pass of their own accord, but are the legitimate results of the negro domination over the white people of this State, and they are all a part and parcel of his prearranged plan of persecuting whites to the verge of desperation and robbing them to the all extent of their means. Thus and thus only could the negro fill the measure of his brutal hate of his former masters, and only by witnessing this political degradation and pecuniary bankruptcy of the white could he show his superiority. Hating his superior intelligence and [envying] his possession of greater wealth, the negro instead of attempting to elevate himself, concluded that it was easier to drag the white man down to his own level. And now we, having grown weary of tame submission to this most desolating war of the negro upon *us*, propose to take a bold stand, to assert the dignity of our manhood, to say in tones of thunder and with the voice of the angry elements. STOP! THUS FAR SHALT THOU GO, AND NO FURTHER!

We are met with the babyish wail and old maidish horrified whine of, "*Oh! Please don't! You will array the two races in conflict.*" Who has arrayed them in conflict? Who has been preaching a crusade of race for seven years? And what we do care if it does become necessary to array them in conflict? The conflict is only a political one, and if he wants to change its character or to provoke us to the point of exchanging ballots for more forcible weapons, who fears the result or has any misgivings? We would deeply deplore any such issue of our efforts to save our State from irrevocable political damnation, and we would counsel a resort to violence only when it was forced on us as it was at Colfax, but we are not to be deterred from a bold and outspoken advocacy of our ideas because such a conflict *might* take place.

The white men have the wealth and intelligence of this country and their political disfranchisement can last no longer. Their wealth and intelligence must be represented in this government, and it never will be until they take just such a stand as we propose for them to take in this approaching campaign.

Questions to Consider:

1. *Leaving aside the racist views of the editors of the* Caucasian, *was there a legitimate constitutional and political argument to be made against the Republican state government during Reconstruction?*

2. *How were the views expressed by the editors Democratic party propaganda?*

Sources:

1. "Our Position," *Caucasian* (Alexandria, LA), April 25, 1874. Library of Congress, Chronicling America, https://chroniclingamerica.loc.gov/lccn/sn86053765/1874-04-25/ed-1/.

2. "The Conflict of Races," *Caucasian* (Alexandria, LA), May 23, 1874. Library of Congress, Chronicling America, https://chroniclingamerica.loc.gov/lccn/sn86053765/1874-05-23/ed-1/.

1891–1896:
Populism in Louisiana

A combination of declining commodity prices in the 1880s and frustration over a lack of response by politicians led farmers associated with the Farmers' Alliance to launch the People's, or Populist, Party in 1891. The organization of the party in Louisiana took place in Alexandria in October of that year. Among the ideas promulgated by the Populists included plans to inflate the nation's monetary supply and government control of the nation's railroads. In Louisiana, like the rest of the South, the Populist movement could not avoid the issue of race, as the party alternated between allying with black farmers, who faced the same hardships as white farmers, and adhering to the era's mantra of white supremacy. Louisiana's Bourbon Democrats naturally saw the formation of the party as a betrayal of their triumph in wresting control of the state from Republicans and freedmen during Reconstruction and put pressure on white farmers to stay loyal to the Democrat creed. The climax of the Populist movement in Louisiana happened in 1896, when a fusion of the party with the remnants of the state's Republican Party posed a serious threat to Bourbon rule. In the gubernatorial race that year, wealthy Republican sugar planter John M. Pharr headed the Republican/Populist ticket against incumbent Bourbon governor Murphy J. Foster. Foster was re-elected, but not without substantial voter fraud in heavily African American northern parishes along the Mississippi River.

In the selections below, the address of the Louisiana Populist Party makes an appeal to white Democratic farmers and black Republican farmers to unite behind a party the vows to take on the moneyed interests that had been the cause of their economic hardships. Nevertheless, excerpts from a leading Populist newspaper show that the party had no hesitation in invoking white supremacy to rally white farmers in north Louisiana when necessary. Finally, excerpts from the leading Shreveport Democratic newspaper demonstrate the concern the party felt over the Populist/Republican challenge in the 1896 campaign.

Address of the Populist Party of Louisiana Alexandria, October 3, 1891

To the Voters of the State of Louisiana, irrespective of class, color or past political affiliation: Friends and fellow citizens—That we are on the eve of a momentous political, economic and industrial revolution in this great republic few will dispute. None can yet foretell whether this revolution shall be accomplished by peaceable means, by appeals to the reason of the dominant element of our population, by a continued agitation that will convince this element that the great multitude of wealth producers enjoy their full share of the responsibility, resulting from years of their toil, their sufferings and their privations, or whether a deaf ear will still be turned to their warning representations, until their long-suffering patience, finally exhausted, they, the people, rise in their mighty wrath, and with swift retributive strokes, beat down the gates of that bastile [*sic*] of monopoly, stock jobbery and corruption, that has so long protected their oppressors, and hurl the monstrous edifice to the ground, burying in its ruins those whom it has sheltered so long.

A revolution by violence, no matter how sacred its aim, must be accomplished by horrors and injustice, at which a civilized community shudder.

A revolution by ballot will cost not a hair from the head of the guiltiest tyrant, not a single tear from an innocent victim.

We call on you to aid the revolution by the ballot. If you heed not this appeal, you will ere long send forth a different summons, or resign yourselves and your children to the utter bondage that is being prepared for us all.

What hope of relief can you entertain from the existing political parties? You white men, who have hitherto loyally followed Republican leaders cannot point to any legislation by them that has permanently benefited the real wealth producers. You cannot close your eyes to the fact that Republican rule has resulted in building up colossal corporate monopolies, and fabulous individual fortunes, such as the world never saw and never dreamed of before.

You colored men, who in your natural exuberant gratitude to the party that claimed the exclusive merit of freeing your race from the bonds of slavery, furnished the votes that have kept the Republicans in power so many years, and whose continued allegiance they claim on account of what they have done for you, you must feel that you have fully repaid all you owe them by your long and voluntary abject political servitude. You must now realize that there is no hope of any further material benefit to you from the Republican party, and that if you remain in it you will continue to be the hewers of wood and drawers of water in the future as you have been in the past.

Both of you, white and colored [Republicans], know that the Republican party has degenerated into a machine controlled by the money kings and used by them to gather into a few hands the enormous accretions to the wealth of the country resulting from the daily toil of millions. Concentration of political power, concentration of corporate power, concentration of money power is to-day [*sic*] the creed of Republicanism. How can we, then, the pawns upon the chess board; [*sic*] hope to win by it?

And you, Democrats, who have so long allowed yourselves to be guided by self-constituted leaders that you seem to have now lost the capacity for that self-assertion displayed so nobly in the past, can you disguise from yourselves that this much vaunted democracy has degenerated into a name to conjure by? Are not THE WALL STREET MILLIONAIRES as much controlling spirits in the Democratic as in the Republican councils? Have you not the testimony of Jay Gould himself that he is a Republican where Republicans control legislation and a Democrat where the Democrats are in power? Has not Grover Cleveland put himself on record as throwing in his lot with Wall Street against the toiling millions when he went out of his way to declare himself opposed to the demonetization of silver? Have you not the experience of uninterrupted Democratic rule in this state? What has it done for you? Are your taxes being reduced? Are your advantages being increased? Are your children growing up better equipped for the battle of life than you were? Are your institutions equal to the demands made upon them? Have your public finances been honestly administered?

The specter of negro supremacy has been used to keep you in the toils of scheming machine politicians as effectually as the voudou [*sic*] is employed to terrify the credulous negroes themselves. That specter can no longer be summoned. While the bloody shirt was waved by our equally deceived and confiding brothers in the north and west, the dreaded threat of negro supremacy was potent in maintaining a solid south for Wall Street to handle through willing tools. . . .

Again we ask: What relief can you expect from the existing political parties? Will you still remain the willing SERFS OF MACHINE POLITICIANS? Shall Louisiana not join in that ringing shout for liberty and reform that started in Kansas, is re-echoed in Ohio, and will soon reverberate over the length and breadth of the land? We do not, we will not believe it. The manhood of this great state cannot remain deaf to the summons. Come forward and aid in the impending struggle! Louisianians, who have ever nobly responded when duty called, will rally to and follow in its victorious course the standard of the people's party of reform.

Excerpts from the *Louisiana Populist*

October 25, 1895

The key stone to the "Solid South," and the key note of success to the Democratic party, the supremacy of the Caucasian race, is fast leaving that party. . . .

The recent action of the Democratic parish committees in DeSoto and Red River, in allowing negroes to vote in their nominating primaries; the refusal of the Democratic congressional committee of this district one year ago, to submit their candidate to a white primary, and the election of that candidate in the November election by negro votes, are straws—yea burrs and branches—that show which way the wind is blowing.

Not only is the Democratic party of this State afraid to submit its ticket against the Populist ticket in a white primary, but the machine Democracy, the leaders who now fill the offices and control the organization of the party, will not submit their chances for re-nomination inside the party to a white vote. . . .

Verily the Democratic party is no longer a party of white supremacy.

November 1, 1895

You Democrats, white men of pure blood, who have devoted your money, your life work, and in many cases, risked your lives in battle, for the principle of white supremacy, how do you regard this betrayal of your interests by the Democratic party?

You did not make your sacrifices for office, nor did you get office, but the men who have filled the offices drawn, the fat salaries, while they made your labor sell cheap, until they begin to think that the offices belong to them, these men are dragging the negro back into politics to dominate you because they can no longer hoodwink and control you.

These same men condemned the Republican party and hunted its white leaders down like dogs because it used the negro vote when honestly cast for that party. But now when the white people are demanding some reform for their patient party service, and refuse to support the Democrat party unless they get it, these leaders and office-holders propose to fill their places with negroes, and force the Democratic party to follow in the footsteps of the Republican party in this State.

Will Caucasians submit? We think not.

Excerpts from the Shreveport *Evening Judge*

November 18, 1895

There is no longer any doubt but the Republicans and Populists will, despite their professions for ballot reform, combine to defeat the suffrage amendment, simply because it is a Democratic measure and which, if adopted, will hereafter place the elections in the hands of the intelligent people of the State. The object of the combination between the Republicans and Populists is not so much to defeat the amendment as it is to defeat the Democratic party. . . . We say the planning and conducting of the campaign will be done by Republicans for the reason there is not a man in the Populist party of Louisiana competent to map out and successfully conduct a district campaign much less a State campaign. . . .

The Populists of Louisiana, the rank and file, are not politicians. They are a lot of honest, good meaning but misguided people who have been led off from the Democratic party by designing and wholly unprincipled demagogues, who at one time affiliated with either one or the other of the old parties.

The mass of Populists, incited by their leaders, have become so prejudiced and embittered against the Democratic party that it will be a very easy matter to induce them to combine with old Satan himself to annihilate the Democratic party. As we already said, the Populists as a class are not politicians. They are simply the prey of politicians. Because of their intense hatred for the Democratic party they blindly follow the leadership of a few crafty fellows who are Populists for what there is in it, and are shrewd enough to see their only hope of ever [holding] a State office is to combine forces with the lily white and charcoal Republicans.

The ostensible object of the fusion is the defeat [of] the suffrage amendment but the true purpose of the Republican managers with their Populistic [*sic*] puppets, is to defeat the Democratic party, and the suffrage amendment will be their shibboleth.

But the Democrats of Louisiana are not going to be taken unawares. After the State Nominating Convention will have adjourned the Democrats with a united party, will inaugurate a vigorous and uncompromising war on Populism and Republicanism and will win one of the most complete and overwhelming victories in the history of the State. . . .

March 6, 1896

At Washington, La., a few days since, this old political monstrosity [John N. Pharr] addressed a crowd of whites and negroes, of which the latter were largely in the majority. At that place he indulged in some very strong and incendiary language, which is calculated, if it was not intended, to inflame the minds and passions of the negroes against their white friends, and if adhered to logical sequence would be the shedding of much blood and the killing of thousands of negroes who are now and have been for years living at peace and contentedly with their white friends and neighbors. If such an unfortunate state of affairs should be brought about vengeance should not be visited upon innocent negroes, but upon the men who incited them to commit wrong and violence. . . .

December 15, 1895

It is the religious duty of Democrats to rob Populists and Republicans of their votes whenever and wherever the opportunity presents itself and any failure to do so will be a violation of true Louisiana Democratic teaching. The Populists and Republicans are one legitimate political prey. Rob them! You bet! What are we here for?

Questions to Consider:

1. *How did the Populists imply that both white and black farmers were misguided?*
2. *How did the Bourbon Democrats view the farmers, both white and black, who supported the Populists?*
3. *Read contextually in the* Evening Judge, *the last line was likely written in jest. Populists, nevertheless, took it seriously. Why would they not find it a joke?*

Sources:

1. *National Economist* (Washington, DC), October 17, 1891. Library of Congress.

2. *Louisiana Populist* (Natchitoches, LA), Louisiana State University Libraries Special Collections.

3. *Evening* Judge (Shreveport, LA), Louisiana State University Libraries Special Collections.

1896:
Plessy v. Ferguson

The most important United States Supreme Court case to originate in Louisiana is *Plessy v. Ferguson*, which in 1896 affirmed the constitutionality of southern segregation laws. In 1890 the Louisiana legislature passed the state's first segregation bill, the Separate Car Act, which required that railroads provide separate cars for white and black passengers. As a state senator from St. John the Baptist Parish, Henry Demas was one of four remaining African American Republicans in that chamber. In response to the act, leading members of the Afro-Creole community in New Orleans formed the *Comité des Citoyens* (Citizens Committee) to challenge the legality of the act. On June 7, 1892, Homer Plessy bought a first class train ticket from New Orleans to Covington and boarded the white passenger car. A private detective hired by the committee ensured that the conductor had him arrested for violating the Separate Car Act, and the test case began. After losing both in a local court and the Louisiana Supreme Court, the case was appealed to the US Supreme Court. In a 7-1 decision, the Court upheld the constitutionality of the Separate Car Act, asserting, among other points, that it was a reasonable exercise of the state's police power to maintain the health, safety, and morals of its citizens. Associate Justice John Marshall Harlan, however, saw through the reasoning behind the law and the majority opinion, and declared in the most famous dissenting opinion in the history of the Court that the decision established second-class citizenship for African Americans in the South. Through the "separate but equal" rule, that accommodations for each race had to be roughly the same in quality, Jim Crow laws came to dominate southern race relations until overturned fifty-eight years later by *Brown v. Board of Education.*

"The Separate Car Bill," *Daily Times-Democrat* July 8, 1890

The Southern whites, in no spirit of hostility to the Negroes, have insisted that the two races shall live separate and distinct from each other in all things, with separate schools, separate hotels and separate cars. They would rise to-morrow against the proposition to educate the white and black children together; and they resist any intercourse in theatre, hotel or elsewhere that will bring the race into anything like social intercourse. The quarter of a century that has passed since the war has not diminished in the slightest degree the determination of the whites to prevent any such dangerous doctrine as social equality, even in the mildest form. They give the Negroes schools; but these must be separate; and the cars also should be separate, in order to keep the races as far apart as ever. We cannot afford to surrender anything in this case.

The law—private not public—which prohibits the Negroes from occupying the same place in a hotel, restaurant or theatre as the whites, should prevail as to cars also. As a matter of fact, one is thrown in much closer communication in the car with one's traveling companions than in the theatre or restaurant with one's neighbors. Whites and blacks may there be crowded together, squeezed close to each other in the same seats, using the same conveniences, and to all intents and purposes in social intercourse. A man that would be horrified at the idea of his wife or daughter seated by the side of a burly Negro in the parlor of a hotel or at a restaurant cannot see her occupying a crowded seat in a car next to a Negro without the same feeling of disgust.

The Louisiana Senate ought to step in and prevent this indignity to white women of Louisiana, as the Legislatures of other Southern States have done.

It is not proposed to refuse the Negroes any right to which they are entitled. They are to have the same kind of cars, but separate ones. The man who believes that the white race should be kept pure from African taint will vote against that commingling of the races inevitable in a "mixed car" and which must have bad results. . . .

Speech of Hon. Henry Demas, on the Separate Car Bill, Delivered in the Senate, at Baton Rouge, La., July 8, 1890

Mr. President, the bill which we now have under consideration is one that, in my opinion, has not been properly framed. This is obvious to all who will read it carefully over. It places the entire Negro race upon one common level and makes no distinction between the ignorant and the illiterate, and those who, by education, refinement and culture, have raised themselves above the standard of their race. This bill, also, Mr. President, panders to class legislation,—and, by two sharply drawing the line between the races, destroys that harmony which should exist at all times between them. It is an undeserved stigma upon the Negro. The prosperity of Louisiana depends in a great measure upon his industry and toil. . . .

Mr. President, this State is peopled by a far larger number of cultured and wealthy colored people than is conjectured, and, owing to the intermingling of the races, it is not frequently a difficult matter to determine,—from a standpoint of color,—the white from the Negro. Would it not be unjust, I ask, to relegate this class to a coach occupied by those much inferior to them in life, and by thus doing humiliate a people accustomed to better surroundings. It would be forcing them to associate with the worst class of Negro element, and would be an unmerited rebuke upon the colored man of finer sensibilities. . . .

Mr. President, the occurrences of the past by which we should be guided, I believe, and which should prove a forecast for the future, show that the Negro is coming to the front rapidly. Twenty-five years ago when the yoke of slavery was removed from him, the Negro was an ignorant, illiterate and unenlightened man; with praiseworthy ambition, he resolutely set to work to ameliorate his condition and, if coming events cast their shadows before, the next decade will witness a remarkable change for the better in his moral and mental condition. He may be trampled upon by arbitrary laws, but his advancement to a higher plane of citizenship and civilization cannot be checked. Persecution cannot down him, and in his invincible march to a better and more elevated goal, his advancement has been steady and continuous.

Mr. President, who are the enemies of the colored people? Is it the educated and refined white? No, it is that class who have no social or moral standing in the communities where they live, and therefore they with keen sensibility feel their inferiority, and to acquire cheap notoriety they are willing to resort to any measure, they care not how insignificant, perfidious or oppressive it may be against the Negro, in order to carry out their unholy and hellish designs. . . .

Like the Jews we have been driven from our homes and firesides, from our churches and school-houses, [from] our civil and political liberties, and from the elevated avenues of livelihood, and now in order to reach the lowest depth of infamy, in order to surpass all other indignities heaped upon us, you are willing to forget you are men and vote for the passage of this bill.

Mr. President, when this bill shall have passed it is the last indignity left for you to [heap] upon us. You have exhausted every indignity, you have inflicted upon us every oppression known to your race, and we have born it with a patience unknown to other races without a single word of resentment, because we desired the security of peace, prosperity and happiness for all. But the time will and must come in our case, as it has in the history of other races, when we will rise and strike, for our liberties, let the chips fly where they may or consequences be what they will.

Associate Justice John Marshall Harlan's dissent, *Plessy v. Ferguson*

It was said in argument that the statute of Louisiana does not discriminate against either race but prescribes a rule applicable alike to white and colored citizens. But this argument does not meet the difficulty. Everyone knows that the statue in question had its origin in the purpose, not so much to exclude white persons from railroad cars occupied by blacks, as to exclude colored people from coaches occupied by or assigned to white persons. Railroad corporations of Louisiana did not make discrimination among whites in the matter of accommodation for travelers. The thing to accomplish was, under the guise of giving equal accommodations for whites and blacks, to compel the latter to keep to themselves while travelling in railroad passenger coaches. No one would be so wanting in candor as to assert the contrary. The fundamental objection, therefore, to the statue is that it interferes with the personal freedom of citizens. . . . If a white man and a black man choose to occupy the same public conveyance on a public highway, it is their right to do so, and no government, proceeding alone on grounds of race, can prevent it without infringing the personal liberty of each. . . .

The white race deems itself to be the dominant race in this country. And so it is, in prestige, in achievements, in education, in wealth, and in power. So, I doubt not, it will continue to be for all time, if it remains true to its great heritage and holds fast to the principles of constitutional liberty. But in the view of the Constitution, in the eye of the law, there is in this country no superior, dominant, ruling class of citizens. There is no caste here. Our Constitution is color-blind and neither knows nor tolerates classes among citizens. In respect of civil rights, all citizens are equal before the law. The humblest is the peer of the most powerful. The law regards man as man and takes no account of his surroundings or of his color when his civil rights as guaranteed by the supreme law of the land are involved. . . .

The arbitrary separation of citizens, on the basis of race, while they are on a public highway, is a badge of servitude wholly inconsistent with the civil freedom and the equality before the law established by the Constitution. It cannot be justified upon any legal grounds

If evils will result from the commingling of the two races upon public highways established for the benefit of all, they will be infinitely less than those that will surely come from state legislation regulating the enjoyment of civil rights upon the basis of race. We boast of the freedom enjoyed by our people above all other peoples. But it is difficult to reconcile that boast with the state of the law which, practically, puts the brand of servitude and degradation upon a large class of our fellow citizens, our equals before the law. The thin disguise of "equal" accommodations for passengers in railroad coaches will not mislead anyone, nor atone for the wrong this day done.

"Equality, But Not Socialism," *Daily Picayune* May 19, 1896

The Louisiana law which requires that the railways operating trains within the limits of the State shall furnish separate but equal accommodations for white and Negro passengers was passed upon in the Supreme Court of the United States, and was yesterday declared to be constitutional.

The decision holds that the statute in question does not abridge any of the constitutional privileges and immunities of the plaintiff, because it does not create any inequality between the citizens of the State and the citizens of the United States, or between citizens of different race or color. It provides equal privileges to all on all the railroads engaged in intrastate transit. It does not discriminate unfairly between citizens of the United States or between citizens of the State, of whatever color or race. It was legislation which it was competent for the State to enact as within the police power. The Supreme Court has held that the legislature determines the necessity for, and the courts the proper subject for, the exercise of the police power which extends to the protection of the lives, limbs, health, comfort, morals and quiet of society, private interests being subservient to the public.

As there are similar laws in all the States which abut on Louisiana, and, indeed, in most of the Southern States, this regulation for the separation of the races will operate continuously on all lines of Southern railway. Equality of rights does not mean community of rights. The laws must recognize and uphold this distinction; otherwise, if all rights were common as well as equal, there would be practically no such thing as private property, private life, or social distinctions, but all would belong to everybody who might choose to use it.

This would be absolute socialism, in which the individual would be extinguished in the vast mass of human being, a condition repugnant to every principle of enlightened democracy.

Questions to Consider:

1. *Contrast how the* Times-Democrat *and Senator Demas envisioned the role of African Americans in Louisiana society.*

2. *Contrast the understanding of equality put forth by Justice Harlan and the* Daily Picayune.

Sources:

1. "The Separate Car Bill," *The Daily Times-Democrat* (New Orleans), July 8, 1890.

2. *The Crusader* (New Orleans), July 19, 1890, Nils R. Douglas papers, 1893–1967, Amistad Research Center at Tulane University, New Orleans, Louisiana.

3. *Plessy v. Ferguson*, 163 U.S. 537 (1896).

4. "Equality, But Not Socialism," *The Daily Picayune* (New Orleans), May 19, 1896. Library of Congress.

1898:
A New Constitution and Disfranchisement

The Republican/Populist ticket in the 1896 governor's race was a serious challenge to Democratic power in Louisiana. The Bourbons realized that electoral fraud and voter intimidation, tactics employed since Reconstruction, had diminished in value. The remedy was a new state constitution, whose purpose was to shrink the number of black voters in the state. The main obstacle in this drive by Democrats throughout the South was the Fifteenth Amendment to the US Constitution, which prohibited the denial of voting rights on the basis of race. Beginning in 1890, Mississippi found a way around the amendment through a literacy test for voters. Other southern states began to follow suit, with Louisiana joining in 1898. To allow illiterate white citizens to vote, the constitution included a "grandfather clause," which permitted them to register if their father or grandfather was a registered voter in 1867. As former slaves did not have voting rights in the state at the time, the racial animus of these suffrage provisions was clear. Despite this exception, many poor white farmers, who would have likely supported the Populists in recent elections, dropped out of the electoral process, another benefit for the Bourbons. In addition, another device used by southern states like Louisiana were poll taxes, which required the payment of a tax to register to vote that could be a burden to poor citizens. The result of these new voter restrictions was dramatic. From 1896 to 1904, white voter registration in Louisiana dropped from 164,088 to 91,716, while the number of black voters fell from 130,344 to 1,342. Per legislative arrangement, this new constitution went into effect without ratification by the citizens of the state. Rev. Benjamin Palmer gave the opening prayer of the convention. Convention president Ernest B. Kruttschnitt was the chair of the Louisiana Democratic Party's central committee and the nephew of Judah Benjamin. The convention was held at Tulane Hall in downtown New Orleans, which was known previously as the Mechanics' Institute, site of the 1866 massacre.

Booker T. Washington's Open Letter to the Louisiana Constitutional Convention

Since the war, no State has had such an opportunity to settle for all time the race question, so far as it concerns politics, as is now given in Louisiana. Will your Convention set an example to the world in this respect? Will Louisiana take such high and just ground in respect to the Negro that no one can doubt that the South is as good a friend to the Negro as he possesses elsewhere? In all this, gentlemen of the Convention, I am not pleading for the Negro alone, but for the morals, the higher life of the white man as well. For the more I study this question, the more I am convinced that it is not so much a question as to what the white man will do with the Negro, as to what the Negro will do with the white man's civilization.

The Negro agrees with you that it is necessary to the salvation of the South that restriction be put upon the ballot. I know that you have two serious problems before you: ignorant and corrupt government on the one hand, and on the other, a way to restrict the ballot so that control will be in the hands of the intelligent, without regard to race. With the sincerest sympathy with you in your efforts to find a way out of the difficulty, I want to suggest that no State in the South can make a law that will provide an opportunity or temptation for an ignorant white man to vote and withhold the same opportunity from an ignorant colored man, without injuring both men. No State can make a law that can thus be executed, without dwarfing for all time the morals of the white man in the South. Any law controlling the ballot that is not absolutely just and fair to both races, will work more permanent injury to the whites than to the blacks.

The Negro does not object to an educational or property test, but let the law be so clear that no one clothed with State authority will be tempted to perjure and degrade himself, by putting one interpretation upon it for the white man and another for the black man. Study the history of the South, and you will find that where there has been the most dishonesty in the matter of voting, there you will find today the lowest moral condition of both races. First, there was the temptation to act wrongly with the Negro's ballot. From this is was an easy step to dishonesty with the white man's ballot, to the carrying of concealed weapons, to the murder of a Negro, and then to the murder of a white man, and then to lynching . . .

I beg of you, further, that in the degree that you close the ballot-box against the ignorant, that you open the school house. More than one half of the people of your State are Negroes. No State can long prosper when a large percentage of its citizenship is in ignorance and poverty, and has no interest in government. I beg of you that you do not treat us as alien people. We are not aliens. . . . While I do not presume to be able to advise you, yet it is in my heart to say that if your Convention would do something that would prevent, for all time, strained relations between the two races, and would permanently settle the matter of political relations in our Southern States, at least, let the very best educational opportunities be provided for both races: and add to this the enactment of an election law that shall be incapable of unjust discrimination, at the same time providing that in proportion as the ignorant secure education, property and character, they will be given the right of citizenship. Any other course will take from one-half your citizens interest in the State, and hope and ambition to become intelligent producers and taxpayers—to become useful and virtuous citizens. Any other course will tie the white citizens of Louisiana to a body of death.

Ernest B. Kruttschnitt, President of the Constitutional Convention, Opening Address to the Convention February 8, 1898

We have here none of the clash of faction. We have here no political antagonism, and I am called upon to preside over what is little more than a family meeting of the Democratic party of the State of Louisiana. . . .

My fellow-citizens, we are all aware that this convention has been called by the people of the State of Louisiana principally to deal with one question, and we know that but for the existence of that one question this assemblage would not be sitting here today. We know that this convention has been called together by the people of the State to eliminate from the electorate the mass of corrupt and illiterate voters who have during the last quarter of a century degraded our politics. I care nothing for details. . . . With a unanimity unparalleled in the history of American politics, they have entrusted to the Democratic party of this State the solution of the question of the purification of the electorate. . . .

Only a few years back, it might have been considered impolite to say what I am now saying, but there are men standing high today in the councils of the nation, who have seen the doors of the White House barred to them by the ignorant and corrupt delegations of Southern negroes, and we know that they cannot but feel a sympathy with us in our aspirations and efforts.

My fellow-delegates, let us not be misunderstood! Let us say to the large class of the people of Louisiana who will be disfranchised under any of the proposed limitations of the suffrage, that what we seek to do is undertaken in a spirit, not of hostility to any particular men or set of men, but in the belief that the State should see to the protection of the weaker classes; should guard them against the machinations of those who would use them only to further their own base ends; should see to it that they be not allowed to harm themselves. We owe it to the ignorant, we owe it to the weak, to protect them just as we would protect a little child and prevent it from injuring itself with sharp-edged tools placed in its hands. . . .

May this hall, where, thirty-two years ago, the negro first entered upon the unequal contest for supremacy, and which has been reddened with his blood, now witness the evolution of our organic law which will establish the relations between the races upon an everlasting foundation of right and justice.

Suffrage and Election Provisions, 1898 Constitution

ARTICLE 197

Every male citizen of this State and of the United States, native born or naturalized, not less than twenty-one years of age, and possessing the following qualifications, shall be an elector, and shall be entitled to vote at any election in the State by the people, except as may be herein otherwise provided.

SEC. 3. He shall be able to read and write, and shall demonstrate his ability to do so when he applies for registration, by making, under oath administered by the registration officer or his deputy, written application therefore, in the English language, or his mother tongue, which application shall contain the essential facts necessary to show that he is entitled to register and vote, and shall be entirely written, dated and signed by him, in the presence of the registration officer or his deputy, without assistance or suggestion from any person or any memorandum whatever, except the form of application hereinafter set forth; provided, however, that if the applicant be unable to write his application in the English language, he shall have the right, if he so demands, to write the same in his mother tongue from the dictation of an interpreter; and if the applicant is unable to write his application by reason of physical disability, the same shall be written at his dictation by the registration officer or his deputy, upon his oath of such disability. . . .

SEC. 4. If he be not able to read and write, as provided by Section three of this article, then he shall be entitled to register and vote if he shall, at the time he offers to register, be the bona fide owner of property assessed to him in this State at a valuation of not less than three hundred dollars on the assessment roll of the current year in which he offers to register, or on the roll of the preceding year, if the roll of the current year shall not then have been completed and filed, and on which, if such property be personal only, all taxes due shall have been paid. The applicant for registration under this section shall make oath before the registration office or his deputy, that he is a citizen of the United States and of this State, over the age of twenty-one years; that he possesses the qualifications prescribed in section one of this article, and that he is the owner of property assessed in this State to him at a valuation of not less than three hundred dollars, and if such property be personal only, that all taxes due thereon have been paid.

SEC. 5. No male person who was on January 1st, 1867, or at any date prior thereto, entitled to vote under the Constitution or statutes of any State of the United States, wherein he then resided, and no son or grandson of any such person not less than twenty-one years of age at the date of the adoption of this Constitution, and no male person of foreign birth, who was naturalized prior to the first day of January, 1898; shall be denied the right to register and vote in this State by reason of his failure to possess the educational or property qualifications prescribed by this Constitution; provided, he shall have resided in this State for five years next preceding the date at which he shall apply for registration, and shall have registered in accordance with the terms of this article prior to September 1, 1898, and no person shall be entitled to register under this section after said date.

ARTICLE 198

No person less than sixty years of age shall be permitted to vote at any election in the State who shall not, in addition to the qualifications above prescribed, have paid on or before the 31st day of December, of each year, for the two years preceding the year in which he offers to vote, a poll tax of one dollar per annum, to be used exclusively in aid of the public schools of the parish in which such tax shall have been collected; which tax is hereby imposed on every male resident of this State between the age of twenty-one and sixty years. Poll taxes shall be a lien only upon assessed property, and no process shall issue to enforce the collection of the same except against assessed property.

ARTICLE 200

No person shall vote at any primary election or in any convention or other political assembly held for the purpose of nominating any candidate for public office, unless he is at the time a registered voter. And in all political conventions in this State the apportionment of representation shall be on the basis of population.

From William Wright Heard, Inaugural Address, May 21, 1900

The wise limitation of the suffrage, under the present constitution [*sic*], to a property owning and intelligent electorate, has served to eliminate from the exercise of the suffrage the vast mass of venality and ignorance which has heretofore been a constant menace to good government.

The elective franchise now being confined to the intelligence of the state, the fear of corruption in the conduct of public affairs has passed away, and the citizen, with a feeling of confidence and security, will find more encouragement to exert himself in the development of the industrial and agricultural interests of our fertile domain.

The elevation and purification of the electorate, while it promises, and will eventually advance and secure these great material advantages, yet places on those entitled to suffrage, the greater duty to see that the moral, social and material interests of the whole people shall be carefully guarded.

These limitations and restrictions of the franchise, eliminate from the electorate a large portion of the negro element, thus committing the destinies of the commonwealth to the hands of its white citizens.

This was done for the purpose of protecting not only the white, but the colored race as well, from the evils of corrupt government and to preserve the rights and liberties of both. It therefore becomes an imperative duty, now more than ever before, to deal justly and fairly with this class of our people, and to see to it that they are fully protected in the enjoyment of their rights of person and property, and to insure the betterment and elevation of their moral and material condition.

Questions to Consider:

1. *The US Supreme Court ruled that restrictions on voting imposed by southern states during this time were constitutional and did not violate the Fifteenth Amendment. From the language of the suffrage sections in the 1898 constitution, how could the court make this determination?*

2. *How did the Democratic Party justify their goals at the constitutional convention?*

3. *How does Booker T. Washington's appeal to the convention mirror the rhetoric of the Democrats? How was his appeal ignored by the state?*

Sources:

1. Booker T. Washington, "An Open Letter Addressed by Booker T. Washington of Tuskegee, Ala. to the Louisiana Constitutional Convention, February 19th, 1898," 2–3, 5–6. Alabama pamphlets collection, LPR131, Alabama Dept. of Archives and History. http://digital.archives.alabama.gov/cdm/ref/collection/voices/id/6606.

2. *Official Journal of the Proceedings of the Constitutional Convention of the State of Louisiana, held in New Orleans, Tuesday, February 8, 1898* (New Orleans: H. J. Hearsey, 1898), 8–10.

3. *Official Journal of the Proceedings of the Constitutional Convention of the State of Louisiana, held in New Orleans, Tuesday, February 8, 1898* (New Orleans: H. J. Hearsey, 1898), 379–81.

4. *Constitution of the State of Louisiana: adopted May 12, 1898; with amendments including the Extra Session of the Louisiana Legislature held August 12, 1912.* Annotated by Theodore Contonio (New Orleans: Louisiana Publishing Co., 1913), 225–28, 232–34.

5. Sidney J. Romero, ed., *"My Fellow Citizens…": The Inaugural Addresses of Louisiana's Governors* (Lafayette, LA: Center for Louisiana Studies, University of Southwestern Louisiana, 1980), 228–30.

1900:
Robert Charles and the New Orleans Race Riot

Race riots were an unfortunate feature of American history in the early twentieth century. Defined as an event in which mobs indiscriminately attack African Americans or other minorities and destroy their property, often in urban areas, race riots in Atlanta in 1906, St. Louis in 1917, Chicago in 1919, and Tulsa in 1921 stand out. The most significant one in Louisiana took place in 1900. The man at the center of the riot was Robert Charles. Originally from Mississippi, Charles arrived in New Orleans in 1894 and worked as a laborer. He also was active in organizations promoting African American migration to Liberia. Late on the night of July 23, Charles and a friend were waiting to meet their girlfriends on the steps of a house when three white police officers approached. An altercation between Charles and one of the officers occurred, and both men fired shots, each receiving superficial wounds. Charles then fled to his residence and fatally shot two officers who arrived to arrest him. After evading capture, he went into hiding. Incited by local newspapers, mobs soon organized and began to assault African Americans on the streets of the city. On July 27, police ascertained Charles's whereabouts, and while the officers searched the house, Charles fatally shot two more policemen. Soon, about a thousand police, special deputies, and armed citizens surrounded the house and laid siege for the next two hours. Firing from various points in the house, Charles killed three more individuals and wounded nineteen. Only when the house was set on fire did Charles try to flee and was killed. Over the course of these four days, white mobs left at least twelve African Americans dead and more than sixty-five injured, along with the burning of two black schools. By September, journalist and civil rights pioneer Ida B. Wells wrote her account of the violence in the pamphlet *Mob Rule in New Orleans*, excerpted here, which she based on reports from New Orleans newspapers.

Mob Rule in New Orleans

The bloodiest week which New Orleans has known since the massacre of the Italians in 1892 was ushered in Monday, July 24, by the inexcusable and unprovoked assault upon two colored men by police officers of New Orleans. Fortified by the assurance born of long experience in the New Orleans service, three policemen, Sergeant Aucoin, Officer Mora and Officer Cantrelle, observing two colored men sitting on doorsteps on Dryades street, between Washington Avenue and 6th Streets, determined, without a shadow of authority, to arrest them. One of the colored men was named Robert Charles, the other was a lad of nineteen named Leonard Pierce. The colored men had left their homes, a few blocks distant, about an hour prior, and had been sitting upon the doorsteps for a short time talking together. They had not broken the peace in any way whatever, no warrant was in the policemen's hands justifying their arrest, and no crime had been committed of which they were the suspects. The policemen, however, secure in the firm belief that they could do anything to a Negro that they wished, approached the two men, and in less than three minutes from the time they accosted them attempted to put both colored men under arrest. The younger of the two men, Pierce, submitted to arrest, for the officer, Cantrelle, who accosted him, put his gun in the young man's face ready to blow his brains out if he moved. The other colored man, Charles, was made the victim of a savage attack by Officer Mora, who used a billet and then drew a gun and tried to kill Charles. Charles drew his gun nearly as quickly as the policeman, and began a duel in the street, in which both participants were shot. The policeman got the worst of the duel, and fell helpless to the sidewalk. Charles made his escape. Cantrelle took Pierce, his captive, to the police station, to which place Mora, the wounded officer, was also taken, and a man hunt at once instituted for Charles, the wounded fugitive.

In any law-abiding community Charles would have been justified in delivering himself up immediately to the properly constituted authorities and asking a trial by a jury of his peers. He could have been certain that in resisting an unwarranted arrest he had a right to defend his life, even to the point of taking one in that defense, but Charles knew that his arrest in New Orleans, even for defending his life, meant nothing short of a long term in the penitentiary, and still more probable death by lynching at the hands of a cowardly mob. He very bravely determined to protect his life as long as he had breath in his body and strength to draw a hair trigger on his would-be murderers. How well he was justified in that belief is well shown by the newspaper accounts which were given of this transaction. Without a single line of evidence to justify the assertion, the New Orleans daily papers at once declared that both Pierce and Charles were desperadoes, that they were contemplating a burglary and that they began the assault upon the policemen. It is interesting to note how the two leading papers of New Orleans, the *Picayune* and the *Times-Democrat*, exert themselves to justify the policemen in the absolutely unprovoked attack upon the two colored men. . . .

Legal sanction was given to the mob or any man of the mob to kill Charles at sight by the Mayor of New Orleans, who publicly proclaimed a reward of two hundred and fifty dollars, not for the arrest of Charles, not at all, but the reward was offered for Charles's body, "dead or alive.". . .

This authority . . . would have been no news to Charles, nor to any colored man in New Orleans, who, for any purpose whatever, even to save his life, raised his hand against a white man. It is now, even as it was in the days of slavery, an unpardonable sin for a Negro to resist a white man, no matter how unjust or unprovoked the white man's attack may be. Charles knew this, and knowing to be captured meant to be killed, he resolved to sell his life as dearly as possible. . . .

The first colored man to meet death at the hands of the mob was a passenger on a street car. The mob had broken itself into fragments after its disappointment at the jail, each fragment looking for a Negro to kill. The bloodthirsty cruelty of one crowd is thus described by the *Times-Democrat*:

> "We will get a Nigger down here, you bet!" was the yelling boast that went up from a thousand throats, and for the first time the march of the mob was directed toward the downtown sections. The words of the rioters were prophetic, for just as Canal Street was reached a car on the Villere line came along.
>
> "Stop that car!" cried half a hundred men. The advance guard,

heeding the injunction, rushed up to the slowly moving car, and several, seizing the trolley, jerked it down.

"Here's a Negro!" said half a dozen men who sprang upon the car.

The car was full of passengers at the time, among them several women. When the trolley was pulled down and the car thrown in total darkness, the latter began to scream, and for a moment or so it looked as if the life of every person in the car was in peril, for some of the crowd with demoniacal yells of "There he goes!" began to fire their weapons indiscriminately. The passengers in the car hastily jumped to the ground and joined the crowd, as it was evidently the safest place to be.

"Where's that Nigger?" was the query passed along the line, and with that the search began in earnest. The Negro, after jumping off the car, lost himself for a few moments in the crowd, but after a brief search he was again located. The slight delay seemed, if possible, only to whet the desire of the bloodthirsty crowd, for the reappearance of the Negro was the signal for a chorus of screams and pistol shots directed at the fugitive. With the speed of a deer, the man ran straight from the corner of Canal and Villere to Customhouse Street. The pursuers, closely following, kept up a running fire, but notwithstanding the fact that they were right at the Negro's heels their aim was poor and their bullets went wide of the mark.

The Negro, on reaching Customhouse Street, darted from the sidewalk out into the middle of the street. This was the worst maneuver that he could have made, as it brought him directly under the light from an arc lamp, located on a nearby corner. When the Negro came plainly in view of the foremost of the closely following mob they directed a volley at him. Half a dozen pistols flashed simultaneously, and one of the bullets evidently found its mark, for the Negro stopped short, threw up his hands, wavered for a moment, and then started to run again. This stop, slight as it was, proved fatal to the Negro's chances, for he had not gotten twenty steps farther when several of the men in advance of the others reached his side. A burly fellow, grabbing him with one hand, dealt him a terrible blow on the head with the other. The wounded man sank to the ground. The crowd pressed around him and began

> to beat him and stamp him. The men in the rear pressed forward and those beating the man were shoved forward. The half-dead Negro, when he was freed from his assailants, crawled over to the gutter. The men behind, however, stopped pushing when those in front yelled, "We've got him," and then it was that the attack on the bleeding Negro was resumed. A vicious kick directed at the Negro's head sent him into the gutter, and for a moment the body sank from view beneath the muddy, slimy water. "Pull him out; don't let him drown," was the cry, and instantly several of the men around the half-drowned Negro bent down and drew the body out. Twisting the body around they drew the head and shoulders up on the street, while from the waist down the Negro's body remained under the water. As soon as the crowd saw that the Negro was still alive they again began to beat and kick him. Every few moments they would stop and striking matches look into the man's face to see if he still lived. To better see if he was dead they would stick lighted matches to his eyes. Finally, believing he was dead they left him and started out to look for other Negroes. Just about this time some one yelled, "He ain't dead," and the men came back and renewed the attack. While the men were beating and pounding the prostrate form with stones and sticks a man in the crowd ran up, and crying, "I'll fix the d— Negro," poked the muzzle of a pistol almost against the body and fired. This shot must have ended the man's life, for he lay like a stone, and realizing that they were wasting energy in further attacks, the men left their victim lying in the street. . . .

Mob rule continued Thursday, its violence increasing every hour, until 2 p.m., when the climax seemed to be reached. The fact that colored men and women had been made the victims of brutal mobs, chased through the streets, killed upon the highways and butchered in their homes, did not call the best element in New Orleans to active exertion in behalf of law and order. The killing of a few Negroes more or less by irresponsible mobs does not cut much figure in Louisiana. But when the reign of mob law exerts a depressing influence upon the stock market and city securities begin to show unsteady standing in money centers, then the strong arm of the good white people of the South asserts itself and order is quickly brought out of chaos.

It was so with New Orleans on that Thursday. The better element of the white citizens began to realize that New Orleans in the hands of a mob would not prove a promising investment for Eastern capital, so the better element began to stir itself, not for the purpose of punishing the brutality against the Negroes who had been beaten, or bringing to justice the murderers of those who had been killed, but for the purpose of saving the city's credit . . . With the financial credit of the city at stake, the good citizens rushed to the rescue, and soon the Mayor was able to mobilize a posse of 1,000 willing men to assist the police in maintaining order, but rioting still continued in different sections of the city. Colored men and women were beaten, chased and shot whenever they made their appearance upon the street. . . .

The press of the country has united in declaring that Robert Charles was a desperado. As usual, when dealing with a negro, he is assumed to be guilty because he is charged. Even the most conservative of journals refuse to ask evidence to prove that the dead man was a criminal, and that his life had been given over to lawbreaking. The minute that the news was flashed across the country that he had shot a white man it was at once declared that he was a fiend incarnate, and that when he was killed the community would be ridden of a black-hearted desperado. The reporters of the New Orleans papers, who were in the best position to trace the record of this man's life, made every possible effort to find evidence to prove that he was a villain unhung. With all the resources at their command, and inspired by intense interest to paint him as black a villain as possible, these reporters signally failed to disclose a single indictment which charged Robert Charles with a crime. Because they failed to find any legal evidence that Charles was a lawbreaker and desperado his accusers gave full license to their imagination and distorted the facts that they had obtained, in every way possible, to prove a course of criminality, which the records absolutely refuse to show. . . .

The life, character and death of Robert Charles challenges the thoughtful consideration of all fair-minded people. In the frenzy of the moment, when nearly a dozen men lay dead, the victims of his unerring and death-dealing aim, it was natural for a prejudiced press and for citizens in private life to denounce him as a desperado and a murderer. But sea depths are not measured when the ocean rages, nor can absolute justice be determined while public opinion is lashed into fury. There must be calmness to insure correctness of judgment. The fury of the hour must abate before we can deal justly with any man or any cause.

That Charles was not a desperado is amply shown by the discussion in the preceding chapter. The darkest pictures which the reporters could paint of Charles were quoted freely, so that the public might find upon what grounds the press declared him to be a lawbreaker. Unquestionably the grounds are wholly insufficient. Not a line of evidence has been presented to prove that Charles was the fiend which the first reports of the New Orleans charge him to be.

Nothing more should be required to establish his good reputation, for the rule is universal that a reputation must be assumed to be good until it is proved bad. But that rule does not apply to the Negro, for as soon as he is suspected the public judgment immediately determines that he is guilty of whatever crime he stands charged. For this reason, as a matter of duty to the race, and the simple justice to the memory of Charles, an investigation has been made of the life and character of Charles before the fatal affray which led to his death.

Questions to Consider:

1. *What does Wells assert about justice and fair treatment by police for African Americans in the South in 1900?*
2. *What does she assert about Charles's depiction in the New Orleans press?*

Source:

Ida B. Wells-Barnett, *Mob Rule in New Orleans: Robert Charles and His Fight to Death, the Story of His Life, Burning Human Beings Alive, Other Lynching Statistics* (Chicago: 1900). E-book provided by Project Gutenberg, www.gutenberg.org.

For Further Reading

Arnesen, Eric. *Waterfront Workers of New Orleans: Race, Class, and Politics, 1863–1923.* New York: Oxford University Press, 1991.

Barnes, Donna. *The Louisiana Populist Movement, 1881–1900.* Baton Rouge: Louisiana State University Press, 2011.

Billings, Warren, and Mark Fernandez. *A Law unto Itself? Essays in the New Louisiana Legal History.* Baton Rouge: Louisiana State University Press, 2001.

Cutrer, Thomas W. *Theater of a Separate War: The Civil War West of the Mississippi River, 1861–1865.* Chapel Hill, NC: University of North Carolina Press, 2017.

Davis, William C. *The Pirates Laffite: The Treacherous World of the Corsairs of the Gulf.* New York: Harcourt, 2005.

Faber, Eberhard L. *Building the Land of Dreams: New Orleans and the Transformation of Early America.* Princeton: Princeton University Press, 2016.

Fairclough, Adam. *The Revolution that Failed: Reconstruction in Natchitoches.* Gainesville, FL: University of Florida Press, 2018.

Follett, Richard. *The Sugar Masters: Planters and Slaves in Louisiana's Cane World, 1820–1860.* Baton Rouge: Louisiana State University Press, 2005.

Frazier, Donald S. *Fire in the Cane Field: The Federal Invasion of Louisiana and Texas, January 1861–January 1863.* College Station, TX: Texas A&M University Press, 2009.

Hair, William Ivy. *Bourbonism and Agrarian Protest: Louisiana Politics, 1877–1900.* Baton Rouge: Louisiana State University Press, 1969.

———. *Carnival of Fury: Robert Charles and the New Orleans Race Riot of 1900.* Baton Rouge: Louisiana State University Press, 1976.

Hogue, James. *Uncivil War: Five New Orleans Street Battles and the Rise and Fall of Radical Reconstruction.* Baton Rouge: Louisiana State University Press, 2006.

Hollandsworth, James G. *An Absolute Massacre: The New Orleans Race Riot of July 30, 1866.* Baton Rouge: Louisiana State University Press, 2004.

———. *The Louisiana Native Guards: The Black Military Experience during the Civil War.* Baton Rouge: Louisiana State University Press, 1995.

Hyde, Samuel. *Pistols and Politics: Feuds, Factions, and the Struggle for Order in Louisiana's Florida Parishes, 1810–1935, 2nd Edition*. Baton Rouge: Louisiana State University Press, 2018.

Johnson, Walter. *River of Dark Dreams: Slavery and Empire in the Cotton Kingdom*. Cambridge, MA: Harvard University Press, 2013.

———. *Soul by Soul: Life inside the Antebellum Slave Market*. Cambridge, MA: Harvard University Press, 2000.

Kastor, Peter J. *The Nation's Crucible: The Louisiana Purchase and the Creation of America*. New Haven, CT: Yale University Press, 2004.

Kelley, Blair L. M. *Right to Ride: Streetcar Boycotts and African American Citizenship in the Era of* Plessy v. Ferguson. Chapel Hill, NC: University of North Carolina Press, 2010.

Kukla, Jon. *A Wilderness So Immense: The Louisiana Purchase and the Destiny of America*. New York: Alfred A. Knopf, 2003.

Lane, Charles. *The Day Freedom Died: The Colfax Massacre, the Supreme Court, and the Betrayal of Reconstruction*. New York: Henry Holt and Co., 2008.

Long, Alecia P. *The Great Southern Babylon: Sex, Race, and Respectability in New Orleans, 1865–1920*. Baton Rouge: Louisiana State University Press, 2004.

Malone, Ann Patton. *Sweet Chariot: Slave Family and Household Structure in Nineteenth-Century Louisiana*. Chapel Hill, NC: University of North Carolina Press, 1996.

Marler, Scott P. *The Merchants' Capital: New Orleans and the Political Economy of the Nineteenth-Century South*. New York: Cambridge University Press, 2013.

Nystrom, Justin A. *New Orleans after the Civil War: Race, Politics, and a New Birth of Freedom*. Baltimore, MD: Johns Hopkins University Press, 2010.

Ostendorf, Ann. *Sounds American: National Identity and the Music Cultures of the Lower Mississippi River Valley, 1800–1860*. Athens, GA: University of Georgia Press, 2011.

Perman, Michael. *Struggle for Mastery: Disfranchisement in the South, 1888–1908*. Chapel Hill, NC: University of North Carolina Press, 2003.

Pierson, Michael D. *Mutiny at Fort Jackson: The Untold Story of the Fall of New Orleans*. Chapel Hill, NC: University of North Carolina Press, 2008.

Prushankin, Jeffrey S. *A Crisis in Confederate Command: Edmund Kirby Smith, Richard Taylor, and the Army of the Trans-Mississippi*. Baton Rouge: Louisiana State University Press, 2005.

Remini, Robert V. *The Battle of New Orleans: Andrew Jackson and America's First Military Victory*. New York: Viking, 2001.

Robertson, Henry. *In the Habit of Acting Together: The Emergence of the Whig Party in Louisiana, 1828–1840*. Lafayette, LA: University of Louisiana at Lafayette Press, 2007.

Rodrigue, John C. *Reconstruction in the Cane Fields: From Slavery to Free Labor in Louisiana's Sugar Parishes, 1862–1880*. Baton Rouge: Louisiana State University Press, 2001.

Sacher, John. *A Perfect War of Politics: Parties, Politicians, and Democracy in Louisiana, 1824–1861*. Baton Rouge: Louisiana State University Press, 2003.

Schafer, Judith Kelleher. *Becoming Free, Remaining Free: Manumission and Enslavement in New Orleans, 1846–1862*. Baton Rouge: Louisiana State University Press, 2003.

———. *Brothels, Depravity, and Abandoned Women: Illegal Sex in Antebellum New Orleans*. Baton Rouge: Louisiana State University Press, 2011.

———. *Slavery, the Civil Law, and the Supreme Court of Louisiana*. Baton Rouge: Louisiana State University Press, 1994.

Scott, Rebecca J. *Degrees of Freedom: Louisiana and Cuba after Slavery*. Cambridge, MA: Harvard University Press, 2008.

Seck, Ibrahima. *Bouki Fait Gombo: A History of the Slave Community of Habitation Haydel (Whitney Plantation) Louisiana, 1750–1860*. New Orleans: University of New Orleans Press, 2014.

Thompson, Shirley Elizabeth. *Exiles at Home: The Struggle to Become American in Creole New Orleans*. Cambridge, MA: Harvard University Press, 2009.

Tregle, Joseph G., Jr. *Louisiana in the Age of Jackson: A Clash of Cultures and Personalities*. Baton Rouge: Louisiana State University Press, 1999.

Tunnell, Ted. *Edge of the Sword: The Ordeal of Carpetbagger Marshall H. Twitchell in the Civil War and Reconstruction*. Baton Rouge: Louisiana State University Press, 1991.

Part III

Twentieth- and Twenty-First-Century Louisiana, 1897–2017

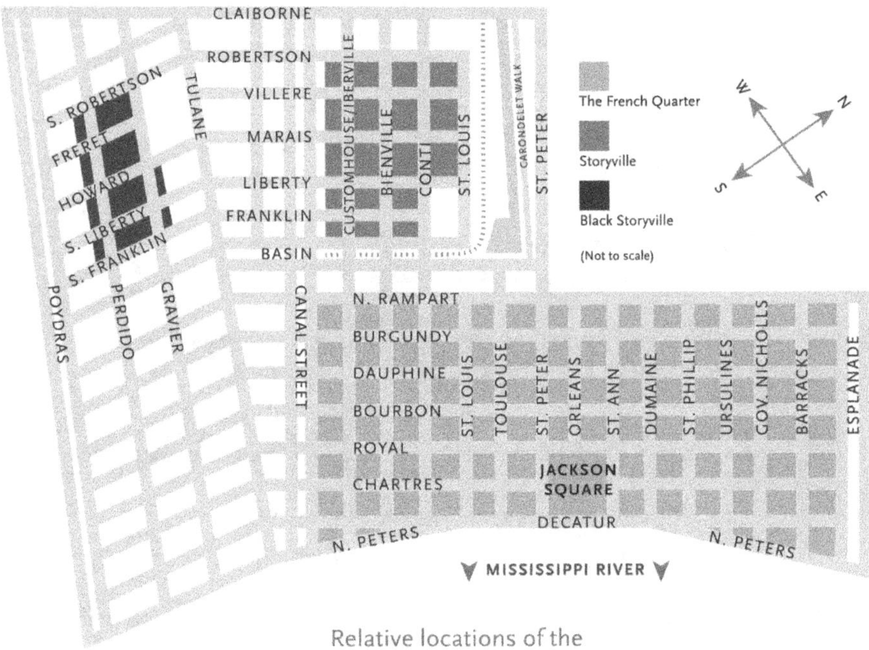

Relative locations of the French Quarter and the two vice districts in the Storyville era

From: Pamela Arceneaux, *Guidebooks to Sin: The Blue Books of Storyville, New Orleans* (Historic New Orleans Collection: New Orleans, 2017).

1897–1917:
The Story of Storyville

Storyville was the nickname of a legal red-light district that existed in New Orleans from 1897 until 1917. Corralling prostitution by allowing it within the limits of a certain part of town (usually a predominantly-minority district) was a common method of regulating what had become an increasingly prominent profession for women. Other river and railroad cities in Louisiana—Lake Charles, Crowley, and Shreveport—established similar districts that included not only legalized prostitution but gambling, too.

New Orleans's district, named for the man behind the ordinance, Alderman Sidney Story, was by far the biggest, fanciest, and most famous in the South. Storyville's main street, which housed the most luxurious brothels, fronted a train depot—prime real estate for servicing male customers traveling on business. At the other end of the district were cribs, tiny rooms containing little more than a cot and a washbasin that part-time prostitutes rented for the night, just long enough to earn rent or grocery money.

The image on page 286 come from annual guidebooks called Blue Books that listed the girls and their assets. The other two excerpts below come from two weekly newspapers that focused on the sporting life in Storyville. The regular daily papers in New Orleans paid little attention to Storyville but would cover stories involving arrests or deaths in the district resulting from other crimes like robbery (patrons often complained of being robbed), assault, public drunkenness, selling liquor without a license, or creating a disturbance. Sometimes clients would be arrested, too, for being drunk and disorderly, but often the john got off scot-free. Due to an outbreak of sexually transmitted diseases among the soldiers and sailors, Storyville was closed during World War I by order of the US Navy.

"The Scarlet World" in the *Sunday Sun's* Society Column

Minnie Rosenthal is now living with Miss Jessie Brown, 1542 Customhouse Street. Boys, she is the goods.

Romey Young from Galveston, Tex. is expected in a few days, and has engaged rooms with Miss Margaret Bradford.

Nettie Garbright, who for a number of years kept a sporting house at 139 Customhouse Street, and retired to private life, is back on the turf again, comfortably situated at No. 1537 Customhouse Street.

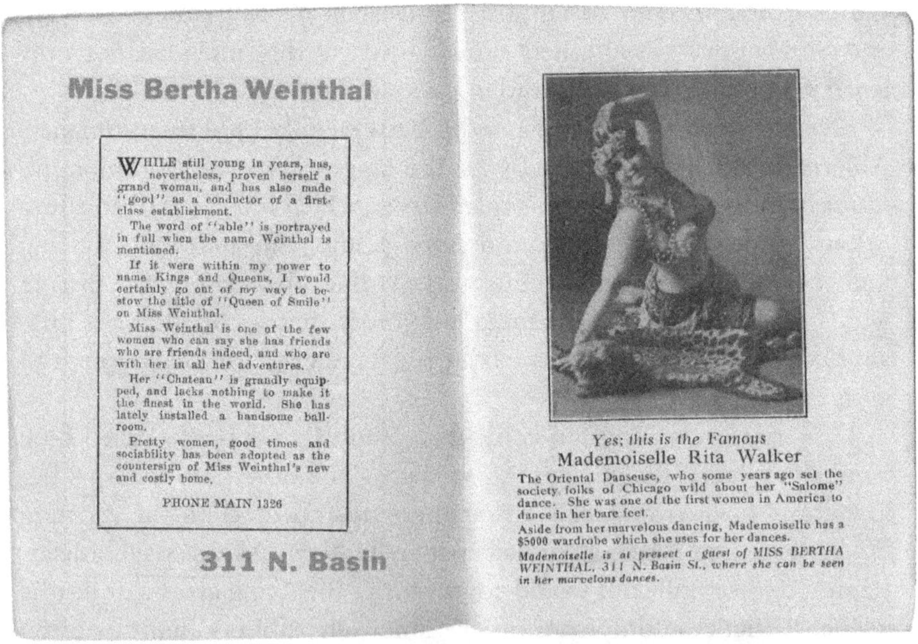

Miss Bertha Weinthal

WHILE still young in years, has, nevertheless, proven herself a grand woman, and has also made "good" as a conductor of a first-class establishment.

The word of "able" is portrayed in full when the name Weinthal is mentioned.

If it were within my power to name Kings and Queens, I would certainly go out of my way to bestow the title of "Queen of Smile" on Miss Weinthal.

Miss Weinthal is one of the few women who can say she has friends who are friends indeed, and who are with her in all her adventures.

Her "Chateau" is grandly equipped, and lacks nothing to make it the finest in the world. She has lately installed a handsome ballroom.

Pretty women, good times and sociability has been adopted as the countersign of Miss Weinthal's new and costly home.

PHONE MAIN 1326

311 N. Basin

Yes; this is the Famous
Mademoiselle Rita Walker

The Oriental Danseuse, who some years ago set the society folks of Chicago wild about her "Salome" dance. She was one of the first women in America to dance in her bare feet.

Aside from her marvelous dancing, Mademoiselle has a $5000 wardrobe which she uses for her dances.

Mademoiselle is at preseet a guest of MISS BERTHA WEINTHAL, 311 N. Basin St., where she can be seen in her marvelons dances.

A page from one of the Blue Books where prostitutes (and the producers of the books) used veiled language and code words to advertise the girls' services in such a way as to avoid censorship. Particularly appealing to clients were exotic women like Rita Walker, who adopted the persona of an Oriental Danseuse.

Among the landladies who have become very popular is Miss Vivian who keeps a modern establishment at No. 325 Basin Avenue. In this place of joy there can be found a bevy of girls who are not only fine lookers but entertainers in the art. Boys, visit this house for a good time.

"A Redlight Row," New Orleans *Daily Picayune* July 29, 1904

Viola Donovan and Maggie Mahoney, two tough propositions, who were taken out of a dive on North Robertson Street by Detectives Schultz and Reynolds are in jail, charged with entering in the daytime and petty larceny.

Though they confess that they did just what has been charged against them, there was cause for it, as Nellie Thornton, who lives at 2110 Calliope Street, had roused them.

The three women, according to the detectives, have been visiting the dive on North Robertson Street, in the Redlight District and often visited each other in their uptown homes, which they regarded as private. It was while Nellie was absent from her place a day or so ago that Viola and Maggie, noisy from drink, went to the place on Calliope Street and raided the room of the Thornton woman. They stole a good deal of clothing and a gold-plated medal valued at $10.70.

When the Thornton woman found out what had been done, she made inquiries and got a description of Maggie and Viola, whom she knew, and complained to the police. Detectives Schultz and Reynolds went to the dive on North Robertson Street, where the women were in a drunken slumber, and took them.

Viola acknowledged the theft and said that she took the goods because the Thornton woman had done her out of some money and she was getting even with her. Then she gave out a number of stories about her enemy and declared that there would be a charge of larceny made against Nellie Thornton, and when the time came she would be a witness against the woman. They turned over some of the stolen property to the detectives, who took them to the Saratoga Street Station, where they were booked last afternoon and subsequently turned over to the First City Criminal Court.

Questions to Consider:

1. *In what ways did Storyville reinforce hierarchies of power?*

2. *In what ways did Storyville transgress hierarchies of power?*

3. *Review the map of Storyville (p.284). Where are the two vice districts relative to the railroad? Why would the vice districts be separated by race?*

Sources:

1. Al Rose, *Storyville, New Orleans: Being an Authentic, Illustrated Account of the Notorious Red-Light District* (Tuscaloosa: University of Alabama Press, 1974), 131. Source appears by permission.

2. "A Redlight Row," *Daily Picayune* (New Orleans), July 29, 1904.

Images:

Pamela Arceneaux, *Guidebooks to Sin: The Blue Books of Storyville, New Orleans* (Historic New Orleans Collection: New Orleans, 2017).

1898/1903: The Convict Lease System

The leasing of penitentiaries to private entities preceded the Civil War, when the state decided it did not want the expense of maintaining prisons. The most infamous lessee, Major Samuel L. James, held the contract with the state for more than thirty years beginning in 1867. He paid the state no more than $25,000 per year in return for enormous personal profits earned by exploiting prisoners at his West Feliciana Parish plantation Angola, named for the African country that was the homeland of many of the slaves who had previously toiled on the estate. Though convicts sometimes worked on levees and on railroad construction, most of their labor went toward the cultivation of James's cotton crop. As many as 20 percent of them died each year. Governor Murphy J. Foster, elected as a reformer in 1896, threw his support behind the enemies of the lease system. Foster also championed the disfranchisement of African American voters and the destruction of the Louisiana lottery, a notorious source of corruption. The Louisiana Constitution of 1898, passed on his watch, accomplished all these goals, specifically prohibiting the leasing of convicts and turning the prison over to state control.

Prisoners, however, probably did not notice much of a change. The previous warden was kept in place, the plantation manager was S. L. James's son (James had died in 1894), and the chairman of the penitentiary board was the executor of James's estate. Angola continued to be run as a working plantation, and the state continued to profit from their labor, now enhanced without the middleman.

Constitutional Convention of 1898, Proceedings from Day 1

Up to this time, and it will be so until the penitentiary lease expires, the convicts confined within the walls of our State prison are farmed out, as it were, treated harshly and often made to suffer many unnecessary ills. But we determined to change all that, and hereafter there will be no leasing out of convicts, who, from that time on, will be under the care of the State itself. We have also established for the first time in this State a board of control over all charitable and correctional institutions within our borders, and that we did in the interest of humanity. Heretofore we have been compelled to rely solely upon the reports of grand juries who have investigated these various institutions, and their reports and recommendations were scarcely ever heeded. But this new board will have authority to make estimations and report to the Governor, who, in turn, will submit such report to the legislature for action by that body.

We have also so changed the judicial system that the delays which have so often resulted in a man being hung by a mob will disappear, that every one accused of a crime may secure a speedy trial, and, if found guilty, receive his just punishment at the hands of the legally constituted authorities.

"Prison Reform's Louisiana Progress Told at the Association's Annual Meeting Yesterday," New Orleans *Daily Picayune* March 19, 1903

Mr. Heymann spoke of the Industrial School in charge of Frances Joseph and said it would relieve the situation at the [state-supported Boys' House of Refuge] materially by taking the colored boys.

Mrs. Joseph was present, and was invited to tell of the school which she had founded by her personal effort. She said they had twenty-three children which had been committed by the city, and forty-one which came from other places. Two separate departments were maintained. She told of the successful efforts to train and mold the children, so that they would become useful to the community. There were five instructors, only three of whom were under salary.

Prof. J. M. Dillard delivered an address on "the Central Principle of Prison Reform."

"There is abundant evidence that we are thus contributing effectively to the fostering of public sentiment in support of further reforms, as well as of the very great reforms that have already been accomplished. The abolition of the convict lease system, the placing of the Penitentiary entirely in the State's care [i.e., abolishing the private for-profit prison system], the passage of a bill for a boys' reformatory, the building of the new jail in New Orleans are the great reforms that have already been effected. All this has been done within the last five years, and the good work will stand to the lasting credit of the legislative and executive officers who have accomplished it."

After discussing the principles of prison reform, Prof. Dillard continued:

"The true theory is that those who are in prison should be treated as human beings capable of betterment; that they should be dealt with in the spirit of helpfulness, with the distinct object in view of trying to awaken whatever good may be latent, to encourage and enforce regular habits and thus to lay the foundation for a better character. In brief, it is the introduction of education into prison discipline.

"From this point of view, it is easy to see the tremendous importance of the separation of the young from the old. It is not only that different educative methods are to be employed, but that the young may be saved from any possible contact with the influence of the more confirmed evil habits and evil character of the older lawbreakers and criminals.

"So far as facts are available for forming a judgment, so far as experience has gone in the way of prison reform, the testimony of experts and of judges is strongly to the effect that the actual practice of the new method of dealing with prisoners supports the humane theory on which it is based. Thus the growth of public sentiment against the merely brutal and vindictive treatment of prisoners which has begun and is carrying on the general movement for prison reform will surely be more and more supported by the evidence of practical results until finally society will cease to make criminals more criminal and will clear itself from a long, black record."

Questions to Consider:

1. *Did reformers modernize the prison system after abolishing the convict lease system? Explain.*

2. *Besides ending convict lease, what other reforms of the prison system did these two excerpts describe?*

3. *What similarities are there between modern private prison companies in Louisiana and the convict lease system?*

Sources:

1. *Official Journal of the Proceedings of the Constitutional Convention of the State of Louisiana, held in New Orleans, Tuesday, February 8, 1898* (New Orleans: H. J. Hearsey, 1898).

2. "Prison Reform's Louisiana Progress Told at the Association's Annual Meeting Yesterday," *Daily Picayune* (New Orleans), March 19, 1903.

1910:
Jean Gordon and Social Justice for Children

New Orleanian Jean Gordon typified a wing of Progressive reformers in the United States in that she raised alarm bells about children employed in mines, mills, and factories. She and her sister, Kate, worked with the National Child Labor Committee (NCLC), headquartered in New York City; it investigated and sought legislation to end child labor in corporate settings. As southerners, the sisters balked at a federal amendment abolishing child labor, fearing that it would be applied to black and white children alike. Anti-child labor activities did not overlap with reform of the South's racial structure.

Jean's work led to the passage of the Child Labor Act of 1906 in Louisiana, which mandated (among other things) safe stairways, the provision of bathroom facilities, and seating for female employees. In 1908, she helped to secure the passage of an act that prohibited the employment of children under fourteen.

The first excerpt traces Gordon's work in this realm of the reform movement. The second shows that despite the Child Labor Act, the situation was not fully alleviated by 1913, when the NCLC issued a report based on an investigation by Edward F. Brown, a Special Agent for the NCLC, and famed photographer Lewis Hine.

New Orleans *Times-Democrat*
June 14, 1906

The women in New Orleans who have been dealing with its civic problems have been hoping earnestly for the appointment of a woman factory inspector and that it will be Miss Jean Gordon. She is sympathetic, observant and absolutely fearless in the discharge of any trust committed to her, and it is expected that the Governor will name her for the position.[1]

The child labor question was thoroughly discussed to-night before the House Committee on capital and labor. . . . The first bill taken up was House Bill No. 104, by Mr. Hughes, which prohibits the employment of any child under the age of fourteen in any mill, factory, workshop, laundry, millinery or dress-making establishment, freight or passenger elevator, or in the transmission or distribution of messages, either telegraph or telephone, or merchandise. Hours of labor for persons under eighteen are limited to ten hours, to include the lunch or dinner period. No boy under sixteen or girl under eighteen shall be employed before 7 in the morning or after 6 at night. There is also a provision requiring seats for the use of female employees, at the ratio of one chair to every three females. There is a further provision requiring appointment by the Mayor of a factory inspector in incorporated cities and towns.[2]

Another bill on the same subject by Mr. Kaliski was also considered. This bill is less drastic than that of Mr. Hughes, and is described by Miss Jean Gordon as having been drafted in the interest of manufacturers.

Prof. Cheevis of Calcasieu, the first speaker, asserted that children between six and eighteen should be in school. Any other system tends to mental degradation. The American people are given too much to commercialism; to begin too soon to enter the financial struggle of life. The boy at eleven who undertakes to work and go to school for a half-day is half-dead at his books.

Miss Jean Gordon next addressed the committee and told how two years ago she had asked for the passage of a factory inspection bill. Since then

1. Gordon was indeed appointed Louisiana's first factory inspector and served from 1906–1911. *Times-Democrat,* January 13, 1907.
2. In practice, only New Orleans did this.

she had attempted to gain admission to mills and failed. At that time Mr. Gilmore, city attorney, suggested the ten-hour law.

Miss Gordon then gave her experience as an inspector, telling how girls who had been discharged from factories because they had lost speed were at twenty-five worn out women and a burden to the community. The speaker then analyzed the bills before the committee, which she said were modeled upon those of other States. New York, Missouri, Illinois and Colorado had eight-hour laws on this subject. The law now in force was impotent. The law proposed by the labor unions, she said, might just as well have been framed by the manufacturers.

Miss Gordon then attacked the messenger boy system as the most wicked in the United States—a system where boys are employed at two cents an hour.

She then paid her respects to the Federation of Labor, which she said was enjoying an eight-hour law and had recommended a ten-hour law for women. She then asked if that is the way the men of Louisiana intended to protect their women.

As to certificate of age in the Federation of Labor bill it played absolutely into the hands of the manufacturers. No girls under sixteen ought to be rolling cigars for ten hours a day, and it was a dreadful thing that girls were allowed in this unhealthy industry and should give up their chances of motherhood to furnish men something to smoke.

She paid her respects also to department stores, where there is only one seat for ten girls. "To listen to cotton mill men," she said, "you would imagine the best place on earth is a mill, but everybody who knows anything of hygiene, knows that a damp and hot room, filled with lint, is a breeder of consumption. When the poor women fall by the wayside, they don't see them. We see them and have to care for them."

[Mr. Gilmore argued that her bill would force factories and mills to close because they could not compete with other states that don't have such laws, and that children would be turned out on the streets to become criminals.]

Mr. Gilmore favored uniformity of laws, equally applicable in all States. He did not believe children should work when they are under age. Fourteen years was a safe limit and was already on the books. Every safeguard has been provided in that law. "The law now under discussion was framed by laboring men; haven't they some rights? Why should you undertake to regulate their children?"

John Dymond, Jr., addressed the committee on behalf of an interest outside of New Orleans, which is satisfied with the laws of 1906, this is the oyster industry. There were twelve canning factories in the State, he said, representing an investment of over $1,000,000. The labor employed was brought down from Baltimore and New York and at the end of the season the workers went back. Opening oysters furnished satisfactory and easy employment to children. Chairs for women to sit down and restrictions of child labor would destroy the industry.

Mr. Dymond said he had seen children as young as seven years shucking oysters. They were with their mothers and came and went as they pleased.

Mr. Odenheimer, representing the New Orleans Cotton Mills and as delegate from the Progressive Union and the manufacturers of New Orleans, said Miss Gordon's bill would destroy the manufacturing industries of New Orleans.

"Miss Gordon's minimum age limit is sixteen years," said the speaker. "This is higher than in any other State in the Union." . . .

"Miss Gordon is not practical. Miss Gordon reproaches women who allow their children to work. Miss Gordon believes in education and freedom from early labor. So does the speaker, but some must work. Great men have begun working at twelve years [old]." . . .

Major Hughes closed the discussion for the bill. The law of 1906 was simply to permit the appointment of a female factory inspector. The law was not otherwise changed. The law was a dead letter since 1880, but never until a female inspector was appointed was the law enforced.

Mr. Hughes said the injunction feature of the bill was a necessary feature and is enjoyed by every official in the State. "Miss Gordon is doing wonderful work at considerable expense to herself, as her salary will not suffice for the expenses she incurs. In New Orleans children eight, nine, and eleven years, are working and taught to say they are fourteen. We are going to find out how old the children are. The motto of the factory is 'Work the children to death and save our profits.'"

The Child's Burden in Oyster and Shrimp Canneries

The investigator [Brown] counted at one plant 24 children 14 years old and younger, male and female, the youngest a girl of six. "These children all started work when the factory whistle blew at five-thirty this morning and at two o'clock they were still at work, expecting to finish in a half hour," he reported. The children's hands were red and often had cuts in them. Some of the children did not speak English and thus could not make their hardship known to the investigator.

The superintendent said:

> We don't drive the kids to work. It's the parents who do. I have seen them whip their children when they would not stay on the job. It's better for them to be at work than in mischief, I think. But the parents want the kids to work. We don't pay them much, and if the children were not allowed to work, the people would not come out. If there are three or four children in a family, all working, they can make $2.00 or $2.50 per day, when there is work.
>
> This is a very poor season, and we have not had much work for the people to do. At times they get unruly because, when there is no work, they must eat just the same. So in such cases we advance them credit at the company store. Then when they get work they must pay back. If they knew work was so scarce, they would not come down. Every year I go to Baltimore with the boss, and we promise the people steady work, and nice houses, and good pay, and work for the children. Then when they come down, they expect all these things. During a good year we can keep everyone busy for five months straight.

Sophie and Ferna Wisakarawish, 10 and 9 years respectively, were found at work shucking. Their mother died of heart trouble in one of the company houses, while out on the plant this season. She was buried in a cemetery maintained by the company in the village. The father works around the plant, shoveling oysters at $1.50 per day. According to the father, these children never went to school. Neither of them could speak a word of English. In the summer they work in the berry fields. Steve Bogt, a local American boy of 12, said he goes to school "when there ain't no shucking to be done." Steve worked to-day from 5:30 A.M. till 2 o'clock; filled four pots at 5 cents, earning 20 cents.

The Polish padrone at Dunbar said to me:

> These little children never go to school. They grow up and know nothing—not even to speak English. In the summer they work in the fruit fields, and in the winter they work here. They are travelling all the time and don't get a chance to go to school. The fathers don't make much and everyone must work. *My* children *go* to school. They don't work at shucking. Sometimes the children get up at three o'clock in the morning and work all day. They don't complain because they know if they don't work they can't eat.

Mike Max, a Polish worker, stricken with rheumatism (35 years old), said:

> They ought to make those kids go to school. They never learn nothing. They grow up like me. I can't read and write, so I must work for 50 cents a day. If I was smart I would be a boss and get $3.00 a day. I shuck all day and don't make more than 50 or 75 cents. The little children—they make 10 or 15 cents.

[Hine and Brown visited Morgan City's canning factory which, this particular year, happened to be putting up shrimp. The superintendent told Brown:]

> We did use children as young as 8 years picking shrimp, but the Health Department inspector came around and told us we were violating the law. So after that we did not give checks to children or employ them. They would come with their mothers and pick a little, and it would all go on the mother's check. We will have about fifty Polish families here when work commences. We can run our plant without children, but the parents won't come unless they can work their little children. When the Polanders come, and there is little work for them to do, they start trouble. A short time ago they went on strike, and the men even refused to bring the boats back from the reefs. I went out there and told them if they did not go to work I would blow their heads off; and when they saw I had a gun, they got to work. . . .

In Louisiana game has been the subject of protective legislation as early as 1857, and amendatory legislation has continued unto the present day. It was not until half a century after the first game protective statute that Louisiana saw the need of a child labor law. When, after a most discouraging fight, a child labor law was finally enacted, the machinery provided was and is now so inadequate as to render almost ineffectual the legislative intent which sought to preserve children from premature toil.

From August 1910 to June 1911, the Louisiana Board of commissioners for the Protection of Birds, Game and Fish spent in its work of conservative approximately $128,180. During the same period of time only $900 was spent for one factory inspector [Jean Gordon], and that only in the Parish of New Orleans. This niggardly grant of $900 could hardly serve the health, safety and comfort of upwards of 76,165 wage earners, a sum equivalent to twice as much as the Louisiana Oyster Commission spent for postage in one year ($441.58).

The annual report of the Louisiana Oyster Commission for 1911, in its forward, says:

> Almost everyone admits the necessity of laws for the conservation of our natural resources in the way of game, fish, oysters, shrimp, and water sites.

And believing in this principle, the state passed an elaborate code for the protection of its shellfish supply. Yet Louisiana has not yet apparently reached the point when it recognizes the propriety, economy and right of the child to legal protection, and the enforcement of that right by an adequate staff of competent officials.

An interview with Dr. Mayer Newhauser, Medical Inspector of the State Board of Health, Louisiana, in *The Daily States*, March 9, 1912, on conditions in the canning factory at Violet, La., reports:

> Dirt and filth, filth and dirt wherever one turns. Here, a low ramshackle affair which serves as a dwelling place for ten or fifteen families. Across the way are the rickety shacks of negroes and whites, and a sudden turn in the road shows us a rather boxlike wooden structure, and as we approach nearer its rotten architecture is evident.
>
> We pass on, across a floor lined with incrustations of dirt, puddles of water and an occasional stray oyster, to a little door, which opens into—well, into Hell itself, if the appellation can be so applied, for it is with a shudder and a cry to God for mercy that we see the baby slaves of Louisiana working out their poor little bodies for a corporation known as the Julian Canning Factory, with headquarters in Biloxi, Miss. Children, mind you, six, seven, eight and nine years old, opening oysters with jack-knives, there being no

discrimination as to sex, and their poor little hands bearing mute testimony in the form of cuts and callous to the hardships they have seemingly become inured.

The insanitary conditions surrounding this factory vie with the Black Hole of Calcutta. The toilet accommodations are, strictly speaking, unprintable. The five-roomed rickety wooden structure which serves as such, with no seats but plain running board, is used by men, women, and children, and with its coincident accumulation of feces, which appears to have been there since the toilet was erected, and the horrible stench arising therefrom causes us to shrink unvoluntarily from such sordid surroundings, the like of which is hardly believable in this age of civilization. From the toilet back to the shucking of oysters and placing them in tin cans, without washing hands, is a most common occurrence. . . . [As we are leaving] we catch a glimpse of another row of ramshackle buildings, which these poor creatures call home, and with hearts crying for justice leave this village of child slavery.

Questions to Consider:

1. *In what ways is Gordon making a gendered argument?*

2. *What were the arguments for and against child labor?*

3. *In what ways did employers evade the 1906 child labor law?*

4. *What did the superintendent promise workers in Baltimore that made them decide to move? Did the promise match the reality? Explain.*

5. *In what ways might these conditions for laborers have intensified their exploitation by employers, especially since many were immigrants not born in the United States?*

Sources:

1. *Times-Democrat* (New Orleans), June 14, 1906.

2. Lewis W. Hine and Edward F. Brown, *The Child's Burden in Oyster and Shrimp Canneries*, National Child Labor Committee Publication 193 (New York: 1913).

1912: Brotherhood of Timber Workers and the Grabow Riot

Timber workers in Louisiana and Texas faced worse conditions than existed in lumber camps outside the South. They worked longer hours for lower wages, were gouged in company stores (which workers sometimes called "robberserries"), were charged excessive insurance and hospital fees, and were given inadequate housing and sanitation. In logging camps, the workers (all men) lived in hastily constructed bunkhouses that lacked the room to get to their own bunk without crawling over other workers. Three to four square feet of living area was the average allowed each man, and they were expected to bring their own sleeping gear. One ex-logger said:

> When I worked in the woods we were packed into bunkhouses like sardines. You had to be an acrobat to get into your bunk. There were no bathing facilities in the camp and the camps were so lousy the louses were lousy [meaning filled with lice]. Can you imagine men were actually carrying their whole households on their backs while they were looking for jobs?[1]

In more permanent camps (like mill towns), the company provided family-style houses, but they were little more than shoddily built shacks. Sometimes workers' wives and families moved into the house with them. This helped to keep them in the camp for longer than they

1. Philip Foner, *History of the Labor Movement in the United States*, vol. 4, *The Industrial Workers of the World* (New York: International Publishers, 1965), 215.

might otherwise have agreed to. For most camps, there was a single mess hall and one cook, but the food was terrible and often rotten.

Workers earned from $1.50 to $1.75 per day for an eleven-hour day, six days a week (or a 66-hour week). Mills paid monthly when they paid regularly, and all paid either entirely or in part in scrip, non-legal tender printed by the company and good only at company-owned property. Sometimes workers got a "time check," an IOU to be cashed at some future specified date. If the bearer cashed it early, he was docked a fee, yet because mills often paid irregularly and infrequently, workers couldn't make it from one payday to the next without cashing them.

In response, workers began organizing strikes and won victories like a ten-hour day without a reduction in pay. Mill owners formed a cabal, the Southern Lumber Operators Association (SLOA) "to resist any encroachment of organized labor."[2] Within six years, SLOA represented eighty-seven companies in seven southern states. The organizer and president, John H. Kirby, was the largest lumber operator on either side of the Sabine River.

Yet the workers felt they had no other option to improve their pay and conditions but to form a union, the Brotherhood of Timber Workers (BTW), which came into existence December 3, 1910, in a meeting near DeRidder. The BTW was unusual in many respects. For one thing, it was the only union in the history of southern lumbering that seriously undertook to organize both white and black workers. African Americans had their own lodges and met separately but had to turn over the dues money to the white leadership. Wives and daughters of the lumbermen were also permitted to join the union and to vote.

The BTW's loose qualifications for membership were also unusual. It allowed many who were not directly engaged in the lumber industry to join, including local farmers and a lot of socialists. The SLOA used this as ammunition to portray them as violent revolutionaries who wanted to overthrow democratic governments—none of which was true.

---

2. Connie Elizabeth Berry, "The Brotherhood of Timber Workers and the Grabow Incident in Southwest Louisiana" (Master's thesis, McNeese State University, 1976), 19.

The BTW's first statewide convention met in Alexandria, Louisiana, in 1911, and adopted a constitution. The first document is the preamble. The second document is a list of the Brotherhood's demands, published in local newspapers.

At the organization's second meeting in Alexandria in 1912, the members voted to become affiliated with the International Workers of the World (the IWW, or the "Wobblies"). The group followed the IWW's lead and did away with the practice of black and white members meeting in different rooms. Unfortunately, the BTW's affiliation with IWW allowed the timber workers to be painted as dangerous radicals. Over time, the SLOA's smear campaign ramped up, as illustrated in the third document.

The lumber companies hired thugs to break up strikes. These thugs were responsible for the deadly incident at Grabow, a small mill town near DeRidder, where the union held a rally on July 7, 1912. The Grabow "riot" (as the lumber operators called it), or the "massacre" as the workers saw it, was the beginning of the end for the BTW. The *Industrial Worker* printed an account of the event, which appears here as the fourth document.

After the incident, Sheriff Henry Reid and his deputies from Lake Charles rounded up sixty workers believed to be involved. They were denied bail and put into filthy conditions in an overcrowded jail. All of the men shared a single room with one faucet and one toilet. During the worst heat of summer, the sewer system barely functioned. It was described as a cesspool, a "chamber of horrors."[3] The men endured these conditions for months. Despite the horrific conditions, none of them ever broke ranks. They stood in solidarity with those who had not been arrested and encouraged their brethren to push on to victory.

Fifty-eight union men were indicted, and nine of those went to trial. The jury deliberated only one hour and returned an acquittal. Charges against all the other men were dropped, but the union was broken by the expenses of supporting these men and their families for months and paying attorneys' fees.

3. Charles R. McCord, "A Brief History of the Brotherhood of Timber Workers" (Master's thesis, University of Texas, 1959), 71.

The mill owners reacted by hiring more armed guards and fencing in their property. In Merryville, after a plant fired fifteen men who had been involved in the Grabow trial, the workers called for a general strike, the largest in BTW's history. The owners fought back viciously and brought in scabs (largely black, and all from out of the area, most from out of state) to continue operating at full capacity.

On February 16, 1912, the company unleashed a crowd of drunken men with weapons to destroy the union's facilities and to beat up the leaders. One leader who had not been at that scene, A. L. Emerson, was hunted down in Singer, Louisiana, more than a year later and given a severe beating by company guards. No one was ever prosecuted for the violence.

The owners had won, completely. The BTW got nothing for the workers, whose conditions and wages continued to deteriorate, despite an investigation by the Louisiana Department of Labor in 1916–18, reprinted below as the fifth excerpt, that concluded that the workers were right, and that redress of grievances was needed. The situation persisted until demand for lumber increased during World War I.

The Constitution and By-Laws of the Brotherhood of Timber Workers

> The Brotherhood of Timber Workers is hereby organized and instituted to improve the conditions of those who are engaged in the labor connected with the timber and lumber industries. Its membership shall be composed of all persons, regardless of vocation, who may be in sympathy with the labor movement, and who comply with the constitution, rules and by-laws of the organization, excepting only officers and employers in the above industries and those whose livelihood is obtained by questionable means.
>
> It is our aim to elevate those who labor—morally, socially, intellectually and financially. We intend to correct and mitigate the abuses of employers in these industries, of whatever kind and wherever found. It is our purpose to use every legitimate effort

to remove and correct such obvious and patent abuses as compulsory doctor's fees, hospital dues, the unfair insurance system so universally practiced, the inordinately high commissary prices, the long and trying hours of labor, the high rents charged for the use of houses, and any and all other unfair and unjust impositions now fastened upon us by employers in these industries.

While demanding our rights, we, at the same time concede, that the employer is entitled to, and we promise him, an absolutely square deal in every sense which this implies. We ask for nothing which we are not willing to grant. To secure justice we must do justice. Violence, in all of its forms, shall be discouraged. Property rights shall be respected, and thrift and moderation among our membership encouraged. Personal violence shall be frowned upon, in whatever guise it may assume. Our appeal shall be to reason and enlightened humanity; it shall be our instrument in establishment of those rights which are common to all mankind, and which we solemnly assert we do not now enjoy. In every struggle in which we may engage, it shall be carried forward with energy, and by every legal means, to accomplish the fundamental purposes of this organization. In the fierce industrial struggle, in which those who labor in every trade and industry are engaged, in order to preserve their very lives, it is our purpose to give sympathy and every proper assistance. At all times, and in all things, we shall be glad to meet and counsel with those who employ us, and by the acts of reason, justice, and persuasion, try to convince them of the righteousness of our cause. We demand:

- Recognition
- Equal rights
- A living wage
- A just consideration of abuses
- Exact and equal justice to those who work with their hands, and who contribute so much to the comforts of mankind, and who get so little in return.

"Truth About Timber Trust" by Covington Hall, *The Rebel* (Hallettsville, TX), February 8, 1913

Demands of the Brotherhood

1. a minimum wage of $2.00 per day, the work day not to exceed ten hours in duration
2. a two weeks pay-day in United States and not commissary currency
3. the right of free trade, the workers not to be forced to buy from company stores, where prices are 33 1/3 percent to 50 percent higher than in surrounding "free towns"
4. a discontinuance of the practice of discounting wages
5. reasonable rents
6. a revision of insurance, hospital and doctor fees, the right to elect their doctors, to see the insurance policy and to have representatives on a committee that is to control these funds. [Doctors typically served several lumber communities and often could not be found in an emergency; if a worker was injured in the woods, his only hope was that the injury might be minor. There was no hospital or clinic in any company town, and drivers and railroads were not allowed to transport an injured worker to the closest one, St. Patrick's in Lake Charles, for fear a lawyer might find out and initiate a lawsuit.]
7. a general improvement in the sanitary and living conditions of the lumber towns and camps
8. the disarming and discharge of all gunmen
9. the right of free speech, press and assembly

St. Louis Lumberman, August 1, 1911

Judging from the demands which have thus far been made upon millmen, the movement is in the hands and under the direction of men seeking to impose extraordinary and impossible conditions upon the employer. The changes sought are, in fact, so revolutionary that no yellow pine manufacturer could do business under them. They include not only impossible demands as to wages and hours of labor, but embrace also every fad of the impracticable dreamer on the labor question. It is a movement run wild.

> That the manufacturers will oppose, with every resource at their command, the introduction of the proposed labor system into the plants goes without saying. They have no objection to unions as such, provided their aims and purposes are reasonable and fair. But they are utterly opposed to labor associations of the character and of the lack of sanity with which they are now confronted, and rather than submit to their demands wholesale shut-downs of plants will be ordered.

Industrial Worker, July 18, 1912

Not content with maiming and mangling the peons in their slave camps in the lumber district the Southern Lumber Operators' Association has turned loose who dare to struggle for better conditions.

As a sequel to the degenerate actions of Kirby's thugs there are three men lying dead in Grabow, La., and 20 others are wounded. Some of the latter are not expected to live

Among those placed under arrest as the result of the battle between the scabs and the BTW men are A. L. Emerson, president of the Brotherhood of Timber Workers, and J. T. Calloway, president of the Galloway Lumber Co. The dead are A. T. Vincent, scab; Roy Martin Cates Hall, and two unidentified men, unionists; the fatally wounded being Ed Brown and J. Tooley, union men, and Bud Hickman, farmer.

The union men were from DeRidder and nearby points. They had gathered under direction of Emerson to hold demonstration in front of the non-union mills. The objective point was Grabow, where the Galloway plant is located.

Following a series of meetings, one of which was held at Carson, amid the jeers of the company thugs and the continual din created by hoodlums hired by the Kirby interests, the band of union men marched to the Galloway mills.

There Emerson commenced to address the non-union men, asking them to be men rather than peons and to stand up for their class. The beating of tin cans and other noises created by company hirelings drowned out his voice. Suddenly an oath was heard high above all other noises and a shot pierced the body of a union man standing just beside Emerson. The shot came from the company office, it is alleged. This was a signal for action and the scabs and thugs of the Lumber Trust had access to the guns and ammunition stored close at hand and the shooting became general.

After a battle lasting over ten minutes Emerson and the union men were forced to break for cover. They gained the woods and made their way to their homes.

It is said that more than a score of arrests have been made upon the charge of murder. The militia has been called out, despite the protests of many persons. Especially strong in denouncing the calling of the troops are Wm. D. Haywood and Covington Hall, who were in New Orleans on business for the B. T. W. at the time of the outrage. It is thought that the presence of troops will add to the tenseness of the situation.

The feeling against Kirby's hired murderers is growing and its echo is heard in Eastern Texas. In Oakdale, La., the company gunmen shot at H. G. Creel, leading writer for the National Rip-Saw. Creel has been instrumental in exposing Kirby's blacklist and also is spreading broadcast the story of the shameful conditions in the Southern labor camps. Along with the leaders of the B.T.W. there is a price upon his head, it is alleged, offered by the Lumber Trust. . . .

The Southern Sawmill Operators' Association has its headquarters at St. Louis, from which point it has been directing a bitter warfare against the B. T. W. The weapons used have been the boycott of B. T. W. sympathizers, the blacklist of B. T. W. men, the mysterious shooting of active union men, the lockout of 5,000 men from their plants, and now open warfare on the B. T. W. and I. W. W. organizers at the hands of hired murderers, while the instigators of these cowardly deeds skulk in their palatial offices.

The B. T. W. is built of the same kind of men as the I. W. W. and against the spirit of revolution that springs alike in their breasts the guns of Kirby's thugs are powerless.

Instead of breaking up the B. T. W. these damnable actions will awaken the spark of manhood in those who have been mere onlookers and the result will be ONE BIG UNION of toilers which will soon have control of the forests and the mills now being despoiled by Kirby and his breed of degenerate coyotes.

Ninth Biennial Report of the Department of Commissioner of Labor and Industrial Statistics, Louisiana, 1916–1918

Investigations have thoroughly convinced us that some law should be passed regulating the operation of company stores or leased commissaries since conditions show conclusively the real sufferer in the final analysis is the laborer. Similar laws have been passed by sister states and proven a blessing and saving to those who ordinarily receive a low rate of wages. Statistics show that leased commissaries are even worse than those operated by employers themselves. . . .

If such places were properly conducted, that is, sell laborers such goods and wares as were necessary and furnish same at cost of maintenance or even at a small margin of profit, no adverse comment would come from this office, but ordinarily these conditions do not exist. It is true that some of the more humane employers are doing this, while a few claim to be operating stores at a slight loss, but the average company store or leased commissary is operated as a money-making proposition and prices are fabulously high. . . .

It is no hard task to solve who are the real sufferers under such conditions as these. What profit is derived by the laborer even though wages are increased ten, twenty, or even thirty per cent if there are no restrictions thrown around such conditions as these and unscrupulous employers and their allies are permitted to literally rob them by charging exorbitantly high prices?

Questions to Consider:

1. *Do you think the fact that the BTW sought to organize across racial lines was a main reason that it was defeated, or were there other more important factors at work? Explain.*

2. *Does an employer have the right to suppress workers' freedom of speech, press and assembly?*

3. *What parts of this story indicate the sentiment of the local population toward the union? Does it seem like public opinion tended to fall one way or another, or does it seem divided? Why might locals have supported workers? Why might they have supported the company?*

4. *Why do you think none of the hired musclemen were indicted or brought to trial for their actions? What does this tell you about the idea of justice being "blind" to class and race differences?*

Sources:

1. *Constitution and Bylaws of the Brotherhood of Timber Workers* (Alexandria, LA: n.p. 1911).

2. Convington Hall, "Truth About Timber Trust," *The Rebel* (Hallettsville, TX), vol. [2], no. 83, ed. 1 Saturday, February 8, 1913, https://texashistory.unt.edu/ark:/67531/metapth394731/, University of North Texas Libraries, The Portal to Texas History, crediting UT San Antonio Libraries Special Collections.

3. *St. Louis Lumberman*, August 1, 1911.

4. *Industrial Worker*, July 18, 1912.

5. Louisiana, Department of Commissioner of Labor and Industrial Statistics, *Ninth Biennial Report, 1916–1918* (Baton Rouge; Department of Commissioner of Labor and Industrial Statistics of the State of Louisiana, n.d.).

1912:
Eleanor McMain and Kingsley House

Eleanor McMain, a native of Baton Rouge, moved to New Orleans to train with the Episcopal Church's Free Kindergarten Association. Out of this came Kingsley House, a settlement house in the Irish Channel neighborhood of New Orleans. Kingsley House was the brainchild of the pastor of Trinity Episcopal Church, and Trinity provided nearly all its original funding and donations of land and buildings. It was established to help the surrounding community at the time, which were German, Italian, and Irish immigrants, to overcome barriers as they settled in New Orleans. McMain became head resident in 1901 and spent that summer in Chicago studying with Jane Addams at Hull House, considered the model settlement in America.

Within a year, McMain made Kingsley House non-sectarian for several reasons. For one, it served a largely Catholic population, and from Jane Addams McMain learned to teach immigrants to respect their own religion and heritage. By that time, too, Kingsley House was receiving financial support from a variety of sources, and members of many faith traditions supplied residents and volunteers.

Just as Addams affiliated with the University of Chicago, Kingsley House formed a partnership with Tulane. Beginning in 1914, McMain's Southern School of Social Science and Public Service (now the Tulane School of Social Work) offered the first classes in social welfare in the Deep South on the Kingsley House campus.

McMain served as head resident for more than thirty years. During that time, she rolled out a variety of services for the poor in the surrounding neighborhood. Many of these services provided a model for New Orleans's city planners. For example, after Kingsley House created a park nearby where the children could play (supervised by one of its residents), interested citizens put pressure on Mayor Martin Behrman to do likewise. He established a playground commission which included McMain and other Kingsley House volunteers or staff. Within a few years, they had opened up more than two dozen public parks throughout the city—for white people only. African Americans could not receive services at Kingsley House (though they could at another settlement house in the city run by Methodist women, St. Marks).[1]

Eleanor McMain received the *Times-Picayune* Loving Cup in 1918 for her significant contribution to the quality of life in New Orleans, and in 1932 a public high school for girls was named in her honor.

The first excerpt below is from one of Eleanor McMain's annual reports to the board. The second is a history of Kingsley House listing its accomplishments. The third is a newspaper story describing Kingsley House's expansion and McMain's achievements as of 1925.

The Kingsley House, New Orleans, 1903–04, Report of Head Resident, Eleanor McMain

Kingsley House is situated in one of the densely populated portions of New Orleans. It is surrounded by factories, mills, tenements and foundries.

[Tenements] have certain features in common:

1st. The alleys and small court yards are damp, and pervaded by a musty, unwholesome odor.

2nd. The water supply is from cisterns that are seldom cleaned, and must of necessity be laden with dust and germs.

3rd. The houses are jammed together and have no side windows.

4th. There is only twenty-five per cent yard space to the entire lot. . . . In these buildings live forty grown people, twenty children, and there is no yard space at all.

1. However, since the 1940s, Kingsley House has actively provided programming for children of all races.

5th. When there are three or more rooms the middle ones are without means of ventilation.

6th. The sanitary arrangements, or rather the lack of any modern sanitary accommodations, creates a condition that is often beyond description.

Many of the streets are unpaved, and clouds of dust are sent up by every passing vehicle. The open gutters are usually clogged and filled with trash, sometimes so completely that the water from the factories finding no means of exit backs up into the alleys, there to lie until some of the men who live on the street devote a Sunday morning to opening the gutter. . . .

Under such conditions, is it any wonder that cleanliness comes to be a virtue difficult of attainment? That the proper kind of home life cannot be developed in places where there is no privacy, nor any of the adjuncts that help to make neat, attractive homes?

Should we be surprised when we come to know that the children of this neighborhood are as a rule, small, undeveloped physically? Or that tuberculosis is so very prevalent?

Forces Working Against a High Standard of Life

Some of the forces, then, that are operating to lower the standard of life in our midst are:

1st. The housing conditions.

2nd. The generally unsanitary condition of the public thoroughfares.

3rd. The precariousness of the livelihood of the wage-earners. The majority of the men are unskilled laborers making from $1.25 to $1.50 per day. Work is not always steady, sickness or accident at times befall them. For these contingences they can make no provision, except through their insurance companies or benevolent associations, and it is a question whether these are not often an added ill condition rather than a benefit.

If they pay their rent, feed and clothe their families (usually large ones), they are doing all that can be expected of them.

4th. The illegal traffic in lottery tickets.

5th. The evasion of law regarding the sale of intoxicating liquor to minors.

6th. Most menacing of all the temptation which comes to parents to exploit the labor of their children.

Possessed of few educational advantages themselves, they fail often to appreciate what educational advantages mean to their children. They have an idea in fact that the "book-learning" for them and for their children is of but little practical value. They and their children have no need for any but the most elementary knowledge in the work they will have to do.

We have no compulsory education laws; often the children who are not at work are kept from school for the most trivial causes.

The child-labor laws that we have are ineffective in as much as evasions of the law seem to be so easy. We have no inspectors, and no educational qualification. Most important of all, the social conscience of the community is not fully awake to the responsibility which the community should feel for its children. Nor does the community seem to have fully assimilated the fact that "It is a foolish and short-sighted people who will use up the strength of its citizens before they are grown to manhood."

Kingsley House, 1896–1925

What is Kingsley House?

It is a Social Settlement.

It is primarily an educational institution.

It is a demonstration of democratic living.

It belongs to **all** of the people of the community, irrespective of their religion, politics or economic condition.

The rich, the poor and the fairly well-to-do are all equally welcome.

It is theirs to use and to enjoy to the enrichment and beautifying of life in their community.

It has **no** propaganda save neighborliness.

Its only watchword is service. . . .

A brief summary of the notable items in this [historic Kingsley House] record follows:

In the Interest of Health:

Gathered facts about the prevalence of tuberculosis in the neighborhood. Verified these findings with the City Board of Health. Direct outgrowth of this activity was the formation of the Anti-Tuberculosis League.

Maintained clinics at the House for mothers and babies long before the founding of the Woman's Dispensary or the Child Welfare Association. Stressed proper feeding of babies in lectures by physicians.

Instituted physical examinations for all children going to Camp Onward.[2]

Made an intensive study of the neighborhood housing conditions. Secured the passage of an ordinance which mitigated some of the most flagrant housing evils. Established a connection between bad housing and tuberculosis.

Residents of Kingsley House served as volunteer inspectors for the Housing Commission for three years. Also sat in with the committee that revised the building code.

Took children of pre-school age to the dentist regularly, and also saw children through adenoid and tonsil operations.

Acted as volunteer nurses when occasion demanded in the days before there was any organized visiting nursing service. Both House residents and neighborhood mothers gave this service to their neighborhood whenever it was needed.

Operated a diet kitchen during the flu epidemic [of 1918–19].

In the Interest of Education:

Worked with the neighborhood schools for better school attendance and for a longer school life for each child.

Sought to enrich the educational experiences of the neighborhood by

---

2. A camp on the North Shore of Lake Pontchartrain to which Kingsley House women took hundreds of underprivileged children every summer.

offering classes not included in the school curriculum. For example, maintained a kindergarten until the Board of Education put kindergartens in the neighboring schools.

Maintained manual training and hand-work classes for boys and girls before any such courses were offered in the schools.

Taught chair caning and basket weaving to many public school teachers.

Introduced folk dancing. Held classes for teachers and other group leaders as well as for settlement groups.

Through story-telling, chorus singing, dramatics, sought to strengthen the cultural side of life in the neighborhood.

Maintained a vacation school for four years, then turned it over to the Board of Education.

Gave individual instruction to ambitious boys and girls, helping them to qualify for higher positions.

Maintained courses in training for social work. Operated same for three years. During the war [World War I] merged it into training course for home service workers. This work was absorbed by the Red Cross and the University.

Before the Board of Education opened evening schools, took care of the overflow from the Sophie Wright night school. This work was immediately turned over to the Board of Education when evening schools were provided.

In the Interest of Industrial Relations:

Helped to pass the State Child Labor Law. A Kingsley House mother went with the committee to the Legislature. Her impassioned plea for her own and other women's children did much to win the day for the bill.

Worked in neighborly fashion with neighborhood industries. Furnished a sort of middle ground of understanding between capital and labor.

In the Interest of Recreation:

Opened the first playground in New Orleans (1903).

Featured recreation not only for children but for grown-ups.

Ran Saturday night dances regularly supervised by the neighborhood council.

Opened a fresh-air camp where from five to six hundred children have a twelve days' outing each year [Camp Onward].

Opened the first children's gardens in New Orleans.

Maintained game rooms, reading and study rooms.

Offered an athletic program to neighborhood boys and men.

Community Work of Women's Clubs:

Took charge of Second Ward [Irish Channel] in campaign to eradicate yellow fever.

Canvassed Second Ward in educational campaign against tuberculosis.

Canvassed Second Ward to help the Woman's Dispensary.

Helped in tag day for Milne Home [for Girls].

"New Kingsley House Social Center Opens; Williams Gets *Times-Picayune* Loving Cup," New Orleans *Times-Picayune*, May 27, 1925

Frank B. Williams, lumberman and financier, got the 1924 Loving Cup for his donation of $300,000 for the new Kingsley House and Day Nursery at 1600 Constance Street. "It's the greatest settlement house in America," Albert J. Kennedy, executive secretary of the National Federation of Settlements said after looking it over. "There is nothing to compare with it, and only Hull House approaches it. As the boys say, it's the cat's eyebrows."

"The most wonderful development of the settlement house idea there is anywhere," said Miss Harriet E. Vittum, head of the Northwestern University settlement. "The great open space in the center and the small unit buildings which surround it will prevent it from ever becoming an institution. It is splendid that it should be headed by Miss Eleanor McMain, who is known and loved by every settlement worker in the country."

Mr. Kennedy said, "I am greatly impressed with the features and the outlook of this plant as well as Miss McMain's marvelous work here and in France. She is a national figure in social work." The $300,000 provided by the benefactor provided both land and buildings. The grounds are green, simple, cheerful, airy and clean. There are several buildings, one of which has the child welfare clinic on the ground floor and upstairs the girls' department with a library, domestic department, and a model flat to help little housekeepers learn the home making game. The day nursery has sleeping porches with green-striped awnings. There's also a shop building to teach trade work to men. . . .

Questions to Consider:

1. *Imagine yourself a small black child living near Kingsley House. Write about how you would feel watching white children go in and out of Kingsley House grounds, parks, and buildings while you were not allowed to enter. How might this have affected the trajectory of your life as you grew older.*
2. *What reforms did Kingsley House residents jump-start in New Orleans and/or in Louisiana?*
3. *In what ways did Kingsley House partner with other progressive reformers?*

Sources:

1. "The Kingsley House, New Orleans, 1903–04, Report of Head Resident, Eleanor McMain," Kingsley House Papers, LaRC-360, Louisiana Research Collection (LaRC), Tulane University Special Collections, New Orleans, LA.

2. "Kingsley House, 1896–1925," LaRC-360.

3. "New Kingsley House Social Center Opens; Williams Gets *Times-Picayune* Loving Cup," *Times-Picayune* (New Orleans), May 27, 1925.

1913–1920:
Kate Gordon and Woman Suffrage

Kate Gordon, like her sister Jean, was an influential reformer of the progressive era in New Orleans. Well-to-do Unitarians who never married, the sisters devoted their lives to public service. In addition to supporting white women's rights, Kate was a vocal advocate in the public health effort to control tuberculosis. In 1906, she organized the Louisiana Anti-Tuberculosis League, and later she managed the New Orleans Anti-Tuberculosis Hospital located in the Gentilly neighborhood.

Kate established the Equal Rights Association Club (ERA Club) in 1896, and in 1901 she joined the leadership of the National American Woman Suffrage Association (NAWSA). By this time, the right to vote had been stripped away from African Americans, and both Kate and Jean were intent on keeping it that way. They, like most other southern reformers, remained bitterly racist and bent on buttressing white supremacy.

Over the next twenty years, Kate Gordon opposed a federal suffrage amendment, preferring that decisions about who qualified to register to vote be left up to the states. To make her opposition to federal enfranchisement clear, Gordon resigned from the NAWSA board and in 1913 formed a rival organization, the Southern States Woman Suffrage Conference, dedicated to state-controlled suffrage. Gordon saw the federal amendment as a threat to white supremacy because she feared that the state's recently enacted poll taxes and literacy tests (designed to keep black people from voting) would be ended by federal enforcement.

In the first excerpt below, however, the New Orleans *Item* opined that a federal amendment should not be concerning to supporters of woman suffrage because there were "exactly 86 registered negro voters in New Orleans" and the number was unlikely to change much if women were enfranchised.

The Woman's Suffrage Party of Louisiana supported the Nineteenth Amendment (previously called the Anthony Amendment for Susan B. Anthony), and in their publicity campaign argued that enfranchising women would "automatically give this state the benefit of many thousands of intelligent progressive white voters with a lively interest in education, sanitation, good roads, civic betterment and progress to offset the ignorant negro and foreign elements which have handicapped us in the past. It is, besides, a measure of right and justice to the women who pay taxes, obey laws, teach, toil, and serve in every capacity needed by men, and who to-day are supporting the war and all its activities with signal patriotism."[1]

New Orleans *Item*, March 19, 1914

It is not likely there would be very many more negro women voters. In case the suffrage were granted to women, the same educational qualifications and the payment of poll taxes and length of residence in wards now required for men would necessarily be applied to women voters. On the other hand, as has been pointed out by the sincere advocates of white supremacy, the number of white women who would be able to qualify, and who would qualify and vote if given the chance, would be so much greater than any proportion of colored women who could meet these requirements that the net result of the enfranchisement of women in the Southern states would be to INCREASE the total white vote beyond any possibility of negro domination. It is facts like these that make one doubt the reality of the pretensions of certain political leaders to be genuine advocates of either woman suffrage or white supremacy.

1. Letter from Woman's Suffrage Party of Louisiana Publicity Chair (unsigned), October 23, 1918, LaRC-700.

New Orleans *Times-Picayune*
January 14, 1918

[The newspaper quoted Gordon from a speech she gave at a meeting of the ERA (Equal Rights Amendment) Club held on the Tulane campus]:

Miss Gordon explained that by a federal amendment negro women would be placed on the same par with white women and that while white men would be willing to club negro men away from the polls they would not use the club upon black women. "If the white men of the South are not willing to raise their women above the negro men, then the federal ballot will not do it. . . . Should a federal amendment be ratified dealing with the suffrage, then the national government will supervise our elections, and we shall have the reconstruction period over again. The reason Mr. Wilson has made such a wonderful president is because he knows history, and he knows that the rights of the states are the fundamental principles of this government." [President Wilson, elected in 1912 and again in 1916, was a southern Democrat who sympathized with the states' rights argument.]

Questions to Consider:

1. *What arguments did the pro-suffrage forces use in favor of the federal amendment?*
2. *What arguments did Gordon and her allies use against the federal amendment and in favor of state-controlled suffrage?*
3. *How did racism figure into the arguments of both groups?*

Sources:

1. *Item* (New Orleans), March 19, 1914, Women Suffragettes papers, LaRC-700.

2. *Times-Picayune* (New Orleans), January 14, 1918, LaRC-700.

1930:
A Union Organizer's Memories

Clinton Clark was a black sharecropper who became an organizer for the Southern Tenant Farmers' Union (STFU). He was born in 1903 on a plantation in Pointe Coupee Parish near the little town of Fordoche, Louisiana, the youngest of seven children in a family of creole-speaking sharecroppers. Pointe Coupee suffered terrible damage in 1912 when the Atchafalaya Basin flooded. Clark's family, along with many other sharecropping families, nearly starved because what relief was provided to the parish went to white families, not to black families, and there was no legal redress for those denied relief. The injustice of this stayed with him for life.

Because he hated how hard people had to work on the former slave plantations in return for little money and constant debt, Clark joined a sister in California in the 1930s. In Sacramento, he learned about organizing the poor and was introduced to the Communist Party of the United States of America (CPUSA). The CPUSA (whose members were largely American citizens) assisted African Americans as they sought equal justice. Clark, like many other union organizers in the 1930s, saw the CPUSA as an ally in the struggle.

He returned to his native Louisiana to work with the STFU and in 1937, Clark formed the Louisiana Farmers Union along with Clyde Johnson, a white man he referred to as Claud. Clark recruited African Americans and Johnson enlisted white workers into the LFU. The union helped workers file for back wages and organized tenant farmers' co-ops that bought fertilizer and other staples from distributors rather than from plantation commissaries. Clark also assisted tenant farmers displaced by the Agricultural Adjustment Administration to get the checks that landowners were withholding from them.

The following excerpt was taken from Clark's autobiography. Dialect and misspellings from original have been preserved.

[When I was young] the women had to work in the planters house for $1.50 a week and one quart of milk and most of the time would have to work from 6 O'Clock until 10 P.M. And until this day the women are still getting $1.50 a week. Their have to clean the house and wash all the cloths and go in the fields and hoe when their get the work done around the house. And in these community if you don't say Yes Sir and No Sir to the White man or the White women, the mob will be sure to get you and take you in the woods and put you in a tree. At one time around Villeplatte La. One of the planter had sold one quart of milk to a Negro sharecropper and the planter claim that the sharecropper hadn't paid for the milk. And the sharecropper said he had paid the planter for the milk. So the planter said that a nigger called him a lie [liar]. The planter went home and came back with two more planters with shot guns and kill the poor sharecroppers and left his poor widow with 10 children to support. And nothing was ever did about the matter, and no Negroes was allow to say anything about the killing. If any one would be caught saying something about this killing the same would happen to them. And if any contractor would come through there putting up some kind of job, no Negroes would be allow to work on the job. The contractor would have to hire White or the contractors would catch hell with the mob gang. So the Negroes never knew anything about working on public jobs, nothing but plantation work for 40 cents and 35 cents a day working from dark to dark.

To day around this section you cant find four Negro sharecroppers out of ever[y] hundred can sign his own name. . . . But the sharecroppers are still looking to the good lord. That the day shall come when the bottom rail shall come on top, and the top rail shall come on the bottom. . . .

The only chance you had getting on public jobs was when the Standard Oil Co. would open up new jobs putting down pipes. Or you could go in the woods and cut trees from sun to sun, for one dollar a day. So I went to work on the plantation for 60 cents a day. I hated to do that, because I knew that 60 cents a day couldn't buy enough to eat for one person and was much harder to feed a family on that amount. And buy shoes and clothes. I had one little sister who we wanted to continue going to school. And my parents were anxious for me to go to school. They wanted us to get an education. Because during those days the rural schools' terms was very short, we Negroes would only get three months schooling in each season. And too the conditions were so bad for the poor farmers, because the planters would refuse to give the sharecroppers money for the crops they would make during the year no matter how much cotton the sharecroppers would make. The times was no better with the sharecroppers if the cotton was selling for 40 cents a pound. The planters always had his robberserrry to take what his sharecroppers made each year in the fields. . . .

I went to Lettsworth La in pointe coupee parish where the first farmer union local was organize and had been 500 strong and was well organize[d]. And our state sec'y [Director] Gordon McIntire [from Arkansas] had been sick [with tuberculosis] for some time. . . . That reason the members[hip] had died down. So while I was in Washington D.C. the committee to aid Agriculture workers had given me $200.00 to buy a car to continue my work. I travel all over the parish in my car, calling meetings in every community getting the dead local going with full speed again and two or three new ones on start. I would travel night and day working to build a strong union all over the state. We would go and have conferences with the FSA and the AAA agents and invite them to our meeting. And whenever the FSA agents would have meeting in the parish, I would always attend their meeting and make speeches in their meeting. And would have all the members of the farmers union to attend these meeting. During my organizing in pointe coupee parish, I came across a large plantation by the name of rexmere plantation. About 75 sharecroppers family living in peonage. The owner of this plantation live up in Chicago. This plantation was surrounded with bob wire fence. A big gate kept lock at all time. No one was allow to enter on this plantation unless they get the permesson from the plantation boss.

And no sharecroppers was allow to come off the plantation unless their get permesson from the plantation boss. On this plantation there was one of the most beautiful fishing lake in the country. Whenever the sharecroppers went fishing on this lake, they would have to give one half of the fish they get to the plantation boss. And if there was no work to be done the sharecroppers would some time go in the woods and pick moss to sell. They would also had to give of the moss they pick to the plantation boss. Also the plantation boss would buy each family his house hold goods and have them to pay for them out of their crops. But when the sharecroppers was ready he would have to leave the household goods on this plantation. And it was no way for the sharecroppers to run away because he had to go through the gate and the plantation boss had the key and they sure had go by him because he live near the gate. And no visit was allow unless he get permission and had to tell who he wants to see and what for and if he get permesson he would be limit. And this rule was the same on the sharecroppers.

Also there was a big store on this plantation where the sharecroppers had to get they food and pay double price for what ever they get out of the big store. And no sharecroppers ever know what a government check was alabout. The plantation owner would go back and forward to Chicago. He had a beautiful home on the plantation. He had a united states flag hanging over his home. When ever he would be going to Chicago the flag would be hanging up. And when he would be at his plantation home the flag would be down.

Leon Smith and Nelson Connady said, If the sharecroppers would work six days in the week, they would always be short of a day when they goes to get they pay. And when they would go to the Overseer and ask about they time, the overseer would tell them that he was going to pay them what was on the book. And at the same time the overseer would get angry. Some time the sharecroppers would work until 10 O.Clock at night and would not get any pay for the overtime they worked. When it would rain the overseer would have some of the sharecroppers cleaning the tracter and greaseaing the tools and would not get any pay for this work. When the sharecroppers would protest about pay for this work, the overseer would tell them that a man has the right to clean his tools what he worked. . . .

I went to Franklin, La., where there was a large sugar cane plantation working the labor under the wages hour law [The Sugar Act of 1937]. I began to get a local started. We were organizeing in secret because the sugar cane planters was doing everything their [they] could to keep the labor unimform [uninformed] of the wages hour law. Many of the labor was paid below the wages hour law. I travel all over the cane belt and find the same condition on ever cane plantation. The planters was against the wages hour law. They would have the big store to get even with the labor when they would come to the big store to get their food. Very little cash the labor would have when they would get their pay envelope on pay days. Mr. McIntire our state Sec'y of the La. F.U. had collected thousand of dollars for the sugar cane labors in the cane belt. He even fought hard to get wages hour law to act for the sugar cane labors and was success to get it to act.

McIntire never lost one minute fighting for the poor farmers while he was in the fields. Many night he slept in his car on the high way waiting for the day to brake so he could have a meeting on some case that they por farmer had give him to take up with the government official in the county seat. . . . He sure know what to do with these big planters when they are stealing form us poor farmers. The planters don't like him because he stood up for our justice and kept them from taking government money from us. . . .

The sharecroppers are still talking about how the planters was talking about killing McIntire and tried to bluff McIntire but their couldn't do that. McIntire stood on his ground for the right of the sharecropper. McIntire lost his health by staying out night and day fighting for the right of the poor farmers both White and Negroes [he was in the hospital in New York City as Clark wrote]. When the rent rise was stop and the back money was collected, it was collected for both White and Negroes.

Most of my experience came from McIntire. He would never let me miss an opportunity where ever it was a chance for me to get some experience. My first trip to Washington DC McIntire had the La. F.U. to send me there to the agriculture department to tell the condition of the poor farmers in the State of Louisiana. There must have been the sum of 37 tenant in the agriculture department from the south. We had conference with the head of the AAA, WPA, FSA, and the relief agents and many other government official in Washington D.C. When McIntire taking sick, I work hard as a bee to hold the farmers union members together along [alone] by myself. Had a couple of union members to come and take McIntire but was unexperence and the job went bad for awhile. But I never lost one minute fighting to keep farmers union rolling.

Many time I have been offer another job and a good one two if I would let that union business alon[e]. I know if that was did it would mean that I had sold my class to the boses. Like Judas did Christ, sold him out for a piece of sliver [silver]. I know that I was in the working class and will always stay in my class. Many times the planters had threaten to kill me and also McIntire. We never stop because they threaten our life because we know we was on the right track. Our work was for justice and not to penetrate our class into the bosses class.

Questions to Consider:

1. *Explain the factors Clark identified that prevented tenants from looking for better opportunities off the plantation.*

2. *How might Clark's lack of fluency with standard English have hampered his abilities as an activist? In what ways did providing limited educational opportunities to African Americans serve the white power structure?*

3. *Why do you think Clark made a point of saying he was not trying to overturn the capitalist class (the owners) and replace them with working-class people?*

Source:

Clinton Clark, *Remember My Sacrifice: The Autobiography of Clinton Clark, Tenant Farm Organizer and Early Civil Rights Activist*, eds. Elizabeth Davey and Rodney Clark (Baton Rouge: Louisiana State University Press, 2007), 7, 14–15, 89–95.

1929:
Articles of Impeachment against Huey Long

Huey Long, a controversial Democratic politician from Winnfield, Louisiana, built a powerful political machine on the votes of poor white citizens, particularly farmers, outside New Orleans. Winn Parish was a relatively poor parish in an area of concentrated populist and socialist activity, and it seems clear that the ideas Long imbibed around him shaped his own brand of populism. After winning the gubernatorial election of 1928, Long immediately moved to raise taxes to finance those things he had promised his supporters, such as free textbooks and paved roads. This move produced a revolt in the legislature, particularly when he asked for a levy of five cents a barrel on refined petroleum products to help, in his words, "the lame, the halt[1], the blind, and the little school children of the state."[2] The revolt was in part stirred up by the object of this tax, Standard Oil, Huey Long's longstanding enemy. Long's attempt to control the special taxing session resulted in a veritable brawl in the House. A representative managed to bring order back to the House, but the next day, the House brought nineteen resolutions of impeachment against Long; all but eight were dropped and sent to the Senate, where the trial would be held. The first charge was litigated and dropped. Before the second charge was presented, a round-robin document signed by fifteen senators—two more than enough to block a two-thirds conviction—de-

1. Meaning someone who walks with a limp.
2. "Legislators Hold Actions Indefensible," *The Shreveport Times* (Shreveport, LA), March 22, 1929.

clared they would not vote to convict Long on the remaining charges because those charges had been filed after the legislative session had ended. This ended the attempt at impeachment.

Long maintained that he had done nothing different than the governors before him except that his goal was to help the poor of Louisiana, while previous governors were only interested in helping rich people like themselves.

Although Long remained in office, a look at the charges brought against him provides insight into the types of corruption that Long and his machine were alleged to have employed.

House Resolutions and Articles of Impeachment

Be it resolved by the House of Representatives of the State of Louisiana that Huey P. Long, Governor of the State of Louisiana, be impeached of high crimes and misdemeanors in office, incompetency, corruption, favoritism, extortion, and gross misconduct, and that he be brought to trial on an article of impeachment. . . . [Repeated before each article.]

That on March 20, 1929, the said Huey P. Long did, in a public place, to wit, the State House of the State of Louisiana, in the city of Baton Rouge, Louisiana, threaten to publish and make known the infirmity of a member of the family of Charles P. Manship, that is to say, publish and make known the fact that Douglas Manship, a brother of Charles P. Manship, was insane and an inmate of the East Louisiana Hospital for the Insane, with the intent to extort from the said Charles P. Manship a benefit, advantage, and immunity to the said Huey P. Long, to wit, to coerce the said Charles P. Manship, editor and owner of the Baton Rouge *State-Times* and the *Morning Advocate* . . . to cease opposing the wishes and the efforts of said Huey P. Long in the enactment of legislation then pending before the legislature of the State of Louisiana, or about to be introduced in said legislature, and to coerce and compel the said Charles P. Manship through the mediums of the two newspapers of which he was the owner and publisher, to support and advocate the legislation which the said Huey P. Long favored and advocated. . . .

That on the 17th day of April, 1928, Adolph Gueymard was duly elected and thereafter qualified as a member of the House of Representatives of the State of Louisiana from the Parish of Iberville.

That during the year 1928, in the latter part thereof, and in the city of Baton Rouge, Louisiana, the said Huey P. Long, Governor, did then and there corruptly offer a bribe and attempt to bribe the said Adolph Gueymard, member of the House of Representatives, by offering him remunerative employment in order to influence the judgement of the said Adolph Gueymard in the discharge of his official duties and to cause him in consideration of the remunerative employment offered to him by the said Huey P. Long to violate his oath of office and to give his vote as a member of the Legislature on matters then and there pending before the legislature of the State of Louisiana and to discharge his official duties with bias and partiality and for the benefit and at the pleasure of the said Huey P. Long. . . .

That during said session held at Baton Rouge the said Huey P. Long did then and there offer to place him, Adolph Gueymard, in a position where he could get any amount of money that he needed for his business and did inform him that he had several big positions vacant (meaning thereby public office under the State of Louisiana) to which no one had yet been appointed and did then and there offer to obtain credit and money for the said Adolph Gueymard for the purpose of carrying on his private business and to appoint him to a remunerative position and to give him profitable employment under the State of Louisiana. If the said Gueymard, acting in his capacity as a legislator of the State of Louisiana, would in said Legislature, vote for and support the bills and measures then pending or to be introduced in the Legislature of the State of Louisiana which he, the said Huey P. Long, Governor, favored.

[There followed similar articles for several other members of the House.]

That on the 26th day of October, 1928, Huey P. Long, in his capacity as Governor of the State of Louisiana, was authorized by the Board of Liquidation of the State Debt, upon the allegation of a grave emergency existing, to borrow the sum of six thousand dollars for the entertainment of the Governors of various states of the United States who were to hold a conference in the city of New Orleans from November 20th to November 24th, 1928.

As a condition of said authorization to borrow the Governor was required to obtain from the members of the legislature of the State of Louisiana written authority to borrow said amount from the fiscal agent banks of the State of Louisiana.

That thereafter the said Huey P. Long, Governor, did obtain from a majority of the members of the Legislature written authority to borrow said sum of six thousand dollars.

That thereafter the State Treasurer, through A. L. Junod, Assistant Treasurer of the State of Louisiana, issued a check of the Treasury Department of the State of Louisiana, dated November 28, 1929, and payable to Huey P. Long, Governor, for the sum of six thousand dollars on the Louisiana National Bank of Baton Rouge.

That thereafter the said Huey P. Long paid to Guaranty Development Co., Inc. in the city of New Orleans, Louisiana, the entire expenses of the visiting governors aforementioned, that is to say, the sum of four thousand dollars or thereabouts.

That the said Huey P. Long, Governor of the State of Louisiana, did thereafter convert to his own use and use in a manner other than that directed by law the balance of $2000 and did fail and refuse and has continued to the present time to fail and refuse to account for the balance. . . .

That said Huey P. Long, Governor, by coercive measures forced and compelled the Board of Administrators of the State Colony and Training School to end and terminate the employment of the said F. D. Richardson, the Secretary-Treasurer of the said institution, and to elect one B. F. Eubanks to the said position, paying to the said Eubanks the same salary and maintenance that had been previously paid to the said F. D. Richardson, and in order to accomplish the illegal removal of Richardson from his office and employment, the said Huey P. Long did pay to Richardson one year's salary amounting to three thousand dollars and maintained this rate of $200/month making a total of $2400, an unnecessary and wasteful payment of the funds of the State Colony and Training School, all of which the said Huey P. Long did illegally and unlawfully and knowingly use public funds of the State of Louisiana in a manner otherwise than that directed by law.

That the said Huey P. Long, Governor, in his said capacity, opened an account with the Bank of Baton Rouge, which account was known as the account of "Huey P. Long, Governor."

That the said account contained, among other things, the moneys appropriated by the State Legislature for the Maintenance and Repairs of the State House, for the Maintenance and repairs of the Governor's Mansion, for the Governor's traveling expenses and for other appropriations made for special and specific purposes.

[There followed similar articles purporting that Huey Long paid W. O. Long as his chauffeur contrary to law, that he charged the state for the purchase of his law books, and that he diverted other funds to his personal use that were not authorized by law.]

The House of Representatives of the State of Louisiana do now impeach Huey P. Long, Governor of the State of Louisiana, for incompetence in the conduct of the office of Governor in this: that he is and has shown himself to be incompetent and temperamentally unfit for said office, and that he has so shown himself to be by the various specifications of fact heretofore recited in the articles of impeachment brought against him by this House of Representatives and the testimony adduced in proof thereof and also in various other ways hereinafter set forth.

And more particularly that W. D. Gardiner, Waldo M. Pitkin and Sidney Fruedenstein, A. L. Shushan and Joseph Haspel were on the 6th day of August, 1928, appointed by Huey P. Long, Governor, members of the Orleans Levee Board, a Board created and organized by the statutes of the State of Louisiana. That after their appointment on the 6th day of August, 1928, as aforesaid, and before their commissions were issued to them by the said Huey P. Long, Governor, they were required by Huey P. Long, Governor, and did deliver to the said Huey P. Long, Governor, their resignations signed and undated. And that after the delivery of said resignations the said Huey P. Long did deliver to them their commissions as members of the Orleans Levee Board.

That thereafter on the . . . Day of . . . Huey P. Long, Governor, did date and file the resignations of W. D. Gardiner and Waldo M. Pitkin and did declare their offices vacant. . . .

That as further evidence of the incompetence of Huey P. Long, Governor, it is shown that he has been insulting and abusive to public officials and citizens and that he has not conducted himself with the dignity and propriety due to the great office which he holds. And to this end it is shown that during the month of September, 1929, the said Huey P. Long, Governor, did use profane, vile, indecent and scurrilous language to and concerning one Mrs. J. M. Lumbly, who was then employed as a telephone operator in the office of the Louisiana Highway Commission at Baton Rouge, Louisiana. . . . [3]

3. Long, according to the charges, commanded O. K. Allen, head of the Highway Commission, to fire her for listening to a telephone conversation between the two men.

Questions to Consider:

1. *Create a list and group the articles under three or four different rubrics. What patterns emerge? Which of the charges seem the most serious? Why?*

2. *Pundits have often drawn parallels between the political styles of Huey Long and later politicians. Can you think of any? How do they compare or contrast with Long?*

Source:

Louisiana Legislature, Senate, *Official journal of the proceedings of the Senate of the State of Louisiana at the Fifth Extra Session of the Legislature Under the Adoption of the Constitution of 1921: Begun and Held in the City of Baton Rouge, March 20, 1929. And the Official Journal of the Proceedings of the Senate of the State of Louisiana Sitting as a Court of Impeachment for the Trial of Huey P. Long, Governor of the State of Louisiana, Beginning Saturday, April 6, 1929* (Baton Rouge: Ramires-Jones Print., 1929), 54–83.

1933:
Excerpts from Huey Long's *Every Man a King*

This excerpt comes from Long's autobiography, penned as he positioned himself for a run at the presidency in 1936. Assassinated in Baton Rouge in 1935, he did not live to complete that run. Because his life was cut short, it's difficult to assess the impact his Share Our Wealth plan, calling for an income floor below which Americans would not be allowed to fall, might have had as it was never implemented. President Roosevelt's Second New Deal created several laws and organizations that included many of the causes that Long championed, such as Social Security, the Works Progress Administration, and the Farm Security Administration. Today, many countries also offer a kind of income floor like Long proposed, which is often referred to as "universal basic income."

As you read, pay attention to Long's rhetoric and the way he attempted to land his arguments.

Chapter IX. Campaign For Governor, 1928

On July 8, 1927, a political conclave was held in the City of Alexandria, composed of all groups opposed to me becoming Governor, for the purpose of drafting some candidate possessing outstanding qualifications, the principal requirement being his probable ability to beat me. It was declared that Governor Simpson was not strong enough to make the grade, and that another and stronger man must be had. With considerable glamor, newspaper headlines, trumpeteering and barbecues, all participants unanimously went on record as calling for the candidacy of Congressman Riley J. Wilson to save the State from Huey P. Long.

Mr. Wilson, like myself [*sic*], had been born in the Parish of Winn, and raised a country boy. He had moved to the eastern part of our parish where he taught school, became judge, ran for and was elected to Congress. He was then serving his fourteenth consecutive year. His friends claimed he had put forth great effort to secure flood control, which was at that time quite a lively issue among the people of the State. It was announced that his candidacy would largely be based upon what he had done and what he proposed to do in the work of flood control.

Our forces waited about one month after this conclave in Alexandria and advertised a meeting to be held in the same city to open my campaign for Governor. Our rally was attended by an even larger crowd than the meeting of our opposition.

The newspapers and interests behind the calling of the Alexandria gathering against us had generally announced that the meeting would be composed of men of affairs in the business and politics of the State. They heralded their gathering as a meeting of "the better element."

We thereupon paraded throughout the State the announcement of our meeting to be held in Alexandria with a display of banners reading: "EVERY MAN A KING, BUT NO ONE WEARS A CROWN."

. . .

In answering the clamor that Congressman Wilson should be elected Governor by reason of his flood relief work, I said:

"So they seek to elect the gentleman because of his flood record! What is that flood record? Why, he has been in Congress for fourteen years and this year (1927) the water went fourteen feet higher than ever before, giving him a flood record of one foot of high water to the year, if that's what he's claiming credit for."

. . . It was in the speech that I delivered under the historic oak where Evangeline waited for her lover Gabriel, as described by Longfellow, that I said:

> And it is here under this oak where Evangeline waited for her lover, Gabriel, who never came. This oak is an immortal spot, made so by Longfellow's poem, but Evangeline is not the only one who has waited here in disappointment.
>
> Where are the schools that you have waited for your children to have, that have never come? Where are the roads and the highways that you send your money to build, that are no nearer now than ever before? Where are the institutions to care for the sick and disabled? Evangeline wept bitter tears in her disappointment, but it lasted through only one lifetime. Your tears in this country, around this oak, have lasted for generations. Give me the chance to dry the eyes of those who still weep here!

My political opposition pointed out early in the campaign that even if I were elected Governor the Legislature would be 3 to 1 of men opposed to me.

"Those men will never stand for what Huey Long is advocating. They will impeach him before he is Governor a year," they said frequently.

War broke out between L. E. Thomas, the Mayor of Shreveport, and myself again.

The Mayor, in an especially advertised meeting, accused me of what vices there remained (if any) of which he had not already accused me in previous campaigns.

I announced a special meeting to reply to his attack. After accusing him of exaggerations and other things I said:

> Why, ladies and gentlemen, a Chinaman, a Fiji Islander, and Thomas made a bet as to which one could stand to stay locked up the longest with a pole cat [skunk].
>
> The Chinaman went in the room with the animal and stayed ten minutes. Then he had to come out. He couldn't stand it any longer.
>
> Then the Fiji Islander went in and stayed fifteen minutes with the pole cat and came out a very sick man.
>
> Thomas's time came. He went in and stayed five minutes and the pole cat ran out.

This and other things were too much for the Mayor of my home city. He had me arrested the next day. Later the district attorney filed bills of information.

By accident the charges against me failed to specify that the Mayor was a man "of good repute," a necessary allegation to prosecute one for slander in Louisiana.

The court dismissed the charge on that account. Mayor Thomas was disgusted at this technical failure to have left out the words that he was "of good repute." He had cooled off and declined to refile the charges. . . .

In the first primary election, occurring January 20, 1928, the vote was as follows: Long, 126,842; Wilson, 81,747; Simpson 80,326. . . .

I have lost New Orleans in all my campaigns, but I think I am one of the very few candidates who has never claimed to have been counted out there. . . .

All three of the candidates for governor, however, Wilson, Simpson and I, declared in favor of letting the final contracts for the free bridges over Lake Pontchartrain.

"You will have to take me on my record in this matter," I said, in speaking of this and other issues.

"I had an uncle," I continued, "who late in life started to join the Baptist Church of which many of my family are members. On the day my uncle was to be baptized, his wife and small boy sat on the bank of the creek happy over his conversion. As my uncle was led out of the water by the preacher, there floated out of his pocket face up, the ace of spades, and a few moments later, the king of spades. As the preacher was just getting ready to take hold of him, there floated behind those cards the queen and jack of spades, and then out came the ten of spades. His wife saw the situation and screamed:

"'Don't baptize him, parson, my husband is lost … my husband is lost!"

"But the young boy on the bank yelled out excitedly:

"'No he ain't ma! If pa can't win with that hand, he can't win at all!'

"So if my record will not win on this point, there is nothing I can give you."

There were prominent leaders in the campaigns of both Wilson and Simpson either friendly to or entwined with the toll bridge owners whose influence was feared to be such as to thwart the building of free bridges by either of them should they be elected, regardless of their good intentions. It is significant that the interests behind this toll bridge fought only my election.

Under Governor Simpson the Highway Commission had drifted into rather bad repute and there were misgivings as to what might be expected from that body insofar as letting final contracts for "free bridges" over Lake Pontchartrain were concerned.

When my election as the next Governor of Louisiana was conceded, I was given a banquet by the business interests of the City of New Orleans.

My friend Judge Foster was one of the speakers. He said:

"I first looked upon Huey Long as a bad boy making faces at authority, but I later learned he knew his cases and studied the law."

There were other equally complimentary remarks. A few presents were tendered me, including a chest of silver, on which my wife's initials were engraved. The interests behind the toll bridges were among those present, and they expressed the wish that my administration would be successful.

I did not wait to become Governor, but asked Governor Simpson to begin the operation of free ferries parallel to the toll bridge immediately. Governor Simpson was later to become part of my administration. He ordered the free ferries. The bridge company went into the hands of a receiver soon after I became Governor. It is in such a situation today. It's possible $8.40 charge has since fallen to 60c.

Chapter XXX. The Effort to Spread the Wealth Among the Masses

I had come to the United States Senate with only one project in mind, which was that by every means of action and persuasion I might do something to spread the wealth of the land among all of the people.

I foresaw the depression in 1929. In letters reproduced in this volume, I had predicted all of the consequences many years before they occurred.

The wealth of the land was being tied up in the hands of a very few men.

The people were not buying because they had nothing with which to buy. The big business interests were not selling because there was nobody they could sell to.

One per cent of the people could not eat any more than any other one per cent; they could not wear much more than any other one per cent; they could not live in any more houses than any other one per cent. So, in 1929, when the fortune-holders of America grew powerful enough that one per cent of the people owned nearly everything, ninety-nine per cent of the people owned practically nothing, not even enough to pay their debts, a collapse was at hand.

God Almighty had warned against this condition. Thomas Jefferson, Andrew Jackson, Daniel Webster, Theodore Roosevelt, William Jennings Bryan and every religious teacher known to this earth had declaimed against it. So it was no new matter, as it was termed, when I propounded the line of thought with the first crash of 1929, that the eventful day had arrived when accumulation at the top by the few had produced a stagnation by which the vast multitude of the people were impoverished at the bottom.

There is no rule so sure that one that the same mill that grinds out fortunes above a certain size at the top, grinds out papers at the bottom. The same machine makes them both; and how are they made? There is enough—yea, there is more—than the entire human race can consume, if all are reasonable.

All the people in America cannot eat up the food that is produced in America; all the people in America cannot wear out the clothes that can be made in America; nor can all of the people in America occupy the houses that stand in this country, if all are allowed to share in homes afforded by the nation. But when one man must have more houses to live in than ninety-nine other people; when one man decides he must own more foodstuff than any other ninety-nine people own; when one man decides he must have more goods to wear for himself and family than any other ninety-nine people, then the condition results that instead of one hundred people, that one man, through his gluttonous greed, takes over ninety-nine parts for himself and leaves one part for the ninety-nine.

Now what can this one man do with what is intended for ninety-nine? He cannot eat the food that is intended for ninety-nine people; he cannot wear the clothes that are intended for ninety-nine people; he cannot live in ninety-nine houses at the same time; but like the dog in the manger, he can put himself on the load of hay and he can say:

"This food and these clothes and these houses are mine, and while I cannot use them, my greed can only be satisfied by keeping anybody else from having them."

Wherefore and whence developed the strife in the land of too much, beginning in the year 1929.

I was standing in the lobby of the Roosevelt Hotel in New Orleans on the 23rd day of October, 1929, at lunch time. Mr. R. S. Hecht, President of the powerful Hibernia Bank & Trust Company, walked to the middle of the lobby, approached me and said:

"Governor, hell's broke loose; the biggest crash of everything that you have ever seen. It is going to be sixty days before this country will get back to normal."

"I have expected this crash for three years," I replied. "It is here for many, many years. It cannot end until there is a redistribution of wealth. Make your plans on that basis."

We argued and wrangled for some moments. A few days later I was informed by a member present that at a meeting of the board of directors of his bank he had repeated, without approval, what I had prophesied. I made known my opinion of the then prevailing cause of the national collapse to the people generally. Time is bearing out all I then said.

Chapter XXXI. Beginning Agitation in the United States Senate to Shorten Hours and Limit Fortunes

My philosophy for sharing the work and sharing the wealth by shortening hours and limiting fortunes was first delivered in the United States Senate on April 4, 1932:

> Machines are created making it possible to manufacture more in an hour than used to be manufactured in a month; more is produced by the labor of one man than was formerly produced by the labor of a thousand men; fertilizers are available whereby an acre of

land can be made to produce from two to three or even four times what it formerly produced; various other inventions and scientific achievements which God has seen fit to disclose to man from time to time make their appearance; but instead of bringing prosperity, ease and comfort, they have meant unemployment; they have meant idleness; they have meant starvation; they have meant pestilence; whereas they should have meant that hours of labor were shortened, that toil was decreased, that more people would be able to consume, that they would have time for pleasure, time for recreation—in fact, everything that could have been done by science and invention and wealth and progress in this country should have been shared among the people…

But, oh, Mr. President, if we could simply let the people enjoy the wealth and the accumulations and the contrivances that we have. If, with the invention of every machine, we could secure the education of every man; if with increased production of every kind there could be less toil, more hours of pleasure and recreation; if there could be a happy and contented people enjoying what the Almighty has made it possible to provide; if there could be people clothed with the materials that we have to clothe them with today, and no place to put them; if the people could be fed with the food that we have to feed them with, and no place to put it; if the people could be sheltered in the homes we have today, that the Federal Land Bank has taken away from them because they cannot pay the interest on the mortgages—if that could be done, if we could distribute this surplus wealth, while leaving these rich people all the luxuries they can possibly use, what a different world this would be.

We can do this. If we do not, we will leave these masters of finance and fame and fortune like the man in the book of old, who said to himself, so the Bible tells us:

"I will pull down my barns, and build greater; and there will I bestow all my fruits and my goods.

"And I will say to my soul: Soul, thou hast much goods laid up for many years; take thine ease, eat, drink and be merry.

"But God said unto him: Thou fool, this night thy soul shalt be required of thee."

While the tax bills were pending before the United States Senate in 1932, I proposed a resolution which provided that the tax bills should be so revamped that no one man should be allowed to have an income of more than one million dollars a year; that no one person should inherit in a lifetime more than five million dollars without working for it.

The effect of that resolution was that when a man made one million dollars in a year, the government of the United States would receive the balance; and when a rich man died, he could not leave one child more than five million dollars, and the balance would go to the government of the United States.

This would have meant that much of the taxes would have been paid by the so-called upper classes, and that instead of the funds of the government being sucked from bottom and exploited by the classes at the top, the classes at the top would have paid the taxes to be filtered out to the masses at the bottom, through the various general works and compensations supported by the government.

A Comparison

Consider the horrible way of the gangster, and then compare his practices with the greed of our mighty fortune-holders in America:

The gangsters have killed hundreds, maybe thousands, to carry out their nefarious rackets to extort money.

The hoarders of wealth have destroyed humanity by millions in their quest for greater accumulation.

From the newborn babe to the man bowed with age, some have been denied the sustenance for life: they have been thrown from the shelter above their heads; to keep children warm they have been placed in the ground, to start a life not in the cradle, but in the grave; half naked bodies have been thrown against the winter's wind; some have become beggars, some thieves, and some have been murderers; others have been driven insane and still others to suicide—all in the wake of the drive that the masters of fortunes may own and control so much to wear, people perish in their shadow.

Jefferson, Jackson, Webster, Lincoln, Theodore Roosevelt and [William Jennings] Bryan have clamored to spread our work and our wealth among all the people.

It is the law of God that a nation must free and refree its people of debt, and spread and re-spread the wealth of the land among all the people.

"Wherefore ye shall do my statutes, and keep my judgements, and do them; and the land shall yield her fruit and ye shall eat your fill, and dwell therein in safety." Leviticus, Chapter 25, Verses 18 and 19.

What cycle of events brings the crime wave of robbery and extortion, murder and destruction?

"Who gave Jacob for a spoil and Israel to the robbers? Did not the Lord, for they would not walk in is ways, neither were they obedient until his law." Isaiah, Chapter 42, Verse 24.

In my never changing course for relief and compensation for the Veterans of our wars, livable wages for public employees, a recognition of all hirelings to unite and bargain for the sinews they have to offer,—all to be supported from top heavy accumulations,—I have merely carried through a philosophy to insure diffusing our wealth into the hands of all who must consume our products.

But I saw to it that my views were known to Mr. Roosevelt, then Governor of New York and now President of the United States. Early in his candidacy in a speech delivered in Atlanta, Mr. Roosevelt said:

> The millions who are in want will not stand by silently forever while the things to satisfy their needs are within easy reach.
>
> Many of those whose primary solicitude is confined to the welfare of what they call capital have failed to read the lessons of that last few years and have been moved less by calm analysis of the needs of the Nation as a whole than by a blind determination to preserve their own special stakes in the economic disorder.
>
> We may build more factories, but the fact remains that we have enough now to supply all our domestic needs and more, if they are used. No; our basic trouble was not an insufficiency of capital; it was an insufficient distribution of buying power coupled with an oversufficient speculation in production.

Soon thereafter on the basis of such declarations, I became convinced that the best chance for a solution of America's difficulties was through the election of Franklin D. Roosevelt as President.

Questions to Consider:

1. *Describe Long's rhetorical devices. How would you characterize his rhetoric?*
2. *How does Long describe his opponents in the 1928 gubernatorial campaign? In what ways had they failed the people of Louisiana, according to Long?*
3. *How does Long portray the wealthy elite?*
4. *What solutions to the economic crisis does Long offer?*

Source:

Huey Long, *Every Man a King: The Autobiography of Huey P. Long* (New Orleans: National Book Co., Inc., 1933), 97–105, 290–98. Reprinted with permission from the Long Family.

1942:
Racial Violence during World War II

World War II forced a reconfiguration of race relations in the South, as black soldiers—drafted into a segregated military—went south to train. The sight of black men in uniform often provoked white violence against them, but this time black soldiers fought back. Barely a month after the United States had officially entered the war in January 1942, a melee broke out on Lee Street in Alexandria, where most black entertainment establishments were located. Alexandria, surrounded by three military camps and three airfields—Camp Beauregard, Camp Livingston, and Camp Claiborne—was bursting at the seams, a common reason for racial violence during the war years. Further exacerbating tensions, most of the uniformed black soldiers were from the North. The soldiers had just been paid on Friday, January 9, and were enjoying a weekend's revelry when white military police arrested a black soldier for being drunk and disorderly. Other African Americans in the neighborhood fought back, and a free-for-all resulted. Though African Americans suspected that some black citizens had died at the hands of the white police who arrived to help quell the crowd, those claims have never been substantiated.

Below are excerpts from a white newspaper, the Alexandria *Daily Town Talk*, and a black newspaper, the Kansas City *Plaindealer*. As you read, compare how they cover the incident.

"No Deaths as Result of Saturday Night Clash Here Corps Says," Alexandria *Daily Town Talk*, January 12, 1942

Fifth army corps headquarters at Camp Beauregard today said that none of the 18 negro troops wounded in the Saturday night riot on Lee street had died. Military, city and state police used tear gas, guns, pistols and sticks to quell an outbreak against military authority.

High corps authorities, while requesting that no army officers be quoted, expressed appreciation to the *Town Talk* for the way the story had been handled.

Four of the negroes were reported by corps to be in a serious condition and there was a possibility that an army statement will be issued late today which may include the names of those seriously hurt.

Fifth Army Corps headquarters immediately restricted negro troops to the two camps. Negro soldiers are in a field artillery brigade at Camp Livingston and a negro infantry regiment and tank battalion at Camp Claiborne. Only the married enlisted men of the two outfits are permitted to leave the camp—and, at that, only by special permission.

Broken glass windows—shattered by bullets, bricks and pop bottles—today marked the line of the battle which raged for about two hours along the busiest part of Alexandria's Lee street.

Only one white person was known to have been hurt in the melee. A state policeman suffered a badly injured hand in wielding a flashlight over the head of a negro.

Wisconsin and Michigan troops of the 32nd Division military police company mixed into the battle with full riot equipment. It was an unidentified 32nd Division M.P. who encountered the first trouble with the negroes after he had arrested a negro soldier on a disturbance charge.

City police estimated that from 25 to 30 tear gas bombs were used in clearing out Saturday night crowds from approximately a score of cares and night clubs along the thoroughfare. There was no estimate on the number of shots fired.

Approximately 90 policemen were involved in the battle. Of this number an estimated 60 were from the 32nd Military Police company, 20 from the city police department, and 10 from the state police patrol.

First reports of the disturbance were received by city police at about 8 p.m. and, two hours later, the "situation was under control." At the conclusion of the battle city police covered the entire territory and closed up all establishments. Alexandria's "Little Harlem" had its first Saturday night blackout. . . .

Both white and negro military police have jurisdiction in Alexandria's negro quarters.

Most of the negroes in Camp Livingston, 14 miles north of here, and Camp Claiborne, 18 miles southwest of here, are from Pennsylvania, Illinois and New York. . . .

"I was at supper when headquarters notified me of the trouble," said the chief. "I rushed down to Lee street. All available military and civilian police were called out, and state police also were called. There was considerable shooting, sticks were being used and bricks and rocks were flying through the air. I saw only one negro soldier who had been shot." . . .

Many of the negro civilians, estimated at 3,000 by Chief Gray, fled quickly when the trouble started. Some, however, took part in the fracas.

Chief Gray commented that it was possible that some of the soldiers may have been hit by stray shots fired by negro civilians.

When the shooting started, traffic gave Lee street a wide berth. Shots were heard blocks away.

"Bullets were whistling and bricks were flying," said one witness. "The Japs might as well have been attacking as far as I was concerned. I ducked."

Several of the windows apparently were broken by shots probably in an exchange of shots from inside and outside. The few negroes who were shooting, however had poor aim. Not a policeman, civil or military, was hit.

"NAACP Says War Dept. To Blame For Dixie Riot; Claim Whites Started Riot," Kansas City *Plaindealer*, January 23, 1942

Repercussions are still being heard from the riot between military and civilian police, and Negro soldiers stationed nearby at Camps Claiborne and Livingston. The scene of the turbulent outburst between white officials and Negro soldiers was laid in the heart of the Negro district in Alexandria last Saturday night, allegedly growing out of a white officer's clubbing of a Negro soldier in the front of Ritz theatre on a claim of nonpayment of admission to the theatre.

This was the first race riot of the new world war and was believed cause by the war department's practice of shipping northern Negro soldiers for training into the prejudiced white south. The clash served to climax what it is contended has been a mounting wave of mistreatment by white military and civilian police of colored soldiers. Brig. Gen. B. O. Davis arrived here soon after this riot, presumably on a routing visit, but was expected to probe the situation.

The Alexandria NAACP branch voiced condemnation against the "short-sighted policies of the war department in their refusal to order the arming of efficient colored MPs who would be fully competent to maintain law and order in the colored section of the city." The NAACP declared "It is contradictory and hypocritical to fight Fascism abroad and at the same time allow it to be practiced within our own territorial boundaries, when it is our avowed national policy to carry the four freedoms into every nook and corner of the world including the reactionary south."

According to reports gleaned from witnesses to the open clash, the soldier, when it was claimed he had not paid admission to the theatre, refused to be arrested and an officer began belaboring him. . . . [In the ensuing riot], wholesale damages were wreaked upon Negro businesses.

Questions to Consider:

1. *How did the white and black newspapers spin the event differently?*

2. *The Lee Street Riot was reportedly the first incident of racial violence in a war that became infamous for such violence. Investigate other clashes that occurred around the country after this, perhaps picking one to concentrate on. What did the other incidents of racial violence share with the Lee Street Riot? In what ways were the circumstances different?*

3. *What evidence of the "Double V" campaign, about to be launched by the* Pittsburgh Courier, *is evident in these reports?*

4. *Consider the use of passive voice in the narrative of the* Daily Town Talk *article. In what ways might it shield law enforcement authorities from culpability?*

Sources:

1. "No Deaths as Result of Saturday Night Clash Here Corps Says," *Daily Town Talk* (Alexandria, LA), January 12, 1942. Reprinted with permission from the *Town Talk.*

2. "NAACP Says War Dept. To Blame For Dixie Riot; Claim Whites Started Riot," *Plaindealer* (Kansas City, KS), January 23, 1942.

1942:
Robert LeBlanc and World War II

Brigadier Gen. Robert J. LeBlanc served as a bilingual officer in the Office of Strategic Services, trained to work behind enemy lines with the French Resistance in support of communications with Gen. Patton's 3rd Army for the advance across France, June to September 1944. He was in charge of Special Forces Detachment 11. He was recruited by the OSS in 1943 because he spoke French.

General LeBlanc discusses the role Cajuns, trained by the military in counterintelligence, played in assisting the French resistance during World War II. In the second interview he also discusses the way Cajuns' experiences in World War II sharpened that identity and led to a renewed pride in their culture.

Interview, April 11, 2003[1]

When Pearl Harbor happened, I was in ROTC at LSU. I was in geology and was supposed to go to the University of Colorado for my final course. Instead, I had to go to ROTC camp in South Carolina. I never did graduate.

I got called up in July 1942. I was commissioned at the time. I went to Fort McLennan, Alabama, to the replacement-training center. We went through one training cycle with the cadets. And then, they were recruiting French speaking officers and reading these officers for the censorship school to

1. Jason Theriot conducted the interviews as part of the research for a new book entitled *Frenchie: The Story of the French-Speaking Cajuns for World War II* (forthcoming, UL Press).

go to the invasion of North Africa, because that was a French colony. They were trying to get French-speaking students who could read, write, and speak French to be censors in North Africa. I didn't apply; they just selected me and ordered me to report to school in Maryland. Then, when I completed that school, they sent us to the New Orleans censorship station where we did our intern work in censorship. Don Broussard, from New Iberia, worked in the classification system as a clerk. He was a good friend. . . .

At censorship school, they were teaching us what to look for in soldiers' letters to home, and what to censor. We would take a soldier's letter, and if he wrote something that he shouldn't have wrote, we would cut it out or mark it out with a heavy marking pencil. That's what we did. My job was to read the French letters coming home to decipher what the words were.

In North Africa, we would be censoring the soldiers mail and the French mail. We would censor the postal service of France. That was the plan for us.

I went back to Fort McLennan for another cycle of basic training. After completing that cycle, there was this one recruiter from OSS [Office of Strategic Services, a wartime intelligence agency and the predecessor of the CIA] and called all of us who could speak and write a foreign language; they called us into headquarters and interviewed each of us individually. They asked, "Do you want to volunteer for strenuous mission; we can't tell you about it. We need your knowledge. And you must be willing to parachute." I thought, "Well, I'm at the mercy of Uncle Sam, so whatever I can do to help, I'll do it." So, I agreed.

About a month later, they called me to Washington. We went to OSS headquarters. We were evaluated and they decided whether or not to keep you. Then we went to (what is today) Camp David; it was originally a Boy Scout camp. And that is where they had OSS training, in the mountains of Camp David. We went through all types of additional training: weapons training, additional French classes, and knowing the mores of the French. For instance, the Frenchman does not eat his gumbo like we eat it. He doesn't lift this side of his plate (the left); he lifts this side of his plate (the right). A Frenchman doesn't smoke a cigarette like an American. A Frenchman will take a toothpick, if necessary, and smoke it down to the end. That's some of the techniques that they taught us to avoid being captured by the Germans. And if you smoked, your hands should be brown, and your teeth should be brown. You shouldn't brush your teeth too much.

We went through all of that training and just before the invasion, they decided that there should be a team to determine and collect intelligence from OSS agents in the field. . . . I was fortunate enough to be chosen for Patton's HQ. My team, Special Forces #11, was assigned to Patton's HQ in England for the invasion. Because of this order, we didn't go to jump school, because they needed us immediately for this post-invasion training. We were sending information back and forth to fool the enemy into thinking where we were going to land at the Pais de Calais or Norway. They issued cold weather equipment and clothing, long jackets, so that the Germans would think that we would land in Norway.

. . . When we landed in Utah Beach, Normandy, Gen. Koenig of the French army was appointed to coordinate all special activities in France. Our section was to coordinate the activities between the operational units and the French underground, as they went along.

We moved out past the causeway to get to fresh water to wash off all of our equipment, because we had sealed everything with putty to make it water proof. When we crossed the causeway it was all marsh; much like landing at Avery Island or any other area in south Louisiana; it was a causeway coming out of the marsh. And the whole area was flooded because the Germans had busted open the damns.

The French underground was more active behind the enemy's lines. When we left Perrie, I had the names and location of every French agent all the way to Rennes. Headquarters had briefed us on every agent, where he was, what was his code name, where he could be found, and in addition to how you were supposed to contact him.

All along the southern area, the Germans had removed the road signs in each little town, and all we had were these little maps, no topography maps. There were so many roads and it was hard to identify each road. So we had the French underground provide guides for us. We also had them provide guards for our supply lines and for the German POWs.

After we dropped the bomb on Japan, I had enough points to go home. They wanted to give me a promotion if I stayed in, but I said that I had a wife and baby on the way and I'm gone.

And that is what I did during World War II. After the war I joined the National Guard and I organized Company H here in Abbeville. I ended up at battalion headquarters in St. Martinville as an operations officer. Then I was promoted to battalion commander. From there, I commanded a brigade and then to New Orleans where I was promoted to Brigadier General. I came back to the 256th Infantry Brigade where I was the commander.

Telephone Interview, April 15, 2006

Q: What role did some of these GIs like yourself, Sam Broussard, Curney Dronet, what role did the Cajun veterans play in helping to preserve this language, this culture?

LeBlanc: I feel that the fact that we were prohibited from speaking French on the school grounds encouraged us to speak it off the school ground, maintain the language and maintain the ability to speak to our grandparents, who many of them could not speak English, enable us, when we were overseas, whether you were in French Indochina, whether you were in France, or wherever the French language was spoken, was to be of extreme value to the United States of America, the ability to speak a foreign language, which was not available in the general Army Air Force or Navy personnel who were available at the start of the war.

Even in the drafting of the draftees, the only draftees that could speak French were primarily those, not only, but the majority of them who could speak French came from Louisiana or came from Maine, New Hampshire, in that area up there that's close to the Canadian border. So it was a valuable treasure that the United States had in the linguistic ability of these native Americans who had been born here, but who had followed the culture and followed the language of their ancestors, to be able to provide this technical expertise through the Army commands throughout the world.

Q: With the establishment of CODOFIL in the late fifties, early sixties, can the pioneers of this movement be linked back to the World War II generation, in fact, the folks who we're talking about today?

LeBlanc: I would think so. Jimmy Dimaggio [phonetic] was a World War II veteran. He was one of the few who had resigned his commission, resigned his seat in the House of Representatives to volunteer for the military. When he came back, he was instrumental in trying to push this. [unclear] LeBlanc was a veteran of World War I, and he was pushing this. Martin from St.

Martinsville was another who was pushing this culture, to come in service and show the world that they still had this Cajun culture. All of these people were very instrumental in getting the culture oriented into the American society and American form of government.

Q: Well, I have a pretty good idea of what Cajun means to me today, and it's probably much different than other individuals my age, and I'll assume that you have an idea of what Cajun identity means to you and meant to you. How do those two identities differ over, let's say, half a century?

LeBlanc: Well, the main thing was that the low esteem that we had when we were young with other people, people of other cultures felt we belonged to a culture beneath them, but as I grew through the stage and visited all over the world, I became knowledgeable in what goes on in all the difficult cultures all over the world and realized that the fact that we were not the best speakers of English, we had value both to ourselves and to the country, and this we could demonstrate with our ability, so that it was recognized that these people here in South Louisiana were a valuable resource to the United States.

For instance, it cost us about $30,000 to train a linguist in the military school. Well, here was a readymade, pre-fabricated, no-cost individual would could provide this service, and that, to me, is what "Wild Bill" Donovan demonstrated to the active Army, that there were second- and third-generation individuals throughout the Army and throughout the community, throughout the United States, who had a valuable foreign language ability, and he was able to mobilize this talent, this skill, and get it in operation within a short period of time in World War II. If we'd have gone through the military system, by the time—look what's going on in Iraq today. How many knowledgeable individuals that we have in American Army who can speak the Iraqi language or speak any Arab language?

Q: Not many.

LeBlanc: That's the point that a lot of people don't understand. We have a lot of Arabs in the United States, but not too many have surfaced to be able to be linguists in American Army, and that's been our shortcoming in the Middle East. Now, when we went in World War II and North Africa, the spoken language in Morocco was French, and a lot of American individuals' talents and abilities to speak French was invaluable in that area. So going back again to World War II, I think that was the key that really Americanized the Cajuns here in South Louisiana.

When you look at what our area of travel was before World War II, for instance, my father was a sheriff. The furthest I had traveled was to Galveston, Texas, where there were a hell of a lot of Cajuns, and the only other place I had traveled to was St. Louis for a baseball game with my father. Other than those two areas outside of the Cajun land, New Orleans was the furthest place we had visited, and Baton Rouge was where I went to college, so it was just on the border of Acadiana that we traveled. We didn't travel to New York, we didn't travel to California, we didn't travel to the Midwest or the Far West, so our knowledge of this country was primarily South Louisiana, and the world travels that we were required to do throughout World War II really called to our attention what we had here in South Louisiana was a very distinct culture from the rest of the United States, and that it was something that we needed to preserve.

Rod Theriot [phonetic] was also a World War II veteran. He was one of the big boosters of the Cajun culture, and he pushed it, and he called attention to the rest of Louisiana. And then suddenly the rest of the United States realized that there was a distinguished culture here in South Louisiana, primarily through the foods, but the military people realized that there was also another valuable thing here, and that was the linguists.

Q: And in the twenties and thirties, General, did you and your friends, did y'all associate yourselves with being Acadian or Cajun or strictly just from South Louisiana? How did you understand your identity at that time growing up?

LeBlanc: We really understood we were Cajuns, and our fathers and grandfathers pounded that into us, that we were not English, we were French descendants and we were descendants of the Acadians from Nova Scotia, and they explained *Le Grand Dérangement* completely to us. About that time was when Dolores del Rio made *Evangeline*, and that impressed all of us as to what our forefathers had gone through to be able to settle in this area.

This area, the Depression didn't affect them as much as the urban areas because just about everybody did subsistence farming on their farms. You raised what you were going to eat. So certainly you didn't have any money, but you didn't starve. You milked your cows, you raised a garden, you raised your cattle, you raised your pigs, you raised your chickens, your ducks, which was the methodology which the Cajuns had utilized in Nova Scotia, which were brought down to our grandfathers and fathers, who understood that you had to provide for your family.

Q: Speaking about these generations, two or three generations down the road, what should they remember or what should the history books teach them about the Cajuns from World War II?

LeBlanc: First of all, it's got to educate our children and our grandchildren and our great-grandchildren that there was a lot of sacrifice made by our Cajun descendants of this particular area, and there were a lot of rewards that they got and a lot of achievement that they accomplished in World War II, which was very distinctive of the Cajun culture, and if they can be knowledgeable in that area, it won't encourage all of them to learn French, but it will encourage many of them to learn the French language, or even if they learn another language which would be a valuable asset to the country.

So I feel that those who are teaching our kids need to instill in the Acadian descendants that they need to understand Acadian culture and they need to maximize their knowledge of the language and the customs. Now, most of the emphasis is on the connection with Festival International [in Lafayette] with French-speaking countries all over the world, but how much of it is devoted to expanding that connection into the economic area? In other words, how many of them are being trained to go and be salesmen for Louisiana? None that I know of. There might be. Perhaps ULL is doing that. But that's certainly a task for ULL to develop these foreign-speaking students in English or Spanish or French, some type of language for which we can utilize in commerce. But sometimes I feel the French immersion program does not go far enough.

Questions to Consider:

1. *How did the experience of World War II transform LeBlanc's understanding of his heritage?*

2. *How did the experience of World War II help create support for the preservation and celebration of Cajun heritage and culture? What programs and events exist now that seek to do exactly that?*

3. *What lessons for current military planners did LeBlanc offer?*

Sources:

1. Robert J. LeBlanc Brig. Gen. (Retired), Army of the United States, interviewed by Jason Theriot, April 11, 2003, Jason P. Theriot Oral History Collection, Archive of Cajun and Creole Folklore, Center for Louisiana Studies (CLS), University of Louisiana at Lafayette.

2. Robert J. LeBlanc, interviewed by Jason Theriot, April 15, 2006, Jason P. Theriot Oral History Collection, CLS.

1942–1945:
Higgins Industries

Andrew Jackson Higgins was a shipbuilder who developed the Landing Craft Vehicle Personnel (LCVP) that General Dwight Eisenhower referred to as the boat that won the war. By 1943, Higgins's seven New Orleans plants employed more than twenty-five thousand workers, including women and African Americans. Churning out more than seven hundred boats a month, fully 92 percent of the Navy's boats were designed by Higgins Industries by 1944.

Higgins was born in 1886 near the Missouri River in Nebraska. As a young man he moved to Mobile and then to New Orleans, where he established a lumber company on the industrial canal and subsequently a shipyard to repair the sea-going craft used to haul the logs and lumber. As the oil companies moved into the Mississippi River corridor, Higgins focused on developing sturdy floating equipment that could operate in the shallow waters of the marshes where sand bars, submerged logs, and other obstacles frequently broke ships' hulls and propellers, leaving them stranded. Higgins developed a boat that could slide over those obstructions, was almost impossible to capsize, and which could retreat off a shore and turn around on a dime. Though he said the LCVP was inspired by the aerodynamic body of whales, others credit his observations of the pirogue, a lightweight dugout used by Cajuns in the bayous and swamps for more than a century.

Besides their utility to commerce, the shallow draft boats changed the nature of warfare because they could move troops, equipment, and supplies onshore without using existing ports or docks. The Higgins landing craft were critical to amphibious invasions in both the Pacific and European theaters, especially the D-Day invasion of Normandy in 1944. The National World War II Museum is located in New Orleans because of Higgins Industries' importance to the Allied victory.

Like many other industries that boomed as a result of the war, Higgins Industries suffered from labor troubles and strikes when the war was over as defense contracts ended. Higgins resisted unionization and ultimately closed most of his plants. He died in 1952.

David McGuire, Higgins Industries' public relations director, produced the publicity materials below while the war was still underway. The story begins with the opening of a facility in 1939 on St. Charles Avenue in the heart of posh New Orleans.

Trolley wires on the Avenue neutral ground were moved so the 70-foot boats could be moved out on big truck trailers. Orleanians gaped at the boats rolling along Canal Street, to be dropped into the Mississippi River.

Higgins had started something new in boat building—something the experts had said couldn't be done. For the first time in history, boats were being built by moving manufacturers [i.e., moving production line]. He had also established his boat yard away from water. Later, when his huge City Park plant was dedicated, someone asked Mr. Higgins why this plant, too, was away from water. His reply was characteristic:

"It was the best location for a plant I could find. Being on or off water doesn't make any difference. It's just as easy to move a boat five miles as five inches."

Before the war New Orleans was principally noted for its port and its famous French Quarter. Today the city is the center of the Gulf Coast boat-building industry. Here seven manufacturing units of Higgins Industries and its subsidiaries have developed and manufactured 64 different products. With 20,000 employees, comprising one fifth of the industrial payroll of New Orleans, Higgins has made the city a major industrial factor and one to be reckoned with after the war. He has proved his contention that efficient and economic manufacturing can be done in the deep South.

Best known and most familiar of the Higgins products are the famous 36-foot ramp landing boats and swift-striking, torpedo carrying PT boats. These all-wood craft are turned out on moving production lines at the City Park plant. Also made in this plant are the deadly little LCS rocket boats and offshore patrol boats.

Coming off the production lines of this plant at the rate of 25 a day, these craft are taken by flatcar and truck trailer to the nearby Bayou St. John plant where they are launched, outfitted, tested and shipped out to the armed services. . . . The "FP" boat is used to transport troops and supplies in the shallow water among islands and rivers where deep-draft vessels cannot go. Drawing only 8 feet of water, it will carry 800 tons of cargo. . . .

In addition to these manufacturing units, the company sponsors a boat operator's school [entirely at the company's expense] where thousands of men have been trained as landing boat operators. . . .

[Due to his outsized productivity, Higgins was given the "E" Award, the Army and Navy Production Award, in September, 1943.]

Until the development of the Higgins boat, the landing of an invasion army on an enemy beach head was considered an impossible military task. In previous wars invasion was confined to attacks upon fortified boats with deep water channels. After the fall of France, Hitler marched to the English Channel and failed to cross (as had Napoleon before him) for the want of a landing boat.

In this war the great "secret weapon" of the United Nations has been the successful operation of amphibious warfare. This is a new kind of warfare, combining for the first time in history naval, land, and air forces in an attack upon the enemy from the sea. It is invasion—the kind of warfare we are carrying to the enemy in every theatre of activity.

History will record that Higgins Industries, Inc., under the leadership of A. J. Higgins, his sons and other associates, pioneered in the development of the landing boat . . . the boat which has revolutionized modern warfare. The background of Mr. Higgins and his development of the boat which was later to become the standard Navy landing craft is a familiar story, and we will not repeat it here. Suffice it to say that only the most determined will power could have succeeded over the years in perfecting the boat which was first used in Louisiana Coastal waters by lumbermen, trappers, and oil companies to navigate areas where conventional boats could not go. . . .

[In addition to Higgins Industries,] twenty-five other companies are now making Higgins boats from the designs and patents which their owner has turned over to the government, royalty-free, for the duration. . . .

But of all the things in which he takes pride, Mr. Higgins is proudest of these. . . . The loyalty and affection of his men [i.e., workers, some of whom were female]. . . . That production has surged on without stoppage of even one minute because of strike or controversy, . . . That the boat plants are company-owned without a cent of government ownership or subsidy—and that their production is better and faster and cheaper than anyone else's—And the sincere words of praise of the brave young men who man and land in the boats. . . .

Questions to Consider:

1. *At the height of the war, Higgins's industries were among the largest in the world. Identify the factors that explain why "the boats that won the war" were built in New Orleans. Why did his success not continue after the war? (You may need to do outside research to answer that completely.)*

2. *What new production techniques did Higgins develop that helped him fill the enormous demand for his vessels?*

Source:

David R. McGuire memorial collection, David R. McGuire Papers, LaRC-271.

1943:
Governor Sam H. Jones's "Report to the People"

Sam Houston Jones, an attorney from Lake Charles, backed by "good government" forces in the state, narrowly defeated Earl Long in the election of 1940 in the wake of the revelations of the "Louisiana hayride" scandals. Jones had been born in a log cabin in Merryville, a lumber town near Texas (hence his name). After a stint in the military during World War I, he returned to DeRidder in time to be elected the youngest member of the Constitutional Convention of 1921. Thereafter he became a prosecuting attorney and moved to Lake Charles.

Drafted by a group of anti-Longites for the gubernatorial race in 1940, he saw himself as a public servant whose job was to govern in the interest of the people of Louisiana, not to feather his own nest, line his own pockets, or further his own political career. He had the good fortune to preside over the state as the Great Depression ended and prosperity returned—in no small part due to federal spending associated with World War II. Louisiana received more than its fair share of federal money during that war—the largest per capita amount in the country according to Jones—for which he naturally claimed credit. Much federal money went into training troops at the 40 or so military installations in the state by war's end. Jones claimed credit for that, as well, comparing it to the two—a cantonment at Alexandria and Chennault airfield at Lake Charles—in the state when he was elected.

Clearly the mobilization effort for this massive war was a tremendous asset for Louisiana, but it did not "just happen," Jones pointed out, without his efforts: "Your Governor made many trips and spent many days in Washington and New York arguing and convincing government and industrial leaders that Louisiana was the right place for training programs, ship building, chemical industries and war plants in general . . . It is not an exaggeration to say that new industries locating in Louisiana, defense plant and private, have added a half billion dollars in new capital investment. This is more than we had done all told in 15 years prior to my administration."[1] In the series of speeches excerpted below, Jones boasted of the accomplishments of his administration.

Prevented from succeeding himself by the constitution he had helped to write, he retired to private practice in Lake Charles. When he ran against Earl Long in 1948, he was crushed. His political career ended, he remained a prominent anti-Longite activist and served on the boards of good government organizations such as the Public Affairs Research Council (PAR) and the Council for a Better Louisiana.

Not all of his reforms stuck. Civil service, for example, was wiped out by the Longites and had to be re-established under later governors.

"Report to the People"

In this series of talks you'll learn about the redemption of Louisiana from its shame. How it has been elevated from the quagmire of scandal. How its finances have improved. How honesty has been restored. How your public servants have been freed from bondage and pillage. How your colleges have been freed from politics. How the high courts have removed the corrupt judges. . . .

You'll learn how your airports have increased from 7 to 37 without expenditure of the state's money. How your air lines have jumped from three to seven. How Louisiana has progressed more in the same period than in any State in the Union. . . .

In addition to all this you'll find that the abuses you fought against have been eliminated. That deducts are out. That Civil Service is in. That dual office holding is gone. That State officials don't profit on State oil leases [as the Longs did]. That big-shot politicians don't build fine homes on the Gold Coast. . . .

1. *Report to the People*, 4, 27.

[Under the previous administrations,] [y]our local officials had been virtually taken over the Statehouse. No deputy, clerk, ditch-digger or technician could be hired or fired in any parish, city or town without Statehouse approval. Every single employee of every political subdivision was under the thumb of one man in Baton Rouge. . . .

Tyranny prevailed in its rankest form. A force existed which made and broke banks and financial institutions. Which by spite and vengeance drove industry out of the state, or catapulted it to fabulous wealth as it chose. Which by whim or caprice denied men and women the right to practice their professions and trades or granted that right without regard to qualification. Which held the destinies of private citizens in its hands with no less power than that exerted by the tyrants of Europe.

The rights of free speech and free and peaceable assembly were threatened because people were afraid. They gathered in dark and secret places to discuss their rights as citizens—even as the underground organizations in the conquered nations of Europe gather today.

So dark was the picture that any man who dared oppose the regime had to be prepared to leave the state if his fight was unsuccessful. That was the horrible picture we were fighting to erase in the memorable campaign of 1940.

Today this horrible nightmare is gone. . . .

[Jones pointed proudly to the fact that he had fulfilled most of his campaign promises, detailed below.]

The first plank contained these pledges: A tax system that will reduce automobile and truck licenses; wipe out nuisance licenses on small business; lift the burden off the laboring man, and provide a real homestead exemption. Let us now compare the performance:

The automobile license has been reduced to three dollars for all alike. The truck license has been cut by forty per cent. Small business pays one license instead of four or five. The social security tax has been lifted from the laboring man, saving him millions of dollars annually. And the homestead exemption has been steadily kept at two thousand dollars, to which it was raised during my campaign.

The second plank called for the doing away of over-lapping and ghost boards and provisions for the retirement of the huge State debt. . . . Thus it can be said that this is the first administration in history that leaves fewer agencies than it started with. The State bonded debt has been reduced . . . and we have a surplus of more than seven million dollars in the general fund. So it can be said this administration is the first in 40 years which did not increase the public debt.

The third plank called for a guarantee of fair elections and fair representations at the polls. In compliance with this we purged the registration rolls; wrote a new registration law. . . . We provided voting machines in the City of New Orleans. . . .

The fourth plank called for elimination of dictatorship and return of power to the people. In response to this we repealed the laws which gave Baton Rouge power over local officials. We enacted Civil Service which, with one fell swoop, took away the Governor's control over State employees, and which took away the Mayors control over the employees of the City of New Orleans.

The fifth plank called for the destruction of the political spy system, the elimination of machine guns from public buildings and discarding of martial law for political purposes. [That has been done.]

The sixth plank pledged to take LSU out of politics; to retain free school books and to provide well-paid school teachers free from political control. The university's depoliticization is written into the Constitution by your votes. The free school books are still with us. And the school teachers have received an average increase of approximately 30 per cent, while the State allocation of school funds to the parishes has been even greater.

The seventh plank pledged the elimination of dual office holding and the system of legislators holding jobs in the executive department. The double dipper law is on the books and has resulted in hundreds of people giving up dual jobs. . . .

The eighth plank called for abolition of favoritism in State contracts and the establishment of a system of free and competitive bidding. The fiscal code did this in this most thorough way. When I came in about 200 firms were getting nearly all the business. Now more than seven thousand are getting it. . . .

The ninth plank sought to eliminate the deadheads and the padding of payrolls. In compliance with this our payroll today has reduced by 7500 those who were on the rolls in February 1940. There has been a net reduction of better than 30 percent in number and 4 million dollars in amount.

The tenth plank pledged the abolition of the infamous deducts system by which public employees were compelled to contribute to political slush funds. This system was killed on May 14, 1940, by an executive order. It was killed in the first session of the Legislature by a special law. It was killed by Civil Service ratified by the people. . . .

The eleventh plank called for public records and the outlawing of closed books. The Public Records Act passed in 1940 is complete compliance.

The twelfth plank pledged impartial audits. We have had many complaints about too much auditing—none about too little.

The thirteenth plank sought to foster conservation laws to do away with waste and called for an end to favoritism in handling of State oil leases. The finest conservation statute in America passed by us has just been validated by the Supreme Court. Under it millions of dollars of wealth have been saved to the State. Favoritism in State leases has passed into the realm of forgotten things. The State has profited by millions of dollars.

The fourteenth plank pledged a farm to market road system; paved roads at half the cost; the public buildings free from scandals. [This was put into effect.] Nearly five million dollars of public buildings and works have been constructed, out of current funds, and without a breath of scandal.

The fifteenth plank called for increased old age pensions [from the state]; reduction of waste and payment of back Confederate veterans pensions. [This has been done.]

The sixteenth plan provided a guarantee for the rights of labor; fostering of agriculture with better prices, and better market facilities. We gave to labor its own commissioner who has diligently protected its rights and enforced its law. Agriculture income has increased nearly 100 per cent. State market facilities have been set up provided by State appropriations.

The seventeenth plank pledged the depoliticalization of the New Orleans Dock Board and the restoration of its rank as second place. The first pledge was enacted in a constitutional amendment which gives the control to business organizations in New Orleans. The second was brought about by good management which lifted the port from 16th to second place in the nation.

[During the 1940 campaign,] I was characterized as the man who would immediately on my election outlaw the free school books for the poor people. And being so out of sympathy with the underprivileged people, they told you I'd cut out the free school lunches in one fell swoop. . . . They fabricated the story that I would cut out the free poll tax. . . .

[The record gives the lie to charges, Jones continued. He explained that he doubled the old age pension, vastly expanded the free school lunches, ended the poll tax, increased appropriations for hospitals and public health units, and increased the severance tax.]

Questions to Consider:

1. *Which of Jones's accomplishments were the result of his efforts as governor, and which were likely the result of federal wartime stimulus money and the end of the Great Depression? In other words, which of these things might have occurred no matter who occupied the governor's chair?*

2. *What groups of people in Louisiana were not part of Jones's reform program and why?*

3. *Jones described himself as a "progressive conservative," one who wanted sound fiscal policies and procedures but who also supported "a system of aids and services to the people uncorrupted by political ambition," as he said in his inaugural address. Why do you think Jones would take that approach, as opposed to a slash-and-burn policy that other conservatives favored?*

4. *Does it appear that Jones may have been taking credit for accomplishments begun under his predecessors?*

Source:

"Report to the People," a series of 10 radio talks delivered by Sam Jones, Dec. 10–23, 1943, Chapters 1 and 2, William Walter Jones collection of Sam Houston Jones papers, LaRC-409.

1947:
Willie Francis's First Trip to the Chair

Willie Francis was sentenced to death for the murder of Andrew Thomas at the age of sixteen in 1945. He survived his first execution attempt in 1946. His lawyer appealed his case citing cruel and unusual punishment, taking it all the way to the US Supreme Court, though the court rejected the appeal. Francis was executed on May 9, 1947, aged eighteen.

They tell me that this is the first time anyone ever had a chance to tell the story of how it feels to go to the electric chair and know that you might have to go back there. This is the first time I ever told the whole story and I hope that by at last telling it people will understand what it means to go through what I went through. . . .

A lot of people write to me and ask me to tell them something about what I did when I was young. I am only eighteen now, so I guess they mean when I was very young. I was born in St. Martinville, Louisiana. It's just a little town where everybody knows everybody else. We have two sections, one for white people and the other for the colored, and everybody gets along fine. The whites tend to their own business and the colored tend to theirs. It isn't often something exciting happens there and when something does happen like when Mr. Thomas gets killed, everybody gets real excited and wants to know who did it. I don't want to talk about the killing of Mr. Thomas. When they asked me to write this story I said I would only if I didn't have to say anything about that part. I was tried and convicted of the killing, and as far as I think, that's all over. But I will tell you about the electrocution.

I guess from the first minute I was born I gave people something to worry about. Maybe you will think I am superstitious. I guess I am, because I have a lot of reasons to be. I was the thirteenth child of my father, Frederick Francis, and my mother Louise Fancies. I was convicted of the murder on the thirteenth of September, 1945. Then the United States Supreme Court turned me down on January thirteenth of this year.

. . . I was baptized Willie Francis. That's what they always called me, anyway, I guess I grew up just like my other colored friends. I belong to the Catholic Church in St. Martinville and my pastor was Father Maurice Roussere. He was there at my electrocution. He comes to see me now and then and tells me how my family is. Every day or whenever he can he goes to see them.

. . . When you live in a house with that many people in it, things aren't as crowded as you would think. All my brothers and sisters got along fine together because we had to. We knew it wasn't any use fighting or fussing because everybody had to stick together if we were going to all be happy. My father worked in a sugar factory in the cane season and does odd jobs during the rest of the year. He made enough money to keep us all fed and nobody ever starved, that I know of. When things went right and he had a nickel to spare we had a bottle of red pop. For me it was ice-cream.

. . . After they sentenced me on September thirteenth, they drove me to the Parish Prison here in New Iberia, Louisiana. They said I would like it much better here because the death cell is bigger and more comfortable than in St. Martinville. It didn't make much difference. They hadn't said when they were going to kill me, so I didn't care where they put me. The cell where I am now is on the top floor of the Court-House. I have one window to look out over the house-tops of New Iberia in two directions. My walls are bright pink. I like the color but I wish the walls weren't behind the paint.

I stayed up here for a couple of months without anything happening. My family and a few friends would drop in on me now and then. I spent and spend most of the time reading books and magazines my family and other people brought me. When nobody else could come my father did, and brought me little things like tooth-paste. One day he brought me a Bible my mother gave him for me. It's pretty well worn out now.

My pastor, Father Roussere, couldn't come to see me often because he lives in St. Martin, and I didn't have a priest to talk to. One day when I was looking out my cell door window I saw a man walking down the corridor of the jail who was dressed just like a priest. I yelled and waved my arms, and when he looked I asked him to come over to my cell. I guess he thought I was crazy because of the way I acted, but he came in anyway. His name was Father Charles Hannegan and I found out he had been confessor to a lot of men who had to die like I had. From what he told me later I was lucky it was the electric chair and not hanging. About that I don't know; I will just say that I have been lucky.

. . . I knew it had to come sometime, so when they told me it was the third [of May] it didn't make much difference. Time began to pass quickly for me. Boy, you sure feel funny when you know you're going to die; almost like you know something only God should know.

The day before I was to go to the electric chair I was plenty scared. Father Hannegan came to see me. He knew I was scared. He told me something funny: He said I was lucky because I knew when I was going to die, and so I could prepare myself in time. I had never thought about dying that way before. All I could see was that I wouldn't be alive any more. What he said made me feel a little better. He said he might fall down the jailhouse steps and break his neck, or maybe he would die between clean sheets in his rectory that night. Anyway, he would never know and I would. He said I had a new life to start when I got up from that chair the next day, and I shouldn't start it like a little cry-baby. Even though I was only sixteen, he said, I had this one big chance to prove I was able to die like a man. It is one of the hardest things to make yourself learn how to die right.

He told me that the chair would only tickle me for a little while and then it would all be over for me. I didn't have any idea what the chair looked like or what it could do besides that it would kill me, and when I went to sit down in it I was hoping it would tickle me like Father Hannigan said. When it was all over and they asked me how it felt I told them that; that it tickled me. But I'm telling you that chair sure isn't full of feathers. I guess people have the idea it tickled the way you feel when you laugh.

When he left me and I was alone I kept thinking about what he told me. I read in my Bible until the sun went down. Then I thought a lot about dying. I wasn't going to be a cry-baby; I was going to be brave and act like he said was the only way. I was worried about my mother because she was sick in bed at the time. They didn't tell me this—that's why I knew there was something wrong at home.

. . . I kept thinking that tomorrow I will be dead and they will bury me in a cold cold grave. I wondered what it would look like and I tried to see myself in my mind looking at my own grave-marker. Later on I got on my knees and said my prayers for what I thought would be the last time. I said, "God, tonight is the last time I will sleep in a bed because tomorrow I will have to sit down on that chair and die. Please help me to die."

. . . A little while after eleven o'clock the Sheriff came in with one of his deputies. Everybody got quiet. He asked me if I was ready because it would take us some time to drive over to St. Martinville. . . .

I was dizzy and going down in the elevator seemed to make things worse. Everybody was so quiet and I was thinking about how scared I was so loud I thought they almost heard what I was thinking. They opened the door downstairs and we walked through the lobby to the outside. The sun was real bright and hurt my eyes. There was a black sedan waiting at the curb with the door already open. I tried to walk straight and bravely like Father Hannegan said. The deputy got in and I took a last look up at my window, then got into the car. The Sheriff got on my other side and they started the car. I saw some other policemen around us.

While we drove I kept thinking about not crying or being a baby. I didn't want to die but I wasn't going to say anything about it. They didn't talk to me very much. It wasn't like the joking in my cell at all. I didn't feel much like talking anyway; my tongue was stuck to the top of my mouth, and my ears were ringing. I looked out the windows at all the places we passed. I knew the whole road very well and I couldn't make myself believe I wasn't going to see any of the scenes again. I knew I was going to die, because I was so scared, yet there was something in me that said, Willie, you aren't going to die. About half way to St. Martinville the deputy said to me, "Don't worry, Willie—it won't hurt you very much. You won't even feel it!" I wasn't worried at all whether it would hurt me, I was more worried about the fact it is going to kill me. . . .

The closer I got to St. Martinville the harder my heart beat and the more my knees jumped. When we did get there I noticed the driver turned down into the colored section. I sat up in my seat when I saw we were going to pass my house. I don't know if the driver knew it was my house or not, but it seemed to me he kind of slowed down when we got real near it. But we were still going too fast for me to see anything but the front part of it. I was hoping I would get to see somebody in front—maybe my mother—but nobody was there. It was nice to see it again. I'm glad I didn't see anyone I knew or anyone in my family in front of it. Dying would have been harder if I had, I see now.

When we got closer to the court house the first thing I saw was a large bunch of people gathered around all the doors of the court house. There were both colored and white. And when they saw us pulling up to the curb, they ran up and tried to look into the car. It seemed like everybody in St. Martinville had come out to see me. I upset their way of living so much I guess I was worth a last look.

I got out and looked around the crowd for my father. They had written to me he would be there. Afterward they told me he had to borrow an awful lot of money to rent a hearse and buy a coffin and grave-stone for me. I didn't see him or the hearse, but I saw the truck that had brought the electric chair. As I started to walk forward its motor started and got louder and louder. I could even see some wires leading up to a window where I guessed the chair was. I wished I had seen my father instead. He's a good man, and I know I caused him and the family a whole lot of misery. . . .

They took me up to the execution room. I never knew so many people could get in a room that small. It was shaped like an "L," and there, almost against the wall was the chair. It was almost like any other chair but a lot heavier looking and it had straps on it. It even scared me to look at it. Nobody said anything and everyone kept looking straight at me. I guessed they wanted me to sit on the chair so I started to sit down on it. But the Sheriff grabbed my arm and pulled me away. I was glad for a minute I had done the wrong thing.

He led me into one of the cells. Father Roussere was inside waiting to talk to me. They closed the door and left us alone. Father started telling me I shouldn't be afraid and asked me if there was any doubt in my mind about dying. He told me a lot of nice things and he said he would take care of my family and help them to try and get over my passing away. That seemed to be about all, so I got up and they opened the door. Everybody was watching me as I walked out. I looked at the Sheriff and he nodded, so I walked across the room and sat down in the chair. He took the handcuffs off and the men began strapping me into the chair. They put one strap around my leg and around my waist and tied my arms down, too. I knew then how real it was to have to die. I had it in my mind deep. It was so quiet in there everybody was looking at me so funny. It was the realest misery I ever knew, to see them watching me. It seemed like they would come close to my eyes and then move away from me. I wished they had kept still because I was already dizzy. I was cold and my hands were all wet. I couldn't feel my neck and my head but they say I was soaked with perspiration. They kept on fixing the machine and connecting the wires to my head and to my left leg.

Everything seemed to be finished because everybody looked stranger than before. The Sheriff was looking back of me, and when someone said, "All right," he stepped next to me and asked me if there was something I would like to say before they pulled the switch on me. I was thinking about saying I didn't blame anyone for what they were doing to me, but I couldn't talk. I didn't see my whole life in front of me like they say you are supposed to. When Father Roussere held the Cross out for me to kiss it looked real big. He and the Sheriff stepped back and I relaxed as much as I could. I heard something behind me but before I could turn my head to see what it was, I jumped. They had just touched my head with the hood. It was wet and scared me because I wasn't expecting it. It was a little cap that fitted over my eyes and left my nose free to breathe. Not being able to see made me even more scared. I heard moving around and mumbling on all sides of me. Then, off to the side I heard a voice I hadn't heard until then say to me, "Good-bye, Willie!" It was funny the way he said it—like he was telling me good-bye and I was going off on a trip. I wanted to say good-bye, too, but I was so scared I couldn't talk. My hands were closed tightly. Then—I could almost hear it coming.

The best way I can describe it is: Whatmm! Zst!

It felt like a hundred and a thousand needles and pins were pricking in me all over and my left leg felt like somebody was cutting it with a razor blade. I could feel my arms jumping at my sides and I guess my whole body must have jumped straight out. I couldn't stop the jumping. If that was tickling it was sure a funny kind. I thought for a minute I was going to knock the chair over. Then I was all right. I thought I was dead. Father Hannegan had been right, in a little way—it hadn't hurt me too much. Then they did it again! The same feeling all over. I heard a voice say, "Give me some more juice down there!" And in a little while somebody yelled, "I'm giving you all I got now!" I think I must have hollered for them to stop. They say I said, "Take it off! Take it off!" I know that was certainly what I wanted them to do—turn it off. I really thought I was dead then. I could feel hands all over my body. I thought it was funny how you can feel hands the same way when you're dead as when you're alive. I thought it was funny you could think a little, too, because I wondered why they didn't just leave me alone. I was dead and it seemed like they were in an awful hurry to get me out of that chair so they could bury me. They took the blindfold off and I looked around. The straps were off me and I could feel my hands a little bit. Everybody was talking loud and like they were excited. Then I knew I was still alive and wondered if they were going to make me sit down and in a little while try to kill me again. They told me to get up and a man said, "Are you all right?" I was sure glad to be alive and I told him I was all right. The Sheriff took me off into another room and told me to lay down on a cot. The Coroner came in with his bag and listened to my chest. Then he left. The Sheriff asked me if there was anything I wanted, like water or something to eat and I told him no. Then the other Sheriff came in to tell me they had just called the Governor and I had until the ninth of May—six more days—before they tried to kill me again. I didn't like the idea of going through that all over again, but I was so glad to be just alive I didn't say anything. As we walked out of the room the man who must have thrown the switch yelled at me and said, "I missed you this time, but I'll get you next week if I have to use an iron bar!" He was plenty mad, I guess.

On my way outside to the car they sure looked at me funny. It was my turn to look at them. They looked like they were looking at a ghost. They had expected me to come out feet-first, and I can see why they were surprised. I got in the car and we drove back to New Iberia. . . .

Father Hannegan came over in a little while. They had sent for him and when they called he didn't believe it was possible I was still alive. His face was funny when he walked in: almost like he was afraid of me. I was glad to see him and I wanted to tell him how I tried to be brave. He said, "Yes, you were brave, Willie. God has been good to you, son." Then I said something he was the most astounding statement he ever heard. At the same time he was so surprised he couldn't say anything, though. He told me later it showed him because he should have known it better than I did. I just said, "Why Father—God is Always good!" . . .

Later on in the day they let the newspaper reporters in to see me. They were excited and talked so much and so fast I got nervous. They took a picture of me reading my Bible. In the next few days, I began getting letters and telegrams from all over the country. I felt just like a movie star, and didn't have any idea I had so many friends. The people who wrote said they were sure the Lord had a hand in what happened and told me to be sure and keep on praying because they were praying, too. They would send me books to read and Bible tracts and wishes for good luck. They were all very nice to me and I tried to answer as many of them as I could. There were so many I tried to find the time to answer them with the little time I thought I had left. . . .

After the electrocution my father went right away to see a lawyer, Mr. Bertrand DeBlanc, and asked him if he would take my case. He told the lawyer he had no money but he would work to repay him. Mr. DeBlanc said it was all right and we didn't have to pay him anything. He said it would be cruel and unusual punishment to kill me.

I had to agree with him on that.

I was all ready to get used to dying again when Mr. DeBlanc came to see me the day before they were going to kill me the second time. He said the Judge had refused to let me go, but I didn't have to die because he got a chance to take my case before the Louisiana Supreme Court the next morning at ten o'clock. He also told me the Lieutenant Governor had granted me a stay of execution for twenty-nine more days. I was glad and very grateful to him. . . .

I found out the Louisiana Supreme Court couldn't do anything to stop me from being killed. But they gave me permission to go to the state Board of Pardons at the end of the month of May. I remember that day well. I was nervous and lonely both. I didn't have anybody to talk to because Father Hannegan had gone with my lawyer to the hearing in New Orleans. Father Hannegan came over the next day and tried to break it to me gently, but I knew by his face before he said anything that they had turned me down. But he said they were going to take my case to the Supreme Court in Washington, DC.

On the tenth of June they came to me and said, "Willie, the Supreme Court decided not to even listen to your case." Well, I felt pretty bad about it, but after a while I got used to the idea. Then a couple of hours later, they came in laughing and said, "They made a mistake, Willie. Somebody put your papers in the wrong place and they are going to listen to your case in October."

Well, I sure felt glad. When they said I had to die I was disappointed, and when they came in I thought they were going to tell me when. But when they said I didn't have to die at all for a long time I really felt happy. . . .

The business about the thirteenth child came up again. Just after the first of this year—on January 13th, which was sixteen days before my birthday—I heard that the Supreme Court in Washington gave a decision on my case. Five of the justices voted against me and four for me. That was pretty close to happiness, I guess. I am not complaining or anything like that, because I know down in my heart everybody has tried to do the right thing for me and everybody else. It is just that there has never been another case like mine before and I see how hard it is to say what is the right thing in my case.

If I ever get to Heaven I guess I'll get to know.

That is just about all I have to say right now. Mr. Montgomery says that in writing this I may have helped someone, somehow. I hope so. He has written the story of my life and it is much longer than this. I wonder if I will ever get to read the thing.

Questions to Consider:

1. *How might a document like this have been used?*
2. *What does this document show about the treatment of death row prisoners in Louisiana in the 1940s?*

Source:

Willie Francis, *My Trip to the Chair, as told to Sam Montgomery* (Lafayette, LA: 1947), Afro-American Pamphlets, Part 3 (1827–1948), Rare Book and Special Collections Reading Room, Library of Congress.

1948–1960:
A. P. Tureaud, Governor Jimmie Davis, and the Desegregation of Orleans Parish Schools

Alexander Pierre Tureaud, known as A. P., was the chief lawyer for the Louisiana National Association for the Advancement of Colored People (NAACP). He joined Thurgood Marshall and the NAACP's Legal Defense Fund and filed lawsuits against one parish school board after another to try to end discrimination against African American students and teachers. The salary equalization suits won higher pay for teachers in the 1950s, but many other inequalities persisted, as the documents in this section illustrate.

The Orleans Parish School Board (OPSB), which was all-white, denied all petitions sent them. Despite the Supreme Court decision in *Brown v. Board of Education* (1954) which mandated an end to segregation in public education, white authorities from school boards to the governor dug in their heels and refused to comply. This forced a showdown between the local and state government, and another showdown between the state and federal government.

It would take another decade of massive resistance and continued tug-of-war among the three levels of power, as well as more court filings and judicial decisions, before most public schools in Louisiana undertook serious integration plans. By 1970, white flight was draining the public schools of a much-needed tax base, and many closed for lack of students. Rather than stay and be part of the change, white citizens picked up stakes and fled to the suburbs where they could once again send their children to all-white schools, but this time racial segregation was the result of residential rather than legal segregation.

Letter from A. P. Tureaud, Attorney, New Orleans, May 21, 1948, addressed to Orleans Parish School Board

Gentlemen:

On July 25, 1946, a petition was presented to your honorable body setting forth eleven items of inequalities existing between the white and Negro schools of this Parish. At this meeting assurance was given the petitioners that due consideration would be given to their petition. After two years of patient waiting, on the part of these petitioners who are parents, citizens and taxpayers of this City, for the relief prayed [a legal term for petitioned] for, little, if any action has been taken by your honorable body with respect to the inequalities complained of; and from all indications, it now appears that the Negro school children of New Orleans face another year of disappointment and frustration, unless definite action is immediately taken to remove these inequalities. Much of the forbearance of these petitioners was due to their confidence in your honorable body and in the representations made by the Honorable Lionel J. Bourgeois, Superintendent.

There still exists in the public schools of this parish discrimination against Negroes in the matter of the following:

1. Pupil-teacher ratio
2. Building facilities
3. Number of periods per teacher in high schools
4. Visiting teachers
5. Kindergarten classes
6. Special classes
7. Vocational curriculum
8. Gymnasium
9. Business education
10. Night high school

Beginning with the 1948–49 term of school, there will be approximately 1109 Negro children graduating from elementary schools for which there will not be adequate housing facilities.

In the elementary schools Negro teachers, in some instances, have as many as 60 pupils per teacher, as compared to white teachers with slightly over 30 pupils per teacher; in the high schools the ratio in Negro high schools is in excess of 30 and in the white schools the ratio is 22 to one.

As citizens, taxpayers and parents of Negro children attending the public schools of New Orleans, these petitioners are entitled to immediate relief; that any delay on the part of your honorable body will be attended with irreparable injury. . . .

It becomes necessary, therefore, to advise that unless these inequalities herein complained of are removed immediately we shall be compelled to take such legal action as may be warranted in the premises.

There is attached hereto a copy of the petition which was presented to your honorable body and discussed at the meeting held with you on July 25, 1946.

Respectfully submitted:
A. P. Tureaud, Attorney for Petitioners

Petition from the Citizens Committee on Equal Education of New Orleans, 1950

This petition on behalf of Negro parents and taxpayers of the city of New Orleans submitted through the Citizens Committee on Equal Education of the New Orleans Branch NAACP shows:

1. On July 14, 1949 superintendent of schools issued a statement to the President and Members of the Orleans Parish School Board relative to the operation of our city schools all of which are concurred in by the board of superintendents.

2. That on May 4, 1946 through this same committee the OPSB was notified of the discrimination existing in the Negro schools in violation of the equal protection clause of the 15th Amendment of the United States Constitution and the School Board has been made the defendant in a cause of action in the Federal Court.

3. The statement issued by the superintendent of schools on July 14, 1949, recommends additional classrooms to the Lockett, Macarty, McDonogh 32, Lee Station, Nelson, Sylvania Williams, and Ricard Schools. We are unalterably opposed to the erection or extension of frame school buildings for any of the children of Orleans Parish. In a like manner we strongly oppose additional classrooms for the Ricard school; it is obsolete and is not conducive to study and industry.

4. The newspapers of August 9, 1949, revealed that the OPSB instructed the Department of Superintendents to arrange double shifts for Negro pupils in over-crowded Negro schools. This is done despite the acknowledgment by the superintendent that some of the white schools are not being utilized to their fullest capacity and the pupil-teacher ratio is 15:1. The superintendent further admits that the reason more of the white schools were not consolidated was because of antagonism and pressure. The Negro Community feels that if the citizenry has elected a School Board that reacts to antagonism and pressure instead of a full day schooling under ideal conditions for all pupils, then we are ready, and ready now, to start our antagonism and pressure. We, therefore, urge you to continue the consolidation-conversion program to eliminate the need of double shifts in the 1949–1950 school session. This recommendation is made only to eliminate the double shift plan; and we want the board to know that the conversion of second-hand white schools to Negro use is not equality. . . .

5. The statement proposes the erection of eight field houses for white students and none for Negroes. This is not in keeping with the equalization program and we urge that the money allocated for the erection of the field houses be divided so as to provide field houses for Negro students . . . The statement also shows that for the 1947–48 Session, the cost per white elementary pupil was $174.69 against the Negro elementary pupil cost of $108.74. . . .

6. We ask for an explanation of the following differences:

   a. Cost of Negro High School site . . . $90,000; cost of the white technical high school site—$150,000.
   b. Furniture and equipment for Negro High Schools $102,000. . . . Cost of equipment for White High Schools $750,000. . . .

The committee submits that a ten year proposal is not considered a reasonable time and that the patience of the Negro Community is at an end.

We are determined to secure absolute equality and nothing less than complete equality is acceptable to our community.

The latest decision regarding equal educational facilities and opportunities adjudicated by the USSC eliminated any waiting period; and when the question of reasonable time was raised the Court said, "NEGROES ARE ENTITLED TO EQUAL EDUCATIONAL FACILITIES AND OPPORTUNITES AT THE SAME TIME THEY ARÉ AFFORDED WHITES." [Caps in original.]

Mr. President and Members of the Board, we respectfully submit this petition on behalf of the Negro Citizens, parents and taxpayers of New Orleans, and request an answer at this time.

CITIZENS COMMITTEE ON EQUAL EDUCATION OF NEW ORLEANS BRANCH NAACP

Irma Landix, Chairman

Letter from Jack Gremillion, Attorney General, to Lloyd Rittiner, President, OPSB, August 2, 1960

It has come to my attention that in your official capacity you have called a special public meeting of the Orleans Parish School Board for the purpose of considering a report of Dr. Redmond on conditions that will exist upon the closing of schools in the City of New Orleans. This report, I understand, is to be made so that the school board my make plans for such an eventuality.

I take this means to notify you that under the law of Louisiana, as you must now well know, the Governor of the State of Louisiana shall take over the active administration and control of the public schools as of September 8, 1960, and that thereafter the operation or closing of schools will be entirely in his hands. Therefore, any attempt on the part of the Orleans Parish School Board to make plans concerning the closing of schools is as much beyond the school board's authority as the planning for the integration of the schools.

It appears that you may render yourself and the board either subject to contempt proceedings or further injunctive proceedings if you persist in holding such a meeting. . . .

I certainly hope that it will not be necessary on the part of the State of Louisiana to resort to further prosecution either for contempt or otherwise which would only add to confusion and result in embarrassing predicaments. Your kind cooperation is anticipated.

Sincerely yours,
Jack P. F. Gremillion
Attorney General

Governor Jimmie Davis Executive Order #1

August 17, 1960

1. In accordance with the provisions of Act 496 of 1960, I, the Governor of the State of Louisiana, in my sovereign capacity, do hereby supersede the Orleans Parish School Board and do hereby take over the exclusive control, management and administration of all the public schools in the Parish of Orleans formerly under the jurisdiction of the Orleans Parish School Board, as of this date.
2. I do hereby direct that the public schools in the Parish of Orleans shall be opened on September 7, 1960.
3. I do hereby designate James F. Redmond to act on my behalf and as my Agent to operate all of the public schools for the Parish of Orleans.
4. I direct that registration of all new students desiring admission to the public schools of the Parish of Orleans be effected [*sic*] in accordance with the following procedure:
    a. For students entering the first grade: Notify by US Mail, addressed to Mr. James F. Redmond, 703 Carondelet Street, New Orleans, Louisiana, the name of the student seeking registration, school in which registration is sought and school of second choice in which registration is sought, present address, where and when born, number of the birth certificate, exact year of birth, sex and race, mother's maiden name and occupation, father's name and occupation, physician who delivered child, any illnesses. The above notice shall be postmarked on or before 12:00 o'clock midnight, September 2, 1960, and such notice

shall be accompanied with a certified copy of the birth certificate of the student and a vaccination certificate, or evidence of same, of the student.

b. For students entering other than the first grade: Notify by US Mail, addressed to Mr. James F. Redmond, 703 Carondelet Street, New Orleans, Louisiana, the name of the student seeking registration, school in which registration is sought and school of second choice in which registration is sought, present address, where and when born, number of the birth certificate, exact year of birth, sex and race, mother's maiden name and occupation, father's name and occupation, physician who delivered child, any illnesses, and proper evidence of school credits previously attained by the student. The above notice shall be postmarked on or before 12:00 o'clock midnight, September 2, 1960, and such notice shall be accompanied with a certified copy of the birth certificate of the student and a vaccination certificate, or evidence of same, of the student.

In witness whereof, I have hereunto set my hand and caused to be affixed the Great Seal of the State of Louisiana, at the Capitol, in the City of Baton Rouge, on this the 17th day of August, 1960. Jimmie H. Davis, Governor of Louisiana.

Questions to Consider:

1. *In what ways did the petitioners summon the ghost of* Plessy v. Ferguson*?*
2. *Describe the techniques and strategies used by black New Orleanians to try to get educational opportunities equalized. Why did they use those strategies?*
3. *In what ways did Jimmie Davis's order, though it sounded race-neutral, disadvantage black students and in effect perpetuate racial discrimination?*

Sources:

1. Letter from A. P. Tureaud, Attorney, New Orleans, May 21, 1948, addressed to Orleans Parish School Board, Orleans Parish School Board Collection (MSS 147), Desegregation Files, Louisiana and Special Collections, Earl K. Long Library, University of New Orleans.

2. Petition from the Citizens Committee on Equal Education of New Orleans, 1950, Orleans Parish School Board Collection (MSS 147), Desegregation Files, Louisiana and Special Collections, Earl K. Long Library, University of New Orleans.

3. Letter from Jack Gremillion, Attorney General, to Lloyd Rittiner, President, OPSB, August 2, 1960, Orleans Parish School Board Collection (MSS 147), Desegregation Files, Louisiana and Special Collections, Earl K. Long Library, University of New Orleans.

4. Jimmie Davis Executive Order #1, State Archives (P1986-11), Executive Orders, Box 1.

1948–1970: Representative F. Edward Hébert on Civil Rights

F. Edward Hébert, Louisiana's longest-serving US Representative, was elected from New Orleans's first congressional district for eighteen consecutive terms from 1941 until he retired in 1977. After graduating from Tulane in 1924, he entered a career in journalism at the *New Orleans States*, covering Huey Long and the Louisiana scandals of 1939 that exposed the corruption of the Longites, including Governor Richard Leche, who ultimately served four years in federal prison. Hébert was a Democrat of the traditional white supremacist variety who, not surprisingly, opposed virtually every civil rights measure championed by a new generation of Democrats, with whom he vigorously disagreed. A member of the House Armed Services Committee and, perhaps more important, the House Un-American Activities Committee, Hébert linked progressive reforms with communist subversion.

The excerpts below come from his weekly radio addresses between 1948 and 1970. Repetitious phrases have been removed.

The first excerpt discusses the 1948 Democratic convention in Philadelphia, where incumbent President Truman's supporters got civil rights measures written into the platform, at which point southern Democrats bolted the convention and formed their own third-party challenge—the State's Rights Party, popularly known as the Dixiecrats. The Dixiecrats' nominee, South Carolina's Strom Thurmond, championed one issue only: opposition to civil rights. The Democrats' civil rights planks were influenced by Americans for Democratic Action, a national organization that supported progressive policies and candidates; Hébert derided the group in his speeches as a communist front organization. In addition to the language he refers to in the excerpt below, the platform also called for an anti-poll-tax bill, an anti-lynching bill, and for the establishment of a permanent Fair Employment Practices Committee (FEPC).

The second excerpt indicates that Hébert's stances had changed very little in two decades. It shows his response to the proposed 1968 Fair Housing bill, one of the last legislative initiatives of President Lyndon Johnson's "Second Reconstruction."

Finally, in the third excerpt, from 1970, Hébert directly ties communist revolution and civil rights reform together.

August 16, 1948

Tonight I want to read you two excerpts from two declarations of principles and philosophy from the people of two great and powerful nations.

"The Democratic Party is responsible for the great civil rights gains made in recent years in eliminating unfair and illegal discrimination based on race, creed or color.

"The Democratic Party commits itself to continuing its effort to eradicate all racial, religious and economic discrimination."

You undoubtedly recognize that language as the language of the so-called "civil rights" plank in the platform adopted by the Democratic Party at Philadelphia under the insistence and direction of the Americans for Democratic Action [ADA].

That is exactly what it is: The civil rights plank which tore the Democratic party asunder and which was so obnoxious to the South and particularly to members of the Louisiana delegation.

This is the plank in the Democratic Party platform adopted at the urging of the Americans for Democratic Action which defiantly says to those of us in the South, those of us in Louisiana and those of us in New Orleans, "We are going to tear and break apart all your laws of segregation. You must have no more segregation signs in your street cars. You must remove all semblance of separation of the races in your public vehicles. Your children must and will attend schools where there is no line drawn between the races. There shall be no distinction in our schools because of color. All children must be assembled together and the distinction of color completely ignored. You must eat together in your restaurants and sit together in your theaters. We, the Americans for Democratic Action, have taken over your Democratic Party and we insist upon these provisions.

"The FEPC is an act which takes away from the employer the right to conduct his own business. An act which furnishes a dugout for radicals to hide. This federal legislation is important to us [i.e., the ADA] because here we are able to take complete control of private business and eliminate the spirit of open trade and competition."

Now let me read you two paragraphs from another document and then suggest you draw your own conclusions as to similarity and expression. I have in my hand an official translation of the Russian constitution of the Soviet Republic as issued by the Russian embassy here in Washington. It reads as follows:

"In equality of laws of citizens of the USSR, irrespective of the nationality or race, in all spheres of economical government, cultural, political and other public activities, is an indefensible law.

"Any direct or indirect restriction of the races of, or conversely, the establishment of any direct or indirect privileges for, citizens on account of race or nationality, as well as any advocacy or racial or nationality exclusiveness or hatred and contempt is punishable by law."

[Hébert went on to discuss his challenger, Lucille Savoie, noting that she was the secretary for the local chapter of the Americans for Democratic Action. Hébert read off her home address, which was also published in the paper.]

There can be no doubt as to the true complexion of the opposition to me [Savoie] in this campaign.

For eight years I have served you well in the Congress. For eight years I have fought against such legislation as anti-poll tax, anti-lynching, anti-segregation and against the so-called FEPC. I have fought against them because I spoke for you and not for any group or clique which is dedicated to the overthrow of what we in the South believe, and who are controlled by sinister figures who take their orders from a centralized headquarters in Washington.

March 31, 1968

In my whole twenty-eight years here in the Congress I have never before received so much mail and protest as during the last three weeks in connection with the proposed so-called open housing bill which came from the Senate and is at the moment before the Rules Committee of the House. I dare say I have received over three thousand letters [from those] who oppose the proposition, an indication of how the people in my own district in New Orleans feel. . . .

Nobody will ever attempt to deny that the real keystone that this country is built on is home ownership. Family life built into community life. The ability to own your own home, your own property and to do with that property and with that home what you please is the very essence of the existence of the type of country in which we live today. . . .

What does so-called open housing mean? This means that you cannot refuse to sell your home to another person because of so-called race, color, or creed. If this isn't dictatorship in the rawest form I don't know what it is.

There are those who will have you believe that this legislation would benefit the colored man or the Negro, [but] this legislation would be most the damning thing against that Negro or that colored man who has worked so hard through his life who has by sheer grit and determination acquired property by paying little by little on it. If he didn't want to sell it to us [white people] because of our race, color, or creed, which is his right, that he could not prevent us from buying that home. Remember, this is a two way street. This is a double-edged sword. I don't have to tell you my position. I have been constant as the Northern star. As far as open housing is concerned, you can depend upon me to be internally, externally, and eternally opposed to it.

March 29, 1970

Good morning, ladies and gentlemen. As I sit here in Washington this morning visiting with you on this Easter Sunday, just a fast throwback of what we have experienced in the last week would indicate to you exactly the haziness and the uncertainty of the future. When I was a youngster during the Russian Revolution [of 1917], it was the talk of the country. It was an expression to say, 'Ah, wait for the revolution.' We laughed at the thought of the day that the revolution worldwide would come. Hasn't it come? Isn't this country in a state of revolution today?

As we look around us, we see a strike against the government by postal employees who are dedicated to get the mail through. We see this group of individuals striking against their government, strangling industry, strangling traffic, delaying the delivery of medicines and checks for the poor. . . . Strikes against the government. If that is not a revolution then I don't know what it is. . . .

The terrible chaos in which we find this country today, the hatreds, the racism, the bigotry, had its genesis right here in Washington in the Supreme Court of the United States in 1954 when nine men, nine men issued a ruling that wiped out all the advances made by the races and turned the white against the black and the black against the white, caused our streets to be streets of blood sores, nine men from millions, nine men, that was a minority and what a small minority. Nine men not elected. Nine men not chosen by their peers. Nine men named for life to hold in the palm of their hands the majority, the vast majority, all the American people.

Questions to Consider:

1. *Why would an openly racist politician like Hébert be elected to his seat even after Congress passed the Voting Rights Act of 1965, which ended discrimination against African American voters?*

2. *Why would Hébert portray liberals as tools of the Soviets? Was there anything to this charge?*

3. *Look up Americans for Democratic Action. What about the group's history undercuts Hébert's contention that it was a communist front organization?*

4. *Hébert argues that the Fair Housing Act hurt black homeowners as much as it would "hurt" white citizens. In what ways is this argument a false equivalency, a logical fallacy?*

5. *How would you answer Hébert's complaint about the role of the Supreme Court in striking down racial segregation laws?*

Source:

F. Edward Hébert papers, LaRC-650.

1959:
Russell Long on Governor Earl Long's Breakdown

In 1959, Louisiana Governor Earl Long was committed by his family and medical advisors to an out-of-state mental institution. US Senator Russell Long (Earl's nephew and Huey's son) prepared this speech to inform the legislature of the circumstances of the governor's hospitalization. Senator Long never presented this version, however, sensing an unreceptive audience. Instead, he gave a much shorter address stating only that the governor was being treated for a breakdown in his health and that Lieutenant Governor Lether Frazar would be acting as governor. The senator's original speech gives a compelling depiction of his uncle Earl, both as a man and as a politician, as well as an insider's view of the events surrounding Earl's confinement.

Friends of Earl K. Long, Members of the Legislature, Ladies and Gentlemen:

Some several days ago the Governor of Our State appeared before one of your committees to urge the merits of certain amendments which he was supporting. From a debater's point of view, he committed every mistake in the book. He directly and personally insulted many of the same legislators whose votes he had intended to woo. He rambled off into matters that were not the least bit relevant to the issue. He discussed matters which are always better left unsaid. He interrupted and treated with discourtesy one of his ablest and most eloquent spokesmen—a man whom he had asked to plead the case. He took the microphone and talked endlessly in a manner . . .

of what I would expect of the last dying gasp of an unsuccessful filibuster. Some of the words he used were disrespectful words of slang which intelligent, respectable men of this state have long ago discarded. There were even words of profanity which he would never have wanted to use under the circumstances. The presentation was so bad that he lost the votes of a considerable number of legislators who have voted with him even if they thought his position was not plausible.

This matter was shown over television to the people throughout the State. Anyone who had arrived from Washington after the incident occurred, I must tell you I was aghast when I saw this played back by film over television. I could not believe my eyes and ears. I believe I have some idea how it came to happen but I could never have actually believed it had I not seen it. Frankly, on afterthought I was surprised that the station would have permitted such a speech to be shown in its entirety. The laws of this Nation do not permit the use of profane language particularly some of the words the Governor used. Nor do I believe the Federal Communications Commission would permit a man to go on television and describe matters involving the personal lives of individuals, living and dead, which they nor their worst enemies would have cared to have discussed in an open meeting. Frankly, I must object that the television stations permitted these matters to be shown to the people and the nation. . . .

On the following day, the Governor returned, anxious to make a contrite apology. He was advised by his friends that he should not attempt to do so. He insisted. They agreed after they had extracted a promise from him that he would limit himself to ten minutes and that he would not depart from a prepared text. He promised to read his prepared statement and then decided to add a few additional words. Unfortunate words indeed. If you want to apologize, let me suggest that you leave the word "but" out of your apology. Don't say, "I'm sorry, but" because everything that comes thereafter will spoil your apology. Unfortunately, the Governor talked for more than an hour after he said the word "but." While I did not see this second presentation, his friends tell me that it was worse than the first. When he concluded, he needed the help of his friends to leave the chambers. His enemies were outraged, his friends were in tears. Not so much because their fate was linked to his as the fact they were seeing a man whom they loved devotedly destroy himself, perhaps forever, whipping himself until his mind, his lungs, his throat, his heart were nothing more than bruised and inflamed tissue.

. . .

Friends of the Governor knew this type of thing could not continue. They attempted to persuade him to take a prolonged rest and submit to medical treatment. One of the things we know about our Governor, those of us who know him well, is if he prescribes his own rest if often times results in a greater strain on his system than his work. Let me illustrate his last weekend vacation. As a lover of horse racing, he asked me to make reservations at a Washington hotel and obtain tickets to the famous Preakness Races at the Pimlico Track. This was to be a long week-end for him. He would attend the races on both Friday and Saturday. After a hard day's work on Thursday, he drove to New Orleans, boarded an Eastern Airlines plane and flew all night in a chair. Knowing the man, I know, he did not sleep on that chair except perhaps for a moment or two. The tension under which he was existing would not permit it. Inasmuch as the plane arrived somewhat early, he was at the baggage counter when I arrived. I saw him squatting on a small rack about six inches high, entertaining a small child. When we went to the hotel, he felt too much on edge to go to bed. He wanted to talk for awhile. After an hour, during which he did most of the talking to his assembled friends around the room, I departed to get some much needed rest. When I went to work, I found that it was time for the Governor to leave for the races and he had not been to bed unless it was for less than one hour. He was late leaving for the races because he was on the telephone discussing more than a hundred matters which were on his mind. He returned from the races, engaged in interviews, more telephone calls, continued to talk to his friends, received very little rest, perhaps two hours at the best, and was on the telephone at 9:00 o'clock urging me to join him for the Preakness Race on Saturday. Unfortunately, I did not feel that I could go. I had a bad cold and an extremely hoarse throat and was scheduled to make a somewhat lengthy speech on Monday. It seemed better to stay in bed and get over the cold. The Governor demanded that I come to the hotel, let him take a look at me and permit him to decide whether I was in sufficiently good health to make the race. I am sure that some of you realize how futile it is to argue with Earl Long when he thinks you should do something. As a long-time friend and admirer, the best way to get out of it is to stall and fail to show up. That was my course. Again he was late leaving for the races, talking on the telephone incessantly, expressing himself about the issues of his conversations and his general point of view on everything under the sun until the races had already started. They were half over by the time he arrived. In his usual fashion, he was taking the attitude that when you do something, you should REALLY do it. Not only had he made a study of every horse running at Pimlico and his record for the past two years, he had done the same thing with regard to the two other race tracks, one in New York and one somewhere else. Not content to bet on the races at that track where he was attending, he was betting on every race at the other two tracks, a total of twenty-seven races. When I next saw him, he was entering my apartment for the purpose of bidding me a brief adieu. It was then 11:00 o'clock. He entered the door and dropped on the first chair he could find. It happened to be near a telephone. I suggested that in view of his weary condition, he should recline on my bed and rest for awhile. He told me he was too tired to drag himself there. He preferred to stay where he was. Within five minutes he had picked up the telephone and was calling everyone under the sun. First to find out how he had made out on his other bets, then to discuss various sundry matters of interest. He showed some irritation to the fact the other guests were attempting to converse among themselves during these interminable telephone conversations. Eventually we managed to move him to the bedroom in order to make it possible for other people to talk while he was conversing over the telephone. He completed his conversations by about 12:30. He talked to us until approximately 1:45 A.M., at which time it was necessary for him to leave in order to get on his airplane to fly back to New Orleans and drive to Baton Rouge. That was his week-end's rest.

I tell you this, gentlemen, only to point out that as an indefatigable worker, Earl Long's recreations have nothing to do with the word "rest." He was going so hard that he couldn't possibly stop. As a man who had worked hard and doggedly for everything he ever had, a person with a "never say die" attitude, a man with the strongest sense of willpower I had ever witnessed, he has gone beyond the point of no return. He couldn't sleep because he had had no sleep. He couldn't rest because he had had no rest. He had permitted himself to become so obsessed with his determination to do a job, he couldn't conceive of a task being performed adequately without him. Every friend he had was urging him to stop it and take a long rest. His doctors advised him he would never live through this session of the Legislature unless he slowed down. His answer was the typical, "yes, I understand your good intentions, but there will be plenty of time to slow down next month." He had been warned repeatedly that he would face a breakdown or perhaps sudden death if he continued longer. He had used his machinery far beyond the point of maximum term. He had worn it until he was getting less than no return whatever from it. At the time he last appeared before you he had reached the point where the doctors could no longer tell him of his condition. He was no longer facing a breakdown. He had had it.

Therein lies the problem, gentlemen. You can tell a man he's facing a breakdown and he can understand you. There comes this type of breakdown when you can't tell him he has had it. He wouldn't believe it. He thinks it is still in front of him even after it has passed. It was for those reasons that his most devoted friends felt that they must save him before his enemies could destroy him. They attempted over a period of thirty-six hours to persuade him to rest. He was willing to agree provided it did not upset his important schedule. . . .

Those of us who have done this thing realize that we have assumed a dangerous undertaking. If we were right, then we are his best friends, his devoted and most faithful followers who would do their duty for him even if it should mean that it might cost us the positions which we hold and even though it may cost us the friendship of the man whom we love above all others. If we are wrong, then we are indeed stupid, ignorant and unworthy of the positions in life which the people and our friends have accorded us. If we prove wrong, then we have forcibly seized a Governor from his State, elected by the people to hold the highest and greatest power which can be entrusted by a free people to a single man, power intended to be exercised for the good of all, including myself. If we are wrong, then we have made the Governor of a sovereign people a prisoner in his own mansion, flown him against his will to a neighboring State where his powers do not exist, imprisoned him in a hospital room against his desires. If we prove to be wrong, then the apology which he read for his presentations here on Wednesday and Thursday is small indeed compared to that which we owe to him. I do not believe that we are wrong. It is my primary and fervent hope that the Governor of Louisiana will come to realize that we are his best friends, not some group of misguided, deluded fools. I hope that he will realize that we were seeking to save him from a failure of his health which could never be repaired. We did not take this step without the benefit of medical advice as to the necessity thereof.

. . .

The main purpose of my speech here tonight was to tell you just these brief words. Earl Long is a man who was giving everything he had to public service. He has served us as Governor longer and more times than any man in the history of Louisiana. His ambition to serve well has been his highest desire. When he committed the almost unpardonable mistake of making a horribly bad presentation before your body, he did so because he thought he was fighting for the common man and woman. He did so because he thought that he was fighting to prevent dear old men and women, many of them his loyal supporters, from being disfranchised because of their inability to answer technical questions or provide proper answers to the difficult and complicated provisions the Constitution of the United States and the State of Louisiana, some of which even good lawyers cannot explain without consulting their libraries. . . .

Either Earl Long's health would have completely broken and he would have been carried away for treatment when it was too late to repair the damage or he could have died on the spot. . . .

Questions to Consider:

1. *What does Russell Long's word choice regarding Earl Long and his actions indicate about the purpose of this speech?*
2. *Based on this source, how does Earl Long compare to the politicians of our time? Do today's news organizations air speeches similar to the ones delivered by Governor Long that got him in trouble? Be specific.*
3. *Following his breakdown, Earl Long ran successfully for Congress in 1960 with the campaign slogan, "I Ain't Crazy." He won the election, but died before he could assume office. What does Long's 1960 election tell us about the priorities of Louisiana voters?*
4. *What does Senator Long's speech tell us about the responsibilities of office?*

Source:

Russell B. Long Collection, Mss 3700, Louisiana and Lower Mississippi Valley Collections, Louisiana State University Libraries, Baton Rouge, LA. Reprinted with permission from the Long Family.

1960:
Testimony of John Scott on Voter Registration Requirements

John Henry Scott, a minister and a farmer, advocated for black voting rights. Scott lived in East Carroll Parish in northeast Louisiana his whole life. The parish's population was almost entirely black. In 1960, it had 4,690 potential African American voters but zero black voters on its roles, while 99.7 percent of eligible white citizens were registered (2,836). Despite repeated death threats and attempts on his life, Scott led a twenty-five-year struggle to rectify that injustice. Klan members burned crosses in front of his home. In 1962, he was wounded by a shotgun blast. Although the FBI investigated the incident, no culprit was identified.[1] Working with the NAACP, Scott convinced Attorney General Robert Kennedy to sue the town and the state.

In addition to pastoring a Baptist church founded by his great-grandfather, Scott was president of the East Carroll Baptist Association, president of the local NAACP for thirty-three years, and chairman of the East Carroll Ministerial Alliance for about five years. Following the testimony below, his church was razed by an arson attack. Scott had completed his education at United Theological Seminary, Leland College, and Southern University (all in Louisiana), and was clearly capable of passing the literacy test. Because he lived in the parsonage, he owned no real estate. He had been attempting to register since 1946. The committee members quizzed him about what happened each time he tried. What follows is a condensed version of the testimony, omitting most of the questions. Each time he went, there was at least one other minister with him.

1. Adam Fairclough, *Race and Democracy: The Civil Rights Struggle in Louisiana, 1915–1972* (Athens, GA: University of Georgia Press, 1995), 307, 341.

John H. Scott's Testimony, September 27, 1960, Before the United States Commission on Civil Rights Hearings on Voting Rights Violations in Louisiana, Held in New Orleans

Rev. Scott: We didn't exactly know where the registration office was, so finally we went upstairs, and we got to the door, and I said, "Paul [Mason], here is the door," and we went to the door, and the registrar of voters say, "Go to the next door." So we went to look for another door, and when we got back, the door was locked. So we didn't make any attempt to go in. We gave up that time.

The next time I tried to register must have been about 2 years later, around 1947; the Reverend Mason and I went together. Went to the same place, the same registrar. She was very nice. She gave us the card to fill. When we filled it she looked at it and said, "Well, we wouldn't know where to find you all," or something, so we went out, and a little later on I decided to go back.

So I decided that probably trying to be a Democrat was making it difficult for me to register.

So I decided to put on my next card "Republican." The registrar of voters looked in the office, and she picked out a card, and she looked at it, and she said, "Well, on this card you said you were a Democrat. On this card you are saying you are a Republican." She said, "What are you?"

I said, "Well, I am not anything until you register me."

So she said, "Well, don't you know you can't change your party that fast?"

So I had to go out.

So, later on, about 1950, I believe, Reverend Mason and several others went in, decided to try again, and she gave us all a card, and we filled them out, and she told Reverend Mason that his was perfect, but he would have to get someone to vouch for him or sign, identify him. All of which he was successful, but that didn't work, either.

Vice Chairman Storey: Could I ask how many signed recommendations or [people] vouched for him?

Scott: Well, just one. But they didn't accept that one [so] I came on out.

Vice Chairman Storey: Did you attempt to register again?

Scott: Yes. Reverend Henderson and I went together, and she told him his was right, and he was fortunate to get a white person to go up there that had not been brought up to the proceedings. And he was turned away, after he had gone down, and they told him what he should do, I guess, and what he shouldn't do. So he went away. So we were not able to get anyone to come, and if we got them it was to no avail because they had made their mind up not to register anybody. So recently they put a new man or they put a man in office after our present registrar resigned or went on retirement, and we thought we would try him, I believe last September, and several of us went. About five. He asked us how long we had been living there. Most of us had been living there all of our life. He handed us a form and he said, "You will have to get two qualified electors, from your ward and precinct to identify you." So he didn't register. So the lady that was with me, she said, "I can get two to identify me." I said, "Well, you think you can, but you can't." She said, "But I know I can," she said, "I have some white friends, and we are all Christians." I said. "But Christians and this registration business is different. Nobody's a Christian when it comes down to identifying you."

So we decided to go back, I believe, in July. A group of us, about 21. The registrar of voters asked us what did we want. We said we wanted to register. He said, "Do you have anybody to identify you?" I says, "We can identify each other." I said, "We identify folk at the bank and at the post office." I say "We have come around and got folks out of jail and signed, went on their bond." I said, "We be here long enough to be known."

So we could not register. I never did think that in America or that a citizen would have to do all of this for an opportunity to vote.

Vice Chairman Storey: Now, tell me how long have you lived in this county? Since what date?

Scott: Oh, I have been there since 1901. That is when I was born.

Vice Chairman Storey: Did you ever have any trouble being identified at banks or the courthouse or any other place?

Scott: No. My great-grandfather lived there; my grandfather lived there; my grandfather was a minister, and I mean, we are all very well known, everybody.

Vice Chairman Storey: The records show that there are no Negro registrants in your parish. Is that true?

Scott: That's right.

Vice Chairman Storey: Why do you want to vote?

Scott: Well, I have always felt like that was a responsibility that belonged to the citizens. It always gives recognition; I noticed the streets where they [people] vote, they were fixed, and the officers of the law respected them and treated them different from the people that didn't vote, and after reading Negro newspapers [the *Chicago Defender*], traveling quite a bit, I felt like that it was a responsibility, and after my brothers—I didn't go because I was a minister—went to the Army, and back there in World War I, when the President was talking about making the world safe for democracy, and everybody had the right and privilege to participate, it always had been a burning zeal and desire within my heart, and I have never been able to tell my children the reason why that Negroes should be treated in such a way or be cast about.

Vice Chairman Storey: Reverend Scott, have you been arrested in your lifetime?

Scott: No.

Storey: Do you know of any impediment that disqualifies you from voting or registering?

Scott: No.

[The next line of questioning revealed that an NAACP lawsuit against the registrar of voters had been erroneously thrown out of court in 1954 and had not been revived. Questioning revealed that many black veterans of the armed forces lived in the parish and had not been allowed to register.

Scott was asked if he had ever been threatened or intimidated because of his voter registration activity.]

Scott: Well, slightly. I don't like to talk about intimidations. I would rather forget them. They told me not to say anything about that. . . . I just go on, go on because I fell like I am right, and I know where I am going. I know what I am talking about, and I don't care what happens. Whatever happens, I got to go to heaven, and if I go for my people or for the right to vote I would be perfectly satisfied, so that's the way I feel about it.

Storey: No further questions. Thank you, Reverend Scott.

Exhibit A-1. Official registration statistics for Louisiana from 1888 to 1960

Louisiana voter registration, racial statistics, totals—1888–Nov. 30, 1958

	Number			Percent of total registered	
	White	Colored	Total	White	Colored
1888	126,884	127,923	254,807	49.8	50.2
Jan. 1, 1897	164,088	130,344	294,432	55.7	44.3
Jan. 1, 1898	74,133	12,902	87,240	85.0	14.8
Mar. 17, 1900	125,437	5,320	130,757	95.9	4.1
Oct. 8, 1910	116,349	730	117,993	98.6	.6
Oct. 2, 1920	257,282	3,533	260,815	98.6	1.4
Oct. 6, 1928	376,963	2,054	379,270	99.4	.5
Oct. 8, 1932	480,406	1,591	481,997	99.7	.3
Oct. 3, 1936	641,609	1,981	643,590	99.7	.3
Oct. 5, 1940	701,659	886	702,545	99.9	.1
Oct. 7, 1944	721,043	1,672	722,715	99.8	.2
Oct. 2, 1948	896,417	28,177	924,705	97.0	3.0
Oct. 4, 1952	945,038	107,844	1,056,720	89.8	10.2
Mar. 1, 1954	648,764	89,755	738,519	87.8	12.2
July 27, 1954	736,900	112,789	849,689	86.7	13.3
Oct. 1, 1955	785,299	127,231	912,530	86.1	13.9
Dec. 17, 1955	884,733	155,460	1,040,193	85.1	14.9
Mar. 17, 1956	896,498	161,410	1,057,908	84.7	15.3
Oct. 10, 1956	903,959	152,578	1,056,546	85.6	14.4
Aug. 31, 1957	744,916	117,911	862,827	86.3	13.7
Sept. 30, 1957	709,010	113,657	822,667	86.2	13.8
Nov. 30, 1957	714,628	112,442	827,070	86.4	13.6
Dec. 31, 1957	723,717	115,021	838,738	86.3	13.7
Jan. 31, 1958	726,679	113,669	840,348	86.5	13.5
Feb. 28, 1958	747,302	118,922	866,224	86.3	13.7
Mar. 31, 1958	743,573	117,598	861,171	86.3	13.7
Apr. 30, 1958	724,422	117,046	841,468	86.1	13.9
May 31, 1958	790,011	124,994	915,005	86.3	13.7
June 30, 1958	792,344	125,589	917,933	86.3	13.7
July 31, 1958	806,449	128,255	934,704	86.3	13.7
Oct. 4, 1958	816,643	129,624	946,267	86.3	13.7
Nov. 30, 1958	808,872	129,902	938,774	86.2	13.8

(Parish registration statistics by race for the years 1952,1953, 1954, 1955, 1956, 1958 are on file in the offices of the Commission.)

State of Louisiana Board of Registration report for month ending April 1959

Parish	Total number of registered voters	Number of white voters	Number of colored voters	Parish	Total number of registered voters	Number of white voters	Number of colored voters
Acadia*	21,992	18,492	3,500	Natchitoches	7,684	6,270	1,414
Allen*	8,901	7,135	1,766	Orleans*	194,223	162,660	31,563
Ascension*	9,502	7,522	1,980	Ouachita*	23,054	22,280	774
Assumption*	6,784	4,791	1,993	Plaquemines*	5,901	5,856	45
Avoyelles*	15,401	13,549	1,852	Pointe Coupee	4,115	3,456	659
Beauregard*	7,891	6,851	1,040	Rapides*	28,313	25,550	2,763
Bienville*	4,720	4,693	27	Red River	2,362	2,346	16
Bossier*	10,535	10,052	483	Richland	4,702	4,513	189
Caddo*	56,149	51,567	4,582	Sabine*	9,170	7,678	1,492
Calcasieu*	42,782	36,333	6,449	St. Bernard	10,305	9,842	463
Caldwell	2,776	2,735	41	St. Charles*	7,527	5,831	1,696
Cameron	2,167	2,085	82	St. Helena	2,921	1,830	1,091
Catahoula	2,679	2,466	213	St. James*	6,368	4,138	2,230
Claiborne*	5,733	5,718	15	St. John*	4,785	2,647	2,138
Concordia	4,158	3,867	291	St. Landry*	24,075	16,254	7,821
DeSoto*	6,025	5,527	498	St. Martin*	9,566	7,036	2,530
E. Baton Rouge*	63,987	54,892	9,095	St. Mary	13,234	10,546	2,688
E. Carroll	2,180	2,180	0	St. Tammany*	16,406	14,333	2,073
E. Feliciana*	2,899	2,449	450	Tangipahoa*	21,276	17,795	3,481
Evangeline*	16,090	12,995	3,095	Tensas	1,025	1,025	0
Franklin	6,512	6,158	354	Terrebonne*	12,738	11,683	1,055
Grant	5,351	4,822	529	Union*	4,584	4,207	377
Iberia*	19,179	14,943	4,236	Vermilion*	18,948	17,036	1,912
Iberville*	7,944	6,004	1,940	Vernon	8,297	7,664	633
Jackson*	5,372	5,010	362	Washington*	13,411	11,877	1,534
Jefferson*	68,745	61,713	7,032	Webster	8,688	8,605	83
Jefferson Davis*	10,059	8,475	1,584	W. Baton Rouge	2,795	2,076	719
Lafayette*	19,030	15,754	3,276	W. Carroll	3,918	3,847	71
Lafourche*	23,129	21,180	1,949	W. Feliciana	977	977	0
LaSalle	5,110	4,953	157	Winn	5,758	5,018	740
Lincoln	5,560	5,052	508				
Livingston	8,036	7,366	670	Total	961,192	828,686	132,506
Madison	1,564	1,564	0	Percent	100	86.2	13.8
Morehouse	5,124	4,917	207				

*Permanent registration.

Commission on Civil Rights, Exhibit A-1

Exhibit A-1. Official registration statistics for Louisiana from 1888 to 1960—Continued

State of Louisiana Board of Registration report for month ending July 31, 1960

Parish	Total number of registered voters	Number of white voters	Number of colored voters	Parish	Total number of registered voters	Number of white voters	Number of colored voters
Acadia*	25, 103	21, 040	4, 063	Natchitoches*	10, 400	8, 634	1, 766
Allen*	10, 106	8, 117	1, 989	Orleans*	205, 391	170, 461	34, 930
Ascension*	11, 389	8, 919	2, 470	Ouachita*	24, 527	23, 804	723
Assumption*	7, 528	5, 297	2, 231	Plaquemines*	7, 054	7, 010	44
Avoyelles*	16, 425	14, 436	1, 989	Pointe Coupee	7, 591	5, 287	2, 304
Beauregard*	8, 960	7, 857	1, 103	Rapides*	32, 784	29, 758	3, 026
Bienville*	5, 170	5, 144	26	Red River	3, 440	3, 416	24
Bossier*	12, 412	11, 878	534	Richland	6, 244	5, 997	247
Caddo*	62, 129	57, 394	4, 735	Sabine*	10, 090	8, 467	1, 623
Calcasieu*	50, 403	42, 934	7, 469	St. Bernard	14, 831	14, 054	777
Caldwell	3, 982	3, 892	90	St. Charles*	9, 342	7, 313	2, 029
Cameron	3, 260	3, 100	160	St Helena	3, 698	2, 458	1, 240
Catahoula	4, 468	4, 093	375	St. James*	7, 193	4, 573	2, 620
Clairborne*	5, 751	5, 735	16	St. John*	7, 030	4, 072	2, 958
Concordia	5, 621	5, 246	375	St. Landry*	32, 700	21, 568	11, 132
DeSoto*	6, 356	5, 785	571	St. Martin*	11, 887	8, 814	3, 073
E. Baton Rouge*	76, 860	66, 291	10, 569	St. Mary	17, 572	13, 542	4, 030
E. Carroll	2, 827	2, 827	0	St. Tammany*	19, 259	16, 435	2, 824
E. Feliciana*	2, 492	2, 416	76	Tangipahoa*	23, 385	19, 820	3, 565
Evangeline*	17, 511	14, 118	3, 393	Tensas	1, 990	1, 990	0
Franklin	8, 617	8, 228	389	Terrebonne*	18, 432	16, 680	1, 752
Grant	6, 681	6, 013	668	Union*	6, 465	5, 872	593
Iberia*	21, 502	16, 756	4, 746	Vermilion*	20, 664	18, 500	2, 164
Iberville*	9, 609	7, 142	2, 467	Vernon	10, 383	9, 615	768
Jackson*	6, 212	5, 730	482	Washington*	16, 870	15, 168	1, 702
Jefferson*	80, 498	72, 199	8, 299	Webster	12, 006	11, 881	125
Jefferson Davis*	11, 157	9, 482	1, 675	W. Baton Rouge	4, 479	3, 280	1, 199
Lafayette*	30, 780	25, 343	5, 437	W. Carroll	5, 189	5, 119	70
Lafourche*	27, 003	24, 727	2, 276	W. Feliciana	1, 283	1, 283	0
LaSalle	7, 018	6, 799	219	Winn	7, 426	6, 336	1, 090
Lincoln	7, 435	6, 628	807				
Livingston	12, 913	11, 714	1, 199	Total	1, 138, 088	978, 497	159, 591
Madison	2, 633	2, 633	0	Percent	100	86	14
Morehouse	7, 672	7, 377	295				

*Permanent registration.

Commission on Civil Rights, Exhibit A-1

428 COMMISSION ON CIVIL RIGHTS

Exhibit C. Official forms used in Louisiana for challenging procedure

PROOF OF IDENTITY

(Section 7, Article 2, Act 45 of 1940)

STATE OF LOUISIANA, PARISH OF ----------

REGISTRATION OFFICE

Personally came and appeared before me --------------------------------, (deputy) registrar of voters in and for the parish of ----------------------, State of Louisiana, ------------------------ and ----------------------, who after being duly sworn do depose and say:

That -- he, she is the identical person whom he, she represents himself, herself to be.

In accordance with the law (Act 45, section 7, article 2) of the State of Lousiana, and that he, she is entitled to be registered.

Affiant are qualified electors in the -------- ward, -------- precinct, of the parish of --

----
(Signature of applicant in full)

(Signature of witness in full)

(Signature of witness in full)

Sworn to and subscribed before me, this ------- day of --------------- 19---

----------------------------------,
(Deputy) Registrar of Voters.

PRINTED CITATION OF NOTICE TO ERASE

STATE OF LOUISIANA, PARISH OF ----------

REGISTRATION OFFICE

Citation To Appear

FROM: ------------------------,
Registrar of Voters,
parish of----------------------
State of Louisiana.

To: ----------------------

You are hereby notified, that on or before the ---------------- day of -------------- 19 ----, a period of ten days from the mailing date of this citation, during office hours, you are to show cause in person if any you have, before the undersigned registrar of voters for the parish of --------------, State of Louisiana, why your name should not be erased from the official precinct register of ward No. ----, precinct No. ----, certificate No. ---- In order to retain your registration you are required to produce three duly registered voters of this parish to make oath before the undersigned that you are legally registered.

----------------------------------,
Registrar of Voters.

LOUISIANA, ---- day of ---------- 19 ---

LETTER OF IRREGULARITY

STATE OF LOUISIANA, PARISH OF ----------

REGISTRATION OFFICE

--------------------, LA., ---------------------- 19---

NAME
Address
, Louisiana.

DEAR SIR: You are hereby notified that our registration office records reflect an irregularity in your registration for the following reasons:

Commission on Civil Rights, Exhibit C

We are enclosing a notice of citation stipulating the period in which you have to appear in person with 3 witnesses at this office and attend to this important matter, otherwise your name will be erased as a qualified voter.

______________________,
Registrar of Voters.

Mailed: ______________ day of ______________ 19__
Advertised: ______________ day of ______________ 19__ for two days.
Affidavit for retention filed ______________ day of ______________ 19__

Order

Let above name be ______________________________
for the following reasons ______________________________
____
________ day of ________ 19__ ______________________,
Registrar of Voters.

AFFIDAVIT IN CASE REGISTRATION OF VOTER IS CHALLENGED

STATE OF LOUISIANA—PARISH OF ____________

Personally came and appeared before me ______________________________ (deputy registrar of voters in and for the parish of ______________________, State of Louisiana, ______________________ and ______________________, who being duly sworn, do depose and say:

That they are bona fide registered voters of this parish; that after reasonable investigation by them, and each of them, and on information and belief, that ______________________________, registered from (Municipal number and street, if any), to whom was issued registration certificate No. ____________, ward ______________, precinct ______________, of this parish, is illegally registered or has lost his or her right to vote in the precinct, ward, or parish in which they are registered, for the following reasons:

____
____
____

and should be erased from the official precinct register of ward ____, precinct, ____; that this affidavit is made for the purpose of causing said name to be erased.

____
____

Sworn to and subscribed before me, on this ____ day of ____, 19__.

______________________,
(Deputy) Registrar of Voters.

AFFIDAVIT OF RETENTION

STATE OF LOUISIANA, PARISH OF ____________

REGISTRATION OFFICE

Personally came and appeared on this the ____ day of ____ 19__, before me, ______________________ (deputy) registrar of voters in and for the parish of ______________ State of Louisiana, ____________ and ____________ and ______________, who being first duly sworn by me, do depose and say:

That they and each of them are personally acquainted with ______________ ______________________________ registrant; that they have investigated the facts of the case and of their own personal knowledge know that said ______________________________ now resides at ______________ Street, precinct No. ______________ ward No. ______________ of this parish, and has continuously resided in said precinct and ward for the past ____ months and during such time has resided at the address aforesaid, and has resided in the parish of ______________ for a period of ______________.

Name______________________ Address______________________
Name______________________ Address______________________
Name______________________ Address______________________

Sworn to and subscribed to by me this ____ day of ____ 19__.

______________________,
(Deputy) Registrar of Voters.

589992—61——28

Commission on Civil Rights, Exhibit C

Questions to Consider:

1. *What factors does Reverend Scott cite in explaining why he sought the right to vote not just for himself but for all African Americans?*

2. *What obstacles did the registrar's office put in front of black registrants?*

3. *What explains the fact that the men who challenged voter restrictions, like many other civil rights leaders in the South such as Martin Luther King and Ralph Abernathy, were Protestant ministers? Why were there no black Catholic civil rights leaders, despite the presence of a large population of black Catholics in Louisiana?*

4. *Based on the statistics in Exhibit A-1, which parishes had the worst record of discriminating against African Americans? In which parishes did African Americans have the best chance of registering to vote? What explains those discrepancies? (You may need to do outside research to answer this question accurately.)*

5. *What years represent the nadir of disfranchisement? When did things begin to change? What helps to explain that? In what ways were these forms designed to deter potential voters, especially minorities, from applying to register? If these forms were required today, would you be likely to register to vote?*

Sources:

1. Hearings Before the United States Commission on Civil Rights: Hearings held in New Orleans, Louisiana, September 27, 1960, September 28, 1960, May 5, 1961, May 6, 1961, Issue 11 (Washington, DC: United States Government Printing Office, 1961), 15–23.

2. Hearings Before the United States Commission on Civil Rights: Hearings held in New Orleans, Louisiana, September 27, 1960, September 28, 1960, May 5, 1961, May 6, 1961, Issue 11 (Washington, DC: United States Government Printing Office, 1961), 424–425, 428–429.

1961:
Report on the New Orleans School Crisis

Louisiana had fewer public clashes as a result of civil rights agitation than did many other southern states, but the white mobs that gathered to prevent desegregation of New Orleans's public schools garnered national attention. The target of their ire was six-year-old Ruby Bridges, who entered first grade in 1960 at the all-white William Frantz Elementary School in New Orleans's Lower Ninth Ward, a largely working-class area. The death threats she and her family received prompted the federal government to authorize federal marshals to escort her to and from school every day as protection from the mobs gathered outside. Excerpted below is the official report about that crisis, as presented to the Louisiana State Advisory Committee on Civil Rights.

PREFACE

This study of the New Orleans school crisis was submitted to the Commission on Civil Rights as part of the 1961 report of its Louisiana Advisory Committee.

The Louisiana Committee is one of the 50 State advisory committees that were established by the Commission pursuant to Section 105© of the Civil Rights Act of 1957. Its membership consists of interested citizens of standing, who serve without compensation.

This report was prepared by the subcommittee on education of the Louisiana State Advisory Committee to the Commission on Civil Rights and adopted by the State Advisory Committee as its report on education.

Louisiana State Advisory Committee

- Hon. J. D. De Blieux, Baton Rouge, Chairman
- Dr. Albert W. Dent, New Orleans, Vice Chairman
- Mrs. Moise Cahn, New Orleans, Secretary
- Mr. Bernard Raynal Ariatti, New Orleans
- Rev. William T. Handy, Jr., Baton Rouge
- Dr. Harold I. Lief, New Orleans
- Mr. John P. Nelson, Jr., New Orleans
- Rev. Alexander O. Sigur, Lafayette

Subcommittee on education

- Harold I. Lief, M.D., Chairman, Professor of Psychiatry, Tulane University School of Medicine
- Paul Hostetler, Assistant Professor of Theatre and Speech, Tulane University
- Edward Rogge, Assistant Professor of Theatre and Speech, Tulane University
- Daniel Thompson, Professor, and Chairman of the Department of Sociology, Dillard University
- Mrs. Betty Wisdom, Board of Directors, "Save Our Schools"
- Mrs. Kathryn Wright, Board of Directors, "Save Our Schools," and Legal Adviser to the subcommittee

INTRODUCTION

In the interest of preserving and strengthening the civil rights of all our countrymen, white or Negro, we would like to tell the story of the New Orleans school crisis, as we see it. To those who object to our views, please remember the words of Alfred North Whitehead: "If it is an uninterpreted fact that you seek, go ask a stone to tell you its autobiography."

. . .

THE ROLE OF LEADERSHIP

The segregationists formed themselves into the White Citizens Council. Using every medium at their disposal, they pictured Negroes as lazy and shiftless, mentally inferior, dirty, immoral, criminal, diseased, violent, savage, "pushy and uppity," conspicuous and boisterous in their behavior, and under the influence of communist-inspired leaders.

These stereotypes, and more, were eloquently expounded by the most rabid segregationists in the State and many influential segregationists from out of the State. In fact, a list of the segregationists who appeared at mass meetings of the White Citizens Council of New Orleans would read like a "who's who among white supremacists." Among the speakers were influential public figures from many other Southern States. Also appearing at these mass meetings at one time or another were the "top" white supremacists of Louisiana including: Judge Leander Perez; Governor Jimmy Davis; State Senator William Rainach; Emily Wagner (school board member); Attorney General Jack P. F. Gremillion; State Superintendent of Education Shelby M. Jackson; and Dr. Emmett L. Irwin (President, White Citizens Council of New Orleans). . . .

The values, traditions, and fears propagandized by this segregationist organization are essentially rural. Consequently, since the Louisiana State legislature is dominated by representatives of rural communities, it began immediately to pass a rash of anti-Negro laws designed to preserve what the lawmakers termed "Southern traditions." Some of these "Black Codes" were obviously unconstitutional, even to the lawmakers themselves. They were passed for the avowed purpose of circumventing Federal court decisions, or at least, as delaying tactics.

Unfortunately the rural conservatism of State politics had a profound effect on the situation in New Orleans as a mayor with a liberal reputation found it necessary to moderate his position in his drive for the governorship. . . . The White Citizens Council took advantage of the absence of official leadership, and by default became the dominant political force in the community in the education crisis. Mayor [DeLesseps S.] Morrison must accept much of the responsibility for the atmosphere thus created.

The main targets of the White Citizens Council were the NAACP, which was labeled as communist-dominated; the United States Supreme Court, which was accused of usurping legislative prerogatives and substituting sociological theory for legal precedents; and white liberals, whom the council subtly accused of being either communists or dupes of communist conspirators. This propaganda is apparently without foundation, because, during the long months of bitter controversy, no concrete evidence to substantiate these accusations has been produced.

Joining in the support of the program of the White Citizens Council were numerous neighborhood organizations, which met regularly in order to give lesser white supremacists an opportunity to express themselves on the issue of public school desegregation. Some of these leaders base their contentions on far-fetched rationales. An example of this is a statement by Mrs. B. J. Gaillat, Jr., president of Save Our Nation, Inc., in which she contends that there is ample evidence that the Bible and the Catholic Church both support racial segregation. She declared, "The issue is not one of hate, violence, or disobedience. Rather it is one of obedience to God's law. God gave Moses the Law of Segregation on Mount Sinai."

Not until spring of 1960 did any white leaders of influence in New Orleans make a public statement in support of maintaining the public schools [i.e., in support of abiding by the court's decision in *Brown*, six years earlier]. Thus, for almost six years of local litigation, the most frequently heard spokesmen in the white community were the segregationists.

Finally, during the spring of 1960, after months of fruitless discussion, a few "moderate" white leaders were able to make themselves heard. Their stated purpose was to "Save Our Schools" (SOS). They made it clear from the beginning that they were not advocating desegregation nor did they necessarily agree with the legality or spirit of the US Supreme Court decision of May 17, 1954. They made it crystal clear that their only purpose was to maintain public education.

Soon after SOS began its campaign to preserve public education in New Orleans, another group, which became known as the Committee on Public Education (COPE) became active. Whereas SOS attempted to recruit to its ranks white leaders from the power structure, COPE was, at the onset, composed mostly of average white parents of public school children.

There was real fear among the two groups formed to maintain public schools in New Orleans that, if the schools were ordered desegregated, they would be closed in accordance with State laws. . . . Nevertheless, they became increasingly vocal. They published pamphlets, called public meetings, issued many statements to the press, and buttonholed important business and professional leaders in their attempt to create a public opinion favorable to keeping the schools open, even if desegregated. Within a short period, they were able to stimulate public debate on the issue of "open" or "closed" public schools.

It was not until Matthew Sutherland ran for re-election to the school board in November that a few important leaders in religion, business, politics, and education began to issue somewhat timid statements to the effect that we must maintain public education "at all costs." A short time before, the members of the Orleans Parish School Board [OPSB], except segregationist Emily Wagner, became publicly concerned about keeping New Orleans schools open. . . . Sutherland, who campaigned on this issue, won an overwhelming victory over the segregationist's prime candidate, John Singreen.

The supporters of continued public education interpreted Sutherland's victory as a mandate from New Orleans voters that the public schools must be kept open despite "token" desegregation. This victory also gave some courage to New Orleans members of the State legislature. Though they still insisted that they were 100 percent for segregation, a majority of these representatives worked diligently to keep the State legislature from "reading out of office" members of the school board and the Superintendent of Schools, who were striving to keep the schools open with four Negro girls assigned to previously all-white schools. Their efforts were most significantly highlighted when they led the fight to prevent the Governor's backers in the legislature from levying a sales tax designed to raise $28 million to support a system of "private" education for white children who might be assigned to desegregated schools.

The peak of the desegregation crisis lasted from November 14 until the Christmas holidays. After that, some powerful businessmen began to join the ranks of those who had struggled so valiantly to keep the schools open in the face of the stiffest opposition from powerful political leaders.

Throughout all this crisis, the most abused leader in New Orleans was Federal Judge J. Skelly Wright. Time after time, it was his difficult duty to set aside State laws, overrule the State administration orders, and place practically every public official under restraining orders to prevent interference with the desegregation of McDonogh No. 19 and William Frantz Elementary Schools.

The January 30th banquet which some private white citizens held in honor of the four "moderate" members of the school board and Superintendent James Redmond, who kept the schools open in spite of all manner of legal, extra-legal, and illegal harassment, may have been the turning point in the desegregation crisis. More than 1600 citizens attended this banquet. The guests of honor were given hearty and sincere acclaim.

THE NEUTRALS

Insofar as the issue of public school desegregation is concerned, by far the largest segment of leaders in New Orleans may be classified as "neutrals." Included in this category are influential leaders in business, labor relations, politics, the professions, and civil and social affairs.

During the long and bitter controversy over the moral, legal, and social aspects of desegregation, the vast majority of the "top" leadership in New Orleans made no public statement in regard to this all-important issue. The truth is that, time and time again, they refused to speak out, despite the fact that certain other responsible citizens begged them to do so. It was not until the school crisis had already developed to a critical point that a "hundred" of these leaders began to issue cautious statements intended to create a favorable climate for the preservation of public education in spite of "token" desegregation. Generally, the statements issued by them were designed to discourage lawlessness.

There may be several reasons why so many of the influential leaders in New Orleans have remained "neutral" during these difficult months of controversy over the public school issue:

1. Since race relations in New Orleans have been relatively peaceful for several decades, some leading citizens seemed unable to conceive of the possibility they would remain so. . . .

2. Some of the most influential politicians in the State have tried desperately to remain "neutral." They are evidently afraid of political retaliations. A few acknowledged that they would like to have taken sides with "Save Our Schools" movement but feared that it would mean "political suicide." Others only reluctantly identified with the segregationists because they were afraid that espousing such an extrem-

ist point of view would definitely lessen their chances of ever achieving national status. . . .

3. Some "top" leaders have remained "neutral" because they fear economic reprisals. They fear boycotts . . . Certain top professional people have failed to take sides because they, too, fear economic reprisals. . . . Even some less influential citizens have tended to remain neutral because they are afraid that they might lose their jobs. This is not an idle fear, because some have, in fact, done so. . . .

4. There is no concrete evidence of this, but it is likely that the fear of social ostracism is the most pervasive reason why so many prominent New Orleanians have remained neutral. [Parents feared their children might be taunted as "nigger-lovers" if they (the parents) spoke in favor of desegregation.]

DESEGREGATIONISTS

The contest between State and Federal authorities over whether or not public schools in Louisiana will remain segregated, become desegregated, or close altogether has been so tense that only a few white leaders, mostly in religion, have dared to identify themselves as desegregationists. Thus, during the several weeks of the most intense crisis, some white religious leaders and a few religious organizations made public pronouncements to the effect that racial segregation is morally wrong and that the United States Supreme Court was legally correct in outlawing it in public education. A handful of white civic leaders made similar statements, but no important white organization so declared itself.

Therefore, by and large, the active desegregationists in New Orleans are Negroes.

. . .

Prior to the crisis (between 1952–58), the NAACP did have occasional mass meetings, at which time reports were made in regard to the *Bush v. New Orleans Board of Education* case. At these meetings, money was raised to support the NAACP. However, there have been no public demonstrations, no lawlessness, no attempts to threaten or intimidate those who opposed the association, and few attempts to publicize the case for desegregation. By and large, Negro leaders have defined this as a legal, constitutional fight which they feel confident will be won by sane, stable local and national leaders.

Perhaps the most serious blunder made by white leaders in New Orleans is that they have failed to utilize the knowledge, wisdom, and insight of established Negro leaders in their attempt to achieve some orderly pattern in the public education controversy. At no time have the city or State officials sought the advice or counsel of informed Negro leaders, despite the fact that on numerous occasions Negro leaders have volunteered their services.

Certain city officials have said that the violence, disorder, and racial hatred that New Orleans experienced during recent months was caused largely by "outsiders" and a few uninformed, irresponsible local whites. They may, in some measure, be right. It seems certain, however, that the ugly mobs would not have formed if they had not felt certain of the approval or at least the indifference of influential white leaders, some of whom appeared to use the crisis for political ends.

Throughout all the bitter racial controversy of the past several months, Negro leaders have remained helpless in the face of the derogatory racial propaganda that has been spread by radio, television, newspapers, pamphlets, handbills, telephone calls, and anonymous letters. They, themselves, have had virtually no opportunity to answer slanderous attacks through public media.

Not only are Negroes silenced insofar as mass media are concerned and ignored by State and city officials when racial issues are being decided, but they are also systematically excluded from the base number of "citizens committees," planning boards, and professional and business societies where public opinion and policies are formulated. Consequently, they have very little opportunity to communicate with "white men of power" or with the white masses. Negro leaders are unhappy and impatient because they have not been able to play a more important part in influencing public opinion. Seldom during this long desegregation crisis have Negroes had an opportunity to address the powerful civic, economic, and professional organizations in the city where community plans are formulated, and which have such a decisive influence on public opinion.

We may conclude then that leaders in New Orleans waited too long to prepare the citizens to respond positively to the desegregation of public schools. They did not react to the invitation by SOS and COPE, the two grass roots organizations, to join forces with them, and to take a stand on keeping the schools open, even if desegregated. It is very likely that, if greater efforts had been made to prepare the minds of citizens for this eventuality, as was done in some other cities, much of the bitterness, violence, and economic loss experienced in 1960–61 might have been avoided.

The timidity of New Orleans' white leadership may be easier to understand if one considers the intense fanaticism that the desegregation issue aroused. This fanaticism is so violent and so completely divorced from reason and common sense, that it must be studied from a psychological, rather than a political, viewpoint.

PSYCHOLOGICAL ASPECTS

Nearly everyone expressing public views on a controversial issue needs group support. The political leaders in this crisis did not lead—they were afraid to step out ahead of the populace. Civic leaders who might have taken over the leadership felt alone and isolated, and it was many months before they were able to band together and express their views publicly.

Those taking a stand, whether on the basis of belief or because they were forced to by circumstances, found themselves becoming firmer and firmer in their convictions with the passage of time. This is partly due to the need to defend oneself against the attacks of opponents and partly to the need to bring one's attitudes in line with one's changed behavior or position on the issue.

. . .

Irrational prejudices towards Negroes are based primarily on the fear of sexual attack and of social transgressions. . . . An analysis of the content of speeches by members of the White Citizens Council demonstrates that this is the major weapon for stirring up fears and hatreds of whites towards Negroes. . . .

Prejudicial attitudes tend to spread from one to other minority groups. The White Citizens Council did not confine its attacks to Negroes but soon centered much of its venom on SOS and similar white groups, which they vilified and whose members they described as being simultaneously Communists, Jews, and Catholics.

One of the important points is that the attitude towards school desegregation often depended on whether the person thought of himself first as an American or first as a Southerner or Louisianian. Those with wider loyalties tended to be desegregationists or at least neutral, while those with intense regional or local loyalties more often tended to be segregationists, usually buttressing their arguments with the issue of States' rights versus the power of the Federal Government. In the latter instance, the Federal Government was seen as the enemy imposing its will on the helpless, defenseless, and misunderstood State....

Questions to Consider:

1. *Look up the members of the advisory committee. How many were white and how many were of African American descent? Did those numbers surprise you? Why or why not?*
2. *How might Louisiana leaders have avoided this public embarrassment? Why did they behave the way they did?*
3. *Compare the behavior of white segregationists with African Americans living in New Orleans who favored the desegregation of public schools. Who were the "rabble-rousers" in this crisis?*

Source:

Louisiana State Advisory Committee to the United States Commission on Civil Rights, *New Orleans School Crisis* (Washington, DC: 1961), 38–50. Historical Publications of the United States Commission on Civil Rights, Thurgood Marshall Law Library, University of Maryland. https://www2.law.umaryland.edu/marshall/usccr/documents/cr12sch6.pdf.

1963:
Ernest "Dutch" Morial, the NAACP, and the Citizens Committee Push for Civil Rights

Ernest N. "Dutch" Morial, a Creole of color born in 1929 and raised in New Orleans's Seventh Ward, graduated from Xavier University of New Orleans and became the first black graduate of LSU Law School in 1954. After college, he continued to rack up an impressive list of "firsts": the first black assistant US attorney in Louisiana, the first black person to serve in the Louisiana state legislature since Reconstruction (1967–70), the first black juvenile court judge, the first black person elected to the Louisiana Fourth Circuit Court of Appeal, and the first black mayor of New Orleans (serving two terms, 1977–1986). A protégé of his law partner, A. P. Tureaud, Morial served as the attorney as well as the president of the New Orleans chapter of the NAACP. He and other civil rights activists formed a committee that pressured the city's white leadership to end racial discrimination in a variety of areas.

When the mayor did not fulfill his promises, Morial and other leaders of local civil rights groups organized a protest for late September 1963, to present a list of grievances to the mayor and city council. Though more than ten thousand people attended the march, no one was at City Hall to greet them. The leaders met with the elected officials, by invitation, the next week to iron out a plan for improvement. Later, Morial himself ran for mayor and won.

As mayor, Morial worked to revitalize old areas of New Orleans, particularly the riverfront and French Quarter, where the Jax Brewery Development, the Convention Center (named in his honor), and the Almonaster-Michoud Industrial District attracted new business. While his tenure as mayor was not without controversy, and he endured criticism from fellow African Americans as well as white New Orleanians, Morial was proud of his successes in adopting set-aside quotas for minorities in city contracts; addressing police corruption and brutality by establishing a citizens' oversight committee; opening up housing to all races in accordance with the Fair Housing Act of 1968; creating a position for a female advisor within his cabinet; firing anyone who engaged in corrupt practices; and supporting and encouraging the arts in the city.

Morial married Sybil Haydel, and the couple had five children. Their eldest son Marc served as New Orleans mayor from 1994 to 2002.

"Dutch" Morial died on Christmas Eve 1989.

Interview with "Dutch" Morial by Historian Kim Lacy Rogers, 1987

[Rogers asked Morial what made him an activist. He replied:]

> My daddy was a cigar-maker, and he was active with the union. And then I went to college with A. P. Tureaud. I grew up in a neighborhood that was racially mixed but we didn't go to school together, couldn't go to the white playgrounds, sat in a different Catholic Church. If we went to the movies it was to the colored balcony. . . . My daddy was kind of a disciplinarian. My mother tried to be a moderating influence. My older brother influenced me, too. He ended up as a school principal.

Q. What drives you?

A. I'm not a gambler, drinker, smoker. I don't play golf. This is my fun: getting stuff done. Solving a problem and seeing solutions come about. Seeing how you affect people's lives, and how they appreciate it, and they come up to you and thank you. We all need that. There's great satisfaction in seeing that you're helping people and that they appreciate it. You're helping people that can't do it for themselves.

Press Release Concerning the Freedom March on New Orleans City Hall

Citizens Committee Headquarters
2319 Third Street
New Orleans, Louisiana

For Immediate Release

The Freedom March on the New Orleans City Hall scheduled for September 30 will not be a demonstration in the strict sense of the word, but a peaceful protest to develop greater public awareness of the grievances of non-white Orleanians, executives of the Citizens Committee said today.

The high point of the march will be the presenting of a petition to city officials asking immediate corrective action, the Rev. A. L. Davis, Jr., chairman of the committee, said in a brief statement of purpose.

The grievances sought to be redressed, Rev. Davis declared, are themselves the denial of a carefully defined constitutional right to equality.

"The City government and members of the majority that have dominated the affairs of this community and its lawmaking machinery for the past century cannot escape responsibility for the years of callous indifference to the demands of the Negro citizens of New Orleans. This indifference created the frustration that now finds expression in this Freedom March," Rev. Davis said.

The grievances which give basis for the Freedom March, Rev. Davis declared, have been called to the attention of Mayor Victor H. Schiro and the City Council several times. He outlined the committee's demands as follows:

1. A statement from the Mayor and the City Council to the effect that they support democratic practices in employment and public accommodations, and that merchants who desegregate their businesses will have the city government support.
2. Abolishment of the dual system of classification in City Civil Service so that qualified Negroes can be considered for jobs in other than Negro institutions, as well as jobs in all levels of city government.

3. The appointment of Negroes to various boards, particularly to the Housing Authority of New Orleans where Negroes constitute a majority of the tenants.
4. The removal of racial signs from municipally-owned buildings, such as City Hall, Civil Courts Building, and the Municipal Courts Building.
5. Repeal of all city ordinances that require segregation of the races, particularly the ordinance requiring segregation in places serving alcoholic beverages, and that the Mayor will not vote the repeal of any such ordinances.
6. The end of racial discrimination at the Delgado Trade and Technical Institute.
7. That henceforth there will be no legal delaying tactics used by the city during the course of the suits once the courts have acted on desegregation.

Rev. Davis concluded:

"We consider this march as but one means of peaceful protest. There are other methods and each will be employed as it will best serve our purposes. It is hoped, however, that the presence of hundreds of footsore and weary Americans at the door of their seat of Municipal Government will prick the conscience of the white community to the extent that they will seek the full freedom for their being by ridding themselves of the unsavory shackles of race hatred and discrimination."

Planning co-ordinator [Arthur J.] Chapital said the march will be peaceful and orderly. "With this in mind, we have already secured a City permit and have fully apprised the mayor, City Officials and the Police Department of our plans," he added.

Excerpts from Judge Morial's Announcement of Candidacy for Mayor

I believe I have the maturity, the experience and the imagination to lead our city, not into an era of radical change, but of evolution; not into a time of false hope and rising expectation, but of well-thought-out solutions that will make sense to reasonable and responsible people; not promises that are bigger and better than those of other men who seek this office, but with a quiet confidence that we can make city government work for you.

The cornerstone of this administration will be citizen input and participation in government. For too long government has become isolated from the problems of average citizens. Government officials have become the captives of the bureaucracy instead of its masters.

The job of controlling and reducing crime is not a simple one. Five hundred additional policemen would cost us 11.3 million dollars per year. This could not be accomplished without drastically increasing city taxes.

However, while I am committed to a better police department dedicated to reducing crime, I will not tolerate the abuse of the rights of individual citizens by police officers in the performance of their duties. I will not try to run the police in the performance of their duties. I will not try to run the police department because that is not good administration. But the person appointed to manage the police department must know and communicate clearly and firmly to every policeman where the line between acceptable and unacceptable conduct should be drawn. I will establish within the office of the Mayor the machinery for expeditious and impartial treatment of complaints of police abuse and misconduct.

A few landlords refuse to make their rental property habitable. These few face an administration determined to improve the conditions under which their tenants must live. Good landlords are taking the rap for slum lords who profiteer at the expense of the poor and elderly who are relegated to living in sub-standard housing because of the inadequacy of available standard housing. This will stop. I will aggressively enforce the city housing code.

Sixty-two percent of New Orleans residents are tenants. They not only desire decent housing to rent, but many of them desire the opportunity to become homeowners. Enlightened redevelopment of neighborhood housing without massive displacement of renters will make our neighborhoods stable and attractive.

To demonstrate my commitment to openness and to the type of administration I will conduct, I will release to you my tax returns, which I requested months ago from IRS, immediately upon receipt.

But disclosure of income tax returns doesn't go far enough. I'm today releasing to the public, a net worth statement disclosing all my assets. This is something that should be done by all other candidates, and I hope the press will make it an issue and keep it an issue in the eyes of the public, because I think it's absolutely critical to honest and open government.

Our educational system severely restricts our efforts to attract new business to our area. The mayor of New Orleans must be a strong moral force for quality education. Although not empowered constitutionally, as mayor I will act as a spokesman and catalyst to develop a cooperative, comprehensive planning mechanism between the Orleans Parish School Board and City Hall.

An improved formal educational system, expansion of the opportunities for vocational-technical training, and manpower programs are essential if we are to attract industry and regain the number of manufacturing jobs we have lost over the last decade. We have a thriving tourist industry which we should continue to develop, and the world's third largest port for which I will be an active advocate and instrument in assisting its Board of Commissioners in efforts to obtain both federal and state financial assistance to expand and improve its existing facilities.

The problem of high utility bills is of grave concern to every New Orleanian. These high bills are not the result of transit losses but the high cost of fuel which is a national problem. I will create a citizens advisory board of inquiry to determine fair utility rates and return on investments and fully staff the Department of Utilities and immediately institute a thorough examination of the needs and uses of energy within the city to determine if needs can be met with conservation and inexpensive alternative sources of energy.

There is a substantial non-resident use of our facilities and it is only equitable that the costs for such facilities be borne by these area non-residents. New Orleans can no longer burden its residents and property owners exclusively for these costs.

We must seek metropolitan cooperation and the removal of the 1974 constitutional restriction to institute a personal income or payroll tax which would be of a reciprocal nature.

I hope my public record and my commitment throughout the 47 years of my life has been a record you can hold alongside the other candidates.

I will not offer false hope. I will offer myself and my record, and my hand to you. If you accept, I will never cease trying to make this city a place where the quality of life is as great as the quality of its people.

Questions to Consider:

1. *What issues raised by Morial and other civil rights activists were unique to the 1960s and what issues do African Americans still struggle with today?*

2. *Why do you think they called their confederation "the Citizens Committee"?*

Sources:

1. Ernest "Dutch" Morial Interview, October 30, 1987, Kim Lacy Rogers Collection, Amistad Research Center at Tulane University, New Orleans, Louisiana..

2. Press Release Concerning the Freedom March on New Orleans City Hall, Ernest "Dutch" Morial papers, 1929–1995, Amistad Research Center at Tulane University, New Orleans, Louisiana.

3. Excerpts from Judge Morial's Announcement of Candidacy for Mayor, Ernest "Dutch" Morial papers, 1929–1995, Amistad Research Center at Tulane University, New Orleans, Louisiana.

1963/1964:
Negro Voter Education Project

In the 1940s and 1950s, African American leaders began to increase pressure on registrars and local officials to allow them to register to vote, a right they had lost in the Constitution of 1898. The response depended on the governor in power. As a general rule, Longites tried to defend black voting rights, but segregationist governors like Robert Kennon and Jimmie Davis allowed African Americans to be purged from the registration rolls, and they signed into law ever-more restrictive voter registration requirements.

The Louisiana legislature passed laws in 1962 that required a citizenship test, a literacy test, and a requirement that the applicant was of "good character." These hurdles were added to existing ones that denied people the right to register based on age, residence, and criminal convictions. State laws mandated the basic content of the process, but the various parishes implemented the law as they saw fit, so the forms used in one parish might look different from those in another parish.

Since determination of who passed or failed and who was of "good character" was entirely up to the whim of the registrars—all of whom were white—white citizens almost always passed regardless of their character and no matter how poorly they performed on the test. The number of black people able to register varied from parish to parish, but as a general rule the larger the black population was in a given parish, the harder it was to register, and very few were allowed to register in parishes where African Americans were the majority.

What follows is an excerpt from a pamphlet prepared by a voter education committee that tried to help African Americans navigate a process designed to ensure that they failed.

"Negro Voting in Louisiana": Prepared by Baton Rouge Committee on Registration Education

This pamphlet has been written to present an historical sketch of the Negro's strive [*sic*] to exercise his God-given and constitutional right to vote in our democratic society. The struggle of the Negro in the Southland to secure this right has been one of humiliation and suffering. Police brutality, political and economic intimidations, and other legal and social impediments have been consistently directed against the Negro in an attempt to maintain the status quo and to prevent him from achieving political and social equality. To eliminate these unjust acts and to secure our just rights, we need more federal legislation and aggressive action in the area of civil rights and liberties, and in voting in particular. But most of all, we need to end fear and apathy among our people and to give them a fighting desire to "register and vote."

It is the sincere hope of those who prepared this pamphlet that, as you read these few pages, you will arrive at a deeper understanding of the necessity of every eligible Negro registering and voting. The struggle has not been easy in the past, nor will it be easy in the future. However, struggle we must, each of us, as individuals, for it is in the individual that the strength and hope of the future lie.

The History of Negro Suffrage in Louisiana
The Vote in Reconstruction

Negro participation in politics began with Reconstruction in 1867. Prior to that time, Negro people in Louisiana had no voice in the policies of their state or of the United States of America. . . . In 1867, Negroes began to register. . . . At the Constitutional Convention, there were 49 Negroes and 49 whites present. Thus, Negroes held the balance of power. . . . They began to campaign for political offices with a zeal and determination that stunned the white population. . . . They did not seek to dominate, but to use the power which was rightfully theirs. Opposition to Negro political power sprang from every corner of the South. By economic intimidation and political assassination, by whippings and maimings, by the knife, whip, and rope, the Klan, and similar organizations, set out to reduce Negroes to political impotence. . . . [These threats landed and significantly reduced black voting strength. Then came the 1898 Constitutional Convention.]

During this Convention, a campaign was initiated to exclude Negroes from the polls. . . .

From 1910 through 1944, the number of registered Negroes never exceeded 1% of the total potential electorate. Toward the close of World War II, Negro registration again began to increase. By 1948, the number of registered Negroes had risen from 1,672 to 28,177. Six years later, the proportion of the voting age Negro population which was registered had risen from 5% to 27%.

This increase brought about new and stronger efforts, on the part of the white citizens, to curtail Negro suffrage. One of the changes is directed at the character of the prospective voter. Convictions for misdemeanors (other than traffic and game law violations), participation in common law marriage, and parentage of illegitimate children constitute "bad character" and are disqualifiers. Moreover, character disqualifiers "shall not be deemed exclusive . . . but said bad character may be established by any competent evidence."

In addition, applicants must now demonstrate that they are "well disposed to the good order and happiness of the State of Louisiana by executing an affidavit affirming that they will faithfully and fully abide by all of the laws of the State of Louisiana." This, of course, eliminates anyone who actively opposes segregation.

During the 1962 session of the State Legislature, additional laws were passed to prevent or severely limit further Negro registration. The State Board of Registration is to design a literacy test on American citizenship which applicants will now be required to pass.

To register to vote in Louisiana, an applicant must be 21 years of age, a resident of the state for one year, a resident of his parish for six months, and a resident of his precinct for four months. He must be of "good character," and he must "understand the duties and the obligations of citizenship under a republican form of government." A special form, the LR-1, must be used when registering. On this form, one must give his exact age (in years, months, and days), color, sex, address, occupation, and previous place of registration. A prospective voter must be able to read and interpret, to the satisfaction of the registrar, any clause of the U.S. Constitution or Louisiana Constitution. He must also be able to prove his identity. Under the Constitution, "If the registrar has good reason to believe that he is not the same person, he may require the applicant to produce two credible registered voters of his precinct to make oath to that effect."

Techniques of Discrimination—Case Studies

Hide and Seek

When Negroes wanted to register in Plaquemines, they were unable to find the registrar. Only after Negroes filed suit in a Federal Court was a permanent office for registration established in Plaquemines Parish.

A witness before the Civil Rights Commission testified that in Madison Parish (where no Negroes were registered) he and several other Negroes went to the registrar's office in July, 1960. Instead of giving them application forms, the registrar told them to see the sheriff. He made two subsequent trips to the office, but on both occasions found it closed.

The Silent Treatment

In some parishes, applicants are not even told whether or not they have qualified to register. Negroes Hester and Eugene Williams live on farms 35 miles from the seat of Bossier Parish. Each time they tried to register, they completed an LR-1 form, which was accepted, without comment, by the registrar. Hester made five trips; Eugene, seven. They were never told whether or not they had qualified to register as voters.

Identification

Reverend Philip Brown, formerly registered in New Orleans, was unable to register in Ouachita Parish because he could not identify himself to the satisfaction of the registrar. When in July, 1960, he presented his driver's license and other papers for identification, he was told that they would not do and that he would have to have two registered voters from his ward and precinct identify him. A voter can only vouch once every twelve months, and Reverend Brown was unable to find two eligible vouchers. He found one who had not vouched for 11 months, but he was not acceptable. The registrar told Reverend Brown, "Well, if you will bring in three documents or bills or receipts of letters showing your name and address at this address, then you will be able to register. When he returned and presented three documents to Deputy Registrar Morin, she refused to accept them because she was not the same person who had waited on him before. Again, Reverend Brown was told that he would have to have two registered voters to identify him.

Identification difficulties are frequent in other parishes. In East Carroll, a well-known life-long resident was told that he would have to secure two "vouchers" from his precinct. Since only whites were registered, this was impossible. . . . The voucher system was expressly designed to prevent Negroes from registering. The registrar of Madison Parish admitted in 1954 that she operated under orders from the sheriff and other public officials, and that she had not yet seen fit to permit Negroes to register and vote.

Intimidation

In St. Helena Parish, Negroes were warned that attempts to vote on their part would result in bloodshed. A Negro testified before the Civil Rights Commission that while he was standing in line to vote in 1952, a white man showed a gun, saying, "Negroes are not going to vote in St. Helena Parish." An FBI investigation remedied the situation and Negroes were allowed to register.

In East Carroll Parish, Negroes were subjected to economic reprisals. Mr. Atlas, a Negro farmer, was not allowed to gin his cotton, market his soybeans, or purchase fuel oil for his home because he attempted to register. Only a federal suit against the firms involved enabled him to resume his farming.

Interpretation

Applicants must be able to interpret any clause of the U.S. Constitution or of the Louisiana Constitution. Whether or not interpretations are correct is left to the discretion of the registrar.

No standards or rubrics.

Joe Kirk of Webster Parish had been registered from 19[illegible] to 1957, when he was disenfranchised. Three times after that he attempted to register but was unable to because of the interpretation requirements. On his fourth try, he was asked whether he had any illegitimate children. When he said no, Registrar Clement said, "You are a damned liar" and flunked him again.

In Plaquemines Parish, a written interpretation, in accordance with an official set of answers drawn up by segregationist leader Leander Perez, must be submitted.

Questions to Consider:

1. *What internal evidence can help determine the date that the document was written?*

2. *In what ways might these African Americans have risked their livelihood or their lives by attempting to register, or suing when they were denied the right to register, or testifying before Congress when they were denied the right to register?*

3. *How might these examples of voter suppression inform your understanding of the current debates about voter ID laws and attempts to suppress the vote today?*

Source:

Baton Rouge Committee on Registration Education, "Negro Voting in Louisiana," National Association for the Advancement of Colored People, New Orleans Branch Collection (MSS 28), Louisiana and Special Collections, Earl K. Long Library, University of New Orleans.

1964:
CORE in Louisiana

Established during World War II, the Congress of Racial Equality (CORE) was a national civil rights organization with affiliated local groups whose stated goal was "to abolish racial discrimination by direct, nonviolent methods." National director James Farmer wrote the following letter to drum up support for the upcoming voting rights drive in the South. New Orleans's local director was Richard Haley, whom another CORE worker, Oretha Castle, married during his service in Louisiana. Volunteers risked life and limb as well as their jobs when they penetrated the delta regions of Mississippi and Louisiana to hold "citizenship schools" and conduct voter registration drives.

Letter from James Farmer, 1964

Dear Friend:

A few weeks ago the Ku Klux Klan burned 150 crosses in front of the homes and churches of Negroes in southern Louisiana. Intimidation is not new to this area. Many, active in the CORE voter registration effort, have lost their jobs . . .

Last month, for the first time since reconstruction, Negroes voted in Tensas and in West Feliciana Parish in Louisiana. This year we registered 17,000 Negroes—more than twice as many as last year. CORE field workers help open parks, public buildings and restaurants, carry on employment and housing campaigns as well as voter registration. They receive only $25 a week for all expenses and yet we turn down requests for field workers because we don't have the funds to hire more.

CORE field workers face daily violence, intimidation and imprisonment in Louisiana, South Carolina and Mississippi. They are willing to risk their lives so that we may all secure our freedom. . . .

Booklet, "An Invitation and a Challenge"

College students, clergymen, workers and businessmen are needed for CORE summer programs in Louisiana, northern Florida, South Carolina and Mississippi. The main concentration will be in Louisiana. Work will be hard, living conditions will be Spartan, opportunities for achievement will be great.

The main purpose of CORE summer programs will be to develop community leadership and strengthen community organization. CORE workers will not enter a community with preconceived plans. They will instead adapt themselves to the community's needs and wishes. They will seek to stimulate the expression of those needs, and organize the kind of groups that will be able to continue activity on a self-sufficient basis after the summer programs come to an end. Program areas include:

Voter Registration
Canvassing, instruction clinics, rallies, transportation to the registrar's office.

Community Organization
Creating community involvement and organization around need for covered sewers, street lights, playgrounds, postal service, libraries, free access to public services and facilities.

Farmers' Leagues
Organizing farmers to deal with their special problems such as elections for County ASCS committees, getting crop loans and farm home loans, setting up marketing cooperatives where these are possible.

Jobs
Working to open jobs at consumer-oriented companies and public agencies by encouraging negotiations, mobilizing community concern through public demonstrations and boycotts.

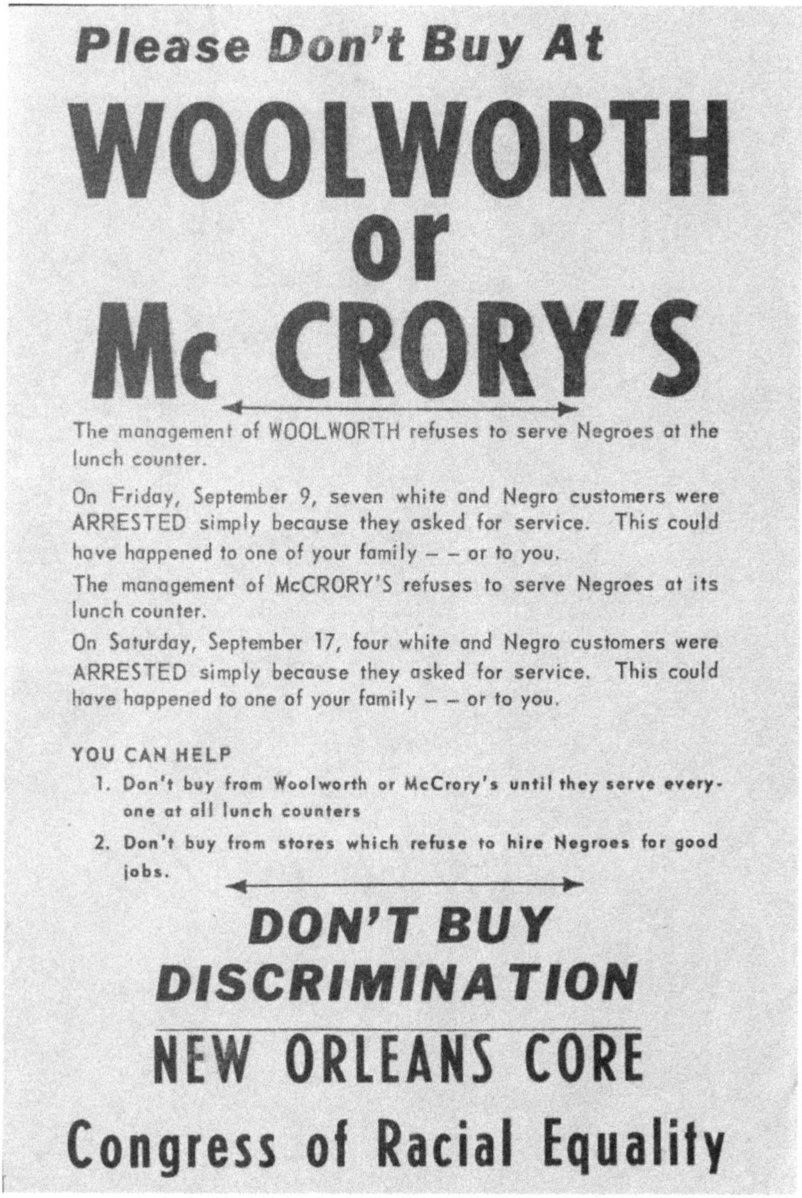

Please Don't Buy At

WOOLWORTH
or
Mc CRORY'S

The management of WOOLWORTH refuses to serve Negroes at the lunch counter.

On Friday, September 9, seven white and Negro customers were ARRESTED simply because they asked for service. This could have happened to one of your family – – or to you.

The management of McCRORY'S refuses to serve Negroes at its lunch counter.

On Saturday, September 17, four white and Negro customers were ARRESTED simply because they asked for service. This could have happened to one of your family – – or to you.

YOU CAN HELP

1. Don't buy from Woolworth or McCrory's until they serve everyone at all lunch counters
2. Don't buy from stores which refuse to hire Negroes for good jobs.

DON'T BUY DISCRIMINATION

NEW ORLEANS CORE

Congress of Racial Equality

Established during World War II, the Congress of Racial Equality or CORE was a national civil rights organization with local branches. As these flyers show, CORE's tactics included boycotts and picketing of stores that practiced racial discrimination. National Director James Farmer, at the bequest of the local branch, gave a rousing talk designed to rally support for demonstrations. Note that two of the meetings took place in African American churches.

NEGROES ON THE MARCH

Because our leaders were jailed on Saturday, March 4, from PUGLIA's Super Market (Caffin & St. Claude Ave.) we are calling upon every fair minded citizen of the City of New Orleans to rally to our support in protest against the illegal arrest of our leaders and these unfair laws under which they commit these acts. Our timetable of activities for Saturday, March 11, follows:

1. Picketing of **PUGLIA's** Super Market at 10:00 a. m.
2. Picketing **McCROY** and **WOOLWORTH STORES** on Canal Street at 12 noon.
3. March from the Canal Street area to the St. James A. M. E. Church, North Roman near Iberville, for instructions at 1:00 p. m.
4. March to the steps of the **CITY HALL** in the Civic Center for prayer and presenting our petition in protest against all arrests made in times past for peaceful picketing.
5. Move over to the **SUPREME COURT** building for presenting a simular petition to the **GOVERNOR** of **LOUISIANA** through the Atty. General in protest against the invasion of New Orleans by the **STATE POLICE** and the **GESTAPO-LIKE** arrest of our leaders (including handcuffing of women) around **PUGLIA's**.

MASS MEETING

March 11 · · St. David Hall

Lamanche near Marais Street

7:30 P. M.

BE PEACEFUL – BE QUIET – BE REVERENT

Wear dark or white clothing for we are in mourning for Our Rights

Sponsored by: THE CONSUMERS LEAGUE OF GREATER NEW ORLEANS and CORE

NEW ORLEANS
CORE
presents
JAMES FARMER
National Director,
Congress of Racial Equality
Thursday
February 13, 1964
8:00 p.m.
New Zion Baptist Church
2319 Third St.
Rev. A. L. Davis, Jr., Pastor
ADMISSION FREE

Freedom Schools, Community Centers
Literacy programs, classes in Negro history, government, current events, nursery programs, drama groups, art. Special need here for trained people.

Medical, Legal Assistance
Programs will have cooperation of Medical Committee for Human Rights, Lawyers Constitutional Defense Committee, CORE Scholarship, Education and Defense Fund.

Summer programs will start with a one-week training session, which is scheduled to open on June 10th. Following this there will be eight weeks of field work ending with an evaluation on August 15th. Participants are expected to be self-sustaining. They will have to pay for their own transportation and room and board, and be prepared for possible bail expenses. The CORE Scholarship, Education and Defense Fund will make a number of Community Development Fellowships available to students in appropriate fields of study who have been accepted for a program. . . .

If you can't join the program, please support it. Contributions are urgently needed.

Questions to Consider:

1. *What techniques or tactics did CORE use to try to unseat white supremacy and create a level playing field in Louisiana?*

2. *How does CORE's strategy differ from the NAACP's strategy?*

3. *Did the fact that CORE was a national organization make any difference in the way it was perceived in Louisiana, do you think? Explain.*

4. *Why were churches a focal point for the civil rights movement?*

Source:

CORE flyers and booklets, National Association for the Advancement of Colored People, New Orleans Branch Collection (MSS 28), Louisiana and Special Collections, Earl K. Long Library, University of New Orleans.

Images:

National Association for the Advancement of Colored People, New Orleans Branch Collection (MSS 028), Earl K. Long Library, University of New Orleans.

1971:
Barbara Scott, Candidate for Representative District 96

Louisiana had a vigorous postwar women's liberation movement, also called the feminist movement. As elsewhere in the country, it was varied, and the women did not see eye to eye about goals or strategies. Among the more centrist organizations was the League of Women Voters, which had existed for years and had chapters across the state. The most famous and longest-lived organization of the second wave (as this era of feminism is often called), the National Organization for Women, had chapters in major cities in Louisiana. Radical socialist groups, centered primarily in New Orleans, had little appeal beyond their small circle. Barbara Scott was not a member of any of those but billed herself as "the feminist candidate" in this race. Owner of a cabaret in the French Quarter, she chafed under state laws that discriminated against women. Like many other residents and tourists who frequented the French Quarter, marijuana was her recreational drug of choice, and she also enjoyed same-sex relationships at a time when both were illegal. She was part of a coalition of French Quarter property owners who organized to prevent the razing of the French Quarter by a group of developers who wanted to run an interstate through it. Her platform reflects forward-thinking positions on those and other issues. Though she gave her opponent a run for his money, the Democratic incumbent won the election, to no one's surprise. Disappointed, Scott left New Orleans to establish a mecca for the LGBTQ community in Eureka Springs, Arkansas. She now lives on the Mississippi Gulf Coast, where she remains politically active.

A STATEMENT BY BARBARA SCOTT: REPUBLICAN CANDIDATE FOR REPRESENTATIVE DISTRICT 96

A major issue in this campaign is discrimination. Just as discrimination against blacks should be eliminated, so should discrimination against other less organized groups.

The State discriminates AGAINST WOMEN. The medieval Civil code which sharply curtails women's control of their finances must be revised. The State must insure equal employment opportunity for women, black and white, and it must require equal salaries for equal work.

The regressive State taxes discriminate AGAINST WORKING WAGE EARNERS. This tax structure must be changed. The poor should not be burdened with heavy taxes on necessities. Their participation in government must be encouraged with representation on all state boards.

The State discriminates AGAINST ALL INDIVIDUALS. The power of the State to dictate personal behavior must be limited.

The State discriminates AGAINST OUR YOUTH. In the face of overwhelming scientific evidence the State continues to persecute young users of marijuana, oftentimes destroying the future of what could be our productive citizens. This persecution must be stopped.

The 96th District is unique. It is one of the few living and growing historical areas in the United States. Furthermore this district generates more tax revenue than any other district in Orleans Parish, and receives far less in return. Yet, preservation continues to be a constant struggle against those forces, some in city government, some in state government, who would rather exploit our district than preserve it. Preservation requires political representation attuned to this struggle.

This is a grass roots campaign. I need your support.

GO YOUR OWN WAY

Questions to Consider:

1. *Does Scott's party affiliation surprise you and if so, what does that say about the historical or political context?*

2. *How would you categorize her platform and seemingly innocuous but politically potent phrases such as "go your own way"?*

3. *We might expect a woman candidate in the early 1970s to be more cautious than a typical male candidate; do these assumptions apply to Scott? How does she defy or match these expectations?*

4. *In what ways do Scott's word choices both reveal and conceal her personal beliefs and personal life to her audience? How do these choices reflect the historical moment? Would the current political atmosphere call for the same choices? Why or why not?*

Source:

"A STATEMENT BY BARBARA SCOTT: REPUBLICAN CANDIDATE FOR REPRESENTATIVE DISTRICT 96," Janet Allured papers, NA-340, Box 1 Folder 4, Newcomb Archives and Vorhoff Collection, Newcomb Institute of Tulane University, New Orleans, LA.

1973:
Going "Behind the Cane Curtain"

"Behind the Cane Curtain" was an award-winning fifteen-part series investigated and written by reporter Patsy Sims that ran in the New Orleans *States-Item* in March/April 1973. It described the work and living conditions of sharecroppers in the sugar cane region south and west of New Orleans. Few people, even those relatively nearby, knew anything about these workers and the conditions they endured year after year. Sims reported: "'No trespassing' signs were often posted on the dirt roads leading to their living quarters, and outsiders, including me, were sometimes threatened with arrest if they dared venture beyond the signs."[1] Sims recreated the dialect of the sharecroppers, most of whom were African American families that had lived on the same plantation since Reconstruction. Most had not completed their formal education, suffered from lack of medical and dental care, and had never been more than a few miles off the plantation, and then only to go to the nearest Charity Hospital if an emergency arose.

Tenant farmers received few paid vacation days, no sick leave, no insurance or pension plans. During peak seasons, they got paid one dollar a day for working from sunup to sundown, about twelve hours, with no breaks. If there was no work to do, they were not paid. Out of their paycheck, the owner took money for gas, electricity, and water, often leaving them with nothing. Tenants frequently borrowed from

1. Patsy Sims, "Cutting Time: Two Generations of Change in Cane Country," *Gravy* (Spring 2019), 32.

the owners to make ends meet, which trapped them in place as they had to stay there until their debt was paid. The only place to shop was in the plantation store, which charged higher prices and interest rates than comparable stores in town, ensnaring them even more.

Owners provided housing but sharecroppers' shacks were substandard by any measure. In some cases, it was an old slave cabin that had been slightly modified to include running water and electricity. Most had no hot water and no indoor plumbing, forcing tenants to use dilapidated, reeking outhouses. Black sharecroppers' houses were made of bare wood, uncovered either inside or out unless the family had tacked up newspaper to cover the cracks in the walls through which the wind whistled. There was little heat and the roofs went unrepaired, allowing rainwater in. Most of the furniture, like their clothing, consisted of cast offs.

One black farmer, the youngest of 10 children, recalled that they bathed in an aluminum tub but everybody used the same water. The adults went first, followed by the children in line. Because he was the youngest, this man recalled, he was probably dirtier after he got out of the water than he was when he went in. In the first excerpt, Sims describes the home of a black sharecropping family led by Henry (who could not read or write) and Edna Cook.

Unlike black tenants, white men were trained for skilled work and could work in the sugar mills tending machinery, welding, as mechanics, etc. Those workers were represented by the Amalgamated Meat Cutters and Butcher Workmen. Because they were unionized, their pay was higher, and their accommodations better. Their houses usually included siding and wall board, indoor plumbing, and sometimes bathrooms.

The owners defended the conditions by saying that they provided housing and sustenance for tenants even when there was no work, and they also transported them to the fields. But the cropping families countered that could not accumulate any savings and they were sometimes turned out of the houses when they got too old or sick to work.

Because sugar growers took subsidies from the Department of Agriculture, the department monitored the wages paid workers. With the assistance of the Southern Mutual Help Association, Inc. (SMHA), based in Jeanerette, Louisiana, two farmers filed suit in 1973 to recover wages they had lost because of President Nixon's wage-and-price freeze. Leading that effort was Huet Freeman, the subject of the second story presented here.

In 1974, they won a landmark decision in *Freeman v. Butz* (Secretary of Agriculture) in a class-action suit. The court froze over $60 million in grower subsidy payments and awarded tenant farmers over $1 million in back wages.

Yet even as there were signs conditions might improve, machinery was in the process of replacing them. However, the new tractors and grinders were dangerous, especially in the mud. A young farmer named Cleveland Benjamin was killed during the reporting of this story when a tractor rolled over in the mud and crushed him. In the third excerpt, Sims talked to a man of sixty-three with no more than four teeth left who reported a similar accident in his past.

When Patsy Sims revisited the area in 2018, she found that civil rights laws, technology, and science had dramatically changed the situation in the cane fields. Most of the shacks were gone, replaced by battered trailers filled with migrant workers who were in the United States legally on the H-2A visa program, which allows the visa-holders to do agricultural work for up to ten months a year. Many of the younger, better-educated black workers had gone to work in towns, and what had once been cane fields were now planted with different crops or were covered with strip malls. Yet sugar production continues to be an important part of the state's economy. Leaps forward in technology and scientific breeding programs have resulted in higher yields and lower costs. In addition, the Department of Labor now polices living and working conditions and set a minimum hourly wage of $10.73 in 2018. These regulations, Sims reports, "are in marked contrast to the lack of protections provided generations of black workers."[2] Children of the men and women she interviewed in the 1970s now have careers in law, in health care professions, in law enforcement, and in engineering. None of that, they recognize, would have been possible for their parents.

2. Sims, *Gravy*, 42.

March 19, 1973

[In the home of Henry and Edna Cook:] Some wire and a couple of clothespins stretch between the posts that hold up the rusted tin roof. A few feet out back, there's a path worn to an outhouse of the same gray planks, an empty pig's pen and a pile of half-charred tin cans and milk cartons. Inside, a bed with a lumpy mattress and the shredded insides of a quilt pulled over it take up most of what is the living room. . . . Framed pictures of John and Robert Kennedy with Martin Luther King in the middle and one of the Last Supper are nailed up over the bed. "These houses" he [Henry] complained between bites [of red beans and rice], "they fix it for the white folks but they don't do nuthin' for us. The white folks they don't have no baths neither but they fixed up better 'n us. . . .

"I ain't got no choice," he shrugged, "and at my age—I'm fifty-one, born July 'leven, nineteen-twenty-one—it be kind of hard to git any kind of job. If I was young, I be off a long time. . . . My daddy took me out of school and I had to work, and I'm sorry he took me out of school. . . . When I went to school, I had to walk," he reminisced, leaning over with his elbows resting on his knees and kind of enjoying remembering he had once gone to school, even if just for a little while. But then the smile left. He still couldn't read and he couldn't write, but he sure wished he could. . . .

March 21, 1973

[About *Freeman v. Butz*:] "I was afraid when we filed that suit," the tall, sturdy twenty-nine-year-old [Huet Freeman] admitted. "I could've lost my house, my job. But it had to be done. I had to take the chance. If no one speaks up, no one will know.

"Most of them is afraid of speakin' up because they is afraid of losin' their job. I don't think they should be afraid, not if you're doing somethin' right. It's time people start doin' somethin'. . . . It's hard enough living here and you don't have to pay rent. Just think about going into town where you have to pay rent. That be just one more bill you have to worry about."

March 22, 1973

[Regarding accidents in the field:] "It be fourteen years ago and the tractor turned over, turned bottom up. It was on top of me but I didn't figure it was serious as it was. I was kinda young then and jist went along with the owner of the place—he's dead and gone now. He kep on tellin me about how 'you don't have to go to the doctor, man. You'll overcome it.' He wanted me for grindin, you know. He wanted me to stay so I could work, running the cutter. Now I wanted to hep him so I limped around and worked. Bout eight years after that it upseted me . . . I stayed in Char'ty Hospital fifty-eight days fore I come out. . . . You see that machine that sittin' down there off the road, that three-leg thang?" he said, meaning the cutter. "I run it, and you KNOW that enough to scare me, that thang!"

March 26, 1973

[In the house of another sharecropping family:] The door opened and two young women in yellow rubber overalls and jackets came in and edged up to the gas heater. Martha introduced the older one—about twenty-six—as her aunt and the twenty-year-old as her cousin. They were working in the fields just during grinding because they could make more money than doing housework. "I make about six dollars a day doing housework," her aunt explained. In the fields, she makes a dollar eighty an hour scrapping cane.

"That," Mr. Williams told me, "is when you foller the cutter and pick it up and throw it on the other side of the road where they putting it at."

"It's nuthin' new for women to do it," the aunt shrugged, pulling off her boots and then her rubber jacket. "They been doin' it . . . my mother used to do it."

"I was nine years old when I started workin' in the fields, pickin' up rice and scrappin' cane. . . . Work all my life, scrappin' and cutting cane, cut rice, load rice, sack it up, done every'thang with it. Now I don't do too much. I'm not able. Wish I could've done housework more than work in the fields."

Questions to Consider:

1. *In what ways did tenant farmers' lives in the 1970s resemble the lives of black sharecroppers in the 1870s?*
2. *In what ways did conditions improve for the tenant farmers between the time the first series ran in the New Orleans newspaper and the year Sims revisited the families in 2018?*
3. *What accounts for those changes?*

Source:

"Behind the Cane Curtain," *States-Item*, March 19, 21, 22, 26, 1973. Capital City Press/ Georges Media Group, and Baton Rouge, LA.

1977:
New Orleans's Gay Rights Community Protests Anita Bryant's Appearance

New Orleans, particularly the bohemian French Quarter, had had a large and visible LGBTQ community since at least the 1920s. Yet the gay community had remained largely politically indifferent, preferring to concentrate on social identity and community within the gay krewes. That changed in part as a response to the announcement that Anita Bryant, a spokeswoman of the Christian Right, was slated to hold a rally in town. Bryant's appearance energized the LGBTQ community in New Orleans, who, with political allies, organized a counter-protest and distributed the flyer excerpted here.

Demonstrate For Human Rights
National Rally & March, Saturday, June 18, in New Orleans
Featured Speaker: Sgt. Leonard Matlovich
Organized by Human Equal Rights for Everyone (H.E.R.E.)

WHY WE PROTEST

Throughout the 1960s and '70s, various minority groups in the United States have stood up to affirm their human dignity, pride and civil rights.

Black Americans organized massive protests in the early 1960s to secure their equal rights. Women have organized to win the legal right to abortion, and are fighting for passage of the Equal Rights Amendment.

And now, gay people have stepped forward to demand that equal protection under the Constitution be extended to their community, as well.

Today, those rights which have already been won, as well as those yet to be won, are under attack. Anita Bryant has stepped forward as a spokesperson for those forces in society that oppose equal rights for gays, women and blacks. In Miami she has formed an organization called "Save our Children." This group, backed by big money interests, has launched an hysterical campaign to overturn a civil rights ordinance in Dade County. That ordinance extends equal access to jobs and housing to people with a gay sexual preference.

What are the facts on homosexuality? The universally respected Kinsey Institute notes that 13% of the adult male population and 7% of the adult female population are predominately homosexual. At an average of 10%, that means 20 million people in the United States and upwards of 100,000 people in New Orleans.

Anita Bryant's principle rationale and justification for her viewpoint is her self-serving interpretation of the Bible. "If God meant for there to be homosexuals," she claims, "He would have created Adam and Bruce."

Recognized religious leaders, however, are far from unanimous on this question. A poll of priests conducted by the independent Chicago-based Thomas More Foundation found that 70% of those responding feel that current pastoral guidelines for homosexuality are "too narrow, unyielding, unrealistic and absurd." In addition, gay rights have been supported by the National Council of Churches, the Protestant Episcopal Church, the United Church of Christ, the Lutheran Church in America, the Unitarian-Universalist Association, and the Society of Friends (Quakers).

In any event, our society is supposed to be governed through the principle of SEPARATION of church and state. This principle exists precisely to prevent extreme religious bigots like Anita Bryant from imposing their views on a secular society, thereby denying freedom of religion (and freedom from religion) to others.

The most revolting and repeated "argument" of Bryant and her Save Our Children crusaders is the myth of child molesting. According to Bryant, "As a mother, I know that homosexuals cannot biologically reproduce children, therefore they must recruit our children." With the charge that all gays are "child molesters," Bryant seeks to bar gays from such jobs as teaching—despite the fact that in 39 communities with teacher employment protection similar to that proposed for Miami, there is not a single letter of complaint on file from either students or parents.

What are the facts on child molesting? All researchers on the subject agree that such behavior occurs in a distinct category of people, mostly men, known as "pedophiles," who are exclusively attracted to children. All these studies note that a majority of those apprehended for molesting young boys also have a history of molesting young girls. Moreover, other statistics, including a recent six year study by the New York Bar Association, show that a greater proportion of heterosexuals than homosexuals commit these crimes—and yet Bryant has remained strangely silent on that phase of the problem.

Why are laws like the Dade County ordinance needed to ensure equal rights for gay people? Anita Bryant claims that "homosexuals are not an oppressed group any more than cigarette smokers." The facts speak otherwise: [gay people] lose their jobs; face dishonorable discharge from the military; [may] be evicted from their apartments; lose custody of their children; and face social ostracism from family and friends afflicted by the same irrational homophobia Anita Bryant is displaying and playing to.

What are the stakes in this fight? Past history shows that when the rights of one social group are denied or taken away, the dynamic does not stop there. Thus, it is no accident that Anita Bryant is linked to the same right-wing forces that oppose the Equal Rights Amendment, legal abortion, and school desegregation. Bryant's anti-gay organization recently joined forces with national anti-ERA leader Phyllis Schlafly to defeat the ERA in Florida.

This fight is thus for EVERYONE's human rights, not just the rights of gay people. We appeal to everyone—and especially women and blacks—to join us in a peaceful, legal protest of Bryant's views on June 18.

The organizers of this protest rally and march are not opposed to Anita Bryant's right to express her bigoted views, her right to perform, her right to free speech, or her right to pursue her livelihood—but we will protest her stated aim TO DENY THOSE RIGHTS OT OTHER AMERICANS. And we will continue to fight her views with every legal means at our disposal, for June 18 is only a beginning.

We are confident that an open confrontation of ideas will find the vast majority of American people on the side of human equal rights, for everyone. JOIN US ON JUNE 18!

Questions to Consider:

1. *Investigate Anita Bryant's background and explain what motivated her anti-homosexual campaign. What impact did her campaign have?*

2. *What parts of this flyer surprised you the most?*

3. *Investigate Sgt. Matlovich and explain why he was a featured speaker at this rally.*

Source:

Demonstrate For Human Rights: National Rally & March, Saturday, June 18, in New Orleans flyer, Mary Elizabeth Gehman papers, Collection NA-142, Newcomb Archives, Tulane University, New Orleans, LA.

1987–1990:
The Oil Slump and Resulting Gambling Legislation

The oil slump of the 1980s was a source of great stress for states like Louisiana that relied on severance taxes on oil drilled from state-owned land for revenue. Oil prices hit a low in 1986 and didn't show signs of recovering. Other Gulf states, like Florida, started experimenting with the idea of a state lottery instead of more traditional sources of income such as raising taxes. All of the following articles were published in the Lake Charles *American Press*.

"Oil Price Skid Compounds State's Fiscal Predicament," December 21, 1987

Louisiana state government, whose fortunes have risen and fallen along with the price of oil for more than 50 years, faces a potentially devastating financial situation if petroleum prices continue downward, officials warn.

Already trying to rally against a deep regression that grabbed the state when oil prices collapsed nearly three years ago, a continued downward swing threatens to dry up state revenue at a time when officials are swinging the budget ax.

At the same time, officials say a renewed oil patch recession could drive up unemployment in a state that has the nation's highest jobless rate.

"I was already facing a $450 million (state budget) deficit," said interim commissioner of Administration Brian Kendrick. "I now face a $500 million to $550 million deficit. I'm not doing anything differently, but it certainly adds urgency to our situation."

Kendrick, who is serving in the administration of Gov. Edwin Edwards at the request of Gov.-elect Buddy Roemer, is trying to find budget cuts and boost efforts to find additional tax money through audits.

Acting at Roemer's request, Edwards recently chopped $40 million in spending and instituted freezes on state hiring, travel and equipment purchases.

The governor-elect, who takes office on March 14, has said his first order of business will be to call a special legislative session to deal with short term budget measures on March 20.

Even before the price of oil dropped nearly $2 a barrel last week, Roemer said the state would run out of money and be unable to pay its routine operating expenses by February or March.

The current $5.9 billion state budget is running short of money because of optimistic budget predictions based upon a price of $20–$21 per barrel.

According to state Senate economist Johnny Rombach, the price of Louisiana sweet crude has averaged about $18.75 per barrel since the fiscal year began on July 1.

Kendrick said for each $1 drop in oil prices, Louisiana loses $30 to $35 million in severance taxes and royalties for production on state owned land and another $10 million to $15 million as the chilling effect cuts business and income taxes.

Despite last week's price downturn that saw Louisiana crude dip below $17 per barrel, Kendrick said Roemer was confident the state could manage its way out of the budget crisis.

But if another price collapse occurs, "We would be faced with a total shutdown of government services." Kendrick said.

"State Support for Lottery Increases" January 12, 1989

More than two-thirds of Louisiana voters favor a statewide lottery despite Gov. Buddy Roemer's strong opposition, according to a poll conducted for the Baton Rouge *State-Times* and *Morning Advocate*.

Support for a lottery has increased significantly in the past two years and cuts across all demographic lines, the survey by pollster Ed Renwick of New Orleans shows.

Majority support for a lottery was voiced in each region of the state, in every age group, among both races and sexes and within all broad religious designations according to the poll.

"The voters didn't go for Roemer's (tax change) plans, but they do favor a lottery," pollster Ed Renwick said. "Roemer, in other words, should attach his cart to the horse."

Proponents say a lottery would be a painless substitute for up to $150 million in taxes. The state has a constitutional ban on lotteries.

Roemer and other opponents say lottery revenue is not dependable and that more gambling would distract voters and government officials from permanent solutions to the state's fiscal problems.

According to the poll, 69 percent of the respondents said they favor a lottery, 23 percent said they were in opposition and 7 percent offered no opinion.

When a similar question was asked two years ago by the same pollster, about 56 percent of the respondents said they favored a lottery and 32 percent opposed it.

In south Louisiana, the lottery is favored by 76 to 77 percent of the voters with only 16 percent to 18 percent opposed according to the poll. Support is weakest in the northern parishes, where about 53 percent is in favor.

The poll, conducted by telephone, included a statewide sample of 883 registered voters. For questions involving the entire sample, the margin of error was 3 percent Renwick said.

"La. Says 'Yes' to Lottery" October 7, 1990

Louisiana voters Saturday approved a constitutional amendment making this the 33rd state in the nation to legalize a lottery.

The lottery amendment was one of 15 proposed changes to the 1974 state constitution on the ballot.

With 1,736 of 3,264 precincts reporting, or 53 percent, the lottery was heading for victory with 408,155 yes votes to 197,315 no votes, or 67 percent approval. "I'm elated," state Senator Ken Hollis said in a television interview. "I think the people have finally gotten an opportunity that they wanted for a number of years. . . . I think they've spoken now."

He said that judging from other states' experiences, it takes about eight months from the time of passage to actually put the lottery system in place.

In decisions on other amendments, voters approved having the Legislature begin its regular session each year in March instead of April. And, returns showed they favored some of the less controversial aspects of Gov. Buddy Roemer's fiscal reform plan, which failed to gain voter approval in April 1989. Opponents said the lottery would breed corruption, draw too much money from the poor and contribute relatively little to the state's $8 billion budget.

Proponents touted Legislative Fiscal Office estimates that it would pump $112 million into state coffers without raising taxes. Even if opponents were right and that figure was closer to $60 million, it would be better than nothing, proponents argued.

As election day neared, those opposed to the lottery on moral, religious and economic grounds formed Coalition against Legalizing a Lottery and claimed to have grassroots support in almost all 64 Louisiana parishes. Still, they acknowledged an uphill battle, with independent polls showing public support for the game.

Hollis, R-Metairie, a chief sponsor of lottery legislation, predicted passage with 67 percent to 68 percent of the vote. He toured the state last week to promote the game and said he found as much backing for it in conservative northern Louisiana as in the more free-wheeling southern part of the state.

"Landrieu: State Should Get $57 Million from Lottery" October 17, 1992

The state will receive about $57 million from the Louisiana Lottery this month, the first quarterly transfer of the new fiscal year.

State Treasurer Mary Landrieu said Thursday that the exact amount will be determined when the lottery board meets next week.

State law requires the lottery to make quarterly payments to the state after its first year. In addition, the lottery is required to transfer at least 35 percent of its gross revenues each year.

The lottery has grossed $540 million in sales. About $270 million went to prizes, and $27 million to retailers.

With the transfer, the state will have received $172 million.

The remaining $71 million covered lottery start-up and operations.

The lottery has transferred $115 million to the state since last December, earlier than the law requires. Lottery President Bonnie Fussell said the lottery turns over everything it doesn't need.

The lottery money goes into the state's general fund and will be available for appropriation by the legislature on Jan. 1, 1993, Landrieu said.

Given the lottery's current pace, Landrieu said state revenue will exceed the $140 million projected by the Revenue Estimating Conference earlier this year.

Questions to Consider:

1. *According to these articles, did the lottery solve the issue presented by the loss in oil revenues?*

2. *Outline arguments for and against the lottery. If you had been of voting age in 1990, would you have voted for it? Why or why not?*

Sources:

1. "Oil Price Skid Compounds State's Fiscal Predicament," *American Press* (Lake Charles, LA), December 21, 1987.

2. "State Support for Lottery Increases," *American Press*, (Lake Charles, LA), January 12, 1989.

3. "La. Says 'Yes' to Lottery," *American Press*, (Lake Charles, LA), October 7, 1990.

4. "Landrieu: State Should Get $57 Million from Lottery," *American Press*, (Lake Charles, LA), October 17, 1992.

1991:
The Race from Hell: Edwards and Duke Debate

Edwin Edwards, a colorful, popular, and witty Democratic politician, was the only governor to serve a total of four terms. His first two terms (1972–1980) were consecutive, and a third term lasted from 1984–1988. Born in Avoyelles Parish in 1927, Edwards was the son of a French-speaking Catholic mother and an English-speaking Presbyterian father. He has been dubbed the "last of the line of New Deal Southern Democrats." He built new infrastructure and appointed more African Americans to office than any governor since Reconstruction.

Ever popular despite a shadow of scandals that followed him everywhere, he decided in 1991 to launch another bid after Republican Buddy Roemer's popularity plummeted due to the decline in oil revenues. Roemer was knocked out of the race during the primary, pitting Edwards against Republican candidate David Duke, a former Imperial Wizard of the Ku Klux Klan, in a campaign popularly called "the race from hell." Duke had founded an organization called the National Association for the Advancement of White People (NAAWP) and had served one term in the Louisiana State House as a Republican. His campaigns depended upon the votes of poor white residents and contributions from small donors, many from out of state. By the time this debate took place, Duke had found religion and described himself as "born-again."

When the votes were counted, Edwards won in a landslide, 61 to 39 percent. Yet allegations of corruption continued to dog Governor Edwards, who had run up millions of dollars in gambling debts and apparently took money from the casinos in return for preferential treatment. Though he always maintained his innocence, in 2001 he was found guilty of racketeering and sentenced to ten years in federal prison.

As for Duke, investigations revealed that he, too, had been using campaign contributions for personal gain and to gamble. After living in Russia for five years, he came home to plead guilty (in 2002) to filing false tax returns and mail fraud (basically defrauding his supporters). He served time in a Texas prison and was released in May 2004. In 2016, he ran for a seat in the Louisiana Senate, and credited Donald Trump for inspiring him to return to politics. Trump was featured on the front page of the KKK's official newspaper, the *Crusader*.[1] In an interview with the *Los Angeles Times*, Duke remarked, "I love it." He continued, "The fact that Donald Trump's doing so well, it proves that I'm winning. I am winning."[2] Duke is portrayed in the 2018 movie *BlacKkKlansman*.

Louisiana Gubernatorial Debate
November 6, 1991

[The debate begins with opening statements.]

Duke: I appreciate this opportunity because I don't have special interest money that Edwin Edwards has, and no big endorsements of political machines operating around the state. I need to reach you personally. We need some changes in our state. . . . Crime has made many people fear on their streets and in their homes. . . . We've had a welfare system that's encouraged crime and hasn't encouraged people to be responsible. . . . It's time for the people to have a voice, and I represent that voice.

Edwards: While my opponent has been traveling all over the country on talk shows trying to establish a national agenda, I have only one interest in

1. Gabe Ortiz, "Former KKK Leader David Duke Is Selling Autographed 'Trump-Duke' Caps For $50," *America's Voice*, October 17, 2016. https://americasvoice.org/blog/former-kkk-leader-david-duke-selling-autographed-trump-duke-caps-50/.
2. Lisa Miscaro, "David Duke and Other White Supremacists See Trump's Rise as Way to Increase Role in Mainstream Politics," *Los Angeles Times*, September 29, 2016. https://www.latimes.com/politics/la-na-pol-trump-david-duke-20160928-snap-story.html.

mind and that is to be your governor. I have been here meeting with you and talking to you and already putting together a coalition of business and industry and labor, fisherman and farmers, people from all walks of life to try to make things better for us in Louisiana. I've met with environmental groups and manufacturing groups at the same time and we've come together in principled compromise. I've worked with educators to put children first. I will work with the legislature to fund the Louisiana Opportunity program for middle class citizens to send their children to college. That's the kind of help we need. I've talked to at least four separate industries that are thinking about coming to Louisiana to assure them that the negotiations that Governor Roemer had begun will be continued by me and I will make every commitment required to get them here because we need the jobs. We have all these people working together for the first time because of the nature of my opposition. We will provide a good, stable, forward-looking progressive government for you for the next four years. I hope you will give me that opportunity. . . .

Q. What three things will you do first, if elected, upon taking office in March, 1992?

Edwards: Reform the tax structure; support the Children First plan for education (started by Roemer); expand kindergarten and Head Start; address environmental issues but also work with industry so we don't lose our jobs.

[Duke began by saying what he opposed, such as a tax increase.]

Reporter [interrupting]: Mr. Moderator, the candidate is not answering the question.

[Duke pivoted and said he would encourage welfare recipients to be responsible, he would put education first and would increase salaries for teachers and support personnel.]

Q. What are your plans to equalize funding between richer and poorer school districts?

Duke: Some communities are willing to tax themselves more to support better schools and we should not ask them to support people in other school districts who are not willing to tax themselves to the same extent.

Edwards: Put a floor underneath all parishes to ensure that there is a minimum amount of funding for all school districts. We need to send money to districts that are having trouble raising the money to improve their schools.

Q. Name five people you've recently had contact with who are CEOs who will bring economic growth to our state.

[Edwards named five; Duke couldn't name one.]

Q. What will you do about the growing budget deficit?

Duke: Louisiana needs to reduce the size of government, eliminate waste and duplication. That will reduce the deficit. We need to reduce the number of employees through attrition by about 10 percent per year.

Edwards: I will talk with legislative leaders to ask them to hold hearings early on to figure out how we can trim this budget. Restructuring should be put to a vote of the people. It should not be crammed down their throats.

Q. [Directed at Edwards] The perception is that while you were governor, you benefited your friends in the legislature by directing contracts that way. Would you support the law that prohibits legislators and other elected officials and their employees from doing private contract work with the state?

Edwards: Absolutely. The perception that legislators had a leg up isn't accurate. If anybody got preferential treatment they weren't my friends. They were somebody else's friends but not friends of Edwin Edwards.

[Questioner interrupted and said they **were** Edwards's friends. Edwards denied that, saying the Board of Ethics prohibits it and that if anyone had proof they should have taken that information to the attorney general. Duke said he has names. Edwards challenged him: "Name some names if you have them." Duke never produced them.

Duke said he didn't have big donors to reward, unlike Edwards. His donations came in small amounts like $15 or $25.]

Q. What work experience do you have that will qualify you to manage a $9 billion budget for the state?

[Duke said the man is implying that he did not work, that he was a small business owner. Questioner said that his runs for political office effectively *were* his job. Duke said he had a mailing list company. He said he was the CEO of a national organization for years. Questioner asked, which one? Answer: NAAWP.

Norman Robinson, black correspondent with WDSU-TV, New Orleans, called him out on his past racist statements.]

Robinson: I'm scared. Why should I and other minorities trust our lives to you?

Duke: There's nobody on this stage who hasn't been intolerant before in their lives, hasn't said anything they later regretted; everybody can be racist. I'm a different person than I used to be. I'm much more tolerant than I used to be.

Q. [To Duke] As I newfound Christian, are you here now to apologize to the people of this state?

Duke: Of course I apologize.

Q.[Still to Duke] Do you repudiate the Klan?

Duke: I do repudiate the Klan and any other racist or intolerant organization that exists, but you don't make up for past discrimination by putting new discrimination on people, such as affirmative action programs and policies. A lot of racism exists in all communities, not just in white communities. There's a lot of violence in the streets directed at white people. There's a lot of fear in this state, people fear becoming victims of violent crime in their homes and in the street.

[Robinson interrupted].

Duke: Mr. Robinson, I don't think you're being fair with me.

Robinson: I don't think you're really being honest, sir.

Duke [exasperated]: You're the one really doing the debate here, aren't you? You aren't asking questions. You're here to put me down and that's your prerogative.

Edwards: Klan people have already announced they are coming down to help their friend Mr. Duke. If any of them get in the way, they will be dealt with harshly. Mr. Duke has given us twenty years of hate and hurt. If he's really reformed let him go back into the community and give us twenty years of healing and help, then come back and ask to be governor.

Reporter: Mr. Duke, you have repeatedly stated that welfare recipients have babies just to increase their welfare benefits. The evidence does not support that. How do you respond?

Duke: There are people who do that.

Reporter: But it's not rampant; in fact it's rare.

Duke: Why are taxpayers paying for welfare recipients to buy lottery tickets and drugs and to behave irresponsibly? We need to get the drugs out of the housing projects!

Edwards: Mr. Duke knows that anybody caught with drugs is kicked out of the housing projects. The drug problem is being addressed. And a welfare recipient who has another baby gets an additional $11 per week. Nobody is going to have another child for that amount of money. It doesn't begin to cover the cost of feeding and supporting that child.

Q. for Mr. Duke: Half of your contributions are from out-of-state contributions. Why is that?

Duke: People all over this country want welfare reform. Most of my contributions have been small, from people who want to end corruption and reduce the size of government, and most contributors live in the state of Louisiana.

Edwards: Forty percent of Duke's contributions come from out of state while only eight percent of my contributions come from out of state.

[Next question concerns environmental issues. Edwards was asked if he had taken campaign money from major polluters in the state. Edwards says no, absolutely not. "I will work with the EPA (federal government) to stop the polluters."]

Duke: I'm suspicious of his answers. Under Edwin Edwards we became the biggest toxic waste dump in the United States. We have some of the highest cancer rates in the country, and the people responsible for that contributed to Mr. Edwards's campaign. I will work with the DEQ (state environmental protection agency) to clean this state up. . . .

[The debate ends with closing statements.]

Duke: I won the Cajun vote. Cajuns are tired of shenanigans and corruption in government. The Cajun people are tired of bigger government, wasteful government, federal intrusion into our lives. We've got to start working to make things better. Economic prosperity will come from less government and more individual freedom and less taxes. Unless we reform the welfare system in this state, we have no future. The system encourages people to have illegitimate children, not to act responsibly. We've got to have honesty in government, clean government. We need to get back to traditional values. We need to stand up for our heritage and our way of life. We're losing the values our nation was built upon. Mr. Edwards, when you were governor last time, you mocked the crucifixion of Christ. I hope you've gotten right with Christ.

Edwards: I never mocked the crucifixion of Christ. I may lose this election because of lies and slurs, but I'm not gonna lose my soul. . . . While David Duke was burning crosses and scaring people, I was building hospitals to heal them. While he was parading around in a Nazi uniform, I was in a National Guard uniform to bring relief to flood and hurricane victims. . . . He has given us twenty years of hate and hurt. If in fact he has a newfound religion, let him go back to our communities and spend some time offering help and serving mankind, then maybe he will come back to us after twenty years, more mature, and showing us that he has become a different person. Don't let him divide us. Don't let him make a mockery of the state of Louisiana.

Questions to Consider:

1. *Like many white southerners, Duke blamed the victims of poverty and discrimination—African Americans—for bad schools and high crime rates in their neighborhoods. Using critical race theory, explain the real causes of those social ills. How, for example, was funding for schools determined?*

2. *Edwin Edwards has often been described as a latter-day incarnation of Huey Long. Would you agree with that either in part or in full? Explain.*

3. *Which Louisianans were likely to support Edwin Edwards? Which were likely to support Duke? Explain why.*

4. *Do you find their proposed solutions to the problems plaguing Louisiana realistic and feasible? Would they have solved the problems? What other possible solutions might these gubernatorial candidates have considered to help reduce the poverty rate in Louisiana and keep well-educated people in the state?*

Sources:

Louisiana Gubernatorial Debates, "Debate 1991: The Governor's Race, No. 2," produced by the Louisiana Educational Television Authority, LPB Collection, http://ladigitalmedia.org/video_v2/asset-detail/LGUBD-19911106.

1992: Dorothy Mae Taylor and the Public Accommodations Ordinance

The youngest of thirteen children of Charles and Mary Delavallade, Dorothy Mae Taylor was a trailblazer for women of color in Louisiana. Educated in Orleans Parish public schools, she graduated from Southern University in Baton Rouge. Despite being a parent to seven children with her husband Johnny Taylor Jr., Taylor became a public figure early in her adult life. She was president of the women's organization in her church, Mount Zion United Methodist, and of two Parent-Teacher Associations (PTAs). A strong advocate of civil rights, women's rights, and social justice, she joined marches and protests that desegregated city facilities and pushed the city to increase funding for the New Orleans Recreation Department's (NORD's) facilities and programs in black neighborhoods. In 1971, she became the first black female elected to the Louisiana legislature. Her first move as a legislator, which was successful, was to call for the elimination of all segregation statutes on the books in Louisiana.

In 1986, voters elected Taylor as the first black woman on the New Orleans City Council, and in October 1988, she brought before the council a highly controversial anti-discrimination ordinance. The ordinance, based on one in New York City that had recently withstood Supreme Court scrutiny, prohibited any club with seventy-six or more members that sponsored public activities from excluding anyone because of race, color, sex, sexual orientation, national origin, ancestry, age, physical condition, or disability. Taylor pointed out that the city expended millions of dollars every year to provide police, fire, and sanitation services during the ten days of Mardi Gras—money collected from all taxpayers in the city, even though most people were excluded from membership in the elite, old line krewes (Mardi Gras clubs).

During the series of public hearings on the proposal, it became obvious that many krewes in New Orleans, particularly the most elite of them, Comus, Momus, and Proteus, openly discriminated against Italians, Jews, women, and people of color.

The three white members on the seven-member city council succeeded in watering down its original wording: the five-month jail term for offending club officers and the threatened loss of liquor licenses for the clubs were rescinded, and fines were reduced to $100. Upset with these changes, Taylor voted against the final version of the bill in February 1992 because she felt that the elimination of a penalty for violators and the absence of required proof of non-discrimination amounted to a weak and ineffective law.

Rather than abide by the new ordinance, Comus and Momus canceled their parades in protest. Taylor was berated as the "Grinch who stole Mardi Gras" but all other krewes paraded as scheduled, and the crowds in 1992 were equal to or larger than in previous years.

Excerpt from Taylor's Press Release December 3, 1991

I believe that in the year 1991, all our citizens regardless of race, sex, creed, or ancestry should be allowed to participate fully in the local economy. If private clubs or carnival krewes contribute to advancement in one's career or profession or lead to economic advancement, then membership should not be denied because a person happens to be, for example, a woman, a Jew, an Italian-American, or a black person. Discrimination in private clubs and carnival organizations has been the subject of discussion and debate in our city for years. Since the Supreme Court ruling in 1988, concerning New York City's anti-discrimination ordinance, I have felt that our city needs to address this discrimination once and for all. If we are to progress, all our citizens should be allowed to participate in and contribute to the local economy by being part of organizations which are integral parts of New Orleans' business and professional community.

Letter to the Editor, *Times-Picayune* March 2, 1992

On December 5, 1991, I introduced an ordinance to address the problems of discrimination which exists in many private clubs and organizations operating in the city of New Orleans. Since that time I have been victimized by threats of violence directed against me, by racial slurs written and verbal, by derogatory caricatures and meanspirited attacks on my character and integrity. Throughout this difficult time, I have refrained from publicly responding to the insults and threats directed against me in the belief that it was most important to have a safe Mardi Gras and to reduce the level of anger and tension which others have sought to raise.

The time has come for me to attempt to explain both the purpose and reasons for the ordinance which others have wrongly dubbed "the Mardi Gras Ordinance." I say wrongly dubbed because this ordinance is not directed at Mardi Gras; it's focus is quasi-private clubs and organizations, many of which it is alleged discriminate in their membership on the basis of gender and race. These clubs and organizations are meeting places where the economy of this community is developed and shared. It is at these clubs and in their organizations that business contacts are made; it is here that entrepreneurs often have time to meet those with the resources to make their dreams become reality. It is here that young people can make the connections in the business community that can open doors, that they otherwise would not even know existed.

We know that historically, women and minorities and in this community principally African Americans, have not enjoyed the same opportunities for economic advancement as others. Among the reasons for this lack of opportunity is the discriminatory practices of certain clubs and organizations whose exclusive policies prevent those excluded from making the contacts necessary in a competitive society to grow and prosper.

This is the reason why I introduced the public accommodations ordinance which has been mislabeled by those who understand that it is not about Mardi Gras at all, but about eliminating the economic barriers which prevent the majority of our citizens from realizing their full economic potential. . . .

It is estimated that Mardi Gras has a 480 million dollar impact annually in this community. If this is true, why are over 100,000 of our citizens living in poverty? Those who are not the beneficiary of this tremendous amount of money coincidentally are the same people who are excluded from membership in certain private clubs and organizations. . . .

The ordinance specifically excludes from its coverage groups with fewer than 75 members, fraternities and societies, church and school groups, fraternal organizations no matter how large, and walking clubs such as the Mardi Gras Indians that do not have liquor or parade permits.

The law is narrow in scope, restricted to those which are large clubs or organizations and where business is part of the character of the group.

In this highly emotional debate, it is interesting to note that those who oppose this ordinance have never explained why they feel a need to discriminate against their fellow citizens. The numerous letters printed in opposition to the ordinance all claim there is a constitutional right to discriminate and that this law infringes on that right. While I do not believe any such right exists in public accommodations, the more basic question that has been completely ignored by my opponents, is why do they want to discriminate? What is it that gives some of our citizens the desire and will to act out their historical prejudices?

I believe our society is better when it is inclusive rather than exclusive. I also believe that it is a proper function of government to eliminate as best we can discrimination that prevents our citizens from competing on a level playing field for jobs, careers, education and business opportunities.

I have no doubt that I will continue to receive hate mail, that the obscene phone calls will persist and threats of violence against me will continue, but be assured that none of this will dissuade me from continuing to pursue a society free from bigotry and racism, a society where a person's individual talent and motivation are the determining factors in how far that person will progress.

Dorothy Mae Taylor

[At about the same time as the controversy over Taylor's public accommodations ordinance, the Liberty Place monument controversy surfaced. The monument, a stone obelisk on a pedestal, had been erected at the foot of Canal Street in 1891 to commemorate the victory of white supremacists (organized as the White League) over the largely black forces of the Metropolitan Police in the Battle of Liberty Place, which took place nearby on September 14, 1874. The battle left about twenty-seven men dead and 105 wounded, but the monument honored only those who fought for the White League. Its inscription and the annual celebration surrounding the anniversary of the battle portrayed it as a fight against tyranny and downplayed the White League's white supremacist motivations.

African Americans began protesting the monument in the 1960s, and when it was moved for street repairs in November 1989, the Human Relations Council, acting at the request of a group of New Orleans citizens, recommended that it not be put back. A group of white citizens led by David Duke, a former Grand Wizard of the Ku Klux Klan, organized as the Friends of Liberty Monument, Inc., sued to have it put back. In the end, Mayor Sidney Barthelemy (who was black), working with state historic preservation officials, agreed to put it in an insignificant spot near Riverfront Park and the Public Belt Railroad tracks. In 2017, it was removed, along with several other monuments to white supremacy, at the recommendation of the city council and Mayor Mitch Landrieu (who is white).]

Template Letter Written by Taylor
July 12, 1993

As you are aware, the Liberty Monument in New Orleans has been a subject of divisiveness and great controversy in our community. The New Orleans Human Relations Commission has concluded that the monument constitutes a nuisance and should be removed from public outdoor display and placed in storage pending a determination of an appropriate place for the monument. I enclose for your information the summary of the recommendations of the Human Relations Commission regarding the Liberty Monument.

On July 15, 1993, the City Council will hold a public hearing on the Liberty Monument and consider an ordinance to order the removal of the Liberty Monument from outdoor public display. This is to invite you to attend this hearing and provide your advice and comments regarding this issue.

Sincerely,
Dorothy Mae Taylor

Lawrence N. Powell, Tulane Professor
Opinion Piece in the *Times-Picayune*, March 17, 1993

Now that the restoration of the Liberty Monument has plunged us for the umpteenth time into racial controversy, it's useful to ask anew why we continue to display this divisive symbol in public. Why not put it in a museum and surround it with the proper demurrals and historical explanations? Why place it in the open to collect angry graffiti and serve as an organizing issue for local white supremacists?

During its 102-year history, the monument has had but a single purpose, to array one part of the community against the other. The time has long passed for entrusting this marble obelisk to museum curators, who know how to use historical relics as teaching tools.

The anti-"political correctness" crowd has sought to turn the Liberty Place controversy into a free speech debate, accusing the monument's opponents of Orwellian thought control. But this confuses the legitimate issue of preserving historical artifacts with every community's right to choose which public symbols it wishes to grace its parks and thoroughfares.

Once erected, monuments don't automatically earn immunity against future relocation. No one in his right mind would insist that the Russian people should leave Stalin's stone likenesses where they are out of respect for "history.". . .

Initiated by a paramilitary group called the White League (which easily overpowered the undermanned, racially mixed Metropolitan Police), the battle was waged to repair cracks in the edifice of white supremacy. White Leaguers would have laughed at contemporary claims that they were struggling only to throw off the yoke of Northern domination.

Their own manifesto, issued just weeks before the battle, frankly urged white men to rally behind a "hereditary civilization and Christianity menaced by a stupid Africanization.". . .

This version of the White League tradition is not what you'll find in Stuart O. Landry's slanted "The Battle of Liberty Place," which defenders of the monument reflexively dust off when seeking historical sanction for their views. But Landry was an arch segregationist whose previous book was a 340-page rant against racial equality. No reputable historian writing today would accept his biased glorification of an insurrection against black democratic rights.

Communities erect monuments to honor historical luminaries or enshrine a usable past. But this particular tradition since its inception has done nothing but foster disharmony. When White League veterans started staging anniversary pageants shortly after Reconstruction, for example, New Orleans' only black newspaper warned prophetically that the commemoration "must always be a red flag shaken in our faces."

The Liberty Monument is not simply another benign historical marker. From the Dixiecrats of the 1940s to the David Dukes of today, white supremacists have instinctively rallied behind its historical symbolism. The whole purpose for erecting the monument was to keep alive an activist tradition of racial subjugation.

Historical monuments are one way a community reminds its members that past ideals are still worth honoring. They define a society to itself. But New Orleans today is a much different community from what it was a century—or even 30 years—ago.

It has become more tolerant and inclusive, and many diehard segregationists have recanted their views. We don't need monuments that encase in stone the prejudices of our great-grandparents, no matter how exemplary their personal characters may have been.

The Liberty Monument doesn't extol home rule, but the right of the white male establishment to rule at home. That elitist notion is a relic of a bygone era. It belongs in a museum along with the marble obelisk that city fathers have foolishly allowed to be re-erected in the bosom of New Orleans' tourist economy.

Questions to Consider:

1. *What arguments did Taylor use in support of her ordinance?*

2. *Though the penalties provided for in the original ordinance were standard penalties for violations of other city ordinances, the city council weakened them. If you were on the New Orleans City Council at the time, would you have voted for the final version of the ordinance? Why or why not?*

3. *Opponents of monument removal are fond of saying that history is being destroyed or rewritten. However, history is always being reinterpreted and rewritten, and monuments are only one way in which we learn and commemorate our past. History is obviously learned from books, too, and is commemorated in pageants, parades, museums, and reenactments. Why does the way we commemorate the past matter?*

4. *What arguments did historian Lawrence Powell use in support of the removal of the Liberty Place monument?*

5. *Why was the history of African Americans not commemorated? How might we change that state of affairs?*

Sources:

1. Dorothy Mae Taylor, Press Release, December 3, 1991, Records of Councilmember-at-Large Dorothy Mae Taylor, 1977–1994, Louisiana Division/City Archives, New Orleans Public Library.

2. Dorothy Mae Taylor, Letter to the Editor, *Times-Picayune*, March 2, 1992, Capital City Press/Georges Media Group, and Baton Rouge, LA.

3. Dorothy Mae Taylor, Template Letter, July 12, 1993, Records of Councilmember-at-Large Dorothy Mae Taylor, 1977–1994, Louisiana Division/City Archives, New Orleans Public Library.

4. Lawrence N. Powell, Opinion, *Times-Picayune*, March 17, 1993, Capital City Press/Georges Media Group, and Baton Rouge, LA.

1998:
Petrochemical Industries vs. the People

This is a story about occupational and environmental health and justice in southern Louisiana. In "Cancer Alley" from Lake Charles to Baton Rouge to New Orleans, chemical companies have produced a variety of materials that eventually proved toxic. In a classic case of "regulatory capture," they influenced the agencies that were supposed to be regulating them for both the safety of workers and the safety of surrounding communities. Hardly transparent, they met evidence of toxicity with obfuscation, silence, and lies. Only attorneys were able to uncover at least a portion of the truth as a result of lawsuits and subpoenas. In 1998, the *Houston Chronicle* published twelve front-page exposés of chemical companies' "toxic secrecy." This is one of those stories, authored by Jim Morris, now of the Center for Public Integrity, a think tank in Washington, DC, as of July 2019.

LAKE CHARLES, La. — Blind and comatose, Dan Ross succumbed to brain cancer on Oct. 9, 1990.

A large and unpretentious man of 46, Ross had spent 23 years at the Conoco—later Vista—chemical plant here. He had made a good living, raised a family, saved for retirement.

After his diagnosis, Ross came to believe that he had struck a terrible bargain, forfeiting perhaps 30 years of his life through his willingness to work with vinyl chloride and other cancer-causing substances.

"Just before he died, he said, 'Mama, they killed me,'" recalled his wife, Elaine. "I promised him I would never let Vista or the chemical industry forget who he was."

She hasn't. Her husband's untimely death set her and a local attorney, William Baggett Jr., on a circuitous course of litigation that led to the industry's well-insulated core.

During the past eight years, Baggett has acquired thousands of previously secret documents, most having to do with vinyl chloride—used to make one of the world's most common plastics.

These documents, and others obtained in recent months by the *Houston Chronicle*, suggest that major chemical manufacturers closed ranks in the late 1950s to contain and counteract evidence of vinyl chloride's toxic effects.

Letters, memoranda and minutes of meetings depict a framework of dubious science and painstaking public relations, coordinated by the industry's main trade association.

There are two dominant themes: avoid disclosure and deny liability.

"There was a concerted effort to hide this material," said Dr. David Rosner, a professor of public health and history at Columbia University who has reviewed many of the documents as part of a research project. "It's clear there was chicanery."

In a prepared statement, the Chemical Manufacturers Association called such charges "irresponsible." The group said that it promotes a policy of openness among its members.

"We took the problem seriously," said Dr. Theodore Torkelson, a retired Dow Chemical toxicologist who chaired the CMA's vinyl chloride panel for 11 years in the 1970s and '80s. "We did what we thought was ethical, scientifically sound and morally responsible."

The documents present another scenario: That the chemical companies, through their silence and inertia, subjected at least two generations of workers to excessive levels of a potent carcinogen that targets the liver, brain, lungs and blood-forming organs.

Although they freely shared health information among themselves, the companies were evasive with their own employees and the government.

They were unwilling to disrupt the growing market for polyvinyl chloride (PVC) plastic, used in everything from pipe to garden hoses. . . .

Put in context by hundreds of interviews, the documents flesh out a story that made headlines during the first half of 1974, only to be overshadowed by Watergate and Richard Nixon's resignation.

And they accentuate the problem of occupational cancer, which, by some estimates, takes more lives (50,000) each year than AIDS, homicide or suicide, but receives far less attention.

To this day, most manufacturers acknowledge only that vinyl chloride causes angiosarcoma, an extremely rare cancer of the liver. They insist that the exposure levels necessary to produce the disease have not been seen in two decades.

As a rule, this is true. Because of government-required controls—controls the industry resisted—vinyl chloride contamination in and around chemical plants has been reduced dramatically.

Significant exposures in some places occurred well into the 1980s, however. And unusual cancers other than angiosarcoma continue to kill chemical workers and retirees prematurely.

On April 30, Henry Tousaint, who had spent 20 years at the PPG Industries plant in Lake Charles, died of mantle-cell lymphoma at age 54.

Tousaint and other PPG workers routinely cleaned chemical storage tanks and mixed pesticides, inhaling vinyl chloride, benzene and other carcinogens in the process. Those who complained of dizziness or breathing difficulties were given cough syrup, kept in gallon jugs, Tousaint said three months before his death.

"We didn't know no better," he said. "But they did."

Officials at the company's Pittsburgh headquarters would not comment.

Baggett won large settlements for both the Tousaint and the Ross families from PPG, Conoco and Vista, none of which admitted culpability. He is building a conspiracy case against 29 other chemical companies, the CMA and the Society of the Plastics Industry, alleging that they obfuscated evidence of vinyl chloride-related deaths and diseases. . . .

By the spring of 1959, the evidence was beginning to accrue.

Manufacturers of vinyl chloride—then known only as an explosion hazard and an intoxicant—came to realize that the compound might be poisoning the people who worked with it.

Dow had been discreetly testing the sweet-smelling, gaseous substance on rats, rabbits, guinea pigs and dogs at its Biochemical Research Laboratory in Midland, Mich.

The results were troubling. Adverse liver effects had been seen in animals that had inhaled only 100 parts per million of vinyl chloride, a fraction of the concentration to which many workers were exposed. . . .

Before Dow began its animal work in 1958, there had been few investigations of vinyl chloride — although acute effects had been seen in guinea pigs as early as 1930, and liver damage had been found in 15 of 45 vinyl chloride workers examined as part of a 1949 study in the Soviet Union.

The Dow researchers published their data in the American Industrial Hygiene Association Journal in 1961, recommending a vinyl chloride exposure limit of 50 ppm.

No one outside of Dow listened. Indeed, a 1963 Yale University animal study sponsored by Allied Chemical found no significant effects below 500 ppm. . . .

(The Occupational Safety and Health Administration didn't come into being until 1970; consequently, there was no government agency to force companies to act.)

In the fall of 1964, Goodrich — which would be commended for revealing a cluster of angiosarcomas at one of its plants a decade later — sought help from the Kettering Laboratory at the University of Cincinnati.

A puzzling hand disability had emerged among workers who cleaned the reactors — huge, blenderlike devices in which vinyl chloride monomer is turned into PVC resin — at a Goodrich plant in Louisville, Ky.

At the time, cleaners entered the reactors without respiratory protection to chip away the residue that built up on the walls. . . .

By 1966, it had become apparent that the hand condition — acroosteolysis, characterized by numbness and swelling of the fingers — was systemic, indicative of vinyl chloride's toxicity. And it was not confined to reactor cleaners.

The following year, an epidemiological study of vinyl workers commenced at the University of Michigan. All company data, it was emphasized, would be held "in strictest confidence."...

Although the Michigan acroosteolysis registry ultimately collapsed from lack of industry cooperation, its keepers managed to convey an important message to the Manufacturing Chemists Association, the trade group that later became the CMA: Get people out of the reactors, or at least limit exposures to 50 ppm.

The recommendation, included in a confidential report to the MCA in February 1969, was not followed. . . .

The wall of secrecy surrounding vinyl chloride was not breached until Jan. 23, 1974, when B. F. Goodrich announced that it had found three fatal cases of angiosarcoma among workers at its PVC plant in Louisville.

Although Goodrich was praised for its candor, it and other manufacturers knew a great deal about the chemical's toxic properties long before Louisville and understood the economic consequences of bad publicity. . . .

The Louisville cancer revelation in 1974 set in motion months of frenetic activity in Washington, highlighted by contentious OSHA and congressional hearings. Labor leaders and public-health advocates spoke of a cover-up by the vinyl industry; the industry accused them of overreacting and threatening its very survival.

OSHA adopted an emergency temporary standard of 50 ppm and later proposed a permanent standard of 1 ppm. A federal ban was imposed on the use of vinyl chloride as a propellant in hair sprays, pesticides and other aerosol products; a proposed ban on PVC liquor bottles was averted when the industry found a way to limit migration of vinyl chloride into the liquor.

. . . A study commissioned by the Society of the Plastics Industry concluded that the new OSHA standard would eliminate at least 1.6 million jobs — from reactor cleaners to plastics fabricators — and have a minimum economic impact of $65 billion.

The SPI challenged the 1 ppm standard before a three-judge federal panel and lost on Jan. 31, 1975.

"I argued that it was arbitrary and capricious to say 1 (ppm), that they pulled that number out of their ear," said [Jerome] Heckman, the society's attorney. "I got killed in court."

In the panel's opinion, retired Supreme Court Justice Tom Clark wrote that "the record shows what can only be described as a course of continued procrastination on the part of the industry to protect the lives of its employees."

Despite the dire predictions, the industry did not disappear.

Using technology developed in Japan in the late 1960s, manufacturers installed reactors that greatly reduced the need for manual cleaning. New ways were found to lower the vinyl chloride content of PVC resin from hundreds of parts per million to less than 1 ppm.

"The industry really, really changed," said Bill Carroll, a vice president with Occidental Chemical in Dallas and an officer with the Vinyl Institute, a trade association. "If you look at how close it might have come to being regulated out of existence — to come from that circumstance to the point of doing what had to be done to make the product safe, I think it's a tremendous success story."

There remained, however, the matter of cancer. . . .

In the late 1980s and early '90s, cancer became an issue for Houston-based Vista, now known as Condea Vista. At least four workers — Dan Ross and another man at Vista's vinyl chloride monomer plant in Lake Charles, and two men at its PVC plant in Aberdeen, Miss. — had developed brain tumors, and there had been other cancers as well.

Vista management held several meetings with workers in an effort to quell fear and mistrust. These were some of the comments received during two sessions in Lake Charles in April 1991, according to a Vista memo:

"Previous explanation about cancer deaths was a snow job, bull----. Our questions were not answered. We believe these employees died because of exposure in the plant. We were told to shut up and not make trouble."

"We think our jobs are killing us. No one listens."

"If the real answer is that Vista doesn't know how much we›re hurt by this exposure, then we deserve some kind of compensation for the agony of not knowing."

"EDC (ethylene dichloride, a suspected carcinogen) drips from the ceiling. When you flush the toilets in the plant and the water fills up again you're overcome with EDC fumes."

Ray Reynolds, Vista chairman of Oil, Chemical and Atomic Workers Local 4-555 and an operator at the Lake Charles plant, said in an interview that the company has been slow to respond to such concerns, despite evidence that chemical exposures have caused illness and death.

"It's all about money," said Reynolds, a gaunt man of 41 with a baffling — and, he thinks, work-related — condition of the nervous system that keeps him fatigued and in pain. "All these years, I believe, they've been killing people, but they've put a dollar figure on it."

Predictably, some of the cancers out of the chemical plants gave rise to workers' compensation claims and lawsuits.

Few of these actions, however, resulted in lucrative judgments or settlements; the burden of proof for occupational cancer was simply too great, and the industry was able and willing to play hardball. . . .

Lake Charles attorney Baggett maintains that the 5,000 or so workers in U.S. vinyl chloride, ethylene dichloride and PVC resin plants aren't the only ones vulnerable to cancer and other serious ailments.

An estimated 120,000 people work in PVC fabrication, turning the white powder into flooring, siding, blood bags and other familiar products. Might they, too, be at risk?

"No one (in industry) is going to study fabricators," Baggett said. "It'll never happen. What if they found something?"

Quite by accident, a Swedish researcher did find something. Three years ago, Dr. Lennart Hardell, an associate professor of oncology and epidemiology at Orebro Medical Center, began distributing questionnaires to testicular cancer victims and a group of controls.

Hardell was searching for possible occupational causes of the disease, on the rise in Sweden and other industrialized countries. By the time he had compiled his data, only one line of work stood out: PVC fabrication.

"We hadn't expected anything on PVC," Hardell said in an interview. "We had no suspicions."

The study was published late last year. Considering the high risk he had observed for PVC exposure, Hardell called for further investigation.

The Brussels-based PVC Information Council responded swiftly and decisively, as its American counterparts had done many times before.

"We do not see a cancer threat for (PVC) workers," the council said.

Questions to Consider:

1. *What can this story tell us about the relationships between corporate power on one hand, and law, science, and good government on the other?*
2. *Why might Louisiana (or any state) have been reluctant to regulate or fine major industries too much, even if there was evidence that they were polluting the environment and killing workers before their time?*
3. *Where did petrochemical plants locate in Louisiana, and why those places?*

Source:

2005: Mary Gehman Survives Hurricane Katrina

Hurricane Katrina made landfall on the Gulf Coast on Monday, August 29, 2005, as a Category 3 storm. New Orleans, on the west side of the storm, seemed to have fared slightly better than places in Mississippi and Alabama—until the levees and floodwalls broke. What follows is an account of the disaster from Mary Gehman, a writer, publisher, and English professor at Delgado Community College in New Orleans.

Gehman's account helps explain why some people stayed. In her case, Gehman had a working automobile and sons who could have assisted her had she decided to evacuate with them. But she had recently bought several houses in the vicinity as rental properties and knew that several of her tenants—all elderly—could not leave. Not only did she want to stay to assist the tenants and protect her property, but she also had two old dogs she could not take with her. Evacuation shelters and first responders would not allow pets into boats or buses. Gehman's hundred-year-old house had survived highly destructive storms before, including one only two years earlier, so she calculated that it would withstand this one, too, and indeed it did. But as the hurricane-force winds began to slow down and the rain let up, the levees and floodwalls holding back Lake Pontchartrain and the Industrial Canal gave way under a powerful storm surge. In a short span of time, 80 percent of the city was under water.

A boat manned by firefighters from north Louisiana plucked Gehman off her roof on Tuesday, a day and a half after the flooding started. She and the others in the boat were dropped off at the nearest interstate, joining several hundred others, the majority of whom were poor, black and/or female—the most vulnerable residents of the city. There was no drinking water or food, and, even worse, no prospect for rescue.

On Thursday, a helicopter dropped cases of water and MREs (Meals Ready to Eat, normally provided to troops), which the crowd shared among themselves, assuaging the worst of their hunger. Yet the sickest among them remained on the verge of death, so others flagged down a helicopter and cleared space for it to land long enough to get the worst-off evacuees out.

This excerpt picks up there.

Thursday, September 1

It was about 3 p.m. and I sat on the curb, my book bag beside me, head in hands. It occurred to me that at this time in the afternoon I would normally be having the second cup of coffee for the day. How good a steaming cup of chicory coffee would taste at that moment! I could look to the right only two blocks away and almost see the roof of my house, though it seemed now miles away. I also wondered why, having done nothing all day for two days in a row I was not bored. And I learned at that instant a very important lesson: people who are in survival mode spend all their time and energy on wondering where their next meal is coming from and how they can scheme to have a place to bed down for the night. They scrounge and forage to keep body and soul together, to find something to keep their children from complaining of thirst or hunger. We middle class people often view the homeless or poor with pity but wonder why they don't take a course to get a job skill or what keeps them from finding at least a minimal job. What we don't understand is that they are busy just figuring out how to get to the next food line! Someone walked past with a fresh bottle of water, and I was off to find out where it had come from.

Friday, September 2

Meanwhile from behind us there arrived several motor boats manned by Texas Wildlife Rangers. I was among the twenty or so evacuees to climb into those boats. We were almost too exhausted to appreciate the exhilaration of the moment. What happened to the obese mother who had moved us to action isn't clear. I have to assume she was rescued soon after. There is also no information available on the several people who nursed dogs during those long, difficult days, nor the old lady in the red upholstered chair. Even the bag lady with the disparate tapes in her head has not returned to her former perch at Canal and Broad. I wonder what shelter took her in. In the rush to leave the overpass, there was no time for good-byes.

Whether our small effort to get that pilot's attention was the only reason we were finally evacuated off the overpass isn't clear. Surely deputies, once they got off the overpass, had reported our plight as they promised they would. Maybe FEMA or whatever power was in charge had gotten around at last to dealing with us. I don't know and probably never will. I just savored the fantastic relief of being in a moving boat going to what we had been told was a bus that would take us out of New Orleans to a shelter. As the boat motored down Broad and turned right on to Tulane Avenue, which now resembled a lake, I could look down the alley and see my house still standing. A lump rose in my throat as I strained to see signs of my dogs on the balcony but there was none. In the past few days I had not allowed my spirit to be crushed by thinking about them. Now I wasn't sure if it was relief or horror that gripped me . . .

[The boat dropped the evacuees off in front of the New Orleans Public Library at Tulane and Loyola and told them to ford through water smelling like piss and vomit towards the Superdome and get in line for a bus.

Contrary to rumors and unsubstantiated news reports, there was absolutely no violence on that interstate overpass, and very little at the Superdome and Convention Center where thousands more had gathered, despite oppressive heat, no electricity, and no working toilets.

The refugees from the overpass joined hundreds of others standing in long lines that wrapped several times around the dome.]

In the bus line at the Superdome

It was about 6 p.m. when our spot in the line reached the open plaza that slopes down into the New Orleans Centre shopping mall. Gradually the line oozed out to the sides and people filled the plaza so there was no longer one clearly defined line but rows of people pushing their way to the front. In the absence of signs, barricades or someone to keep order, it became each to his or her own. The family group ahead of us had a huge flatbed cart piled high with their belongings but were soon forced to abandon the cart because of the crush of people. Our small group stayed together as best we could. Whereas earlier we had thought about having one or two of us go through a line at a table off to the side to procure MRE's that were being handed out there, we decided it was better to stay together and forgo eating. In the heat and close crowd it was hard to breathe. We pushed ahead along side elderly people being helped by their children, babies in strollers, pregnant women and people almost too sick to stand up. It was really our worst nightmare come true. The next two hours spent in that crowd are blurry in my mind, partly because it is painful to remember the pointless agony of it all. Not only were we jammed into a suffocatingly [*sic*] hot and fetid mob of desperate people, but we also had to climb up over at least a foot and a half of debris to advance: mattresses and bed clothes with curtains, all of which appeared to have been blown out of the Hyatt Regency Hotel during the hurricane four days before, folding chairs and military cots abandoned by whomever, and hundreds of empty water bottles. It was very hard to find one's footing, especially for anyone pulling a heavy school bag as I was or for the elderly who had already been standing for hours on end. I recall a middle aged woman to my right, apparently alone, bracing herself stoically, tears falling silently down her cheeks. At that moment I could not think of a word of comfort to offer her. Nothing made any sense, nothing but sheer endurance.

At some point we were close enough to a National Guardsman for me to ask him why no one was controlling the crowd or cleaning away the debris. A man in the crowd had just had a vomiting episode and was shunted to the side to catch some fresh air. When he was told that he could exit at the side stair but would lose his place in line, his family pulled him back into the anonymous crowd. The soldier turned his attention back to my question and looked at me blankly.

"The Army is in charge of getting you all out of the Dome and on to buses," was his reply. When I asked why then was the Army not doing anything to help us, he said so matter-of-factly that at first I mistook it for a joke, "We don't talk to the Army and they don't talk to us." My thought was interrupted by Laura in our group crying out in pain because of a muscle spasm in her back. The stress on us all was mounting; we just didn't know what to do. Fortunately, Bill knew something about massage and was able to gradually relieve Laura's back pain, though she continued to suffer several more bouts during our wait.

Psychologically it was torture to hear someone up front shout into a megaphone "We'll take 500 more for the buses then break for the night." Where was the 500th person in that mob? Would we make it together? Might we be split up? Would we be condemned to spend another night under the stars with the stench of human waste assaulting our senses? Panic spread fast, causing us all to stiffen with resolve to make it to the front as soon as possible. Willie had managed well despite his advanced age. It was hard for him to climb over the mattresses and water bottles, but we all helped by offering him a hand or a shoulder to lean on. When he apologized for steadying himself on my arm, I joked that I didn't mind his being fresh with me—his smile was a ray of light in that dismal day.

As we finally worked our way to the front, the five barricades manned by Army soldiers in full uniform became visible. Beyond the barricades order ruled. An officer in a very authoritative voice called out periodically on a megaphone "Three people from Gate 2, five people from Gate 5," and so on. There appeared to be an attempt to keep families together, so we quickly agreed to call Willie "Grampaw" and insist the rest of us were siblings, an improbable plan but not one likely to be challenged by soldiers under the circumstances. When we thought we could not make it another few minutes, the gate/barricade in front of us opened wide enough to permit us to pass, and we were free!

This group of evacuees went to a shelter in Texas, where the Red Cross and other volunteers were out in force and provided them with badly needed supplies. Why couldn't Louisiana have done this, Mary wondered? Where had the authorities fallen down on their job? That question would not be an easy one to answer. Though the numbers are somewhat disputed, the combined deaths for Louisiana and Mississippi are at least 1,200 and perhaps as many as 1,800 people.

Questions to Consider:

1. *In what ways did the disastrous flood expose fault lines along class and racial lines in the city? In what way did it expose deficiencies in the response of the federal government?*

2. *If you or a family member weathered Hurricane Katrina or a different natural disaster, was your experience similar to Gehman's? Explain.*

Source:

Mary Gehman, "Surviving the Hurricane," *Hurricane Katrina and the Lessons of Disaster Relief*, ed. Michael Powelson (UK: Cambridge Scholars Publishing, 2017), p. 26–35. Published with the permission of Cambridge Scholars Publishing.

2005/2010:
Governor Blanco's Response to Hurricane Katrina

Hurricane Katrina, one of the costliest and deadliest storms ever to hit the United States, struck the Gulf Coast in the early morning hours of Monday, August 29, 2005. At first it seemed as though New Orleans had escaped serious damage, but just when everyone began to relax, a powerful storm surge made its way up several manmade industrial channels, through Lake Pontchartrain, broke through the levees, pushed past the floodwalls and put 80 percent of the city under water within a few short hours. The failure of the manmade levee and floodwall protection system caught everyone off guard. Mayor Ray Nagin, who later went to jail for corruption, had not ordered city or school buses to higher ground before the storm hit, and dozens of them filled with water, useless, in the lots where they had been parked on Friday. Both Mayor Nagin and Governor Blanco came under criticism for not ordering mandatory evacuations sooner. But perhaps the greatest criticism was directed at President George W. Bush and his ill-fated Federal Emergency Management Agency (FEMA) director, Michael D. Brown. On September 12, Brown resigned his position after reporters revealed that he was a political hack with almost no disaster response experience.

What follows are excerpts from two interviews with Governor Blanco five years apart. In the first one, the disaster was still fresh and recovery underway. By the time of the second interview in 2010, President Bush had just published a memoir in which he pointed fingers at both Blanco and Nagin for a failed response that left as many as 1,800 people on the Gulf Coast dead. In both interviews, Blanco defends her actions.

Louisiana: The State We're In, "Gov. Kathleen Blanco Interview - Dec. 30, 2005"

Interviewer, Robyn Ekings:

Q. Where did things start to escalate and go wrong in the days as the storm hit and the full impact of it was realized?

Governor Blanco:

A. Robyn, as you know, Louisiana's resources were maxed out. The city of New Orleans's resources were maxed out to some extent or perhaps not properly directed at certain times. The federal government's resources were not properly applied and I think they were overwhelmed. And there was a sense of urgency. As governor, I recognized all of our entire situation, and I was hollering out begging for more assistance particularly from our federal partners. It was slow in coming except for the National Guard. The governors of all states in the country, the territories, and DC responded by sending guard members. The federal response on troops was a little slow in coming. In fact, they came—there was plenty work to do—but they didn't come during the days of the emergency that I was asking for.

Q. How much do you think of the reaction of the White House in the beginning was partisan?

A. I don't think it was necessarily partisan right at first. I think that they did not understand the magnitude and as many times as I explained it to them, they still just didn't get it. And then when the national media starting attacking the president, the president's people, those around him who are hired to protect him and who feel obligated to protect him, decided that he should not be the target of the angst, and so they turned their machine in our direction.

Q. What part of you being a woman, being the woman governor, do you think played in that?

A. Certainly I think that a lot of times women are underestimated for their strength of purpose and now I'm getting tremendous compliments even from members of Congress who thought I wasn't as strong as some random male. But I think the strength came from my side of the equation as opposed to a lot of other folks. Those stories are all going to be told.

I'm not wanting to live in the past but I know that I did everything possible to lead my people and to ask for the right kind of help in the right time. In the end, Louisiana people were the people who saved our folks. We have a lot of heroes, and the stories are amazing, and I'm not going to let any Congressional inquiry take away from the heroic moments and actions of Louisiana people and those who came to our aid.

Q. Do you think you stretched yourself too thin perhaps at one point?

A. Well, you know when people are in the water fighting for their lives, a governor cannot rest easily. I think perhaps that I was tired certainly showed (laughter) but I wasn't the only soul out there in total exhaustion. No, you don't rest well and your phone rings all night and rescue efforts are so critical and days, hours, minutes, moments mean the difference between life and death, and every single moment I was fighting to save lives while other people were playing politics, and that got me very angry. Other people were out there discussing appearances but I could have cared less about all that and none of that penetrated to my level. My entire focus was on getting all of our folks to safety. The sorrow is that we lost some. Those people by and large stand as a reminder that we always have to do things a little bit better. No matter how prepared we are, natural forces will have its way with us, but I think our citizens have learned a hard lesson that they do need to get out of harm's way when we ask them and beg them to do so, and then we can go back and pick up the pieces.

Q. What has been your most hopeful sign in the recovery so far?

A. I was not very hopeful about Washington, and after my presentation on, I think, the 14th, I understand the White House went into a huge scramble that night to find more money for the levee problems, and that night they announced it.

Q. So you think that was a direct response?

A. I think it was. I think it's very important for the White House to show a real commitment to the Louisiana people. As I explained to the members of Congress, we would not have been there if the levees hadn't broken. The levees are a manmade installation and what man makes, man has to back up. The federal government, through the Corps of Engineers, is responsible for levees. They build our levees, they build bridges and damns all across the country. There are responsibilities that are doled out to different levels of government and levees belong specifically to the federal government. Now having said that, Louisiana has not always, as a state, paid close attention to what's going on in the levee districts, but my new bill creating a coastal protection and restoration authority means that we as a state, at the state level, are going to coordinate all the projects and do an intensive hands-on process to make sure that the levee concerns and the flood protection concerns are properly addressed in the state of Louisiana.

Q. Has this been an education for the rest of the country in the ways to protect a key part of the American economy, Louisiana?

A. It has been. One of the things I like to remind citizens across the country is that our first line of protection is a strong wetland. You know, we have lost coastal wetlands over the years. It has made us more susceptible. We have been begging for the money to restore our wetlands and we had a $14 billion price tag. I laugh about that now because while we were asking for that, all members of Congress—except for our own delegation of course—were looking at us like we were crazy, saying that was a ridiculous amount of money and that we shouldn't even be there talking about it. Fourteen billion dollars, or a commitment to that over a long period of time, would have allowed us to begin the process of building healthier marshes and a healthier coastline, and would have prevented some of the costs and the misery that we're experiencing now.

Q. What did you think about that *60 Minutes* story saying that New Orleans shouldn't be located where it is, that it should be moved because it'll be an island within a certain period of time? Did you see that as accurate or maybe as hurtful?

A. A lot of things are hurtful, but are they saying the same thing about all the coastal cities all around this country? The mudslides in California? Are they saying people shouldn't live on the coast of California, or that you shouldn't live on the Mississippi Coast? They've been wiped out on more than one occasion themselves. No, they're making value judgements about a great and most beloved city. There are engineering ways to do a better job protecting that city from flooding. There are countries in this world, particularly in the Netherlands, that live with water control and I think that we can do it, and that we can build it smart and we can rebuild it, where our citizens are safe and their property is safe. The lessons learned from Katrina will be, I hope, handed down through the generations, so that everyone considers public safety and their personal safety their most important goal. If we do the building codes right—and we passed new building code legislation—and if we have flood plains that are respectful, and are accurate, then I believe we can live wherever we want to live and that we can survive a difficult situation, that is, if the manmade levees are designed properly, and the flood control installations are put in the right places like the floodgates perhaps should be at the lake instead of internally. We've learned a lot about the infrastructure of our own city and our own state and we know that there are bright minds around the world who care about us and who are willing to help us, and I think we are going to accomplish all of those things. . . .

Louisiana: The State We're In, "Former Governor Kathleen Blanco on Hurricane Katrina," November 26, 2010

[This interview was held shortly after the publication of former President George W. Bush's book *Decision Points*, a memoir released in November 2010. The interviewers read a quote from the book in which Bush pointed to Blanco for the failure of security in the wake of the flood. Governor Blanco responded:]

A. The local authorities are in charge of security, not the governor. He wanted to help but he had some mistaken thoughts that he did not express to me in a timely fashion. I needed extra military assistance and he thought I wanted the federal government to take charge when what we really needed was to have the National Guard to be backed up with military assistance, and there was an important reason for that. If he had done it his way as he had first initially indicated, the Louisiana National Guard would have lost law enforcement authority. Local national guards all across the country have the power to back up law enforcement at the local level. They become a part of whoever wants help and they have the same power as police authorities do, but the US Army by federal law does not. There is a law called Posse Comitatus that prevents the US Army from assuming that kind of authority and in those days we were getting rampant reports especially on the cable networks that New Orleans was completely out of control and while we tried to verify every one of the rumors and could find no real verification, there was a national image that was going out and I think that President Bush accepted the media versions that were greatly exaggerated in many, many cases.

Q. We heard reports of lawlessness and chaos, reports showing New Orleans completely out of control.

A. That is right [there were such reports], and then when everyone went back to review the situation, we know that while there were reports of helicopters being shot at, not one single helicopter took a bullet. . . . Reports were exaggerated. I think that he was right, there was miscommunication, and had he stepped forward and stopped his regular schedule and come into Louisiana in a timely fashion, that miscommunication would not have happened.

Q. Was there a power struggle at all?

A. It wasn't a matter of me retaining control. It was a matter of the needs out there. I was getting calls from the New Orleans police—they needed backup—the parish presidents were calling for National Guard. Jefferson Parish ended up asking for the National Guard to have police powers to guard all the neighborhoods in Jefferson Parish. It was a very practical, real problem. If we didn't have police authority, we would not be able to respond properly to the situation as it actually was unfolding.

Q. In the book he says that you and the mayor demanded to meet with him on Air Force One [on Wednesday morning] and that the meeting was tense.

A. Laughs. Well, I do agree that it was tense. We had been in the field battling what felt like a war, as close to a war-zone feeling as you'll ever get on our soil. We were all exhausted, so yes, everybody was pretty upset because he came in five days late and he was asking questions that pretty much had been resolved, he still had not sent the military assistance in, and you know the one thing that could have made everything better was if his FEMA had been able to get the buses in on Wednesday as everyone expected to see happen. The temperature would've calmed down and the people would've been able to leave the Superdome in a timely fashion but there was chaos and confusion in the bureaucracy. I know that he wanted to help. I will always say that he was not reacting from a racist position . . . but his systems fell apart. On the other hand, at the point of that meeting, all of us had been working in the trenches day and night for nearly a whole week. I mean, our work started before the storm, and this was on the seventh day after our work began, and he came in asking questions that we thought surely he knows the answers to these questions. But in that meeting I gave him an updated report and I told him that we had finally begun the evacuation because the FEMA buses had arrived on Thursday at noon, and that we were practically finished evacuating the Superdome and we were beginning the evacuation of the Convention Center so that in another twelve hours or so, all of the commotion would be resolved and then we would get to the hard work of doing search and rescue in all of the houses where we didn't know if people were still trapped in their homes or not.

Q. After that meeting, was there then a teamwork mechanism or did that get deteriorated due to this meeting?

A. Ironically, on Saturday morning, he announced a plan that matched exactly what I asked him to do on Wednesday morning. He did it the way I asked him to do it, and it worked, and in his book he confesses that if he had known how well that would work he would have done that in the first place, or maybe we can say he should have done it.

Q. Are you talking about when General [Russel L.] Honoré [commander of Joint Task Force Katrina] arrived?

A. Well, that's correct, but when General Honoré arrived on Wednesday night, at my question, "how many soldiers did you bring?" He said, "I have a handful of staffers, ma'am. I'm only here to advise." He [Bush] sent a general in without soldiers! The great thing about General Honoré is that he was a great personality and the TV cameras loved him and he was mainly good for the PR part of it. . . .

Questions to Consider:

1. *In what ways might storm preparedness have been hampered by Americans' sense of individual freedom and resentment of government orders?*

2. *In what ways did Hurricane Katrina reveal cracks in the political system?*

3. *Doing your own research, explore what steps have been taken since 2005 to prevent another such catastrophe in the New Orleans area. What would happen if a storm like Hurricane Katrina hit New Orleans today?*

4. *What does the US House of Representatives' investigative report on the storm, "A Failure of Initiative" (available on the internet), conclude about who was responsible for the failures of 2005?*

Sources:

1. *Louisiana: The State We're In,* "Gov. Kathleen Blanco Interview - Dec. 30, 2005," with host Robyn Ekings, produced by the Louisiana Educational Television Authority, LPB Collection, http://ladigitalmedia.org/video_v2/asset-detail/LSWI-2918-01_Blanco.

2. *Louisiana: The State We're In,* "Former Governor Kathleen Blanco on Hurricane Katrina," aired November 26, 2010, with interviewers Charlie Whinham and Shauna Sanford, produced by the Louisiana Educational Television Authority, LPB Collection, http://ladigitalmedia.org/video_v2/asset-detail/LSWI-3411-KathleenBlanco.

2017:
Mayor Mitch Landrieu on the Removal of Confederate Monuments

Confederate statues in Louisiana towns and parishes were erected between 1890 and 1920, decades after the end of the Civil War. As Professor Light Cummins wrote in an op-ed in 2016, "Historical statues tell as much, if not more, about the values of the people who erected them, and the times in which they were erected, than the historical subjects being referenced."[1] New Orleans Mayor Mitch Landrieu, son of former mayor Moon Landrieu, led the effort to remove Confederate statues that dotted public spaces in New Orleans. What follows are excerpts from the speech he delivered after the last of the monuments had been removed.

Representing the men and women of the New Orleans Police Department, Homeland Security, EMS—all of the individuals who have done really hard work over the last month under very difficult circumstances, and Chief Harrison and Tim McConnell, and our entire team at city hall who are here today; and particularly Glenda and Mary, who are sitting at the front desk of city hall that have received all the warm blessings. I think they're watching right now but before I came over here I asked Mary how we were doing. She said, "Well chief," she said, "they called you everything but a child of God."

1. Light Cummins, op-ed, *Herald-Democrat* (Sherman, TX), September 9, 2017.

To Matt Bailey and to US Marine Corps retired Lieutenant Colonel Richard Westmoreland, who have been there every step of the way on behalf of the United States of America. Thank you for being strong.

Pastor Anglim, and to all the ministers who prayed and gave us strength.

To Keith Plessy, from the Plessy family, who brings a history from where it was to where it is today, and along with the Ferguson family who are not here but have demonstrated what reconciliation really looks like.

The descendants of Georgetown slaves.

And to the New Orleans Freedom Riders—Diane Nash couldn't make it today, but Claude Reese is here, who was—give him a round of applause.

I thank you all for coming today.

The soul of our beloved city is rooted in a history that has evolved over thousands of years; rooted in a diverse people who have been here together every step of the way through good and through bad.

It is the history, our history, that holds in its heart the stories of Native Americans—the Choctaw, the Houma, the Chitimacha; Hernando de Soto, Robert Cavelier, Sieur de La Salle, the Acadians, the Islenos, the enslaved people of Senegambia, free people of color, the Haitians, the Germans, both empires of France and Spain; the Italian[s], the Irish, the Cubans, the south and central Americans, the Vietnamese, and so many more.

You see, New Orleans is truly a city of many nations, a melting pot, a bubbling cauldron of many cultures. There is no other place quite like it in the world that so eloquently exemplifies the uniquely American motto: *E pluribus unum*—Out of many we are one.

But there are also other truths about our city that we must confront. New Orleans was one of America's largest slave markets, a port where hundreds of thousands of souls were bought, sold, and shipped up the Mississippi River to lives of forced labor, of misery, of rape, and of torture.

America was a place where nearly four thousand of our fellow American citizens were lynched, 540 in Louisiana alone; where our courts enshrined "separate but equal," where Freedom Riders were beaten to a bloody pulp.

So, when people say to me that the monuments in question are history, well what I just described to you is our history as well, and it is a searing truth. And it immediately begs the question, why there are no slave ship monuments, no prominent markers on public land to remember the lynchings or the slave blocks; nothing to remember this long chapter of our lives of the pain, of sacrifice, of shame—all of it happening on the soil of New Orleans.

So, for those self-appointed defenders of history and the monuments, they are eerily silent on what amounts to historical malfeasance, a lie by omission. There is a difference, you see, between remembrance of history and the reverence of it. For America [and] New Orleans, it has been a long and winding road, marked by tragedy and triumph. But we cannot be afraid of the truth. As President George W. Bush said at the—at the dedication ceremony for the National Museum of African American History and Culture (and I quote): "A great nation does not hide its history. It faces its flaws and" it "corrects them."

So today I want to speak about why we chose to remove these four monuments to the Lost Cause of the Confederacy, but also how and why this process can move us towards healing and understanding each other.

So, let's start with the facts.

The historic record is clear: Robert E. Lee, Jefferson Davis, P. G. T. Beauregard statu[es] were not erected to just honor these men, but as part of the movement which became known as the Cult of the Lost Cause. This "cult" had one goal and one goal only: through monuments and through other means to rewrite history, to hide the truth, which is that the Confederacy was on the wrong side of humanity. First erected 166 years after the founding of our city, nineteen years after the Civil War, these monuments that we took down were meant to rebrand the history of our city and the ideals of the Confederacy.

It is self-evident that these men did not fight for the United States of America; they fought against it. They may have been warriors, but in this cause they were not patriots.

These statu[es] are not just stone and metal. They're not just innocent remembrances of a benign history. These monuments celebrate a fictional, sanitized Confederacy: ignoring the death, ignoring the enslavement, ignoring the terror that it actually stood for. And after the Civil War, these monuments were part of that terrorism as much as burning a cross on someone's lawn. They were erected purposefully to send a strong message to all who walked in their shadows about who was still in charge in this city.

Now, should you have any doubt about the true goals of the Confederacy, in the very weeks before the war broke out, the vice president of the Confederacy, Alexander Stephens, made it very clear that the Confederate cause was about maintaining slavery and white supremacy.

In his now famous "Cornerstone speech," he said that the Confederacy's "corner-stone rests, upon the great truth, that the negro is not equal to the white man; that slavery—subordination to a superior race—is his natural and his normal condition. This, our new government," he said, "is the first, in the history of the world, based upon this great physical, philosophical, and moral truth."

Now, with these shocking words still ringing in your ears, I want to try to gently peel your hands from the grip on this false narrative of our history that I think weakens us and make straight a wrong turn that we made many years ago, so we can more closely connect with the integrity to the founding principles of our nation and forge a clearer, straighter path towards a better city and towards a more perfect union.

Now, last year President Obama echoed these sentiments about the need to contextualize and to remember all of our history. He recalled a single piece of stone, a slave auction block engraved with a marker commemorating a single moment in 1830 when Andrew Jackson and Henry Clay stood and spoke from it.

President Obama said, "Consider what this artifact tells us about history. . . . On a stone where day after day, for years, men and women bound and bought and sold, and bid like cattle; on a stone worn down by the tragedy of over a thousand bare feet." And, "For a long time the only thing we considered important, the singular thing we chose to commemorate as 'history' with a plaque were the unmemorable speeches of these two powerful men."

A piece of stone—one stone. Both stories, history. One story told, one story forgotten—or maybe even purposefully ignored.

Now, as clear as it is for me today, for a long time, even though I grew up in one of New Orleans's most diverse neighborhoods, even with my family's proud history of fighting for civil rights, I must have passed by these monuments thousands of times without giving them a second thought.

So, I'm not judging anybody. I am not judging people. We all take our own journey on race. I just hope people listen like I did when my dear friend Wynton Marsalis helped me see the truth. He asked me to think about all the people who have left New Orleans because of our exclusionary attitudes.

Another friend asked me to consider these four monuments from the perspective of an African American mother or father trying to explain to their fifth-grade daughter why Robert E. Lee sat atop of our city. Can you do it? Can you do it? Can you look into the eyes of this young girl and convince her that Robert E. Lee is there to encourage her? Do you think she feels inspired and hopeful by that story? Do these monuments help her see her future with limitless potential? Have you ever thought, have you ever thought that if her potential is limited, yours and my potential [is limited] as well?

We all know the answers to these very simple questions.

When you look into this child's eyes is the moment when the searing truth comes into focus. This is the moment when we know what we must do, when we know what is right. We cannot walk away from this truth.

Now, I knew that taking down the monuments was going to be tough, but you elected me to do the right thing, not the easy thing, and this is what that looks like. So, relocating these monuments is not about taking something away from someone else. This is not about politics. It's not about blame. It's not about retaliation. This is not about a naïve quest to solve all of our problems at once.

This is, however, about showing the whole world that we as a city, that we as a people are able to acknowledge, to understand, to reconcile, and more importantly, choose a better future for ourselves, making straight what has been crooked and making right what was wrong. Otherwise, we will continue to pay a price with discord, with division, and yeah, violence.

To literally put the Confederacy on a pedestal in our mo[st] prominent places [of] honor is an inaccurate recitation of our full past. It is an affront to our present. And it is a bad prescription for our future.

History cannot be changed. It cannot be moved like a statue. What is done is done. The Civil War is over. The Confederacy lost—and we're better for it. Surely we are far enough removed from this dark time to acknowledge that the cause of the Confederacy was wrong. And in the second decade of the twenty-first century, asking African Americans—or anyone else for that matter—to drive by property that they own; occupied by reverential statu[es] of men who fought to destroy the country and deny that person's humanity seems perverse. It seems absurd. Century-old wounds are still raw because, you see, they never healed right in the first place.

So, here is the essential truth: We are better together than we are apart. Indivisibility is our essence. Isn't this the gift that we, the people of New Orleans, have given to the world?

We radiate beauty and grace—in our food, in our music, in our architecture, in our joy of life, in our celebration of death; in everything that we do. We gave the world this funky thing called jazz. It is the most uniquely American art form that is developed across the ages and from different cultures. Think about second lines; think about Mardi Gras; think about muffaletta; think about the Saints; think about gumbo; think about red beans and rice. By God, just think: All we hold dear is created by throwing everything in the pot—creating, producing something better; everything, everything a product of our historic diversity.

We are proof that out of many we are one—and better for it. Out of many we are one—and we really do love it.

And yet, and yet we still seem to find so many excuses to not do the right thing. President Bush's words once again: "A great nation does not hide its history. It faces its flaws and corrects them." We forget, we deny how much we really depend on each other, how much we really need each other. We justify our silence and inaction by manufacturing noble causes that marinate in historic denial. We still find a way to say "wait, wait, wait, not so fast." Dr. Martin Luther King Jr. said, "Wait has almost always meant never."

We cannot wait any longer. We need to change. And we need to change now. No more waiting. This is not just about statu[es], this is about attitudes; and it's about behaviors as well. If we take down these statu[es] and don't change to become a more open and inclusive society, then all of this would have all been in vain.

While some have driven by these statu[es] every day and either revered their beauty or failed to see them at all, many of our neighbors and our fellow Americans see them very, very clearly. Many are painfully aware of their long shadows, their presence cast not only literally but figuratively. And they clearly receive the message that the Confederacy and the cult of the Lost Cause was intended to deliver.

Earlier this week, as the cult of the Lost Cause statu[e] P. G. T Beauregard came down, world renowned musician Terence Blanchard, who's with us, stood watch with his wife Robin and their two beautiful daughters at their side. You see, Terence went to school on the edge of City Park, at a school named after one of America's great heroes and patriots, John F. Kennedy. But to get there he had to pass by the monument to a man who fought to deny his humanity. And he said (quote), "I've never looked at them as a source of pride. It always made me feel as if they were put there by people who don't respect us. This is something I never thought I'd see in my lifetime. It's a sign that the world is changing."

Yes, Terence, it is, and it is long overdue. Now is the time to send a new message to the next generation of New Orleanians, a message about the future, about the next 300 years and beyond: Let us not miss this opportunity New Orleans and let us help the rest of the America do the same, because now—see, now—is the time for choosing. Now is the time to actually make this city the city we should have always been had we gotten it right the first time.

But, this is a good place to stop for a moment and ask ourselves at this point in our history—after Katrina, after Rita, after Ike, after Gustav, after the national recession, after the BP oil spill catastrophe, after the tornado—if presented with an opportunity to build monuments that told our story or curate these particular spaces, would these be the monuments that we want the world to see? Is this really our story?

You see, we have not erased history. We're becoming part of the city's history by righting the wrong image these monuments represent and crafting a better, more complete future for all of our children, and for future generations. And unlike when these Confederate monuments were erected as symbols of white supremacy, we now have a chance to create not only new symbols, but to do it together, as one people. In our blessed land, we come to the table of democracy as equals.

We have to reaffirm our commitment to a future where each citizen is guaranteed the uniquely American gifts of "Life, Liberty and the Pursuit of Happiness." That is what really makes America great and today it's more important than ever to hold fast to these values and together say a self-evident truth that out of many we are one. That is why we reclaim these spaces for the United States of America, because we are one nation, not two; indivisible with liberty and justice for all, not some. We all are part of one nation and pledge allegiance to one flag, the flag of the United States of America.

And here—And here's the kicker: New Orleanians are in it all of the way. It is in this union, it is in this truth that real patriotism is rooted and it flourishes. Instead of revering a four-year brief historical aberration that was called the Confederacy, we can celebrate all 300 years of our rich, diverse history as a place named New Orleans and set the tone for the next 300 years.

After decades of public debate, of anger, of anxiety, of anticipation, of humiliation and of frustration; after public hearings and approvals from three separate community boards and commissions; after two robust public hearings and a 6-1 vote by our duly-elected city council; after review by thirteen different federal and state judges: the full weight of the legislative, executive, and judicial branches of government has been brought to bear and that is why these monuments are coming down in accordance with the law and will be removed.

So, now is the time to come together to heal and to focus on our larger task—not only building new symbols, but making this city a beautiful manifestation of what is possible and what we as a people can become.

And so, let us remember the once-exiled, imprisoned, and universally loved now Nelson Mandela and what he said after apartheid, "If the pain has often been unbearable and the revelations shocking to all of us, it is because they indeed bring us the beginnings of a common understanding of what happened and a steady restoration of th[e] nation's humanity."

So, before we part let us again state clearly for all to hear: the Confederacy was on the wrong side of history and humanity. It sought to tear apart our nation and subjugate our fellow Americans to slavery. This is a history we should never forget and one that we should never, ever again put on a pedestal to be revered.

As a community, we must recognize the significance of removing New Orleans's Confederate monuments. It is our acknowledgment that now is a time to take stock of, and then move past, a painful part of our history. Anything less would render generations of courageous struggle and soul-searching a truly lost cause. Anything less would fall short of the immortal words of our greatest president, Abraham Lincoln, who, with an open heart and a clarity of purpose, calls on us today across the ages to unite as one people when he said, "With malice toward none; with charity for all; with firmness in [the] right, as God gives us to see the right, let us strive on to finish the work we are in; to bind up the nation's wounds . . . to do all which may achieve and cherish a just, and a lasting peace, among ourselves, and with all nations."

God bless you all.
God bless New Orleans.
And God bless the United States of America.

Questions to Consider:

1. *How were Confederate symbols (flags, statues, and so forth) used to bolster white supremacy in Louisiana?*
2. *Explain the myth of the Lost Cause and why it is a lopsided view of our past.*
3. *How does Landrieu answer the criticism that removing statues is "changing history"?*
4. *What process did the city of New Orleans use before deciding to remove the statues?*
5. *Why does the commemoration of Confederate icons on public spaces matter?*
6. *Do a google search for new movements that seek to rectify the white supremacist commemoration of our history and explain what they are doing to try to correct the record. A good example is the Whitney Museum in Wallace, LA.*

Source:

Mitch Landrieu, "Speech on the Removal of Confederate Monuments in New Orleans," delivered at Gallier Hall, May 19, 2017, New Orleans, LA, television broadcast.

For Further Reading

Aiello, Thomas. *Jim Crow's Last Stand: Nonunanimous Jury Verdicts in Louisiana.* Baton Rouge: Louisiana State University Press, 2015.

Allen, Barbara L. *Uneasy Alchemy: Citizens and Experts in Louisiana's Chemical Corridor Disputes.* Cambridge, MA: MIT Press, 2003.

Allured, Janet. *Remapping Second-Wave Feminism: The Long Women's Rights Movement in Louisiana, 1950–1997.* Athens, GA: The University of Georgia Press, 2016.

Arceneaux, Pamela D. *Guidebooks to Sin: The Blue Books of Storyville, New Orleans.* New Orleans: The Historic New Orleans Collection, 2017.

Becnel, Thomas. *Labor, Church, and the Sugar Establishment: Louisiana, 1887–1976.* Baton Rouge: Louisiana State University Press, 1980.

Bernard, Shane K. *The Cajuns: Americanization of a People.* Jackson, MS: University Press of Mississippi, 2003.

Brasseaux, Carl. *French, Cajun, Creole, Houma: A Primer on Francophone Louisiana.* Baton Rouge: Louisiana State University Press, 2005.

Bridges, Tyler. *Bad Bet on the Bayou: The Rise of Gambling in Louisiana and the Fall of Governor Edwin Edwards.* New York: Farrar, Straus, and Giroux, 2001.

———. *The Rise of David Duke.* Jackson, MS: University Press of Mississippi, 1994.

Brothers, Thomas. *Louis Armstrong's New Orleans.* New York: W. W. Norton, 2007.

Burby, Raymond J. "Baton Rouge: The Making (and Breaking) of a Petrochemical Paradise." In *Transforming New Orleans & Its Environs: Centuries of Change*, edited by Craig E. Colten, 160–77. Pittsburgh: University of Pittsburgh Press, 2000.

Carleton, Mark T. "Four Anti-Longites: A Tentative Assessment." *Louisiana History* 30 (1989), 249–62.

———. *Politics and Punishment: The History of the Louisiana State Penal System.* Baton Rouge: Louisiana State University Press, 1984.

Colten, Craig E., "An Incomplete Solution: Oil and Water in Louisiana," *Journal of American History*, 99 (2012), 91–99.

———. "Making a Lemon Out of Lemonade: Louisiana's Petrochemical Corridor." In *Energy Capitals: Local Impact, Global Influence*, edited by Joseph A. Pratt, Martin V. Melosi, and Kathleen A. Brosnan, 58–76. Pittsburgh: University of Pittsburgh Press, 2014.

———. "The Rusting of the Chemical Corridor." *Technology and Culture* 47 (2006), 95–101.

Cortner, Richard C. *The Kingfish and the Constitution: Huey Long, the First Amendment, and the Emergence of Modern Press Freedom in America.* Westport, CT: Greenwood Press, 1996.

David, Emmanuel and Elaine Enarson. *The Women of Katrina: How Gender, Race, and Class Matter in an American Disaster.* Nashville: Vanderbilt University Press, 2012.

Dawson, Joseph. G. *The Louisiana Governors: from Iberville to Edwards.* Baton Rouge: Louisiana State University Press, 1990.

De Jong, Greta. *A Different Day: African American Struggles for Justice in Rural Louisiana, 1900–1970.* Chapel Hill, NC: University of North Carolina Press, 2002.

Fairclough, Adam. *Race and Democracy: The Civil Rights Struggle in Louisiana, 1915–1972.* Athens, GA: University of Georgia Press, 1995.

Finley, Keith. "Dutch Morial." Available online at *64 Parishes.* https://64parishes.org/entry/dutch-morial.

Frystak, Shannon. *Our Minds on Freedom: Women and the Struggle for Black Equality in Louisiana, 1924–1967.* Baton Rouge: Louisiana State University Press, 2009.

Gill, James. *Lords of Misrule: Mardi Gras and the Politics of Race in New Orleans.* Jackson, MS: University Press of Mississippi, 1997.

Green, Elna C. "The Rest of the Story: Kate Gordon and the Opposition to the Nineteenth Amendment in the South." *Louisiana History* 33 (1992), 171–89.

Hair, William Ivy. *The Kingfish and His Realm: The Life and Times of Huey P. Long.* Baton Rouge: Louisiana State University Press, 1991.

Honeycutt, Leo. *Edwin Edwards: Governor of Louisiana.* Baton Rouge: Louisiana State University Press, 2009.

Kemp, Kathryn. "Jean and Kate Gordon: New Orleans Social Reformers, 1898–1933." *Louisiana History* 24 (1983), 389–401.

Kuzenski, John C. *David Duke and the Politics of Race in the South.* Nashville: Vanderbilt University Press, 1995.

Landau, Emily Epstein. *Spectacular Wickedness: Sex, Race, and Memory in Storyville.* Baton Rouge: Louisiana State University Press, 2013.

Landrieu, Mitch. *In the Shadow of Statues: A White Southerner Confronts History.* New York: Penguin Books, 2019.

LeJeune, Keagan. *Always for the Underdog: Leather Britches Smith and the Grabow War.* Denton, TX: University of North Texas Press, 2010.

Lindig, Carmen. *Path from the Parlor: Louisiana Women, 1879–1920.* Lafayette, LA: Center for Louisiana Studies, University of Southwestern Louisiana, 1986.

Long, Alecia P. *The Great Southern Babylon: Sex, Race, and Respectability in New Orleans, 1865–1920.* Baton Rouge: Louisiana State University Press, 2005.

Maginnis, John. *Cross to Bear.* Baton Rouge: Louisiana State University Press, 1992.

———. *The Last Hayride.* Baton Rouge: Louisiana State University Press, 1984.

Mancini, Matthew J. *One Dies, Get Another: Convict Leasing in the American South, 1866–1928.* Columbia, SC: University of South Carolina Press, 1996.

McCord, Charles R. "A Brief History of the Brotherhood of Timber Workers." MA Thesis, University of Texas, 1959.

Morial, Sybil Haydel. *Witness to Change: From Jim Crow to Political Empowerment.* Winston-Salem, NC: John F. Blair, 2015.

Pfeffer, Miki. *Southern Ladies and Suffragists: Julia Ward Howe and Women's Rights at the 1884 New Orleans World's Fair.* Jackson, MS: University Press of Mississippi, 2015.

Powell, Lawrence N. *Troubled Memory: Anne Levy, the Holocaust, and David Duke's Louisiana*, 2d edition. Chapel Hill, NC: University of North Carolina Press, 2019.

Prejean, Helen. *The Death of Innocents: An Eyewitness Account of Wrongful Executions.* New York: Random House, 2005.

Raeburn, Bruce Boyd. *New Orleans Style and the Writing of American Jazz History.* Ann Arbor, MI: University of Michigan Press, 2009.

Rogers, Kim Lacy. *Righteous Lives: Narratives of the New Orleans Civil Rights Movement.* New York: New York University Press, 1993.

Rose, Al. *Storyville, New Orleans: Being an Authentic, Illustrated Account of the Notorious Red-Light District.* Tuscaloosa, AL: University of Alabama Press, 1974.

Sanson, Jerry Purvis. *Louisiana During World War II: Politics and Society, 1939–1945.* Baton Rouge: Louisiana State University Press, 1999.

Scott, John H. with Cleo Scott Brown. *Witness to the Truth: My Struggle for Human Rights in Louisiana.* Columbia, SC: University of South Carolina Press, 2003.

Shepherd, Sam C. "Eleanor McMain." 2010. Available online at *64 Parishes.* https://64parishes.org/entry/eleanor-mcmain.

Simpson, William M. "A Tale Untold? The Alexandria, Louisiana, Lee Street Riot (January 10, 1942)," *Louisiana History* 35 (1994), 133–49.

Sims, Patsy Sims. *Cleveland Benjamin's Dead: A Struggle for Dignity in Louisiana's Cane Country.* Athens, GA: The University of Georgia Press, 1994.

Sindler, Allan. *Huey Long's Louisiana: State Politics, 1920–1954.* Baltimore, MD: The Johns Hopkins Press, 1956.

Stern, Walter C. *Race and Education in New Orleans: Creating the Segregated City, 1764–1960.* Baton Rouge: Louisiana State University Press, 2018.

Strahan, Jerry E. *Andrew Jackson Higgins and the Boats that Won World War II.* Baton Rouge: Louisiana State University Press, 1994.

Theriot, Jason P. *Frenchie* (forthcoming, University of Louisiana at Lafayette Press)

———. *To Honor Our Veterans.* 3 vols. Houston, TX: J. P. Theriot, 2002.

Tolino, Vanessa "Louisiana State Penitentiary at Angola." 2013. Available online at *64 Parishes.* https://64parishes.org/entry/louisiana-state-penitentiary-at-angola.

Trade Secrets: A Moyers Report (PBS): https://www.pbs.org/tradesecrets/program/vinyl.html.

Tyler, Pamela "Kate and Jean Gordon." 2011. Available online at *64 Parishes.* https://64parishes.org/entry/kate-and-jean-gordon.

———. *Silk Stockings and Ballot Boxes: Women & Politics in New Orleans, 1920–1963.* Athens, GA: The University of Georgia Press, 1996.

———. "Woman Suffrage." 2016. Available online at *64 Parishes.* https://64parishes.org/entry/woman-suffrage.

Wheeler, Marjorie Spruill. *New Women of the New South: The Leaders of the Woman Suffrage Movement in the Southern States.* New York: Oxford University Press, 1993.

About the Editors:

Janet Allured is Professor of History and director of Women's Studies at McNeese State University in Lake Charles, where she teaches courses in the history of women, Louisiana, and the modern United States. She is co-editor of *Louisiana Women: Their Lives and Times, Volume 1,* with Judith Gentry (University of Georgia); *Louisiana Legacies: Readings in the History of the Pelican State*; and co-author of a history of Lake Charles, Louisiana. Her most recent book is *Remapping Second-Wave Feminism: The Long Women's Rights Movement in Louisiana, 1950–1997* (University of Georgia, 2016), and she is currently working on a monograph about southern Methodist women and progressive change.

John Keeling is an assistant professor at McNeese State University. His research and teaching interests include Louisiana history, legal history, and southern history.

Michael S. Martin holds the Cheryl Courrégé Burguières/Board of Regents Professorship in History at the University of Louisiana at Lafayette. His research and teaching interests focus on Louisiana history, public history, and the history of the US South. The author or editor of several books of the Bayou State, Martin also serves as managing editor for the Louisiana History Association's quarterly journal, *Louisiana History.*

www.ingramcontent.com/pod-product-compliance
Lightning Source LLC
LaVergne TN
LVHW040838310126
830341LV00003B/8
9781946160676